RAILA ODINGA AND BURNING BRIDGES IN KENYA

Is Dr William Ruto
the Better Option for
Vision 2022-2032?

Mũthende Ndũũcũ

The Golden Jubilee Enterprises
NAIROBI

Published 2020 by
The Golden Jubilee Enterprises
P.O. Box 7264 – 00300
Nairobi, KENYA
Email: golden020jubilee@gmail.com /
info@goldenjubilee.co.ke

ISBN 978 9966 10 909 5 (eBook)

Cover concept by
Sammy Musyona

Layout and design by
Ediprint Communications
ediprint@yahoo.co.uk

"And I will make of thee a great nation, and I will bless thee,
and make thy name great; and thou shalt be a blessing."
(Genesis 12:2)

Dedication

Kenya was meant to be great. It deserves the best.

For all Kenyans who are zealous about building great genuine bridges.

Contents

Preface

The genesis of this book was inspired by a seemingly shameful occurrence on 29 December 2002 when a sick and tired citizenry threw mud, stones and insults at the outgoing second President of Kenya of 24 years, Daniel arap Moi at Uhuru Park, Nairobi. The scene took me back to 25 October 1969 when the first President, Mzee Jomo Kenyatta, just five years into the office, was similarly treated at the opening ceremony of the New Nyanza General Hospital in Kisumu, following a period of ideological differences with the opposition leader Jaramogi Oginga Odinga. The immediate question that apparently had a ready answer was: Why do leaders who assume the highest state job with utmost goodwill from their subjects suddenly turn their enemy?

For President Kenyatta, I recalled the fireworks in the Nairobi sky that memorable night of Independence Day, 12 December 1963, and the adrenaline-charged nation as the 55,000 foreigners relinquished authority over the eight million Kenyans. At precisely zero hour 00.00, the Union Jack had gone down and the new Kenyan flag went up at the iconic Uhuru Gardens.

Fast forward 22 August 1978 when Moi became the President after the death of President Kenyatta. The country had received him with both hands and excitement beyond measures was felt across the land. Talking biblically, Kenyatta was the people's Moses and Moi was the Joshua; both were expected and had sworn to take their people to the Promised Land. What had gone wrong?

These leaders initially acted true liberators yet for some incomprehensible reasons fell along the way. A simple calculation closed up the matter: From Kenyatta's entry to Moi's exit were exactly a total of 40 years, the same duration the Israelites were taken by their Saviours in circles around some stupid mountain in the desert. Much earlier, another computation had manifested a surprising revelation. Just as the Israelites lived for 70 years in the captivity in Babylon, so was the period of Kenyans' bondage from the British since the declaration of Kenya as its protectorate to independence. White enslavers and black enslavers: what was the difference?

In a civilised African society, hurling missiles and nasty words to leaders and more so the elders is considered immature and is bound to invite a curse. But the people had no alternative to reacting to a betrayed liberation promise. Just as the coronavirus coronaisation of the 21st century has distanced mankind from their economic, political and social expectations, Presidents Kenyatta and Moi had subjected, in the 20th century, a free people from colonial domination, to a neo-colonial distancing or more appropriately, quarantined them from the rich vaults of their land for 40 years.

The term quarantine, isolation, comes from the Latin *quadraginta* and the Italian *quaranta*, both meaning a space of 40 and in the Bible symbolises a period of testing, trial and probation. The reaction was a kind of self-sanitisation. Further, the two had excelled in the art, very un-mankind and un-Godly, of using and dumping in the dustbin, silencing – sometimes eternally –the voices of reason who dared question their selfish governance *modus operandi*. This was the reason, on that afternoon 29 December 2002, a wheel-chair bound from an earlier motor accident Mr. Mwai Kibaki's inauguration as the Republic's third President had an atmosphere comparable to Jesus Christ's entry into Jerusalem for commencement of his mission.

Surprise, surprise! In a mere 10-year two-term tenure, President Kibaki transformed the country in a manner that was hitherto un-thought of in this part of our world. When he took over, the country's GDP was growing at 0.6 per cent, then rose steadily to 7.1 per cent by year 2007, but sadly nose-dived due to the post-election violence in January 2008. The remarkable performance recorded was despite his health challenge and an extremely unco-operative Prime Minister in Raila Odinga. Worldwide, Kenyans were described as the most optimistic people on earth. Mr Kibaki was described as Kenya's best President since independence.

On 9 April 2013, Mr Uhuru Kenyatta, on a Jubilee Party platform, took the reign as the country's fourth President with Mr William Ruto as his Deputy thanks to the new Constitution. The pair, christened UhuRuto, had emerged as the best combination to continue economist

Kibaki's great work and even do much more. Finding an already laid firm foundation to elevate the country to greater heights, the two meant business and business they did especially in their first term in office. The two men demonstrated what kind of stuff a country's top leadership required. You could not ask for more. (I was a strong believer of the Jubilee Promise, to date. Ahead of the UhuRuto re-election for second term, I constituted a team and we made two books and their corresponding documentaries to help in their campaign.)

And the world was taking note of Kenya's road to prosperity, the Bretton Woods institutions no less. In June 2013, the International Monetary Fund's (IMF) Ragnar Gudmundsson predicted that Kenya's economic growth rate would improve to 5.5 per cent up from 4.7 recorded in 2012 and then climb to around 6.6 in 2014. Mr Wolfgang Fengler, the World Bank Lead Economist for Kenya, Rwanda, Eritrea, and author of *Realizing the Kenyan Dream* sounded more optimistic. In an inspiring article, published in the *Saturday Nation* of 22 June 2013 (two months after Jubilee came into power) and headlined "Kenya Economy is on the Runway, Waiting to Take Off", he described Kenya as a country of incredible beauty, dynamism and hope, where a silent revolution was underway for transforming Kenya for the better:

> …The macroeconomic environment was never as good as it is today. Indeed, if Kenya was in the European Union, it would have one of the Union's lowest debt levels… For the first time, it seems that sustainable development is within reach in Kenya. The country is experiencing major transformations… The environment and the timing are right: with smart policies and hard work, Kenya can make it to the next level… Kenya has done moderately well maintaining its spot as the richest country in East Africa.

Mr Wolfgang concluded, still on a positive forecast:

> As I am leaving Kenya next month, the country is at the dawn of a *new development chapter* (italics, mine)… in the future, Kenya should be the place where what you have in your head and heart matters more than what you have in your pockets. That is what true development is all about.

The country's momentum was there, the body was willing and the spirit was willing too. Well, Kenyans were saying: We can't wait to fly!

The same year, 12 December 2013, Kenya marked its 50 years of independence, the Golden Jubilee. Now former President Kibaki advised the nation (*Daily Nation,* same date):

> Kenya's golden jubilee provides us with an excellent opportunity to review five decades of hard work and lasting achievement... And it is the time to plan ahead for an even bigger, better Kenya in which the prosperity agenda can be made more inclusive and, hopefully, with minimal calamity.

Tragically, the good tidings projected by the Bretton Woods agencies, President Kibaki, the Jubilee government, Kenyans and other global fraternity well-wishers were to be short-lived. Back on 1 August 1982 a human political Sisyphus had been born, fated forever to roll a heavy power stone headed for State House that always rolled back to the bottom only for him to begin the process afresh like in Greek mythology; it's every push upwards translated into Kenya moving a step backwards. Presidents Moi and Kibaki administrations had suffered from this curse. The Jubilee government had also tasted several doses until 9 March 2018 when it reached the climax in form of treasonable presidential swearing-in and thereafter the Handshake followed closely by the Building Bridges Initiatives (BBI). Outwardly the new concept looked good except that it lacked a reliable and firm base (Mathew 7:26-27); a once again false route to Canaan destined to end in a *cul de sac*, with dire consequences to the Jubilee manifesto, the Big 4 Agenda, and the people and country.

Arguably, Stephen Hawking, the British physicist, cosmologist and author remains one of the greatest scientists in modern times. He had lived with a motor neurone disease for over 50 years that paralysed him for decades. When he died on 14 March 2018 aged 76 Kenyan journalist, Philip Ochieng, described him as a case study that came to "personify a mind without a body" and who lived a "history-making mental life housed in a physical body so diseased" (*Saturday Nation,* 17 March 2018). History is clear in black and white that Raila's is an extremely dangerous political mind domiciled in a fantastically created body that has a habit of terrorising the country's political, economic and social atmosphere, then hibernating, awakening then terrorising once again... Was President Kenyatta not playing with fire? (Proverbs 6:27-28).

Any patriotic Kenyan would have been very afraid as the voice of German poet Bertolt Brecht in the *Mother* tormented their minds: "On whom is the blame if their oppression stays? On us! On whom does it fall to destroy it? On us!" As if in a dream, the voice of Leslie Brown, an American motivational speaker and author spoke to me: "The graveyard is the richest place on earth, because it is here that you will find all the hopes and dreams that were *never fulfilled*, the books that were *never written*, the songs that were *never sung*, the inventions that were *never shared*, the cures that were *never discovered,* all because someone was too afraid to take that first step, keep with the problem, or determined to carry out their dream (italics, mine)."

Patriotism is ruthlessly courageous. In whatever circumstances, it does not risk the anticipations and visions of a motherland to head to the cemetery, rather it takes a leap of faith and try to find a solution… Kenya deserves the best.

Thus, this book was born.

Mũthende Ndũũcũ
Nairobi, September 2020

Acknowledgements

This book would not have become without reference to various sources and assistance from some institutions and special individuals. I am indebted to them all.

I am full of gratitude to my parents, Ndũũcũ Kariũki and Mary Nyakĩrĩnga who are up there watching. You cannot get better preparers of the way. A heap of appreciation to my wife and children for being a wonderful pillar and believing, like one of our leaders that, prayers is not just a ritual, but indeed is serious business. Thanks to uncle Ngũgĩ wa Thiong'o for his magnificent lesson on keeping on dreaming even in times of adversity.

Of special mention is Duncan Watata; together we embarked on the journey, but sadly he passed on of cancer along the way. God bless his soul.

Josephat Ngamau, Mwangi Karanja, Peter Oloiputari, Albert Gacheru, Luke Mulunda: your contributions are priceless. To Josephine Kiinga who tirelessly typed the manuscript and Jeremy Ng'ang'a for the editorial work. You are terrific.

Going back in time I encounter some of my teachers: Ian Gooch, late Sammy ole Kwallah, Simon Masiea, Charles Kamanja, Captain Francis Wamwea (died in Kenya Airways Douala plane crash, May 2007) and Alfonse Ndamagoe (killed during 1994 Rwanda Genocide). Others are David Carden and Paul Von Hoidoonk. You all left footprints in the sands of time.

To everyone, I am truly grateful. I hereby close with Steve Jobs: "Going to bed at night saying we've done something wonderful… that is what matters to me." Be blessed abundantly.

Abbreviations

AAPC	-	All African People's Conference
ANC	-	African National Congress
ANC	-	Amani National Congress
AU	-	African Union
BBI	-	Building Bridges Initiative
CCM	-	Chama cha Mapinduzi
CNN	-	Cable News Network
CoE	-	Committee of Experts
CORD	-	Coalition for the Restoration of Democracy
COTU	-	Central Organisation of Trade Unions
Covid-19	-	Coronavirus disease 2019
CPC	-	Communist Party of China
CVO	-	Covid-Organics
DNA	-	Deoxyribonucleic acid
EACC	-	Ethics and Anti-Corruption Commission
EFCC	-	Economic and Financial Crimes Commission [Nigeria]
EFF	-	Economic Freedom Fighters (SA)
ESV	-	English Standard Version
EU	-	European Union
FORD	-	Forum for the Restoration of Democracy
GWR	-	Guinness World Records
HIV	-	Hate, Incitement and Violence
IAU	-	International Astronomical Union

ICC	-	International Criminal Court
ICU	-	Intensive Care Unit
IDPs	-	Internally Displaced Persons
IEBC	-	Independent Electoral and Boundaries Commission
IPC	-	International Potato Centre
KANU	-	Kenya African National Union
KCCB	-	Kenya Conference of Catholic Bishops
KDF	-	Kenya Defence Forces
KJV	-	King James Version
KNBS	-	Kenya National Bureau of Statistics
KNCHR	-	Kenya National Commission on Human Rights
LDP	-	Liberal Democratic Party
LSE	-	London School of Economics
MBI	-	Mending Bridges Initiative
MCA	-	Member of the County Assembly
MIT	-	Massachusetts Institute of Technology
MP	-	Member of Parliament
NASA	-	National Aeronautics and Space Administration
NASA	-	National Super Alliance
NAZI	-	Nationalsozialistische (National Socialist German Workers' Party)
NDP	-	National Development Party
NIV	-	New International Version (Bible)
NLT	-	New Living Translation
NPD	-	Narcissistic Personality Disorder
NTV	-	Nation Television
OAU	-	Organisation of African Unity
ODM	-	Orange Democratic Movement

OHCHR	-	Office of High Commissioner for Human Rights
PCR	-	Polymerase Chain Reaction
PDP	-	Perseverance Democratic Party
PEV	-	Post-Election Violence
PLO	-	Palestine Liberation Organization
POWs	-	Prisoners of War
PPE	-	Personal Protective Equipment
PRB	-	Population Reference Bureau
PUI	-	Person Under Investigation (for disease)
ROI	-	Return on Investment
SARS	-	Severe Acute Respiratory Syndrome
SDGs	-	Sustainable Development Goals
SGR	-	Standard Gauge Railway
TJRC	-	Truth, Justice and Reconciliation Commission
TNA	-	The National Alliance
UDHR	-	Universal Declaration on of Human Rights
UNECA	-	United Nations Economic Commission for Africa
UNEP	-	United Nations Environmental Programme
UNESCO	-	United Nations Educational, Scientific and Cultural Organization
UNGA	-	United Nations General Assembly
VE	-	Victory in Europe
VK	-	Victory in Kenya
WFP	-	World Food Programme
WHO	-	World Health Organization
WMD	-	Weapons of Mass Destruction

Opening Quotes

When the angels saw how unfortunate men could not pass those abysses and ravines to finish the work they had to do, but tormented themselves and looking in vain and shouted from one side to the other, the angels spread their wings above those places and men were able to cross. So people learned from the angels of God how to build bridges, and therefore, after fountains, the greatest blessing is to build a bridge and the greatest sin to interfere with one, for every bridge, from a tree trunk crossing a mountain stream… has its guardian angel who cares for it and maintains it as long as God has ordained that it should stand.

Ivo Andric, winner, Nobel Prize in Literature, 1961
The Bridge on the Drina

*   *   *

A book is made from a tree. It is an assemblage of flat flexible parts (still called leaves) imprinted with dark pigmented squiggles. One glance at it and you hear the voice of another person… the author is speaking, clearly and silently, inside your head, directly to you. Writing is perhaps the greatest of human inventions, binding together people, and citizens of distant epochs, who never knew one another. Books break the shackles of time-proof that humans can work magic.

Carl Sagan, American astronomer

*   *   *

The book which the reader now holds in his hands, from one end to another… treats the advance from evil to good, from injustice to justice, from falsity to truth, from darkness to daylight, from blind appetite to conscience, from decay to life, from bestiality to duty, from Hell to Heaven, from Limbo to God. Matter itself is the starting point and the point of arrival is the soul.

Victor Hugo, French writer,
introduction to *Les Miserables*

*   *   *

We are tired of war. We are tired of running. We are tired of begging for bulghur wheat. We are tired of our children being raped. We are now taking this stand, to secure the future of our children. Because we believe as custodians of society, tomorrow our children will ask us, Mama what was your role during the crisis?

Leymah Gbowee,
Joint Nobel Peace Laureate, 2011

*   *   *

Mr. President, my friend. I have told you in private and I will tell you today in public, that you have an opportunity and me as your Deputy will support you, to make sure that Kenya becomes one. You have my unqualified support, all of us; you have our support Mr. President. Under your leadership is my prayer that God shall give us the grace and the favour that never again shall the people of this country shed innocent blood or destroy property on account of political competition.

Deputy President, William Ruto,
Daily Nation (2016)

*　　　　　*　　　　　*

You have enemies? Why, it is the story of every man,
Who has done a great deed or created a new idea.

Victor Hugo,
French writer

*　　　　　*　　　　　*

… New world, big horizon,
Open your eyes, and see it's true,
New world, across the frightening,
Waves of blue…

New world, sun is rising,
We were wise just to see it through,
New world, second chance,
For me and you.

David Wilcox,
New World

*　　　　　*　　　　　*

No!
I will not still my voice!
I have too much to claim…
I have learnt,
From books dear friend,
Of men dreaming and living,
And hungering in a room without a light,
Who could not die since death was far too poor,
Who did not sleep to dream,
but dreamed to change the world,
And so…
I do not sleep to dream,
but dream to change the world

Martin Carter,
Looking at Your Hands

*   *   *

From everything that man erects and builds in his urge for living nothing is in my eyes better and more valuable than bridges. They are more important than houses, more sacred than shrines. Belonging to everyone and being equal to everyone, useful, always built with a sense, on the spot where most human needs are crossing, they are more durable than other buildings and they do not serve for anything secret or bad.

– Ivo Andric, *The Bridges*

Introduction

The path laid out ahead
is long and dark
but the path behind me
Is litered with rubbel
Smoke dots the horizon
Thick black smoke
billowing into the sky
marking the bridges I've burned
Alone and lost
no turning back
no place to call home
No other choice
but to trudge on ahead
Into the dark, into the void

Rebecca Lynn
"Burning Bridges" (February 2015)

*   *   *

Pick a leader who will make their citizens proud. One who will stir the hearts of the people, so that the sons and daughters of a given nation strive to emulate their leader's greatness. Only then will a nation be truly great, when a leader inspires and produces citizens worthy of becoming future leaders, honorable decision makers and peacemakers. And in these times, a great leader must be extremely brave. Their leadership must be steered only by their conscience, not a bribe.

Suzy Kassem,
"Rise Up and Salute the Sun" (2011)

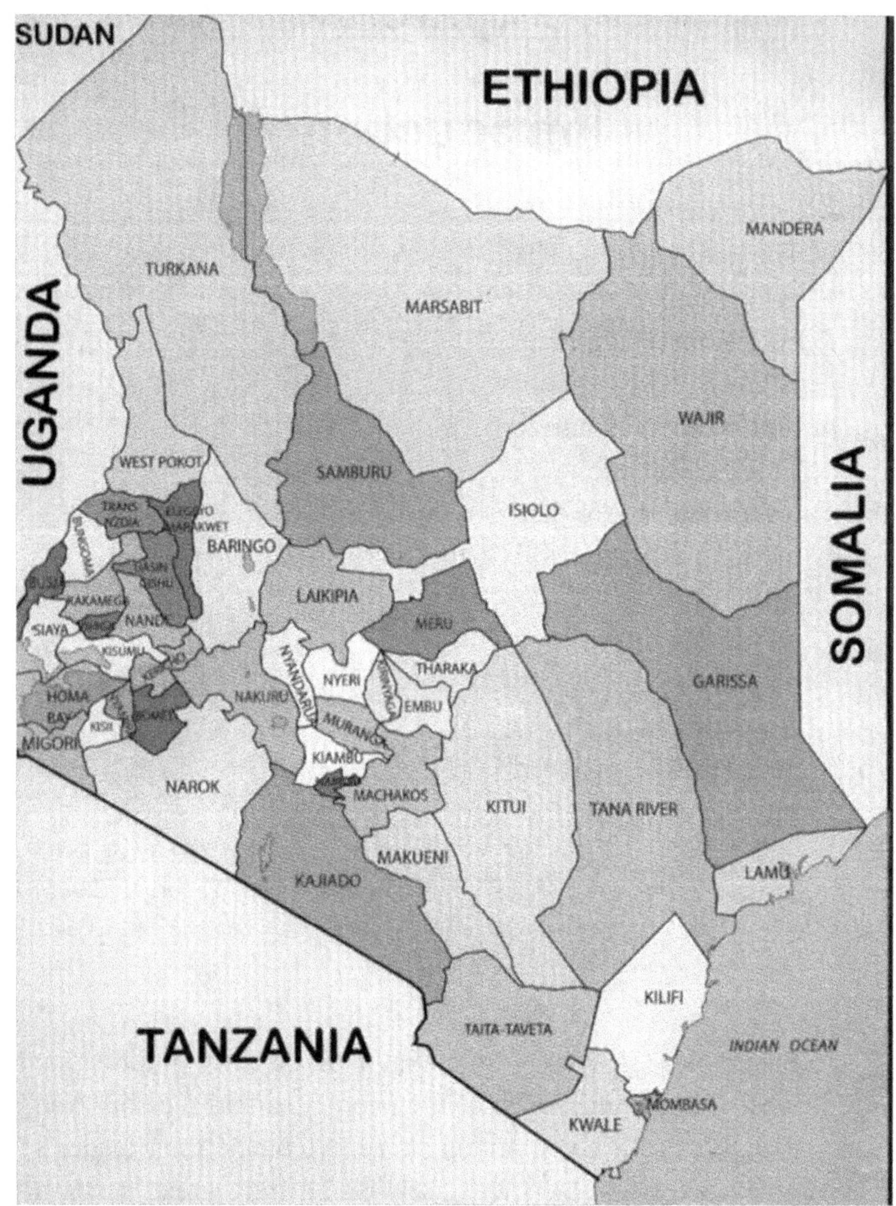

Brand Kenya: Tainted by poor leadership

Time indeed flies fast. It seems like just yesterday that Kenya marked the 50th Independence Anniversary. On 12 December, 2023, the country will be celebrating the Diamond Jubilee of her independence. Ordinarily, diamond is a symbol of human progress and is often used as a marker of the 60th remembrance of a marriage. In Kenya's case, it will commemorate an unbreakable partnership entered into between Kenyans and their government on 12 December1963.

Looking back in time since independence, Kenya has had an assortment of ups and downs – a cocktail of moments of triumphs and defeats. This is however a scenario that obtains in all nations worldwide. It is the way of the world; hence, the reflections from the Kenya of the past provide a perfect description from Charles Dickens' *A Tale of Two Cities*:

> It was the best of times, it was the worst of times, it was the age of wisdom, it was the age of foolishness, it was the epoch of belief, it was the epoch of incredulity, it was the season of Light, it was the season of Darkness, it was the spring of hope, it was the winter of despair, we had everything before us, we had nothing before us, we were all going direct to Heaven, we were all going direct the other way …

The above extract was used to describe the contrasting scenarios between London and Paris during the French Revolution, where the writer, Dickens, expresses a vision that human prosperity cannot be matched with human despair. These images are still present in Kenya today and they will be present in the future. There have been numerous milestones in the country arrived at in the last six decades. However, nothing in the world ever reaches the state of perfection, of finality. A good life basically involves refining the accomplishments, endeavouring to complete work-in-progress, initiating new ventures and correcting the worst of situations.

At this moment in time the major question would be: what main assets or liabilities have shaped Kenya's history? And moving forward, is the Building Bridges Initiative (BBI), unveiled November 2019, the best thing to have happened in the country –maintain the assets, discard the liabilities? The answer is to be found in what could be described as, "A Triple Heritage: the Country, its Master Plans (the BBI) and the Leaders".

HERITAGE I. COUNTRY KENYA

One must love a country before they start building bridges. And the country must be great. Without exaggeration, Kenya is a truly unique country, where the term unique, in the words of Philip Ochieng, a renowned journalist, "…is to have no exemplar, no lookalike, no model…To be unique is to be absolutely alone in your category… Thus a thing or idea is unique if it is the only example of its kind existing…"[1]

Kenya is endowed with abundant blessings from Above. When this is added to the marvellous work of its people's hands, one gets a country teeming with a collection of top global brands. The country is a brand in itself.

Many prominent people have ably described the bright side of Kenya. At one time, a Speaker of the National Assembly, Kenneth Marende, described Kenya as, "A country possibly playing host to God".[2] Gilad Millo, former Israel Deputy Ambassador to Kenya explained that, "In Hebrew, Kenya means 'God's nest' and I think that is reflected in the culture of people here".[3] Years back, American novelist, Ernest Hemingway, described Kenya as "unknowable, unimaginable, unbelievable". All these accolades confirm that Kenya is indeed an invaluable brand. Therefore, it is a country that was undoubtedly crafted from the gold dust, so to say.

HERITAGE II. THE HORIZON (MASTER PLAN/BBI)

Today, perhaps more than ever before, one cannot pretend that all is well. Observing Kenya from a distance through a powerful telescope one would think all there is, is total harmony. A closer look however reveals a dark cloud hanging over the land; deep pits whose digging seems to have no end. Ngũgĩ wa Thiong'o speaks to this state of affairs in his book, *Devil on the Cross*:

> How can we cover up pits in our courtyard with leaves or grass saying to ourselves that because our eyes cannot now see the holes,

---

1 Philip Ochieng, "A thing is unique only if it is the only one of its kind", *Daily Nation*, 8 July, 2016.

2 Quoted in Dennis Lumiti, "Ancestors cannot condone immorality in the Kenyan society", *Daily Nation*, 29 July, 2013.

3 Julius Sigei, "From Beverly Hills to muddying hands with farmers: Envoy's story", Daily Nation, 21 February 2014.

our children can prance around the yard as they like? Happy is the man who is able to discern the pitfalls in his path for he can avoid them.[4]

In one of his regular articles, December 2014, Dr Lukoye Atwoli, a scholar and social commentator, is critical about the situation in Kenya. While commending the country for "still growing in a positive way", he warned leaders that, "…There are areas in which you could do better though … you could begin by acting your age".[5] This is probably where the BBI, birthed by President Uhuru Kenyatta and Raila Odinga, come in. It is the current horizon. Who would not wish for a stable, peaceful, united and prosperous country? The BBI that Kenyans desire is very simple. It should be like a hen sitting on 44 eggs (country's communities) and on the 21st day of hatching all chickens come out alive and kicking.

The BBI's outcome should not be manna from heaven. Kenyans should be given their full human rights, the Golden Fleece – symbol of freedom and sovereignty – they have searched for ages, as envisaged in the Constitution and the 30 articles of the United Nations Universal Declaration of Human Rights (UDHR). The US First Lady, Eleanor Roosevelt, chair of the United Nations Human Rights Commission predicted that the Declaration "may well become the international *Magna Carta* – the Great Charter of the Liberties – for all men everywhere". Then they should be given opportunities as in the words of Archimedes: "Give me a place to stand, and a lever long enough, and I will move the world." Depending on the circumstances, opportunities could be a subset of human rights.

What Kenyans would dislike is a BBI that behaves like the Big Bang theory of the universe origin, a concept that even some of the best minds cannot comprehend. While fixing the struggling economy shall be a priority, the BBI as a matter of priority should begin by killing the HIV – Hate, Incitement and Violence virus - in top leadership:. Then, and only then shall the BBI mean business.

Political violence is particularly one culture that should be shunned. Nairobi City County, the seat of Kenya's government, occupies a significant

---

4   Ngũgĩ wa Thiong'o, *Devil on the Cross* (Nairobi: East African Educational Publishers, 2002), p. 1.

5   Lukoye Atwoli, "Kenya on right track but leaders need to grow up", *Saturday Nation*, 13 September, 2014.

position both locally and internationally. It is the only city in Africa and, indeed in the Southern Hemisphere, to host a UN agency headquarters. The UN office in Kenya is the third largest duty station in the world after New York and Geneva contributing around KES 40 billion annually in foreign exchange. The City also houses the second largest European Union foreign mission after London. Moreover, multinational companies from all over the world have invested billions of Kenya shillings; hence, it is accurate to say that the world is run from Kenya. The world cannot therefore risk to be headquartered in an unstable country.

Centuries ago, a young Greek scholar, Archimedes, leapt out of a public bath tub and ran through the streets of Syracuse, stark naked and in broad daylight, shouting, "Eureka! Eureka! Eureka!" (I Have Found it! I Have Found it! I Have Found it!). He had made a discovery of his life – that the volume of irregular objects could be measured with precision by immersing them in water. In the past, Kenya has arrived at its Eureka moments several times. It has found exactly what ailed it and conceived marvellous plans to remedy the ailments. Such moments have included the Kenya Vision 2030, the Truth, Justice and Reconciliation (TJRC) report, the Constitution and the Big Four Agenda. All were hailed locally and internationally as masterpieces. However, upon the advent of the BBI in 2019 one would have been tempted to ask, what happened to the earlier four initiatives?

While documents get updated once in a while, convincing answers would hardly come by. This gives rise to another question: What could be the problem with Kenya if it cannot be cured of illness even with the best prescriptions in the market?

HERITAGE III. THE LEADERSHIP

In the book, *The Trouble with Nigeria*, novelist Chinua Achebe concluded about his country (Nigeria): "The trouble with Nigeria is simply and squarely a failure of leadership", and went further to add, "There is nothing basically wrong with the Nigerian character. There is nothing wrong with the Nigerian land or climate or water or air or anything else. The Nigerian problem is the unwillingness or inability of its leaders to rise to the responsibility, to the challenge of personal examples which are the hallmarks of true leadership."[6]

---

6   Chinua Achebe, *The Trouble with Nigeria* (Oxford: Heinemann, 1984), p. 1.

Likewise the problem with Kenya is not about its problems, but the leadership. Problems are normally created by the leadership and are not a reflection on the country itself. There is nothing wrong with Kenya. Kenya is not a poor country, for instance, but has been made a country of poor – spiritually, morally and materially – by greedy and incompetent leadership. It is the leadership that leads the country into darkness.

A country will never achieve perfection unless its citizens are converted into angels. That said, the BBI is a fantastic thought. It is a possible jackpot for Kenyans. More critically, it is supposed to have a long life-span. The Initiative will go through and beyond Vision 2030 and Africa's Agenda 2065. Even the Americans are still building bridges among its people over two centuries after independence. Now, the main pilots of BBI are President Uhuru Kenyatta and Raila Odinga. Will they heal the patient? Another question: Among the leading political leaders as currently constituted, who is the better option to drive the BBI agenda, now and in the future?

In the 1970s, Venezuela had a huge oil boom. The then country's Minister of Mines and Hydrocarbons, Juan Alfonzo, predicted: "Ten years from now, 20 years from now, you will see … Oil will ruin us … Oil is the devil's excrement." True, because the leaders at the top were greedy and incompetent to capitalise on the new found riches. As the old adage goes, "Oil is a curse". Today the country is one of the poorest in the world.

Supposing the BBI is oil from the Turkana fields being transported to Mombasa for export. The tanker has the driver and the turn-boy (*makanga*). Somewhere into the journey, the *makanga* takes to the wheels. He has no driver's licence and causes an accident spilling out the oil. The country misses all the petrodollars. Instead of enriching the country the BBI becomes the devil's excrement.

ABOUT THE BOOK

Raila Odinga and Burning Bridges in Kenya is a literary project that takes the form of a Barrel of the Pen. It has been compiled with the sole aim of making Kenya a better place to live in, inspired by a great sense of patriotism. First and foremost, the book is derived from the recognition that *art* is a powerful catalyst in changing a society positively. It is a mirror that makes people know themselves better and spruce themselves up.

On 4 September, 2015, while at the Kenya National Theatre, President Uhuru Kenyatta emphasised the importance of the art:

> ... [Art] gives society an opportunity to examine itself, criticize itself, admire itself, understand itself, laugh at itself, teach itself, and move itself forward to a higher, better social-political and moral plane ... I also encourage more organizations to partner with my government in realizing our aspirations...[7]

Secondly, the work is an appreciation that the subject of building bridges in Kenya requires thousands of pages to tell it adequately. But it must start somewhere, say, by putting together some hundreds of pages. A former US President, Thomas Jefferson, selected some parts of the Bible, which he believed were relevant to him. He told his comrades: "I too have made a wee little book from the same materials which I call the philosophy of Jesus Christ ... A more beautiful or precious morsel .... It is a document in proof that I am a real Christian ... a disciple of the doctrine of Jesus Christ ..."[8] This text is evidence of deep commitment to the Spirit of independence.

Why is this endeavour a barrel of a pen? The country's leaders are obviously the problem and the buck should stop at their doorstep. They deserve the war to be taken right to their doorsteps. Whatever the degree of love we have for them, the country comes first.

In August 2005, Andrew Mwenda, a political editor of the Nation Media Group *Monitor* newspaper was charged with sedition. He had called President Yoweri Museveni of Uganda a villager.[9] His counsel argued that, "The emphasis of the constitution is about the power of the people. If they cannot talk about the leaders, then the law is

---

7   Speech by President Uhuru Kenyatta during the commissioning of the Newly Modernized Kenya National Theatre, A Kenya @50 Legacy Project, at the Kenya National Theatre, Nairobi 4th September, 2015.

8   *"The faith (and doubts) of our fathers" The Economist*, 17 December, 2011. Available: https://www.economist.com/christmas-specials/2011/12/17/the-faith-and-doubts-of-our-fathers

9   *Nairobi Law Monthly* magazine, November 2010.

unconstitutional…" and added, "If there is a law that criticizes whatever someone writes against the President, how would the government change if people loved their president forever? If one accepts a high office, one must grow hard skin to bear criticism." This is the freedom of thought and expression in the constitution.

Kenyans must demand for good leadership. Lee Kuan Yew, the Singaporean Prime Minister from 1959 to 1990. On leadership, Yew believed that "There must be continuous renewal of talented, dedicated, honest, able people who will do things not for themselves but for their people and for the country."[10] During his rule, Singapore was transformed from the Third World to the First World in a single generation. In 1988, two years before he stepped down from premiership, Yew declared, "Even from my sickbed, even if you are going to lower me into the grave and I feel that something is going wrong, I will get up!"[11]

Since independence, Kenyans have been building bridges. To understand what caused the sins of omission and commission, the journey must be written accurately and boldly. It does not need to please everyone. The knowledge about constructing bridges in the past will be an asset to the success of the BBI. More or less, this is what Tom Odhiambo, a literature lecturer at the University of Nairobi, had in mind in his article, published in the *Saturday Nation*, 29 June 2013:

> We need to open up, talk to each other, exorcise the ghosts, pour libation to the ancestors and begin to acknowledge and compose a national history that doesn't have to be agreeable to all Kenyans but is a representative of the various shades of histories found in Kenya.

CRACKING THE BBI RIDDLE

Americans have the term, "one million-dollar question" (or the one million-dollar dilemma) to describe something that needs to be resolved in a make-or-break situation. For Kenyans, it would translate into *Swali la kufa na kupona* (a matter of life and death). This is principally for:

(a)   The Office of High Commissioner for Human Rights (OHCHR) Nairobi, representing the 70-year old United Nations Universal Declaration of Human Rights (UDHR);

---

10 Interview with China Central Television (CCTV) on 12 June 2005.

11 "Lee Kuan Yew: his most memorable quotes", *The Telegraph*, 23 March 2015.

(b)   The Committee of Experts (CoE) on the Kenya Constitution;

(c)   Religious leaders;

(d)   Political scientists;

(e)   Economists; and,

(f)   The BBI Task Force.

The question: Here is a person,

- the most mentioned in the worst human rights violations in the last 40 years, including being accused of treason twice,

- being fronted as the best suited midwife in building bridges among 47 million Kenyans, and

- being proposed President/Prime Minister of a country that holds such immense significance for its people and the global community.

Pray, tell: what or where is the logic behind this mighty riddle? Kenya and the world want to know.

This book is a ruthless conversation about the subject of leadership in the country and how the culture of betrayal is not a menu for human rights and development. It is an invitation to the reader to discover the better leader and the worst leader in the current political dispensation.

CHAPTER TWO

The 'Big Lie' Virus Attacks Jubilee Party

His primary rules were: Never allow the public to cool off; never admit a fault or wrong; never concede that there may be some good in your enemy; never leave room for alternatives; never accept blame; concentrate on one enemy at a time and blame him for everything that goes wrong; people will believe a big lie sooner than a little one; and if you repeat it frequently enough people will sooner or later believe it.

Dr Walter C. Langer,
A Psychological Analysis of Adolf Hitler (1999)

*   *   *

That a lover who is detected in doing any dishonourable act, or submitting through cowardice when any dishonour is done to him by another, will be more pained than at being seen by his father, or by his companions, or by anyone else… And if there were only some way of contriving that a State or an army should be made up of lovers and their loves, they would be the very best governors of their own city, abstaining from all dishonour; and emulating one another in honour; when fighting at each other's side, although a mere handful, they would overcome the world… Or who would desert his beloved or fail him in the hour of danger? The veriest coward would become an inspired hero, equal to the bravest, at such a time; Love would inspire him.

– Plato, Greek philosopher,
Symposium (360 BCE)

*   *   *

Argument is conclusive… but… it does not remove doubt, so that the mind may never rest in the sure knowledge of the truth, unless it finds it by the method of experiment. For if any man who never saw fire proved by satisfactory arguments that fire burns, his hearer's mind would never be satisfied, nor would he avoid the fire until he put his hand in it that he might learn by experiment what argument taught.

Roger Bacon,
British theologian (1219-1292)

Jubilee Party logo: People's Party under virus attack

The Year of Our Lord Twenty Eighteen is when it happened in Kenya. First, politics and science were in a contest. Two opposite poles (North and South), not of a magnet, but politicians, attracted one another. That is normal; the law of science at work that also favours politics. Like when a dog bites a man, it was not news.

Next, two parallel lines – again, politicians – which are supposed to never meet (are always at equidistant) except at infinity, actually did meet. By defying the laws of mathematics, politics became victorious. This was hot news like when you see a man biting a dog. A journalist with a nose for a good story would spare no effort to rush to the epicentre of the drama, record the exciting proceedings, and with haste head to the newsroom. Following this Breaking News, in the immediate foreseeable future, Kenya would never be the same again…

"What was the most important year in human history?" *The Economist*'s Intelligent Life magazine, posed in an article sometime in 2009. Anni Mirabiles, the editor, argued that how we answer says a lot about who we are. Somewhere along the line, Adrian Wooldridge noted: "You don't have to be a believer to recognize that Jesus' birth was the most important event in human history." The article went on to elaborate, "Jesus inspired the world's most popular religion...two thousand years after his birth...a third of the world population calls themselves Christians...It is such a momentous event that it makes other contenders for the most important year look feeble by comparison." At times like these, one can twist the magazine's question and ask: "What was the greatest moment in Kenya's history?"

"MOST IMPORTANT YEAR" IN KENYA'S HISTORY

In matters social-economic-political emancipation, the midnight of 12 December 1963, easily comes top. Feeling on Cloud Nine, Kisoi Munyao hoisted the Kenyan flag on Mount Kenya and memorably declared: "...The Flag is flying. The light is shining all over Kenya." The country was free at last from slightly over 70 years of foreign domination. But another great moment comes to mind, namely the end of the KANU rule.

On 30 December 2002, Mwai Kibaki ascended to the presidency. Inheriting a country he described as having "been ravaged by years of misrule and ineptitude", he sat down to work. In five years, the annual GDP growth rose from 0.6 to 7.1 per cent. He brought the constitution home. He launched Vision 2030. Many, including his fiercest critic like Prof Makau Mutua, called him Kenya's greatest president. And Kenyans were described as the most optimistic people in the world.

Kenya marked the 50th year of independence, the Golden Jubilee, on 12 December 2013. On 4 March 2013, Uhuru Kenyatta and William Ruto had been elected President and Deputy President respectively for a five-year period. It was another moment to behold. Reasons?

1. Two become one

The election to the Presidency of Uhuru-Ruto duo under the new constitution was significant in many ways. First, Uhuru and Ruto had been among the so called the "Ocampo Six", accused of crimes against humanity by the ICC at The Hague regarding the 2007-2008 post-election violence. Before and after the case, millions of Kenyans, nearly all leaders of the 54 African countries and others beyond the continent, had come together to defend the two.

Second: UhuRuto's was a political marriage scripted right from heaven. Where except in Kenya do you encounter the Commander-in-Chief and his Deputy accompanied by their spouses at the swearing-in ceremony kneeling down on pillows for divine intervention in their leadership, while the Generals of the Defence Forces stood behind them?

Third: UhuRuto's was a blessed presidency from the word go. Never in the history of Kenya had millions of citizens suffocated the airwaves with prayers for the country and its leaders. And during the country's Golden Jubilee anniversary, Deputy President Ruto emphasised the importance of prayers: "...But I want to say prayers is not a ritual, it is a serious business. If you are in doubt, ask Uhuru Kenyatta and myself."[1]

Fourth: The Jubilee Party campaign manifesto. It was an ambitious master plan based on a magnificent vision and values to transform Kenyans from all walks of life across the country.

---

1   "Uhuru leads in taking Kenyans' pain to God", *Daily Nation*, 20 June, 2013.

Besides the desire to bring justice to the victims of post-election violence, what the ICC and its local and international acolytes wanted most was probably to separate President Kenyatta and Deputy Ruto and frustrate their joint leadership of the country. The plan flopped miserably. More importantly, the political partnership between the two was informed by their desire to unite the country and make development their utmost signature. In the *Symposium*, Plato speaks to us about relationships meant to have a common destiny:

> After the division the two parts of man, each desiring his other half, come together, and throwing their arms about one another, entwined in mutual embrace, longing to grow into one, they were on the point of dying from hunger and self-neglect, because they did not like to do anything apart... so ancient is the desire of one another which is implanted in us, reuniting our original nature, making one of the two and healing the state of man... Each of us when separated, having one side only, like a flat fish, is but the indenture of a man, and he is always looking for his other half.[2]

The UhuRuto political drama would have qualified for a place in the *Guinness Book of World Records*. Yours truly celebrated the Jubilee victory thus:

> ...perhaps no other national exercise had generated such local and intentional interest than this one...except that of President Obama perhaps no other held the world attention in recent times probably not even the ongoing Vatican drama... so with the stroke of a pen they (electorate) made their decision, the lowly were elevated, the mighty humbled and veterans sent packing.[3]

The President and Deputy enthusiastically settled down to fulfil their mandate. They became like the Siamese twins, a top leadership partnership never witnessed before. Development across the country was addressed, even in those areas that had not voted for them. By the close of the five-year term, the finished and work-in-progress projects were clearly visible. The manifesto pledges were a serious business, it was proved. Kenya and the world were convinced that indeed the

---

2   Plato, Symposium, translated by Benjamin Jowett. Retrieved from: http://classics.mit.edu/Plato/symposium.html. Accessed on 2 June 2020.

3   Mũthende Ndũũcũ, "Behold, a New Dawn for Kenya!" *Daily Nation*, 12 March 2013.

Jubilee Party and its leadership were the best thing to have happened in the country. Truly this was the era of the Golden Jubilee.

Prof. Peter Kagwanja, the Chief Executive Officer, African Policy Institute, wrote:

> In many ways, the launch of the Jubilee Party… signalled the return of mass party politics to make Africa's democracies safe for development…the Jubilee elite realized that stability and inclusion hold the key to long-term planning, sustainability and implementation of government policies. The decision by 12 political parties to dissolve and form the Jubilee Party coupled with the mass defection of 46 opposition members of Parliament, three governors and several senators marked the dramatic rebirth of mass party politics…[4]

In the hierarchy of years, 25 years denotes the Silver Jubilee, 50 years the Golden Jubilee, 60 years the Diamond Jubilee and 70 years the Platinum Jubilee. Jubilee derives its name from the Hebrew traditions and its period occurred every 50 years in which slaves and prisoners would be freed, debts would be forgiven and the mercies of God would be particularly manifested. In modern times, this anniversary denotes an important milestone the world over.

Jamie Rivera (Mary Cruz Mendoza from Philippines) captures perfectly this important model in the song, Jubilee:

> It's a time of joy, a time of peace
> A time when hearts are then set free
> A time to heal the wounds of division
> It's a time of grace, a time of hope
> A time of sharing the gifts we have
> A time to build the world that is one…
> It's the time of the Great Jubilee…[5]

2. Jubilation and Ruto on the Cross

The UhuRuto new era was a sweet jubilation as long as it lasted, that is until the 9 March 2018 handshake. They say the eagle is the

---

4   Peter Kagwanja, "Jubilee mass party to fortify inclusive development", *Daily Nation*, 17 September, 2016.

5   Jamie Rivera, "The Jubilee Song", AZ Lyrics, retrieved from: https://www.azlyrics.com/lyrics/jamierivera/thejubileesong.html. Accessed on 2 June 2020.

coolest bird of prey. Wait until you meet his compatriot, the vulture. Raila Odinga supporters have given him monikers including Nyundo (hammer), Tinga (tractor) and Agwambo (unpredictable or mysterious). One from an animal could as well have done. American master thriller, James Hadley Chase, wrote a novel, *The Vulture is a Patient Bird*. "It does not kill its prey," he said. "It waits for another predator to kill and then swoops down on what is left of the carcass." This large carnivorous scavenging bird of prey has a keen eyesight and can spot a three-foot carcass four miles away on the open plains. Raila's political eye is long-sighted. No matter how hungry a vulture is, it always wait perched on a tree nearby even for days for an opportune moment. Immediately after the IEBC and Supreme Court declined to declare him President in 2017, he had spotted a convenient prey, far away. When time presented itself, Raila took the oath of the Presidency.

A vulture does not attack healthy animals; it prefer the weak, injured, sick or dying ones. Raila knew the swearing in had bruised President Kenyatta seriously. It was time to fly down and devour the meal, the Handshake served generously at the Office of the President. It is also said that the vulture eats from both the king's table and in worse times, scavenges the dustbins for rotten food. Now feasting on the BBI with the President, Raila knew, next stop could be in the streets running away from the police officers' tear gas canisters. The deal had to be absolutely watertight. It is also a fact that when you see a vulture hovering in the sky, the slaughter house or carcass is not far off. Raila was proven right. Life had never felt more promising.

> The Lord is my shepherd; I shall not want. He maketh me to lie down in green pastures; he leadeth me beside the still waters… Yea, though I walk through the valley of the shadows of death, I will fear no evil… Thou preparest a table before me in the presence of mine enemies; thou anointest my head with oil; my cup runneth over… (Psalms 23:1-5)

> Go thy way, eat thy bread with joy, and drink thy wine with a merry heart… Live joyfully with the wife whom thou lovest all the days of the life of thy vanity… (Ecclesiastes 9:7-9)

The invasion, conquer and subsequent partial occupation of the Jubilee House was officially stamped by the Handshake between President Kenyatta and Raila Odinga. The Jubilee Party was now on the Cross. Deputy President Ruto, the Deputy Party leader more or less, became a foreigner in the House. The country was shocked. The ruling party began a painful journey to disintegration.

This tragic saga of Raila gate-crashing the Jubilee House and being given a soft landing by the party leader takes one back to a story in Jomo Kenyatta's book, *Facing Mount Kenya*:

> That once upon a time an elephant made a friendship with a man. One day a heavy thunderstorm broke out, the elephant went to his friend, who had a little hut at the edge of the forest, and said to him: 'My dear good man, will you please let me put my trunk inside your hut to keep it out of this tormenting rain?'

> The man, seeing what situation his friend was in, replied: 'My dear good elephant, my hut is very small, but there is room for your trunk and myself. Please put your trunk in gently.' The elephant thanked his friend, saying: 'You have done me a good deed and one day I shall return your kindness.'[6]

But what followed? Finally the elephant put his whole body in the hut and flung the man out into the rain. After the man complained to the animal kingdom, King Lion established a Commission of Enquiry consisting of the elders of the jungle "To go thoroughly into this matter and report accordingly." As the Commission sat for the hearing, the elephant defended himself wisely thus: "...He invited me to save his hut from being blown away by the hurricane..." Following a lengthy deliberation where man was constantly interrupted, a verdict was arrived at. "...we give you permission to look for a site where you can build another hut more suited to your needs, and we will see that you are well protected."[7] The man was told, to his betrayed hospitality.

This narration is quite familiar. But in the Jubilee scenario where the hut was owned by the two, the party leader was not edged out, but his Deputy. Or was it just a matter of time? Gradually top party lieutenants, and by osmosis millions of members who sacrificed, campaigned and voted it in, started feeling the cold outside. Soon, the House became divided into factions called Tanga Tanga and Kieleweke. US President Abraham Lincoln once warned that a house divided cannot stand.

---

6   Jomo Kenyatta, *Facing Mount Kenya: The Tribal Life of the Gikuyu* (London: Mercury Books, 1961), p. 47.

7   Ibid, p. 51.

In his mind, in particular, Deputy President Ruto found himself in a land similar to one described by the main character in Ngũgĩ wa Thiongo's book, *Matigari* – Matigari ma Njirũngi – when querying the Minister for Truth and Justice. Ruto was wondering loudly where truth and justice had vanished to so soon after his celebrated political bonding with his boss. The story resonates well with one of another man named Karĩanĩme who is a perennial feeder on other people's sweat. Raila was this Karĩanĩme, the master of political exploitation. Matigari ma Njirũngi lamented:

> The builder builds a house,
> The one who watched while it was being built moves into it.
> The builder sleeps in the open air,
> No roof over his head.
> The tailor makes clothes.
> The one who does not even know how to thread a needle wears
> the clothes.
> The tailor walks in rags.
> The tiller tends crops in the fields.
> The one who reaps-where-he-never-sowed yawns for having
> eaten too much.
> The tiller yawns for not having eaten at all…
> Where are truth and justice on this earth?[8]

Flashback, a troubled Father of the Nation. One day, a disturbed President Uhuru Kenyatta paused. Things were not going right in this great nation. Every electoral cycle; violence, madness. Every market has its own madman, but Kenya had gone beyond international standards. And unlike a KEMRI scientist trying to discover a vaccine for the deadly Covid-19, he did not have to look far and wide. Surveying past and present, dead and living politicians, he quickly zeroed in on Raila. Eureka! Therein lies the trouble with Kenya. He crowned him that medal, the Violence-originator.

Secondly, the President had to look forward, his remaining term in office. The problem became a two-fold. What can be done to ensure that every election time people exercise their constitutional right of voting, go home happy and resume their national-building activities without fear of their country turning out hell? The victor and loser becoming one? And will I ever have peace and sound sleep to build on my legacy

---

8   Ngũgĩ wa Thiongo, *Matigari* (Oxford: Heinemann Publishers, 1987), p. 113.

as long as this man from the lake walk on the Kenyan soil an unhappy soul? How can the monster be tamed with all the state machinery having failed? Probably these were the questions that were circling in the President's mind.

Elsewhere, Raila was equally troubled. His Personal Anthem was ringing loudly in his mind: 'In 1982 the lousy Kenya Air Force soldiers planned a miserable coup that was destined to abort – Several presidential elections called – People vote overwhelmingly for me – My competitors rig me out – The IEBC and Supreme Court take side with election thieves – Mass protests and demos fail to spark the Kenyan Spring – January 30, 2018 swearing in becomes messy – I am fast getting old – I will never become president of this country until and unless I cleverly put myself under the wings of President Kenyatta.'

Sooner than later the magnetic forces created by the two men pulled them together. Sometimes even two people with visions running parallel could find something in common, you know. In the spirit of forgiveness and reconciliation they performed the Handshake, followed by the birth of BBI. From that moment on, Raila became the apple of the President's eye. Lay down your claims and arms; I will dry all your tears, give you a new earth and a new world.

The BBI appeared to be the Mother of all previous master plans. This was the real bridge to cross people over to Canaan. President Kenyatta and Raila were the true Miracle Builders. They had declared our self-inflicted slavery a national crime the same way William Wilberforce, the British slave trade abolitionist, had done. He wrote in his diary in 1818: "In the Scripture, no national crime is condemned so frequently and few so strongly as oppression and cruelty, and the not using our best endeavour to deliver our fellow-creatures from them."[9] The two leaders were echoing him in the BBI, exactly 200 years since.

The nine-point agenda addressed in the BBI looked to tackle precisely what the people wanted: national ethos, responsibilities and rights of citizenship, ethnic antagonism and competition, divisive elections, inclusivity, shared prosperity, corruption, devolution, safety and security. These provided the conversation that Kenyans must have been waiting for.

---

9   Robert I. Wilberforce and Samuel Wilberforce, *The Life of Wm. Wilberforce, Volume 4* (London: John Murray, 1839), p. 374.

Then the BBI Party took off. In town halls and stadia rallies, the people deliberated on the nine points, the Kenya they want. Then suddenly it dawned on them: just as the guests in Jesus's first miracle at Cana of Galilee wedding party were first fed with inferior *mũratina* brew, the BBI's party first priority was the creation of the position of Prime Minister and President for certain individuals. A new term was coined: Mending Bridges Initiative (MBI) between two people.

Secondly, the BBI propagation transformed into an arena coated with a solid mission to discredit, soil, insult and give marching orders to Deputy President Ruto. Look, when you shamelessly roast the DP in public like a goat *mũtura*, dig a grave to bury him in while breathing – the second most important national pillar commands millions of followers and the largest number of MPs in the National Assembly – are you building bridges or digging a gulf? Are you uniting or dividing the country?

The introduction of the BBI to Kenyans became synonymous to a husband divorcing the wife of many years of building their household and bringing up children together. "Here," the husband tells the children, "is your new mother. She is better in making *ugali* and brewing *uji* than your former mother." Blood is thicker than water. "No Sir." the children protest to their father. "She is not former, we have her blood; we owe our being to her safe hands and sacrifice. Take this one illegitimate, peace-breaker, bridges-breaker to another planet."

Additionally, the BBI evolved into the killing fields for the Jubilee Party, a national institution stewarded by President Kenyatta and Deputy Ruto, but wholly owned by millions of Kenyans. How do you disintegrate a political bond gluing together more than half the country and claim without blinking an eye that you are building the same country? No doubt the BBI was a two-mouthed ogre; one preaching water, the other wine. To add salt on the wound, Raila and his party, ODM, started playing God and the President Missed in Action.

The Jubilee Party members had always envisioned their party one day joining the club of world giants such as Tanzania's Chama cha Mapinduzi (CCM), South Africa's African National Congress (ANC) or China's Communist Party of China (CPC). Long life-span parties with solid policies of unifying people, economics and maturity make great nations. Less than ten years since formation, Jubilee was being killed slowly. Its Secretary-General, Raphael Tuju, an incompetent and non-performer, was a suspected Raila mole, sleeping on the job and always waiting to see which ship to jump into next. "Tuju is Jubilee's Secretary-General to demonstrate the image of inclusivity and not because he can be relied upon for votes," wrote Oscar Obonyo.[10]

Then there is David Murathe, a ghost worker who adds no value to the party. He had tendered resignation as party Vice-Chairman then hastily brought back to head the Sycophancy and Propaganda Department for the Destruction of Jubilee to speed up the party's death. Seemingly, Raila's virus of breaking political parties at every sunrise had found new willing and accommodative hosts to spread the political pandemic countrywide.

Presumably, what the loud-mouths, modern-day Iscariots, three Axis of Evil of Tuju-Murathe-Atwoli (Francis Atwoli, COTU boss) see in Jubilee is just a seven-letter word. Their ignorance cannot let them decipher exactly what the party stand for. They perceive it as a village slogan, sang by drunkards as they head home in the night.

First, the word and period Jubilee means hope, healing, reconciliation and liberation. It means peace, unity, restoration and God's blessings. In the Catholic Church, Jubilee denotes a special year of remission of sins and universal pardon, reconciliation, solidarity, hope and justice. The name is history of mankind, spiritual, as well as a global brand. Produce a better name for a political party and you possibly qualify for a Nobel Peace Prize.

It is the actual spirit of the Jubilee that UhuRuto right from day one intended and were able to translate into action, Kusema na Kutenda – to make it the goose that lays the golden eggs for the country. But the Party had first to grow, from the grass up. The duo approached the youth, *jua kali* workers, hawkers, *boda boda* riders, women and the rest, from the slums to the villages and every corner of the country as they popularised it. The masses embraced it. The Party was therefore built by the hustlers in the real sense of word.

Meanwhile, big people were busy seeking positions to vie for or making political alliances. The Party was merely their lean-on platform.

---

10   Oscar Obonyo, "Will the new political realignments be the game changer?" *Sunday Nation*, 10 September 2017.

And today it is a confederation cementing together millions of Kenyans. Thus, the Jubilee Party was nurtured, and is maintained to date, not at its Pangani House headquarters, the two Harambee Houses or State House, but by devoted, nationalistic supporters. It belongs to these staunch disciples, specifically the hustlers and not to a handful of double-dealers, enemies of development whose only singsong is "Kusema Bila Vitendo". Any further attempt to annihilate the Party therefore leaves UhuRuto presidency a trivial shell or a one-footed government. It is also a disfavour to the two and significantly a mockery to the passionate prayers they did kneeling down at that Inauguration Day in 2013. And a big blow to the hustlers owners.

Within a short period of time, the masses started perceiving the BBI as doubtful, resisted it and were on the road to rejecting it. Hard questions were being raised. Between Raila and Deputy President Ruto who is the more conversant in building bridges in this country? Ruto has invested tremendously in peace, forgiveness and reconciliation efforts, consistently supporting the President as a trusted, committed and hardworking Principal Assistant in developing the country, in building the Jubilee Party into a monumental national institution imprinted deeply in the hearts and minds of Kenyans, in personal time and money in philanthropic work across the land and in shinning Brand Kenya internationally. No debate about it, Ruto is a huge investor in the country's well-being and logic dictates that high-profile investors are aggressively wooed and provided conducive environment in which to operate upon and rewarded with commensurate Return on Investment (ROI).

What was there in Raila's history to showcase except personal gain and national loss? Raila does not value the work to develop a nation, selfish interests is the in-thing. You can't bring a past-darkened, bankrupt-minded and patriotism-drained individual on board to build bridges in Kenya or anywhere else in the world. You become a laughing stock to the international community. Besides, most propagandists are workaholics. Raila is not. He waits for the tiller to till the land, the planter to plant the seeds and the weeder to weed, then in the dead of the night, with a gunny bag in tow he steals the harvests.

Joseph Goebbels, chief propaganda minister for Germany's Adolf Hitler, believed in the sanctity of work:

> Work is not mankind's curse, but his blessing. A man becomes a man through labour. It elevates him, makes him great and aware, raises him above all other creatures… Men are distinguished by the results of their labour. That is the sure sign of the character and value of a person… Labour means creating value, not haggling over things.[11]

Nevertheless, this was conceivably no big issue. Let the right leader lead. The problem was the elephant, indeed, the camel that was gradually squeezing itself to wholly occupy the Presidency. History is witness. Fairness is just. Raila, the principal architect of the BBI, is ruthlessly unpredictable, migratory more than the Maasai Mara wildebeests, unstable like the bomb-making elements in the chemistry's Periodic Table, a liability in any political marriage…Simply put, his ideas, thoughts, philosophies, intentions, patriotism are totally upside down, and that is his undisputable blood composition. These traits were not suitable in the BBI.

Then something else, the President had been against premature 2022 campaigns at the expense of development. By releasing the BBI, he threw the entire country into a campaign mood full blast. He politicised the civil service. No work but politics. What an unholy trinity that the three-letter word BBI was?

That said, the Jubilee fraternity had yet more unanswered questions. Why in God's name didn't the Party leader consult with his deputy or request mandate from the millions of party members before going to sit for 19 hours and decide the destiny of the country – with a man who had called him drunkard, his party satanic and committed treasonable act by swearing himself the People's President? For how long must one person hold the country at ransom? Kenyans continued to convince each other why Raila was the wrong person for the BBI.

In modern times' narrative, the tent-invading elephant has been largely substituted for a camel. The animal can survive many days without water, a characteristic that make it the desert animal. Raila's political DNA resembles a camel. Invasive, slow, battle-hardened. A desert animal like a camel (or donkey) took 40 good years instead of 40 days to get the Israelites to the Promised Land. For approximately 40

---

11   Joseph Goebbels, "Those Damned Nazis" German Propaganda Archive, Calvin University, 1929. Available at: https://research.calvin.edu/german-propaganda-archive/haken32.htm. Accessed on 2 June 2020.

years, Raila has been a political camel rider. You might have seen the Maralal Camel Derby. The animals pretend to be clocking 100 kph while in reality; they are doing a miserable 20 kph. It is only in Jesus' time that a desert vehicle took a man to spiritual and political glory! You need to come from a community of athletes to learn the ropes of running. It was evident that with Raila's working speed, the BBI was headed nowhere.

3. The bitter waters of Marah

In the second book of the Bible, Exodus, it is written: "So Moses brought Israel from the Red Sea and they went out into the wilderness of Shur; and they went three days in the wilderness, and found no water... And when they came to Marah, they could not drink of the waters of Marah, for they were bitter... And the people murmured against Moses, saying, what shall we drink?" (Ex 15: 22 – KJV)

From the second book of the Bible to the last – Revelation – the Holy Scriptures provided an answer: "The name of the star is Wormwood (curse, in Hebrew); and a third of waters became wormwood, and many men died from the waters, because they were made bitter." (Revelation 8:11 – KJV)

The BBI water was indeed bitter even for human swallow. The President was deep in the BBI. The Deputy had been swept away by its wave. Kenyans, now alone with the tested and untrusted Raila asked themselves: what shall we drink since the water is bitter? Their musical clock started rewinding to the Gathaithi PCEA Church Choir song (banned by President Jomo Kenyatta's government):[12]

Maaĩ nĩ marũrũ	*The water is bitter*
Musa werũ-inĩ gĩthima kĩa Mara,	Moses in the plains at Marah well,
Maaĩ marũra makĩaga kũnyuĩka,	When the water became too bitter to drink,
Kĩrĩndĩ gĩothe gĩkĩũria Musa:	The masses asked Moses:
Nĩ marũrũ, tũkũnyua kĩ?	It is bitter, what shall we drink?
Ona rĩu, maaĩ no marũrũ ...	Even now the water is still bitter...
Nĩ marũrũ, tũkũnyua kĩ?...	It is bitter, what shall we drink?...

---

12 "Maaĩ nĩ Marũrũ" was composed by Ishmael Nga'ng'a, who was also the founder and leader of the PCEA Gathaithi Church Choir. The song had been banned ostensibly because "the fruits of independence could not be equated to the proverbial bitter water that caused concern to the children of Israel". Ishmael died in 2011 of heart failure.

Ta ŭrĩa Musa erirwo nĩ Ngai,	Just like Moses was told by God,
Aikie mũti maaĩ magĩe cama,	To dip a rod so that water may be sweetened,
Tweta Jesu nĩegũtũthondeka,	If we call on Jesus He will treat us,
Kũrĩa kũhĩtanu maaĩ manyuĩke.	So that the water can be drank.

Much later, Moses sent 12 spies to Canaan (Num 13). They found good land there and brought back some fruits. But the land of milk and honey had fierce giants. The Israelites were terrified to hear the bad news. They murmured. They wished to return to Egypt. But Joshua and Caleb urged them on to take the land. Kenyans remembered the liberation trip that is dear to Raila's heart.

President Uhuru Kenyatta had told the nation to read the BBI report and understand the content. They reported back to him: The nine points in the BBI look fantastic. But there is one setback. Which one? There is one giant, the Executive Raila Odinga. Kenyans found a dangerous giant in Raila.

But Raila pressed on. BBI is the Big Apple (like those fruits found in the Promised Land) something regarded as the most significant of its kind, an object of desire and ambition. He told Kenyans to "bet a big apple," that is "to taste the supreme assurance, to be absolutely confident" of the BBI, spicing up with the old English proverb, "An apple a day keeps the doctor away." Meanwhile he crisscrossed the country, hammering and hammering and hammering in the BBI into people's minds.

But Raila was reminded: There was the Kenya Constitution, Vision 2030, the Truth Justice and Reconciliation Commission (TJRC), and the Ndung'u and Kriegler Reports. Add that to the Jubilee manifesto and the Big 4 Agenda. These were constructed using billions of shillings from the taxpayers. Some are in various stages of execution. Others are gathering dust in the shelves. Then the BBI is suddenly commissioned at the Bomas of Kenya on 27 November, 2019. For how long are Kenyans going to make plans which will never see full implementation? How many plans are good enough? What is ever good for us?

Initially, Kenyans were as a matter of fact excited by the BBI trek. But as soon as they arrived at Station Raila Odinga, the shock awaiting them was loudly felt. Raila was the wormwood. He had caused the BBI to be bitter; in fact the bitterest of all former national blueprints, the Bitter Biting Irrigation (BBI) that was ostensibly meant to cleanse the nation. Previously, there were the specialists, Committee of Experts, the Dream Team, Think Tanks, who made ambitious plans. Where were the gurus who moulded the BBI sourced from? Which among the various national plans were Kenyans to trust and follow? Like the hyena who broke his hind legs while following two different scents of *nyama choma*, they risked the same danger!

4.   The Big Lie, a big lesson

Finally, the gospel truth started to emerge: The BBI hidden truth was all about working on who became the President, Prime Minister, Deputy President, Deputy Prime Minister and Cabinet Secretaries. Or wasn't it? The history hit the nail on its head. BBI was nothing but the Big Big Insult (BBI) to people's intelligence. And could Raila care to read George Orwell's *Nineteen Eighty-Four* masterpiece that also celebrated its Platinum Jubilee (70 years) in 2019, the year of Kenya's Big Lie?

The Guardian of 19 May, 2019, termed Orwell's book, one "we turn to when truth is mutilated, when language is distorted, when power is abused, when we want to know how bad things can get." The British publication (founded in 1821 as *The Manchester Guardian*) identified Orwell's core values as honesty, decency, liberty and justice. These were missing in Raila's gospel. And Kenyans were obviously not insane. Orwell stated: "There was truth and there was untruth, and if you clung to the truth even against the whole world, you were not mad."[13] Raila does not give in easily. He boarded the BBI into a Lunatic Express, fuelled it with music and declared that "Nothing Will Stop Reggae" (until Covid-19 struck!)

History does not rot. In Germany, where Raila was a student, the concept of the Big Lie was born. It means that if you tell a lie big enough and keep repeating it, people will eventually believe it. The bigger the lie, the more it will be believed. In his manifesto, *Mein Kampf* ("My Struggle") – a work of propaganda and falsehoods published in 1925, Adolf Hitler explained:

> In the big lie there is always a certain force of credibility; because the broad masses of a nation are always more easily corrupted in the

---

13   George Orwell, *1984* (Planetbooks, 2008), p. 274.

deeper strata of their emotional nature than consciously or voluntarily; and thus in the primitive simplicity of their minds they more readily fall victims to the big lie than the small lie, since they themselves often tell small lies in little matters but would be ashamed to resort to large-scale falsehoods.[14]

To Raila, Kenyans were of simple, primitive minds. In *The Death of Truth* (2018), Michiko Kakutani, an American literary critic, contributes to this subject and notes, "cynism and weariness and fear can make people susceptible to the lies and false promises of leaders bent on unconditional power.[15] In Raila's political career, truth has been an endangered species. He has told all manner of lies to Kenyans. The BBI has some truths in it no doubt. Weren't the simple folks sick and tired of their prevailing circumstances? But if Raila thought that stating, repeating and treating the cocktails of BBI falsehoods will translate into truth and Kenyans fall into the trap, then he had another think coming. The BBI was the Big Lie in Kenya.

Raila has in the past likened himself to great men like Jesus Christ, Nelson Mandela and Galileo Galilei. Scientists tell that no two people are exactly the same, even twins. Yet some coincidences between Hitler and Raila are quite surprising. Adolf Hitler of Germany was born in April and died April 1945. Raila was born in 1945. Hitler launched his national revolution at age 34; Raila at age 37. Hitler died aged 56, BBI was conceived by Raila at year 56 of Kenya's independence.

Adolf Hitler believed that the Jews were enemies of the German people. He used the Big Lie propaganda to turn long-standing anti-Semitism into mass murder of the Jews. He was convinced that he was the Chosen One and was under the protection of Providence. He was also convinced he had a divine mission to redeem his people and lead them to greatness. And he had great fear of death. According to Dr Walter C. Langer's book, *A Psychological Analysis of Adolf Hitler*, "If he cannot achieve immortality as the Great Redeemer, he may seek it as the Great Destroyer who will live in the minds of German people for

---

14   Adolf Hitler, *Mein Kampf*, translated by Ralph Manheim (Boston, Mass: Houghton Mifflin, 1971), p. 231.

15   Quoted in Michiko Kakutani, "The death of truth: how we gave up on facts and ended up with Trump", *The Guardian*, Saturday, 14 July 2018.

a thousand years to come."[16] Raila thinks that the voters, the political competitors and the related electoral institutions are the problems for denying him power. Yet he is the main problem. He believes he is one and only Messiah for Kenya.

The following rather lengthy account of Hitler – the man Germans and other supporting nations thought was the world's greatest bridges builder – is derived from the aforesaid work by Dr Langer that remained a classified document in the archives of the US Office of Strategic Service (OSS) for 56 years until 1999 when it was approved for release. It has been brought to the very first chapter of this book deliberately to demonstrate how dangerous bridge builders can turn the world upside down through the Big Lie. Because Kenya, as a developing nation, is not an island, it needs to look up to others and learn a thing or two. What did they do right? Where did they go wrong? Of what stuff were their bridge builders made up of? For every country has its own Hitlers. Little Hitlers, big Hitlers and the Super Hitlers with their corresponding degrees of madness, destructive and genocidal tendencies.

Italian astronomer Galileo Galilei remarked that, "We can judge our progress by the courage of our questions and the depth of our answers, our willingness to embrace what is true rather than what feels good." The age when leaders sold fear to their people is long gone. Consequently, the true BBI is about positive transformation for the whole country. Therefore, people deserve to ask tough questions and get reasonable answers. What if a Hitler is installed at State House? That is what building bridges is all about, the truth.

This text is a big lesson to Kenyans now and ahead of the 2022 General Election especially on the person of Raila and the BBI Big Lie. The selected pieces are like: Caution! With Raila at the driver's seat of the BBI, you are entering into an extraordinarily unpredictable, unsafe world. It is absolutely important for Kenyans at this juncture since theirs is indeed an honourable country to be left in ruinous hands. Kenyans deserves, if not the best, the better option.

The idea is not to depict Raila as the mass murderer like Hitler, but Raila the carrier of the Big Lie. Or if the foot fits, take both. It's passion for one country, stupid!

---

16   Quoted in Robert Jay Lifton, "The man who wanted to live forever", *The New York Times*, 31 December, 1972.

Begin reading by returning to the first quote of the chapter: "His primary rules were: Never allow the public to cool off…" then proceed. (For guidance, *Author* is Dr Walter Langer, *Self* is Hitler, *Associates* are Hitler's associates, and *Source* is a contributor in the book.)

5. Behold, the Messiah!

"For unto us a child is born, unto us a son is given; and the government will be upon his shoulders. And his name will be called Wonderful, Counsellor, Mighty God, Everlasting Father, Prince of Peace. Of the increase of His government and peace there will be no end." These are the words prophet Isaiah (9:6-7 – NKJV) wrote to foretell the coming of Jesus, the Saviour of mankind. Hitler believed and proclaimed that he was the Messiah to the German people. Furious and devastated by the defeat of Germany in World War I, Hitler joined politics. Bloody politics. He developed ambitions to conquer the whole of Europe and dominate the world.

But Hitler was not a Redeemer or Prince of Peace. He was a dirty warlord. In 1914, the young Hitler prayed and thanked God that World War I had broken out for him to take part! He wrote in *Mein Kampf*: "Overpowered by stormy enthusiasm, I fell down on my knees and thanked heaven from an overflowing heart for granting me the good fortune of being permitted to live at this time."[17]

Raila Odinga: A reflection of Adolf Hitler?

1. Search for role model:

   (a)   Author: "…We find him searching for a strong masculine figure whom he can respect and emulate… he attempted to find great men in history who could fill this need. Caesar, Napoleon and Fredrick the Great… And so Hitler has spent his life looking for a competent guide, but always ends with the discovery that the person he has chosen falls short of his requirements and is fundamentally no more capable than himself."

   (b)   Author: "How a man can lead a nation of 130,000,000 people and keep them in line without a great deal of name-calling,

---

17   Hitler, *Mein Kampf*, op cit. p. 161.

shouting, abusing and threatening is a mystery to him. He is unable to understand how a man can be the leader of a large group and still act like a gentleman. The result is that he secretly admires Roosevelt (US President) to a considerable degree, regardless of what he publicly says about him. Underneath he probably fears him inasmuch as he is unable to predict his actions."

2. At home as a child

In the hands of a violent, drunkard father: Author: "…Not a single good shred is left for humanity, not a single institution is left unattacked; starting with the teacher, up to the Head of the State, be it religion, or morality as such, be it the State or society, no matter which, everything is pulled down in the nastiest manner into the filth of a depraved mentality."

3. The Messiah

    (a) Source: "He feels that no one in German history was equipped as he is to bring the Germans to the position of supremacy which all German statesmen have felt they deserve but were unable to achieve."

    (b) Source: "When a man gets to the point to identifying himself with Jesus Christ, then he is ripe for an insane asylum."

    (c) Source: "He has accepted this God-like role without any hesitation or embarrassment… when he is addressed with the salutation, 'Heil Hitler, our Saviour,' he bows slightly at the compliment in the phrase – and believes it – it becomes more and more certain that Hitler believes that he is really the Chosen One and that in his thinking he conceives of himself as a second Christ who has been sent to institute in the world a new system of values based on brutality and violence…"

    (d) Self: "Unless I have the incorruptible conviction: This is the solution, I do nothing. Not even if the whole party tried to drive me to action. I will not act; I will wait, no matter what happens. But if the voice speaks, then I know the time has come to act."

(e)   Sources: "Hitler's word is God's law, the decrees and laws which represent it possess divine authority… There has arisen a new authority as to what Christ and Christianity really are - that is, Adolf Hitler. Adolf Hitler… is the true Holy Ghost."

4. Two in One

(a)   Author: "This is not a single personality but two which inhabit the same body and alternate back and forth… The other (second) is just the opposite – a hard, cruel, and decisive person with considerable energy –who seems to know what he wants and is ready to go after it and get it regardless of cost… It is the second Hitler who cries in open court: 'Heads will roll' … it is the second Hitler who can order the murder of hundreds, including his best friends, and can say with great conviction: 'There will be no peace in the land until a body hangs from every lamp-post'… And it is the second Hitler who works for days on end with little or no sleep making plans which will affect the destiny of nations…"

(b)   Author: "…It is a kind of Dr. Jekyll and Mr. Hyde personality structures in which two wholly different personalities oscillate back and forth and make the individual almost unrecognisable. This characteristic is common in many hysterics. Under these circumstances it is extremely difficult to predict from one moment to the next what his reactions to a given situation are going to be."

(c)   Author: "He can grapple with the most important problems in a few minutes reduce them to extremely simple terms, he can map out campaigns, be the supreme judge, deal with diplomats, ignore all ethical and moral principles, order executions or the destruction of cities without the slightest hesitation. And he can be in the best of humour while he is doing it."

5. Physical appearance

(a)   Source: "He is formless, almost faceless, a man whose countenance is a caricature, a man whose framework seems cartilaginous, without bones. He is inconsequent and voluble, ill poised and insecure. He is the very prototype of the little man."

(b)   Source: "It was the first time I had seen Hitler close at hand. Face and head of inferior type, cross-breed; low receding forehead, ugly nose, broad cheekbones, little eyes, dark hair. Expression not of a man exercising authority in perfect self-command, but of raving excitement. At the end an expression of satisfied egoism."

6. Oratory, propaganda master

(a)   Associates: "He has a matchless instinct for taking advantage of every breeze to raise a political whirlwind. No official scandal was so petty that he could not magnify it into high treason; he could ferret out the most deviously ramified corruption in high places and plaster the town with the bad news."

(b)   Author: "Hitler's speaking has been described as 'verbal diarrhoea' and 'oral enema.' And for him the masses are fundamentally feminine in character."

Self: "The people, in an overwhelming majority, are so feminine in their nature and attitude that their activities and thoughts are motivated less by sober consideration than by feeling and sentiment."

Author: "In other words, his unconscious flame of reference when addressing a huge audience, is fundamentally that of talking to a woman… Thus he is able to win them to his new view of life which sets a premium on brutality, ruthlessness, dominance, and determination, etc; and which frowns upon all the established human qualities."

(c)   Self: "I follow my course with the precision and security of a sleep-walker."

(d)   Self: "I cannot be mistaken. What I do and say is historical."

(e)   Author: "His power and fascination in speaking lay almost wholly in his ability to sense what a given audience wanted to hear and then to manipulate his theme in such a way that he would arouse the emotions of the crowd:

Source: "Hitler responds to the vibration of the human heart with the delicacy of a seismograph… enabling him, with a certainty with which no conscious gift endow him, to act as a loudspeaker proclaiming the most secret desires, the least permissible instincts, the sufferings and personal revolts of a whole nation."

(f)   Author: "When he began to speak, he usually manifested signs of nervousness. Usually, he was unable to say anything of consequence until he had gotten the feel of his audience:

Source: "The beginning is slow and halting. Gradually he warms up when the spiritual atmosphere of the great crowd is engendered. For he responds to this metaphysical contact in such a way that each member of the multitude feels bound to him by an individual link of sympathy."

(g)   Source: "His oratory used to wilt his collar, unglue his forelock, glare his eyes; he was like a man hypnotized, repeating himself into a frenzy… He was a man transformed and possessed. We were in the presence of a miracle."

(h)   Source: "When, at the climax, he sways from one side to the other his listeners sway with him; when he leans forward they also lean forward and when he concludes they either are awed and silent or on their feet in a frenzy."

(i)   Self: "There is only so much room in a brain, so much wall space, as it were, and if you furnish it with your slogans, the opposition has no place to put up any picture later on, because the apartment of the brain is already crowded with your furniture."

(j)   Author: "He has a magnetic quality about him which, together with his past accomplishments, wins the allegiance of people and seems to rob them of their critical functions. It is a bond which does not easily dissolve even in the face of evidence that he is not always what he pretends to be-in fact is more often than not, the exact opposite."

7. No regard for advisors

    (a)   Author: "He is unable to match wits with another person in a straight-forward argument. He will express his opinion at length but he will not defend it on logical grounds."

        Source: "He is afraid of logic. Like a woman he evades the issue and ends by throwing in your face an argument entirely remote from what you were talking about."

    (b)   Self: "Of secondary importance is the training of mental abilities. Over-educated people, stuffed with knowledge and intellect, but bare of any sound instincts. These impudent rascals (intellectuals) who always know everything better than anybody else… The intellect has grown autocratic, and has become a disease of life."

    (c)   Self: "I have the gift of reducing all problems to their simplest foundations… A gift for tracking back all theories to their roots in reality."

    (d)   Associates: "He became impatient if the details of a problem were brought to him. He was greatly adverse to experts and had little regard for their opinion. He looked upon them as mere hacks, as brush-cleaners and colour grinders."

    (e)   Self: "I do not look for people having clever ideas of their own but rather people who are clever in finding ways and means of carrying out my ideas."

        Associate: "No system in the execution of his thoughts. He wants things his own way and gets mad when he strikes firm opposition on solid ground."

8. Hitler's strange mind

    (a)   Associates: "Anyone who has seen this man face to face, has met his uncertain glance without depth or warmth, from eyes that seem hard and remote, and has then seen that gaze grow rigid, will certain have experienced the uncanny feeling: 'This man is not normal.'"

    (b)   Self: "Every attempt at fighting a view of life by means of force will finally fail, unless the fight against it represents the form of an attack for the sake of a new spiritual direction – masses are as hungry for a sustaining ideology in political action as they are for daily bread – only in struggle of two views of life with each other can the weapon of brute force, used continuously and ruthlessly, bring about the decision in favour of the side it supports."

(c)   Author: "At the climax (of his rages) he rolls on the floor and chews on the carpets… In the worst rages he undoubtedly acts like a spoiled child who cannot have his own way and bangs his fists on the table and walls. He scolds and shouts and stammers and on some occasions foaming saliva gathers in the corners of his mouth."

(d)   Author: "These form the nucleus of the Hitler he consciously knows and must live with. It is in all probability not a happy 'Hitler' but one harassed by fears, anxieties, doubts, misgivings, uncertainties, condemnations, feelings of loneliness and guilt. From our experience with other hysterics we are probably on firm ground when we suppose that Hitler's mind is like a 'battle-royal' most of the time with many conflicting and contradicting forces and impulses pulling him this way and that."

(e)   Author: "He has the 'never-say-die' spirit. After some of his severest setbacks he has been able to get his immediate associates together and begin making plans for a 'come-back.' Events which could crush most individuals, at least temporarily, seem to act as stimulants to greater efforts in Hitler."

(f)   Associate: "I saw this seemingly super-self-confident man actually blush when I broached the theme of German-American relations… This evidently caught him off-guard. He was not used to having his infallibility challenged. For a moment he blushed like a schoolboy, hemmed and hawed, then stammered an embarrassing something about having so many problems to ponder that he had not yet had time to take up America."

(g)   Goebbels: "The Feuhrer does not change. He is the same now as he was when he was a boy."

(h)   Source: "…feels the obligation in accordance with the Eternal Will that dominates this universe to promote the victory of the better and stronger, and to demand the submission of the worse and weaker."

"A stronger generation will drive out the weaklings because in its ultimate form the urge to live will again and again break the ridiculous fetters of a so-called 'humanity' of the individual, so that it's place will be taken by the 'humanity of nature,' which destroys weakness in order to give its place to strength."

Author: "The image Hitler created was a form of compensation for his own inferiorities, insecurities and guilts … All the human qualities of love, pity, sympathy and compassion were interpreted as weaknesses and disappeared in the transformation."

Self: "…If a people is to become free it needs pride and will-power, defiance, hate, hate and once again hate. Brutality is respected. Brutality and physical strength. The plain man in the street respects nothing but brutal strength and ruthlessness. We want to be the supporters of the dictatorship of national reason, of national energy, of national-brutality and resolution."

9. Fear of death

    (a)   Self: On making plans to build a mausoleum for himself… "I know how to keep my hold on people after I have passed on. I shall be the Fuehrer they look up at and go home to talk of and remember. My life shall not end in the mere form of death. It will, on the contrary begin then."

    (b)   Self: "There are still five bullets in my pistol-four for the traitors, and one, if things go wrong, for myself."

10.   Please no sex...but

He insisted that Germany was his only bride. His attempts at intimate and lasting relationships with women proved disastrous. Women he had sexual contacts with either attempted suicide or succeeded. He was suspected of being a homosexual.

    (a)   Author: "It is probably true that he is impotent, but he is certainly not homosexual in the ordinary sense of the term…

derives sexual gratification from the act of having a woman urinate or defecate on him."

(b)   Source: "He (Hitler) is thinking about the peasant girls. When they stand in the fields and bend down at their work so that you can see their behinds, that's what he likes, especially when they've got big round ones. That's Hitler's sex life. What a man."

Hitler as god of war

If Hitler had lived in mediaeval times, he would have qualified for Mars or Ares, the Roman and Greek gods of war respectively (see Chapter Six). By invading Poland on 1 September, 1939, Hitler the NAZI Party leader, Chancellor, Führer (supreme leader) of Germany led to the start of World War II. Eventually over thirty countries participated in the war. By the time it ended six years later, Hitler had annexed/invaded or declared war on close to a dozen countries.

The war left an estimated 60 million people dead (3% of 2 billion world population then) including six million Jews murdered in the Holocaust. Approximately seven million Germans were killed, nine million prisoners of war (POWs) held, infrastructure destroyed and industrial and agricultural outputs reduced by more than half. The defeated Germany was split and occupied by four nations and later divided by half. The succession of events was swift.

Hitler had sensed defeat, hid in an underground Berlin bunker, married on 29 April 1945 and on 30 April both he and wife committed suicide. His body was burned and the ashes scattered around the bunker. On 1 May, 1945, Joseph Goebbels, his Propaganda Minister and his wife also committed suicide after killing their six children. These monsters did not want to risk being captured alive and prosecuted for crimes against humanity.

Germany surrendered on 8 May 1945. The country was divided into four allied occupation zones in June. Hitler's plan was an empire that would last for 1,000 years he called "Thousand-Year Reich"; it only lived for twelve (KANU had dreamt to rule for 100 years). Imagine if the reign had gone for 20 or 30 years, history would be much different today.

In 1919, Hitler had been found guilty of pederastic (sex between two males especially when one is a minor) practices. In March 1920 he had attempted to overthrow the government, arrested, tried for high treason and imprisoned for five years (served nine months). In 1932 he had ran for the Presidency and came second... Thus, this was the Chosen One for you, a Christian no less. Instead of making Germany great, he transformed it into an epicentre of history's most destructive war and unprecedented human suffering. God and the Kenyan voters should not be judged too harshly for rejecting the Raila Presidency. Even with his Messiah Complex, they could be knowing something the rest of the world doesn't.

6. A mandatory mental examination

In the book, *A Psychological Analysis of Adolf Hitler,* Dr Langer termed the study of Hitler as not propagandistic, but "an attempt to screen the wealth of contradicting, conflicting and unreliable material concerning Hitler into strata which will be helpful to policy-makers and those who wish to frame a counter-propaganda..."[18] and called it as objective as possible in evaluating his strengths as well as his weaknesses. The analysis of Raila would follow the same avenue.

In perhaps his most acclaimed book, *The Mind of Adolf Hitler*, Dr Langer advised that such studies when done in good time can help evade some future catastrophes in the nations of the world:

> ... I like to believe that if such a study of Hitler had been made years earlier, under less tension, and with more opportunity to gather first-hand information, there might not have been... studies of this type cannot solve our international problems. That would be too much to expect. They might however, help to avoid some of the serious blunders we seem to have made because we were ignorant of the psychological factors involved and the nature of the leaders with whom we were negotiating.[19]

Take the obvious issue, for instance. Raila has been rejected several times by Kenyan voters as their President. Wild dances at political rallies. Venomous tongue. Violence and all its deadly consequences.

18 Preface, Walter C. Langer, *A Psychological Analysis of Adolf Hitler: His Life and Legend* (Washington DC: Office of Strategic Services, 1968).

19 Walter C. Langer, *The Mind of Adolf Hitler: The Secret Wartime Report* (New York: Basic Books, 1972), p.32.

Then you find him one day in broad daylight at Uhuru Park swearing by the Bible that he was now the President of the Republic of Kenya. This was a man practically ready for war with the whole government machinery and Kenyan people. He did not care a hoot what happened to him or the country. If Armageddon had arrived, so be it. The image was that of a suicidal case. Something has been terribly wrong.

Surely this man was not normal at some particular points in time. In 2017 presidential campaign President Kenyatta called him, "*mũndũ mũgũrũki*", Gikuyu for a madman. The Handshake came less than two months after the swearing and soon the BBI process commenced. Can you make a big blunder and trust such a man with building bridges in a country or with State House? Kenyans are dreadfully frightened by man Raila navigating the BBI.

BEWARE OF THE "BIG LIE"

Experience is the best teacher, it was confirmed long ago. Since Chapter Six in the *Constitution of Kenya 2010* on Leadership and Integrity has failed to live up to people's expectations regarding suitability of leaders assuming positions of monumental national importance, shouldn't the BBI dictate in the Constitution that every future political contestant must be subjected to a compulsory psychological profiling at Mathari Hospital, Nairobi, in order to determine their mental state? The decree would save the country from a lot of predicaments. Besides probable mental shortcoming, majority of our leaders are offensively wanting. In Kenya the leadership is the problem, it is backward, *pihsredael*. "There goes my people." Mahatma Gandhi said. "I must hurry and catch up with them, for I am their leader."[20]

Dr Langer, after completing his study on Hitler concluded that he (Hitler) was "probably a neurotic psychopath bordering on schizophrenia," a weakling masquerading as a bully who almost brought the whole world in ruin.[21] Supposing a psychoanalyst or consultant psychiatrist was hired to work on Raila just before he started campaigning for Langata Constituency MP in 1992? With a publication

20   Brock Brower, "Where Have All the Leaders Gone?" *LIFE*, Vol 17 No 15 (8 October 1971), p. 80.

21   Langer, *The Mind of Adolf Hitler*, op cit. p. 131.

titled, "The Mind of Raila Odinga" out and read by all, he would have been instantly banned from contesting the seat. As a result, Kenya would not have undergone years of political turmoil and today would be sitting comfortably in the table among the Asian Tigers, economically speaking. A mental examination outcome can serve as a warning about evil and lethal leaders.

Come to think of it. Raila has caused distressing devastation in the country for as many years even at times when he was an ordinary citizen. What could become of Kenya with all powers in his hands as President? Or go back in time. The Wazungu labelled Jomo Kenyatta a "leader unto darkness." If Jomo was Raila then they would have rightly called him Premier or the Paramount Leader unto Darkness. And thanks heaven Raila was not among the top figures in the independence struggle. Standing on a firm ground, it is correct to state that the Wazungu would have faced massacre of genocidal proportion with rivers of their blood flowing all the way to Lake Victoria. Or if he was on the side of the colonialists, Africans would have seen hell on earth and independence movement completely frustrated.

And just visualise Kenya without Raila, at least temporarily. Just imagine, could Kenyans do a countrywide fundraiser and give him a fully paid grand tourism package abroad to last five years? Attraction destinations determined by Kenyans themselves to start from Egypt (learn first-hand the story of Exodus) then proceed to Lebanon, Syria, Jordan and Israel (re-enact the journey and arrival at Canaan) move on to India (study the story of non-violence from the source) and to Hong Kong (behold where Kenya would likely be except for his politics). This would be a study, reflection and leisure adventure. Last stop, Jamaica for an authentic taste of the reggae music. The only condition for this offer: absolutely no politics while away, no politicians to accompany or visit him. Of course Raila will refuse categorically to be away even for a couple of months. He is a dead man outside politics. The point is, Raila missing in action would change Kenya for the better. Just a thought.

Another reason of this imagined tour, apart from forcing Raila into exile, is River Jordan. Why did the Israelites' Joshua manage to cross himself and his people over so effortlessly yet our very own Joshua (Raila) has only been marking time on the bank? To begin with Raila would visit museums, consult Rabiis and griots – the very old men knowledgeable in the Hebrew's family tree. From these he would discover what trick was behind Joshua's success. The river was flooding heavily. But Joshua and team walked on the dry land. What has been essentially lacking in Raila's endeavours is the spiritual element, God's hand in his endeavours. This is the lesson.

Surprisingly, Raila is also telling himself a big lie. That he managed to cross Kenyan River Jordan through the Handshake. True, the Handshake wave swept him right to the middle of the torrential river; himself alone, leaving his followers crying after him, tired, hungry, thirsty and hopeless. Without the spiritual drive he will not go further. When the cock crow dawn of 2022 announcing the General Election, the Voice of the People will be pushing him back to the shore he came from. His people will still be there, waiting. What shall he tell them? And did a mention of River Jordon representing a spiritual rebirth and salvation that Raila needs so badly escape the pen?

Kenya was created a great country. Its people were born to be great. You cannot count fast enough the number of "firsts" in the world from this land. Led by its two national emblems: the National Flag and the National Anthem. The National Flag is the global brand most admired piece of cloth as the Shroud of Turin is to the Christians. The National Anthem has been described as "rousing, uplifting, epic, genuine, biblical movie, flown right from a Beethoven or Mozart creation, haunting, cool, world's best" (2016 Rio Olympics).

It is the country whose first Jamhuri Day anniversary on 12 December, 1964, was graced by one of the greatest bridge builders in history. At the Malmen Hotel in Stockholm, Sweden, Rev. Martin Luther King Jr danced the night away with wife Coretta Scott to celebrate the occasion, as the chief guest of the Kenya Government. Two days earlier, Rev King had been awarded the Nobel Peace Prize; at 35 years, then the youngest recipient ever. He called the award "a profound recognition that non-violence is the answer to the crucial political and moral question of our time…" and "peace is more precious that diamonds or gold."[22] A month later, Rev. King talked about the 'birth of a new nation' Kenya that he was proud to be associated with.

---

22   Martin Luther King Jr., "Martin Luther King Jr. – Acceptance Speech", The Nobel Peace Prize 1964 in Oslo, Sweden, 10 December, 1964. Retrieved from: https://www.nobelprize.org/prizes/peace/1964/king/26142-martin-luther-king-jr-acceptance-speech-1964/. Accessed on 2 June 2020.

It was in the same country that, feeling on top of the world, US President Barack Obama, then the most powerful leader on earth, took to the floor and danced to the Afro-pop group Sauti Sol song "Sura Yangu" together with President Kenyatta, First Lady Margaret Kenyatta and US National Security Advisor Susan Rice at State House, Nairobi, on 25 July, 2015. During the three-day trip to the country President Obama had referred to Odinga as a "traitor" to his Commander-in-Chief.

And this is the country that has been handed to Raila, the most dangerous and treacherous politician in Kenya's history to build bridges among its 47 million citizens. My foot! When we present Raila to the world on occasions such as the Washington Breakfast Prayer Meeting, they see a country headed to shredding into smithereens. They recall the tyrannical KANU regime as well as Nigerian award-winning playwright Ola Rotini hilarious play, "Our Husband Has Gone Mad Again". They exclaim silently: Kenyans have gone mad again!

"Our closest relatives are chimpanzees." observed Dr Milford Wolpoff in the *National Geographic* of October 1988. "There's only one or two per cent genetic difference. We're more closely related to chimpanzees than any two frogs you see probably are related to each other." When whites perceive Africans as apes who only recently dropped off from trees, we feel insulted. Yet sometimes they have specific justified reasons to come to such a conclusion.

When President Obama visited Kenya July 2015, his interactions with President Kenyatta brought out one possible scenario. That the two men shared exactly the same chemistry of inspired leadership and concern for their people and the world inside and out. Kenyans envisaged an Obama-style leadership with UhuRuto at the helm. A good thing for the country.

President Obama's successor, Donald Trump, campaigned on a motto of "Make America Great Again". Very fast, the Americans and the world discovered that he was an awful choice for PROTUS. Since his victory, Trump has been described as the most reckless, craziest, ugliest, boastful buffoon, joker, insulting and childish of all US Presidents. A survey reported by BBC on 17 January, 2019, judged the 45th President to be "the worst of the worst… the boss of crime family…his presidency a profile of amorality." The media company added that Trump made the US Presidency more uncouth and untrustworthy, made the Oval Office a focal point of perpetual turmoil and uncertainty; his term as history – defying presidency. The *USA Today* termed him the worst President of all time. On the art of lying – petty lies and big lies – the *Washington Post* had listed more than 7,000 presidential falsehoods by that date.

At home, Raila is the leading autocrat and power-hungry politician and the worst president Kenya never had. For 40 years he has been a prolific liar, using rotten language that rendered untold misery to Kenyans as he tried to reach the pinnacle of power. To quote author George Orwell, Raila "political chaos is connected with the decay of language." For those four decades, again to borrow Orwell's words, Raila has lied to Kenyans: War is Peace, Freedom is Slavery, Ignorance is Strength.

President Trump wants a second term in office. Obama has endorsed Joe Biden for the 2020 election saying he can unify and heal a nation struggling through some of its darkest moments. "I believe Joe has all the qualities we need in a President right now," Obama noted, calling his choice of Biden as his running mate in 2008 "as one of the best decisions I ever made."

President Kenyatta will complete his second and last term in 2022. A while ago, his Deputy Ruto was definitely his best choice for a running mate in 2013. While the Americans are working overtime to throw out Trump, the Father of the Big Lie in the US and bring in Obama's able deputy of eight years, the BBI is doing the exact opposite. It has thrown Ruto under the bus, to the political Siberia, Kenyatta's excellent Deputy of eight years and the better option for Kenyans and dragged Raila, Kenya's Father of the Big Lie on board as the best unifier and healer of the Kenyan nation. Heavens, spare us the pain, can we get an alternative sermon? This is the reason the global citizens are cracking their ribs and noses like the proverbial louse as they try to contain explosive belly laughter at Kenyans. It is a perfect case study of a people who cannot learn from history.

CONCLUSION

Appointing Raila as the chief architect of the BBI smirked serious lack of wisdom. In him, BBI will be another round of problems to the country. Philosopher Plato noted: "Mankind will never see an end of trouble until… lovers of wisdom come to hold political power, or the holders of power… become lovers of wisdom."[23]

Meanwhile, the country is crying tears of blood to see the government prominently displaying Raila – the violent man and the Big Lie man – in their midst as the choicest pathway to their future. There is justifiable fear in the land. And appropriately South African writer Alan Paton speaks to us from the novel, *Cry, the Beloved Country*:

> Cry, the beloved country, for the unborn child that's the inheritor of our fear. Let him not love the earth too deeply. Let him not laugh too gladly when the water runs through his fingers, nor stand too silent when the setting sun makes red the veld with fire. Let him not be too moved when the birds of this land are singing. Nor give too much of his heart to a mountain or a valley. For fear will rob him if he gives too much.[24]

God save Kenya from the BBI, the Big Lie that could burn our fingers as we experiment to know the truth hidden within. Meanwhile the Jubilee Party, the country's largest people's political alliance since independence and an incredible symbol of nationalistic collaboration for a better Kenya, was headed to the ICU thanks to a certain witchdoctor and his high priests. Shame on us all.

---

23   Quoted in Maduabuchi Dukor (ed), *Philosophy and Politics: Discourse on Values, Politics, and Power in Africa* (Lagos: Malthouse Press, 2003), p. 208.

24   Alan Paton, *Cry, the Beloved Country* (New York: Scribner, 1948), p. 73.

CHAPTER THREE

The Handshake, *DeRailafication*, Walls and Betrayals

I know there is a God because in Rwanda I shook hands with the devil. I have seen him, I have smelled him and I have touched him. I know the devil exists and therefore I know there is a God.

Romeo Dallaire,
Shake Hands with the Devil (2003)

* * *

I like to see myself as a bridge builder, that is me building bridges between people, between races, between cultures, between politics, trying to find a common good.

Thomas D. Jakes,
American Bishop

* * *

In 200 years will people remember us as traitors or heroes? That is the question we must ask.

– Benjamin Franklin letter
to US President Thomas Jefferson (16 March, 1775)

*   *   *

There are three signs of a hypocrite: when he speaks he speaks lies, when he makes a promise he breaks it, and when he is trusted he betrays the trust.

Islamic quote

*   *   *

A nation can survive its fools, and even the ambitious. But it cannot survive treason from within. An enemy at the gates is less formidable, for he is known and carries his banner openly. But the traitor moves amongst those within the gate freely, his sly whispers rustling through all the alleys, heard in the very halls of government itself… He rots the soul of a nation… he infects the body politic so that it can no longer resist. A murderer is less to fear. The traitor is the plague.

Marcus Cicero,
Roman philosopher (58 BC)

Shaking hands with the Devil: dangerous!

Every generation has its most memorable historical year. For the 20th and 21st centuries, 1945 certainly stands out from the rest. Wikipedia terms it, "a common year starting on Monday of the Gregorian calendar, the 1945th year of the Common Era (CE) and Anno Domini (AD) designations, the 945th year of the second millennium, the 45th year of the 20th century, and the 6th year of 1940s decade." But the year holds more than the above description.

On the evening of 30 August 1939 man, the Homo sapiens, the most intelligent creature ever walked on earth retired to bed. On 1 September he woke up as the Devil. And for the six years forward, he terrorised his habitat mercilessly including the slaughtering of millions of fellow devils and non-devils and turning his home upside down until he got exhausted a few minutes before midnight on 8 May, 1945, when he transformed back to man.

Looking around, man thought he was experiencing a nightmare. Yet what he was seeing was real. The nucleus of this insanity was Germany. The waking up from senselessness to normalcy was christened Hour Zero. At the Hour Zero (00.00) midnight on 8 May 1945 Germany signed the unconditional surrender officially marking the end of World War II and soon over 30 countries of the world silenced their drums of war.

The end of the six years of brutal warfare and hardship was celebrated by nations around Europe and the world. There was rejoicing at the United Nations. Vehicle sirens blared and church bells rang in world cities in jubilation. Millions of people flooded the streets, homes and pubs as dancing, singing and toasting as well as speeches from the leaders marked the beginning of the hard-won peace. This day, an annual event ever since, was named Victory in Europe (VE) Day.

The relevant definition of Hour Zero from *Merriam-Webster Dictionary* is "the time at which a usually significant or notable event is scheduled to take place or a time when a vital decision or decisive change must be made." In Germany Hour Zero (*Nullpunkt, Pointo Zero, Stunde Null*) has been described variously as "an absolute break with the past and a radical new beginning" or "a sweeping away of old traditions and customs" or "the resetting the clock to start again from the scratch." Aditionally, "Zero Hour was the inaccessible beginning of history, the caesura that separated us from the previous world, the departure from the Holocaust and from everything that had led to it…" (Frank Schirmacher) What the term referred to really was an attempt by Germany to dissociate itself from the evil Nazi regime – a denazification process – and create a new, better Germany.[1] So Germany proclaimed 1945 Year Zero "to reflect the fact that they had been bombed into the Stone Age and also in the hope that the nation might be allowed to start again with a clean slate."[2]

Denazification was a massive programme undertaken by the Allies (Britain, France, US and Soviet Union) that ran to 1951. It was intended to cleanse the German society of all Nazi ideologies and influences in culture, press, economy, judiciary and politics, and wipe out the Nazi Party, institutions, organisations and physical symbols. Additionally, denazification was to make Germans confront the crimes of the Nazi regime and re-educate them. People were required to fill questionnaire relating to their activities and membership in the Nazi Party into five categories: majority offenders, offenders, less offenders, followers and people exonerated. The programme was about reconstruction and development or redemption and rehabilitation. Considering how deep the Nazi evil regime had gone into people's minds and lives, denazification was akin to collecting millions of mental cases and their worlds and hauling them into a correctional centre…

President Uhuru Kenyatta was 13 years old when one of the most peculiar things happened and must have come across this story somewhere later. One day in November 1974 Yasser Arafat, leader of the Palestine Liberation Organization (PLO) was attending the United Nations General Assembly (UNGA) in New York. Wearing a full military uniform and pistol holster, he told the audience: "I have come bearing an olive branch and a freedom fighter's gun. Do not let the olive branch fall from my hands."[3] Arafat's symbolism was that of a man who was ready to make peace or fight a battle.

---

1   See, for example, Andreas Huyssen, *Twilight Memories: Marking Time in a Culture of Amnesia* (New York: Routledge, 1995), pp. 51-53.

2   Keith Lowe, "Was 1945 the world's year zero?" HistoryExtra, 4 June, 2019. Available at: https://www.historyextra.com/period/second-world-war/aftermath-nato-united-nations-america-britain/. Accessed on 10 June 2020.

3   Paul Hofmann, "Dramatic Session", *The New York Times*, 14 November, 1974.

Some 39 years later, Uhuru Kenyatta and William Ruto met at the Afraha Stadium, Nakuru, to launch their election campaign. Each carried an olive branch themselves, and for all Kenyans. Millions of Kenyans participated in the rally either in physical presence or through the media. The gathering was like the "United Nations" of Kenya. Both leaders stated that whether they were elected or not their noble mission was to unite the country. They sailed through the ballot. The message of unity is still part of their agenda to date.

THE HANDSHAKE

Then some 44 years since the Arafat's drama at the United Nations, President Kenyatta and Raila Odinga met in a Nairobi bunker to discuss building bridges. They agreed. The date for the Handshake was set to inform the world about the new get-together. The motivation was apparently the same. Unity of the country. The President was excited to see Raila holding an olive branch. But unfortunately, Raila had his 'gun' in the holster, just in case, permanently held there since 1982. Why hadn't the President known Raila well for all the years?

If the President was keen enough, British Prime Minister Winston Churchill, would have come back to him clearly about his newfound partnership with Raila: "The longer you look back, the further you can look forward."[4] President Kibaki and Raila's messy coalition of Nusu Mkate would also have flashed in his mind. For Raila's 'gun' was real. The olive branch was fake, a collection of withered twigs. And the word 'unity' was a vocabulary to Raila.

What President Kenyatta forgot or did not know was that Raila had never seen or carried an olive branch in his life. Nor will he ever. His statements when the Supreme Court invalidated the August 8, 2017, presidential election should have also alarmed the President. While Uhuru's favourite gospel was "Peace", "Peace", "Peace" and "shake hand with your neighbour," Raila's was different: "They stole our votes … send thieves to jail … we will boycott elections."[5]

---

4   Chris Wrigley, *Winston Churchill: A Biographical Companion* (Santa Barbara, CA: ABC-CLIO, 2002), p. xxiv.

5   Nation TV, "We defeated Uhuru with more than 1.5 million votes, but they stole our victory - Raila Odinga", DailyNation, 5 September, 2017. Available at: https://www.youtube.com/watch?v=CdvppILpkQE. Accessed on 5 June 2020.

Most likely, this was what was transpiring in Raila's mind, that day on the steps of Harambee House as he did the sham handshake: "Year 2022 I will be 77 years old. This Handshake is my last bullet towards the State House. Either they give me the real presidency or premiership or I go down with them all. Must they have forgotten the story of Samson of old? Unless I become the boss, I will show them the works. I will make them sweat blood. I will leave this country in ruins. Kenya can go to Hell for all I care. For me, it is *Aluta Continua* and *Victoria e Certa* (the struggle continues, victory is certain). Year 2022, I will not go to the Supreme Court. I will not swear myself as the People's President. Forcing part of the country to secede and I become the President of the New Republic shall be the ultimate trick. I will never live in the political Siberia again!"

And how was the Handshake received? It was a blessing from the Above to have the country once again in peace. Temporary peace, but at what future cost? In an interview with the *Sunday Nation*, 29 December 2019 Leader of Majority in the National Assembly Adan Duale responded to the question: Do you think the Handshake is part of the President's legacy?

> I don't think that the genesis of the Handshake … was to unite the country politically and socially. I have hoped that the Handshake would set the stage for national reconciliation, connect all bridges of political, ethnic and regional diversity, and create a national ethos. But I am very sad that the Handshake has done the opposite. It has destroyed Jubilee's internal political bridges, destabilised our party's political strongholds, undermined the constitutional office holders … It has sowed seeds of discord, caused confusion and political tensions that have seen the emergency of political gangs, abuse of the rule of law by civil servants and disenfranchisement of communities …[6]

Suspicious handshakes turned bloody

Most assuredly, I say to you, he who does not enter the sheepfold by the door, but climbs up some other way, the same is a thief and a robber… The thief does not come except to steal, and to kill, and to destroy… (John 10:1-10 – NKJV). The ancient Greek called the handshake *dexiosis*, the

---

6   Kipchumba Some, "Duale to Uhuru: Handshake is killing our party and destabilising country", *Sunday Nation*, 29 December, 2019.

representation of two people joining together their right hands. The now universally accepted gesture of greeting or parting carries other deeper meaning as it were in the old days. A handshake symbolises peace and non-aggression – it demonstrate one is not holding a weapon. It shows a bond of mutual relationship. In some instances, it is used as a sign to pledge a commitment to seal treaties in politics, military, business or families. The act becomes like an oath or a promise.

Sometimes the pledge does not work out especially when one of the parties is not sincere about the agenda. When one will be wishing, "Lord help this deal go through" the other one will be, "You idiot, I have got you squarely in my snare." Then sooner or later, the handshake will obey Murphy's first, second, fourth and eighth laws respectively: anything that can go wrong will go wrong. Nothing is as easy as it looks. If there is a possibility of several things going wrong, the one that will cause the most damage will be the one to go wrong. And, if everything seem to be going well, you have obviously overlooked something.

Because of the dishonesty of one party the agreement or alliance collapses. The traitor takes home his loot and the betrayed walk away (that is, if he is not dead already) down-casted humming Elvis Presley song, "You're the Devil in Disguise":

> You look like an angel /Walk like an angel/Talk like an angel/…
> You're the devil in disguise/Oh yes you are/The devil in disguise…/
> You fooled me with your kisses/You cheated and you schemed/
> Heaven knows how you lied to me/You're not the way you seemed…
> /I thought that I was in heaven/But I was sure surprised/Heaven help
> me, I didn't see/The devil in your eyes…

And not only do betrayed handshakes turn painful, violent and expensive, they sometimes become bloody when the Big Lie penetrate the cause they intend to propagate. The two local case study below of pre-independence Kenya demonstrate this.

Buried upside down, alive

Chief Waiyaki wa Hinga, a freedom fighter, allowed Captain Fredrick Lugard to establish a garrison at Fort Smith in Dagoretti, Kiambu for the British caravans en route to Uganda in 1890. The two signed a treaty of blood brotherhood in agreement that the Europeans would not take any land or property from the locals.

They did a handshake. But soon, Lugard's men disregarded the arrangement and started raiding villages for food and women and to occupy the land. This resulted in a relationship of hostility between the hosts and newcomers.

One day, the commanding officer of the British W.P. Purkiss invited Waiyaki for peace talk – a BBI – and promptly arrested him. This was on 14 August 1892. As he was resisting the arrest Waiyaki injured one of the captors. In turn, they wounded his head. He was then quickly tried in a kangaroo court, found guilty and sentenced to deportation.

On 17 August 1892 Waiyaki, now a political hostage and bound in chains, bleeding from the wound and guarded by heavily armed soldiers set off in a caravan for the Coast. Twenty-one days into the journey and almost 400 km away from home the group arrived at Kibwezi (today Makueni County). Waiyaki was shot, buried upside down, still breathing and alive. The Waiyaki Way in Westlands, Nairobi, is named after this patriot.

Shot in cold blood

Koitalel arap Samoei was the Supreme Chief of the Nandi people. He is credited as the founder of the first Kalenjin resistance to colonialism from February 1890 and as Kenya's first freedom fighter.

For eleven years, the Nandi presented a formidable rebellion to the British occupation, winning one war after another. Then the British schemed an evil plan. On 19 October 1905 Col Richard Meinertzhagen, a fierce and ruthless soldier, invited Koitalel for a handshake to negotiate peace. There was one condition: both men had to come unarmed – that is carry an olive branch. Koitalel thought the BBI was about the surrender terms and safe exit from the Nandi country by the British. He was mistaken. He accepted the invitation.

The two men met. Koitalel stretched his empty hand for the handshake, while Col Meinertzhagen extended one with a hidden gun. He shot Koitalel in cold blood. Some 23 among his family and community members were also machine-gunned. Later, his head was chopped off and together with other items taken to England.

In *Detained, A Prisoner's Diary*, Ngũgĩ wa Thiong'o adds on to the murderous nature of Col Meinertzhagen. In Murang'a, a British officer was killed by the locals. The Colonel went to Muruka village on a market day and ordered the whole place surrounded and every soul extinguished, a total massacre. Meinertzhagen wrote in his diary: "Every soul was either shot or bayonetted…We burned all huts and razed the banana plantations to the ground… Then I went home and wept for brother officer killed".[7] The Colonel was never punished for his murderous escapades. Instead, he was later recalled and re-deployed then went on to be promoted and decorated by the Queen.

In 2003, Lieutenant-General Romeo Dallaire of UN Assistance Mission for Rwanda (UNAMIR) released a book about the 1994 Rwandan genocide titled *Shake Hands with the Devil*. Earlier, the *Time* magazine had described on its cover page, "There are no devils left in Hell, they are all in Rwanda."[8] Shaking hands with the devil is normally taken to mean the devil becomes your friend. Pretty soon the world will know whether in the 9 March 2018 Handshake theatrics Dallaire's book title was playing out.

Only a genuine handshake shall bring *sufuria za ugali* to the 47 million Kenyans. Betrayers and traitors do not go about shouting around their true intentions. Oftentimes, you cannot identify them. Jesus Christ was lucky enough to know one in advance and even dropped a bombshell at the Last Supper to his chief campaigners: "…I tell you the truth, one of you will betray me – one who is eating with me." In many ways, humans are not well gifted in prediction matters. Well, this time tomorrow.

Being the ancestors of renowned Seers does not mean we are prophets of doom. But Kenyans must be afraid, very afraid of the aftermath of the Handshake and BBI. Before and after August 2022 General Election winners and losers will emerge. The crucial question comes from Job 34:16-17: "If you have understanding hear this; listen to what I say, can someone who hates justice govern? Will you condemn him who is most just?" (NIV).

---

7   Ngũgĩ wa Thiong'o, *Detained: A Writer's Prison Diary* (Nairobi: East African Educational Publishers, 1981), p. 35.

8   *Time,* magazine, 16 May 1994.

The outcome of the BBI is fairly predictable. After Kenyans have passed the document there will be two rubber stamps. The first one, obviously – the Executive– Implement Pronto. The other one, for about the 47 million Kenyans will read: Pend all till Jesus comes (when funds are available). To stamp-pend the people's desires will resemble Queen Marie Antoinette's (of France) reaction when she was informed that her peasant subjects were starving due to bread shortage. She roared back: "*Qu'ils mangent de la brioche!!* (Let them eat cake!)"

The subject of who will be the President or the Premier is where the real combat will begin, with majority of Kenyans disagreeing with the BBI proposal and process. Gradually, Gerard Butler, as Spartan King Leonidas in the "300" film could come into play:

No retreat, no surrender. That is Spartan law.
And by Spartan law, we will stand and fight…and die.
 A new age has begun; an age of freedom…
The world will know that free men stood against a tyrant,
that few stood against many and, before this battle is over,
that even a god-king can bleed.[9]

This film was released on 9 March, the same date as the Handshake (2018).

Some events travel faster than the speed of light. Soon, it was becoming self-evident that the Handshake was building too many walls and not enough bridges. The very first casualty was President Uhuru Kenyatta himself. Between him and Kenyans of various stations emerged huge social distancing Covid-19 technique. Messiah Kenyatta of yesterday was being labelled dishonest, unreliable, promise-less, selfish, traitor and an economy destroyer. The *Mūtongoria Njaamba* (heroic leader) was being described as an alcoholic who only want to succeed himself. Too early for things to start falling apart.

Though total men do not show regret in public (for dumping Ruto for Raila), a feeling of restlessness was probably slowly encroaching the President, sometimes wishing he could run to Mount Kenya for need of urgent prayers: "*Thaai, Thaai, Thaai, Thathaiya Ngai*". But who cared? Has transforming to a dictator ever killed someone? The

---

9   *300*. Directed by Zack Snyder. Performed by Gerard Butler, Lena Headey, David Wenham and Dominic West. Warner Bros. Pictures. 9 March 2007 (United States).

rule of dynasties in Kenya will last 100 years, *wapende wasipende* (whether they like it or not). Let them eat cake! The same hands that sealed the Handshake were now bleeding heavily. Unfortunately, *maji yakimwagika hayazoleki* (spilt water cannot be gathered). For Deputy Ruto, it was the reverse. Despite being the most betrayed politician in post-independence Kenya, the more they were trying to hurt him the more they drove him to the Hall of Fame (Hebrew 11). "Every betrayal contains a perfect moment, a coin stamped heads or tails with salvation on the other side" was what Barbara Kingsolver advised in *The Poisonwood Bible*.[10] And for Raila, obviously he was laughing all the way to the bank. In case something went wrong, his secret weapon of street battles was ever ready.

What could be the tipping point of this drama? Tipping point is defined by *Merriam-Webster Dictionary* as "the critical point in a situation, process, or system beyond which a significant and often unstoppable effect or change takes place." Conduct a hypothetical laboratory experiment in a Kenyan kitchen. Immerse all the aspiring presidential candidates in a large glass of generous amount of water. To fill up, pour enough concentrated sanitising agent. Stir thoroughly. Then pass the contents through a sieve – *kichungi cha chai* – into another glass. Only Deputy President Ruto will manage to pass through (see Chapter Thirteen) and settle in the new container, as the better option for President of Kenya. The rest will remain stuck in the sieve, as waste.

What a politician like Deputy Ruto need to remember: Right now Raila is like a supernova, a large violent explosion that takes place at the end of a star's life cycle – according to the American NASA. As the star runs out of nuclear fuel, some of its mass flows into its core making it collapse. The result is the giant explosion of a supernova that essentially ends its active lifetime. That is Raila in the BBI age.

As such, Ruto, whom the BBI has brought down, but definitely not out, will need to employ the Soft Power concept developed by Professor Joseph Nye of Harvard University. Soft Power refers to the capacity to get what one wants through attraction or persuasion rather than various forms of hard force. That is the language Kenyans prefer most rather than Raila's use of violence. Ruto will additionally need to be tough as

---

10   Barbara Kingsolver, *The Poisonwood Bible* (London: Faber & Faber, 2008), p. 96.

Mahatma Gandhi would say, "to be strong not with the strength of the brute, but with the strength of the spark of God."[11]

Kenya's Hour Zero (00:00): DeRailafication

Then Saul, still breathing threats and murder against the disciples of the Lord went... As he journeyed he came near Damascus, and suddenly a light shone around him from heaven. Then he fell to the ground, and heard a voice saying to him, "Saul, Saul, why are your persecuting me?" ... Then Saul arose from the ground... And he was three days without sight, and neither ate nor drank. ...And Ananias went his way and entered the house; and laying his hands on him he said, "Brother Saul, the Lord Jesus, who appeared to you on the road as you came, has sent me that you may receive your sight and be filled with the Holy Spirit." Immediately there fell from his eyes something like scales, and he received his sight at once; and he arose and was baptized... Immediately he preached the Christ in the synagogues... (Acts 9:1-20 – NKJV)

Unlike Saul's, Raila's purportedly Road to Damascus that lead to the Handshake did not occur while he was in motion; going to his Bondo rural home, Kibra bedroom or Uhuru Park to pretend to be Head of State. Most likely, it happened in an isolated surrounding that could allow for serious soul searching, probably at his Karen Home, Nairobi.

Stretch imagination and construct a suitable scene sometimes in February 2018. Raila is a gravely unsettled man. The just passed self-swearing in ceremony of 30 January has been an inconsequential climax that misfired totally. President Kenyatta is still sitting pretty at State House. What next? Raila is between the devil and blue sea. *Hakuna mbele au nyuma*. He retraces his life of close to 37 years of search for power from 1982 when he was 37. All these close to 40 years of unforgiving wilderness. Arrest, treason trial, detention, exile. All the past speeches, dances, insults, propaganda, manifestoes for presidential campaigns. All the battles with electoral institutions. All support from foreign friends, donors, organisations and governments. All that running. For how long should one be in *mapambano* (struggles)

---

11 Ramjee Singh and S. Sundaram (eds), *Gandhi and the World Order* (New Delhi: APH Publishing, 1996), p. 242.

to be President? Isn't there another avenue for an immensely popular chief liberator or is this finally the end of the road?

Raila is seated in his study room. For three days, like Saul, he has self-imposed quarantine himself, Covid-19 version. Viewing his NASA co-principals and followers as cowards and traitors for failing to take him shoulder-high to State House on that 30 January, he really need peace of mind. The appetite for food even the favourite *ugali* and fish has evaporated. No urge to read newspapers or watch TV. A pint of Tusker beer or some whisky to ease the mood? Does he smoke? Does he pray or read the Bible (of course not!)?

His mind having hit the blank wall, Raila's thoughts goes to Erik Erikson's eighth stage of psychosocial development: "Would have," "should have," "could have" been. Did I travel the wrong career path? His eyes wanders into the well-stocked library, walks to one shelf and reluctantly picks works of one of his best authors, Marcus Cicero, the Roman statesman, accomplished lawyer, philosopher and great orator. He embarks on a kind of honest self-interrogation or self-trial. Mentally, he is doing an audit of his journey for power. Where did I go wrong? He picks at random Cicero's famous quotes for cross-examination.

The function of wisdom is to discriminate between good and evil. Test failed. Anger is the beginning of madness. Test failed. The higher we are placed, the more humbly we should walk. Test failed. The trial continues: never go to excess but let moderation be your guide. Test failed. Do not hold the delusion that your advancement is accomplished by crushing others. Test failed. Any man can make mistakes, but only an idiot persists the error. Test failed. The harvest of old age is the recollection and abundance of blessing previously secured. Test failed. A life of peace, purity and refinement leads to a calm and untroubled old age. Test failed.

Raila had now failed eight tests. Just as he was about to stop the exercise for revealing a bitter failed history, he sported the 9th quote: Old age: the crown of life, our play's last act! He suddenly stood up as if new life has been pumped into him. Never say die, Cicero had shown the way – the last act, what fools call the kick of a dying horse. If I promised President Kenyatta that I am tired of war, will put down my crude weapons and tame my tongue, won't he receive me with warm open arms? Of course the President will offer you anything under the sun, billions of shillings and VVIP treatment in exchange of peace.

Just as Cicero's 9th quote had commanded, Raila's final act, his last hurrah worked wonders. He set the President's heart aflame with the peace proposition. Name Odinga written backward – Agnido(a) – means "setting on fire, explosive" in Sanskrit language. Therefore, on the 9th March the Year of our Lord Twenty Eighteen, on the footsteps of Harambee House, the Handshake was consummated. What a lucky number nine!

Henceforth, Raila's guns went silent. The country breathed a sigh of relief. A mother would now sleep soundly without worry of her children turning up crippled, in a hospital ICU or mortuary from Raila's *mapambano* assignments. The business community, *Mama mboga* and hawkers would have no fear of their stocks being destroyed by Raila mobs. Motorists would be safer. Tourists and investors would now resume their visits into the country. Police officers, pot-bellied for lack of exercise from chasing Raila's rowdy crowds, would return to normal duties of fighting crime. The government's tear gas canisters budget would drop. People and the birds of the air would feast on clean, pure Nairobi air devoid of noise and tear gas pollution. And more crucial, President Kenyatta would concentrate on important matters of running the state without one nagging politician. Thus, 9 March 2018 Handshaketime became the Victory in Kenya (VK) Day, Kenya's Hour Zero. Hail son of Jaramogi! Raila for President!

One question came to mind. Why didn't the multitudes flood towns and villages to celebrate the VK Day as happened in VE 1945? Or the President declared the day a public holiday? In Europe, Hitler had left the political scene; in Kenya Raila had not, that was the difference. Secondly, Raila's body language and especially facial expression told it all. Previously, Raila had performed other handshakes, which soon turned meaningless. This was not different or special; a lot was hidden between the lines.

Thirdly, Raila's speech left a lot to be desired. He gave a blanket condemnation to all Kenyans as the root problem to a united and prosperous country. He was using "our." At the appearance outside of the Harambee House, what the President had, consciously or otherwise told the world was: "Look, here is the Devil incarnate who has caused

Kenyans untold suffering since the 1990s. I have brought him back home for rehabilitation to become like "us" and pray that the nightmares from him will end once and for all." But Raila was saying "It was not me", but "us." All said and done the President went home with 100 per cent mark score, while Raila took zero or minus per cent. Yet Raila was not done. His pot was fast brewing the Big Lie, like that of Adolf Hitler (Raila written backwards is A-Liar), the BBI, to give the Handshake huge credibility and national appeal.

Still, the key question remained unanswered. What in reality had transpired in Raila between 30th January and 9th March to give a convincing stand that him or the Handshake were genuine? Raila had to be a completely new man for this to happen. Had a miracle happened like in Saul's case? Before the Handshake Raila, in an ideal situation, should have called a press conference or bought space in the dailies and enumerated his dark past, offered apology to the people and the nation then begin afresh from there. In March 2015, President Kenyatta had apologised to the Kenyans for past wrongs committed by his government and previous ones. You can only begin from an honest point.

It did not take long then. The Handshake and the BBI became suspect. The unshakable truth was that on swearing himself President on 30 January 2018 Raila had reached his un-ceremonial Hour Zero. Political Raila was dead as a dodo. He had scored own goal. Considering that it is completely impossible to rehabilitate him, what the country urgently required now was not the BBI, but first to completely wipe away Raila's brand of politics: deRailafication. What would deRailafication involve?

RAILAISM AND DERAILAFICATION

DeRailafication is a proposition of national magnitude. The BBI report require updating and chapter one introduced and appropriately titled, "*Railaism* and *DeRailafication*" to make it a 10-point document. Because of the importance of the new addition, the two terms will find a place in world dictionaries and become a way of life to Kenyans in the immediate future.

One would hypothesise a situation. Suppose Covid-19 sojourned on the earth in mid-1982. On 1 August, the Kenya Government placed Raila in a quarantine that is still in force today. Don't ask why only one person; nothing personal, just business. Then the government committed to meeting all costs related to the virus detention-without-trial, including sound-proof face masks lest Raila attempts to communicate with the outside world and launch *mapambano* while still in isolation. In the total absence of Raila in public, Kenya would have been the Switzerland of Africa. There are many bad things that would NOT have happened in the country.

Paul Thomas Mann, a German novelist and Nobel Prize in Literature winner (1929) was deeply disturbed by the Nazi regime in his motherland. On 8 May, 1945, the day of Germany surrender, he wrote while in exile: "Our shame lies open to the eyes of the world. Everything German, everyone who speaks German, writes German, has lived in Germany, is affected by this shameful revelation… Humanity shudders in horror of Germany!"[12]

In the 1940 book, *Zero Hour*, Mann's daughter, Erika, a refugee, penned an article, "Don't Make the Same Mistakes". In it she urged Americans to confront the danger posed by the Nazi Germany: "Am I going too far?" She wrote. "Am I a stranger? Am I meddling in other people's affairs? There is only one affair-the affair of mankind-and that is my affair as well as yours. In the hands of America, into your hands, God has placed the affairs of mankind. And one man should be forbidden to entreat you: Act! This is your hour, it's the final hour – the Zero Hour!"[13]

Begin with the immediate past and engage a reverse gear. The 30 January 2018 in Kenya was a historical day. A treasonable act was conducted in public in broad daylight. Check the timelines. On 8 August 2017 Kenyans went to the polls. The IEBC declared Uhuru Kenyatta President. Raila rejected the results and headed to the courts. The Supreme Court announced a repeat of the election, which were held on 26 October. Raila boycotted the exercise. Kenyatta won again. Raila went back to the drawing board including considering whether the military could come to his aid.

Then forward. The moment he raised the Bible and announced himself President, Raila had hit his Hour Zero. He had catapulted

---

12   See Stephen Brockmann, *German Literary Culture at the Zero Hour* (Rochester, NY: Camden House, 2004), p. 92.

13   Stephen V. Benét et al., *Zero Hour: A Summons to the Free* (New York: Farrar & Rinehart Inc., 1940), 76.

himself to Stone Age. He looked so small and crazy. He was a man unfit to live in the modern world. He had raped his motherland. He was a person who cared less for women, children, elderly, disabled or the whole nation in case chaos erupted. Instantly, the pseudo democrat was transfigured into a despot, a professed liberator to an oppressor and his oft-pretended journey to Canaan rightly revealed as one to hell on earth. In fact, Raila fell down so fast from whatever level like a monkey sliding on a slippery tree. For what name would you give to a person who could harm your legitimately elected President or who thought mothers' children were rifle targets at Stoni Athi Shooting Range? The level of this primitivism could not go below this point, Hour Zero.

Treason is defined by *Merriam-Webster Dictionary* as "the offense of attempting by overt acts to overthrow the government of the state to which the offender owes allegiance or to kill or personally injure the sovereign or the sovereign's family." In the *Longman Dictionary*, it is "the crime of being disloyal to your country or its government, especially by helping its enemies or trying to remove the government using violence." This is exactly what Raila was attempting to do on that day. Treason. With Raila, citizens or even the President and his family were not safe.

Take huge steps backward to 1 August 1982 when Raila was first tried for treason. These are four decades of one man individually, or with others, orchestrating a deadly show that left the country about 7,000 people dead and approximately Kes 500 billion in economic loss, a situation close to what Germany was called a vast lunatic asylum (**discussed in subsequent chapters**). The ideologies, politics, economies and sociology of Raila collectively termed Railaism have made Kenya; "our shame lies open to the eyes of the world", to copy from Mann.

Railaism has traces of Hitler's genes, and it stinks to high heavens. Whether Raila tries to remove his surface or shed old skin like a serpent, or tries to bend the time to suit the present, burn the archives of his nasty past or have President Kenyatta's two palms cover him up through the BBI, Railaism still stinks. In the twilight of his 23-year rule in the Congo that resulted in deaths of between 10 to 15 million people, massive looting of natural resources and stealing of one million dollars, King Leopold tried to erase historical records that could incriminate him. In August 1908, five months after officially handing over the Congo to Belgium, the king ordered all state archives burned in a furnace. When questioned, he replied: "I will give them my Congo, but they have no right to know what I did there." Reportedly, the records that survived are still safely kept at the Brussels Foreign Ministry marked: "*Ne pas a' communiquer aux chercheurs* – No access to researchers."

Soon after independence, the British Government secretly shipped some 8,000 secret files out of Kenya. These files are said to have given a picture of what went on in the government and military circles in London and Kenya during the Emergency. *The Times* of London of 5 April 2011 indicated there were 300 boxes containing files with 17,000 pages hidden in the basement of the Foreign and Commonwealth Office for the last 50 years marked "most secret" and contained material that "might embarrass Her Majesty's government as well, might embarrass members of the police, military forces, public servants and others."[14] This was until Caroline Elkins wrote *Britain's Gulag: The Brutal End of Empire in Kenya*. The book details the torture the freedom fighters endured and led to the suing of Britain in a London court for torture and sexual abuses. From this process some victims were compensated. The British Government had thought the issue was long dead and buried. Equally one would like to wish Raila's past atrocities as forgotten. They are still fresh in people's minds. The country's mainstream media still have them intact.

Raila is like a rat that bites and blow wind to sooth the pain. If he wishes the past away he is badly mistaken. Even fools cannot accept him into their kingdom now. Though even Jesus demands repentance and salvation before accepting a sinner into his kingdom, Raila is beyond redemption. Even the high temperatures required to refine diamond cannot cleanse his impurities.

For the building bridges to succeed, Railaism has to be wiped out from the face of Kenya. Beginning from people's minds, DeRailafication should involve the dissociation from national, political, economic, cultural and spiritual Railaism in toto. A new beginning.

However, this *fagia fagia* will not be easy. Railaism has penetrated into some people internal and external systems like that nagging couch grass (*thangari* in Gĩkũyũ and *kwekwe* in Kiswahili) that hardly leaves a

---

14   See Ian Cobain, Owen Bowcott and Richard Norton-Taylor, "Britain destroyed records of colonial crimes", *The Guardian*, Wednesday, 18 April 2012.

garden however much one tries, for however diligently Kenyans sanitised themselves and maintained social distancing from him Covid-19 style, Railaism virus always found and infected them with dire consequences.

In *Decolonising the Mind*, Ngũgĩ wa Thiong'o calls the weapon imperialists unleashed daily to annihilate people's beliefs in themselves a cultural bomb. Railaism is a political bomb that trumps on people's constitutional right to choosing their preferred leaders. DeRailafication is an endeavour towards modernity that must be undertaken with utmost zeal.

Another critical point. Hitler boasted that German youth belonged to him. According to *Revisiting Zero-Hour 1945* edited by Stephen Brockman and Frank Trommler, almost all German young people belonged to the Hitler Youth Movement. And they were prepared to die for him anytime. "In songs, poems, speeches, novels, movies, plays and Party Congresses the Nazi celebrated youth at the expense of old age." Why so? To use them.

Railaism perhaps borrowed the same insight from Hitler. To radicalise or indoctrinate youth to become a militant tool for his selfish political destiny since he lacked his own military. "War is young men dying and old men talking," (Franklin Roosevelt) and, "I'm fed up to the ears with old men dreaming up wars for young men to die." (George McGovern) Railaism is barbarism that has no value for the country's youth. It must be brought to a closure.

"We may allow ourselves a brief period of rejoicing," warned British Prime Minister Winston Churchill when the war in Europe halted offering that more toil and efforts lay ahead. BBI is nothing than Bed Blanket Insulator (BBI) for covering Railaism. "If peace be indivisible," noted *The Guardian* editorial of 8 May 1945, "this is not peace, but at least we have stopped the onrush of evil. We have won the right to hope."[15] Railaism has merely gone on a brief slumber. The next round could be volatile like nothing ever seen before: "For one thing is quite certain," Frederick William, The Great Elector, ruler of Brandenburg-Prussia advised his son Frederick II, King of Prussia in 1667. "If you simply sit still, in the belief that the fire is still far from

---

15   Richard Nelsson, "VE Day: 'We have won the right to hope' - archive, May 1945", *The Guardian*, Wednesday, 6 May 2020.

your border: then your lands will become the theatre on which the tragedy is played out."[16]

To repeat, deRailafication shall not be a walk in the park. The powers that be that have given Railaism a sure temporary safe haven are, to quote Sam Mustafa in a review of Christopher Clark's *Time and Power*, "the chess players with a near-infinite ability to alter the balance of the present."[17] The present is the deRailafication, an absolute break with Railaism and a radical new beginning in the words of John: "And I saw a new heaven and a new earth: For the first heaven and the first earth were passed away; and there was no more sea." (Revelation 21:1). Railaism's best bedroom is the three-quarter of the 21st century post-independence modern Africa fast backwards, when aspiring rejected leaders knew military coups and civil wars as the ideal alternative highways to grab the power. DeRailafication should be the Kenya's moment's vision, the unofficial national anthem for building genuine bridges, a national transformation to change national politics appropriately starting from the leadership.

Was denazification a success story? From a world's case study of ruins in 1945 modern Germany is a top democracy, Europe's biggest and the world's fourth largest economy in terms of GDP. In an article published in *The Guardian* titled, "Exorcising Hitler: The Occupation and Development of Germany", the writer admitted that the denazification process was complicated, the road was rocky and there was a big price to pay, but went on to say: "For more than half a century, the rise of modern Germany as an exemplary liberal democracy, as an economic power, as an exporter of decent European values… has been an object lesson in how a violent pariah state can cleanse itself."[18] Calling the rehabilitation a seamless story of redemption earned through good work, the article noted that "The Marshall Plan 'exorcised' Hitler and gave birth to the West German economic miracle."[19] A big lesson to

---

16 See Christopher M. Clark, *Iron Kingdom: The Rise and Downfall of Prussia, 1600-1947* (Cambridge, Mass: The Belknap Press, 2006), p. 66.

17 Sam Mustafa, "Mustafa on Clark, 'Time and Power: Visions of History in German Politics, from the Thirty Years' War to the Third Reich'", H-Net Reviews (July 2019). Retrieved from: http://www.h-net.org/reviews/showpdf.php?id=53975. Accessed on 10 June 2020.

18 Victor Sebestyen, "Exorcising Hitler: The Occupation and Denazification of Germany by Frederick Taylor – review", *The Guardian*, Sunday, 24 Apr 2011.

19 Ibid.

Kenya (see how strangely the country has calmed down since Raila went Missing in Action through the BBI).

BBI CREATED KENYA'S BERLIN WALL

Right from day one of independence President Jomo Kenyatta talked of building bridges. In his Big Three Agenda, he promised to make cross-overs that would move the people from poverty to wealth, ignorance to knowledge, and from a nation ravaged by disease to a healthy one. Sixty years down the line, there are still many bridges to build over rivers to cross people, to better politics, economy and social lives.

Surprisingly, no one told President Uhuru Kenyatta that his hands were already full when he was negotiating the BBI with Raila. What with the work-in-progress and uninitiated items in the Jubilee Manifesto and the Big Four Agenda. His time was running out. Kenyans supported the President fully to fulfil the pledges made for their well-being and his decent and memorable legacy. Likewise, they had the right to warn him that "the emperor is naked" and "was entering a lion's den where angels to rescue him could be scarce" – as long as he was co-driving the BBI with Raila.

Yet by giving Raila some goodies through the Handshake, the President was sure he had blinded him Samson-style. He was wrong. Raila is ruthlessly calculating, a smooth operator who appears on the surface like a calm sea. Raila, the engineer, set down to work. Then the President started ejecting Deputy Ruto's allies from their rightly earned positions and making political alliances left and right. Had premature campaigns suddenly become a priority to development? Raila virus of making different political arrangement every minute had caught him sooner than expected. Kenyatta's brand president built passionately for eight years began a gradual depreciation. Therefore, the moment *Basi ya Baba Iliingia* (BBI) – Dad's bus entered – the Jubilee House, a set of chain reactions was triggered. The biggest was the Kenya's Building Berlin Infrastructure (BBI) plan that was preceded by the conception of the Cold War in the country. Will the latter lead Kenya to the brink of a nuclear war like the two Superpowers did in the early 1960s?

The 10 December 1948 was a special day for the global community. In August 1945 the World War II had come to an end. The world had looked back and asked: how can a civilised people continue living a life of barbarism? This and World War I had left about 75 million people dead. Initiated by people of great vision, the Universal Declaration of Human Rights (UDHR) was established on that December day following the launch of the United Nations Organization (UNO) to, among other things, prevent such conflicts in the future.

The UDHR notwithstanding, wars with weapons were replaced with one that did not involve direct military engagement. The United States and Soviet Union, the two superpowers and their allies, began a war of rivalry over political, economic and military matters. The geopolitical tension, best known as the Cold War, was viewed as a contest between capitalism (US) on the one hand and communism (Soviets) on the other. However, the Cold War exported to Africa and elsewhere was real war where millions of people lost their lives.

The most powerful and enduring symbol of the Cold War was the over 150 km Berlin Wall. Started on the dead of the night on 13 August 1961, its construction was designed to divide West Berlin and East Germany to prevent East Germans from entering the West. Finally, the 28-year old wall was brought down on 9 November 1989. More than two million people from East Germany crossed to West Germany. The people hugged, kissed and cried with joy. They sang, cheered and danced. They toasted champagne. One journalist called the celebration "the greatest street party in the history of the world." The dismantling of the Wall signalled the collapse of communism and the beginning of the democratic wind of change that swept across the world. In October 1990 the East and West Germany were unified to form one German state.

But it was not all that "cold" since 1945. We live in a strange world. Exactly 14 years since the world resolved to live in peace (UDHR formation), the two Superpowers were engaged in the most direct and dangerous confrontation. The US had placed nuclear missiles in Turkey and the Soviet Union had their own in the Cuban Island, 90 miles from the US shores. After a week of intense negotiations between President John F. Kennedy and Premier Nikita Khrushchev, the political and military stand-off was halted. Termed the most dangerous or hottest moment, the two-week Cuban crisis in October 1962 was one of the most significant confrontations that threatened the Cold War to evolve into a full nuclear war.

Back home, Kenya had a taste of its own "world wars" in form of an August 1982 attempted coup, ethnic clashes and election violence. President Kibaki's government brought people together and the new constitution was born in 2010. It was the country's UDHR. Raila was one of the architects of the document. But instead of laying down the arms, he continued with his election-related wars.

Along the line, the street wars proved fruitless to Raila. Ditto swearing himself in as People's President. As a good political engineer, he went back to the production line and came out with the Handshake, quickly followed by the BBI. The war of throwing stones to pedestrians and motorists, mugging, looting and deaths went on a temporary leave. To stand for the real war was a weaponless Kenya's Cold War that came after the BBI.

The Harambee House and Harambee Annex in Nairobi are separated by Harambee Avenue. These are national buildings housing the Office of the President and Office of Deputy President, respectively. They are the places where Kenya is governed from. The '*harambee*' term is as old as independent Kenya and literally means "pulling together" for development. One of the BBI's first visible consequences after Kenya's Cold War commenced was to transform Harambee Avenue into a Berlin Wall. First, the Cold War was turned from one between the Jubilee government and ODM/NASA to between the two public offices. While in normal circumstances the two Harambee buildings occupants worked in harmony, the BBI made them behave like the two bulls of Khayega in Western Kenya once named Obama and Romney. Like the US and Soviets, the two offices installed "nuclear" missiles on their respective sites from where invisible scud missiles were directed to rival office. It is the grass that suffers when two bulls fight.

It does not matter that the Harambee Annex was once occupied by Raila as Prime Minister. Nor is it a secret that Raila would have Deputy President Ruto as the country's President only over his dead body. Actually, rumours have it that whenever Raila drives in close proximity to the Annex he feels like throwing up (not stones, but vomit) or he just closes his eyes.

What matters are important questions: How can a BBI translates into an earthquake in the Presidency? How can a BBI be so keen in dismantling the ruling Jubilee Party and the country's seat of government on the pretext of building the country? How can it create a concrete political wall that divides Kenya's 580,000 sq km right in the middle? Indeed, what was the real spirit or idea behind the BBI? Perhaps world scholars knowledgeable in politics and international studies from distinguished universities like Harvard, Yale or the London School of Economics (LSE) and Political Science will one day unveil this mystery from Kenya.

In the middle of the Cuban Missile Crisis, on 22 October 1962 President Kennedy addressed his nation:

> ...We are prepared to discuss new proposals for the removal of tensions on both sides....But it is difficult to settle or even discuss these problems in an atmosphere of intimidation...My fellow citizens... No one can foresee precisely what course (the path taken) or what costs or casualties will be incurred. Many months of sacrifice and self-discipline lie ahead... our goal is not the victory of might but the vindication of right...[20]

And 10 June 1963:

> So let us not be blind to our differences, but let us also direct attention to our common interests ...For, in the final analysis, our most basic common link is that we all inhabit this small planet. We all breathe the same air. We all cherish our children's future. And we are all mortal.[21]

The global Cold War lasted 45 years, the Cuban Crisis 12 days (16-28 October 1962) and the Berlin Wall 28 years. Kenya is unlucky to lack a leader of President Kennedy's wisdom to give proper direction. The Jubilee Party, Harambee House and Harambee Annex only have the will and the power to decide when their wars, crises and walls will end. One can only trust Raila to add more fuel to the Kenyan Cold War and to the Harambee Houses "Missile Crisis" with a view to putting Kenya on the brink of war. And one can still trust him better to put more steel bars to the Harambee Avenue's "Berlin Wall" to strengthen it further and thus divide more the relationship between President Kenyatta

---

20   Michael Meagher and Larry D. Gragg, *John F. Kennedy: A Biography* (Santa Barbara, CA: Greenwood, 2011), p. 151.

21   Ibid, p. 147.

and Deputy Ruto in addition to unity of 47 million Kenyans. The path and the destination is unknown. The actual causalities are unknown. A mathematician would simplify this awful scenario into an equation: Handshake + BBI = Cold war + Political missiles + A political wall.

IS MARCH THE MONTH OF BETRAYAL?

Wikipedia defines betrayal as "the breaking or violation of a presumptive contract, trust or confidence that produces moral and psychological conflict within a relationship among individuals or organizations". Often, betrayal is the act of supporting a rival group, or it is a complete break from previously decided upon or presumed norms by one party from the others. Someone who betrays others is commonly called a traitor or betrayer.

An act of betrayal, the Wikipedia adds, creates a constellation of negative behaviours, thoughts and feelings in both its victims and its perpetrators. The interactions are complex… Most adults living in liberal democracies place trust in the state of which they are a citizen. When this trust is betrayed, at its worst, the individual can suffer psychological betrayal trauma… Betrayals hurt; they break relationships between individuals, societies or nations. They mess the trust between the leaders and the led. And normally, they bring expensive social, economic and political ramification among the concerned parties.

The Handshake that brought in the BBI was conceptualised in March, the month associated with the world's most famous acts of betrayals. Would a building bridges concept also suffer elements of betrayal? A down memory lane of most notable cases of backstabbing in history and why the BBI could be the newest kid on the block would suffice.

First, take some coincidence of the March dates; for instance, Julius Caesar's Ides in March 44 BC, Jesus Christ's trial in March AD 30, Jomo Kenyatta's betrayal in March 1959, ICC coming into force in March 2003, the "Ocampo Six indicted in March 2011, (General election held in March 2013) and the Handshake in March 2018. The stories in these dates revolve around that one 8-letter word, betrayal. Let's walk together.

Rome, 15 March 44 BC: The Ides of March

"Beware the Ides of March," a soothsayer warned Julius Caesar about his eventual assassination in William Shakespeare's play, *The Tragedy of Julius Caesar*. The actual story happened much earlier on 15 March 44 BC. The soothsayer had alerted Caesar, the Roman emperor and one of the greatest figures in history, about the oncoming misfortune. Caesar was stabbed 23 times by a group of rebellious Senators. He died aged 55. Before his assassination, he had established a new constitution, increased his powers and decreased the authority of other political institutions. The move had angered the Senate seeing it as an attempt to create a monarchical reign. Sometimes back he had told his friends. "It is more important for the state than for me that I should survive: I have long had my fill of power and glory; but should anything happen to me, Rome will not enjoy peace..."[22]

Caesar acquired several titles during his rule: Dictator Perpetuo (Dictator for Life), Prefect of the Morals and Father of the Fatherland. Coins bore his likeness. Described as a conquering general, high priest of an exotic cult, an epileptic and a complex character, the emperor was also considered by some as a war criminal for waging unsanctioned wars. Caesar was known for his exceptional impassionate gestures and high-pitched voice when speaking. "Julius Caesar is seen as the main example of Caesarism," notes Wikipedia, "a form of political rule led by a charismatic strongman whose rule is based upon a cult of personality, whose rationale is the need to rule by force, establishing a violent social order, and being a regime involving prominence of the military in the government."

Adrian Goldsworthy, one of the most celebrated Caesar's biographers, observes in *Julius Caesar, Life of a Colossus*:

> Caesar spent a very large part of his life at war...was at times many things, including a fugitive, prisoner, rising politician, army leader, legal advocate, rebel, dictator... as well as husband, father, lover and adulterer...There is perhaps a lesson for modern democracies in danger of allowing entrenched lobby groups, political parties and other interests to stifle real debate.[23]

---

22   Steve Coates, "Giving Caesar and Augustus their due - Culture - International Herald Tribune", *The New York Times,* 29 December, 2006.

23   Adrian Goldsworthy, *Caesar: The Life of a Colossus* (New Haven: Yale University Press, 2006), p. 7.

In *News and Observer*, Peder Zane previewed the biography thus: "… is a superb and absorbing life of the man, who came, saw and conquered – and he was murdered for his trouble."[24]

Earlier in 60 BC, Caesar, Crassus and Pompey had formed the First Triumvirate, a political alliance that dominated Roman politics for several years. At one time, Caesar threatened to eclipse Pompey who had realigned himself with the Senate.

In ancient Rome, the Ides of the March corresponded with the date 15 March and had Latin roots. It was meant to divide the full moon into two. It was a festive day dedicated to Mars, the god of war, and was also notable as a deadline for settling debts. Since Caesar's murder, the day became linked to the prophecies of misfortune and has been passed down as a mark of an anniversary associated with treachery and doom.

Should Kenyans have sleepless nights because the Handshake was sealed in the month of March, one viewed as unlucky through a 2,063-year old event in Rome? What could be split into two by 2022 (like the moon in Rome): the Jubilee Party, the Kenyatta-Raila alliance or the country? Betrayal is deeply imbedded in human nature. Between President Kenyatta, Deputy Ruto and Raila, who best symbolises Julius Caesar, and who could betray who? Who could be settling some debts? And who could encounter the Ides of March 2022; among the three politicians or the BBI?

Palestine, March, AD 30

Jesus Christ had a grand mission. He wanted to recapture his rightful position as the "President" of the whole earth. The official opposition, headed by Satan had reigned for too long. Jesus started preparations for the campaign at age 12, from the Synagogue. Then at 30 years, he brought together twelve campaign managers. His campaign motto was simple: get baptised, be born again, and get filled with the Holy Spirit. Doing the three translated into voting for him and thus a victory to his BBI for the benefit of humankind.

After three and a half years of selling his manifesto, Jesus was betrayed by one of his managers. "Greetings, Rabbi!" Judas Iscariot

---

24   See book preview of Goldsworthy's *Caesar: The Life of a Colossus*. Available at: https://www.indiebound.org/book/9780300126891. Accessed on 10 June 2020.

gave out the kiss, the Handshake of death that delivered the presidential candidate to the Roman colonialists. Then Iscariot received his 30 coins of silver as a reward, committed suicide thereafter (another biblical source says that he bought a *shamba* – plot of land – with the money, then fell down suddenly and his intestines burst open, dead) and Jesus' campaign on earth ended forthwith and the whole world was literally left at the Satan's official opposition's mercy. Even after walking and working with Jesus for three years, was taught the Good News and witnessed dozens of miracles, Judas opted to forego the eternal life for the thirty coins of silver. Handshakes, when not genuine are dangerously expensive.

Kenya, 16 March 1959

On this date, *Time* magazine reported that the star witness who had testified against Jomo Kenyatta during the Kapenguria Six trial, Rawson Mbugua Macharia, had, in March 1950, confessed that his testimony had been false.[25] The testimony was contained in the trial proceedings that had commenced on 3 December 1952. Jomo Kenyatta had been charged alongside five others with managing and assisting to manage a proscribed society called the Mau Mau. Macharia had testified that he had taken one of the Mau Mau oaths at Kenyatta's hands.

Some 47 men and women were bribed to give false evidence. For his evidence, Macharia was awarded with a two-year paid study in Britain together with subsistence for his family and a promise of a job in the Kenya Government after qualification – all for giving evidence implicating Kenyatta.

The Hague, March 2011 forward

Two people, A and B, have a common enemy C who is dying to destroy them. Not long after, person A makes a fake friendship and moves to cohabit with C. Person A, therefore, becomes B's enemy. This is the story of the ICC Kenyan cases revisited in the wake of the political re-alignment courtesy of the BBI. Is there a time when an angel needs a demon or vice versa?

---

25 Kenneth Kwama, "The 'little shopkeeper' who had Mzee Jomo Kenyatta jailed", SDE, 22 June 2014. Available at: https://www.sde.co.ke/article/2000113519/the-little-shopkeeper-who-had-mzee-jomo-kenyatta-jailed. Accessed on 10 June 2020.

Just before the 4 March 2013 General Election some Western governments and institutions had issued sermons and warnings on how the polls were to be conducted and those who were not to be voted in. They talked of "choices have consequences" and "limited contacts". Although they made a hasty U-turn soon after the results were announced; they sent congratulatory messages and willingness "to work together with President Uhuru Kenyatta and Deputy William Ruto", their latest move was not deemed an honest one.

Locally, there were similar voices, especially from some politicians. Mr Kalonzo Musyoka, the Wiper Democratic Party leader, criticised the IEBC and the Judiciary on their handling of the election. "This IEBC cannot manage the next election. It will be a disaster for this country. If they try to stick with it…." Mr Musyoka said, and added; "In fact I want to ask them to just pack and go because they will not be allowed to handle those elections. We know that billions of shillings were used to compromise certain individuals and that the money was paid through foreign accounts in the Seychelles".[26]

The conduct of the IEBC and the results it released also got a thumping from Prof Makau Mutua: "… (The election) was nothing but a return to the primeval-the primordial tribe de minimis. That is the true meaning of the so called tyranny of numbers. Herd the tribe together and whip it up into an irrational frenzy using bogeymen to 'thumb' your opponent. That was one half of the Jubilee's basic campaign strategy".[27]

But the electoral process had its supporters, including the European Union chief observer Aloiz Peterle, who saw "many positive achievements that Kenyans can be justly proud of." Further, the London-based International Centre for Policy Studies bestowed IEBC Chairman, Issack Hassan, the Electoral Resolution and Conflict Award for conducting a free and fair election.

It all started after the 2007/2008 post-election violence when Justice Philip Waki came up with a secret envelope containing names of six prime suspects, later to be charged by the ICC for crimes against humanity at The Hague, Netherlands. Then known as the Ocampo Six,

---

26 Isaac Ongiri, "Kalonzo: I was to be Uhuru's running mate but Ruto changed mind", *Saturday Nation*, 3 August, 2013.

27 Makau Mutua, "Why Obama has skipped Kenya in his Africa tour", *Saturday Nation*, 22 June, 2013.

after the Court's prosecutor, Louis Moreno Ocampo's name, among them were Uhuru Kenyatta and William Ruto. Meanwhile, the two had declared interest in contesting the country's top seats in the next election… They won… The world was shocked. Raila Odinga fought tough battles to reverse the results with no success.

Many believed that the ICC case was primarily to prevent Uhuru and Ruto from ascending to the country's leadership. Nairobi lawyer, Ahmednasir Abdullahi, noted that right from the mediation process after the violence, chaired by Kofi Annan, some Western powers, especially Germany, France and Britain, were sympathetic to Raila and thus played a partisan role. He wrote: "The ICC case was a targeted political assassination focused solely on Mr Kenyatta and Mr Ruto. The other four Kenyans were collateral damage…The sole aim of the case as conceptualized was to take Uhuru and Ruto out of the political equation in the presidential election".[28]

After the election result, some of those opposed to UhuRuto victory probably thought that Kenyans must have been crazy. How on earth could they defy the mighty West? How on earth, and of all the people, from among the eight presidential candidates, could millions of Kenyans elect persons indicted by the highest court in the world on crimes against humanity to the presidency and deputy presidency? But Kenyans knew the two were the best at that moment in time. And like the Roman brothers, Tiberius and Gaius Gracchus, in 100 BC, they believed that "The voice of the people is the voice of God" – *Vox Populi, Vox Dei*. They had spoken collectively at the ballot box and theirs was final, a constitutional right.

In so doing, the voters had rejected the alternative voice, the Raila Presidency, the one used for wrong motives, like when mobs riot, rape, kill and destroy property, being very close to madness. In Latin, this state translates into *Nec Audiendi Qui Solent Dicere, Vox Populi, Vox Dei Quum Tumultousitas Vulgi Semper Insaniae Proxima Sit*. Quite a mouthful of words. In the meantime, the support for Uhuru, Ruto and Kenya as a whole against the ICC continued to strengthen.

---

28 Ahmednasir Abdullahi, "African Union rightly saw what ICC cases are all about", *Sunday Nation*, 2 June, 2013.

Here, a sitting president and his deputy were being charged in a foreign land, thousands of kilometres away, perhaps a first in world history. It was an unprecedented record. Where else do you find hundreds of MPs from an African country camping in a court in a foreign land, singing their National Anthem, flapping their country's miniature national flags and praying for their charged compatriots? Where else do you find virtually all 54 African countries of one billion people and a few others beyond the continent, coming behind one country to rescue it from the ICC jaws? This was an entire African Union, coming so strongly in solidarity to defend one country. And where do you find the UN Security Council members converging for a special session to deliberate on one African country?

And still, where do you find priests from all religions leading millions of their followers at every opportune moment to pray for their two leaders? The great rallying was overwhelming. Even President Kenyatta appreciated the power of prayers. When the ICC presiding Judge, Chile Eboe-Osuji, warned Kenyan MPs conducting prayer rallies across the country, the President fired back and urged them to continue praying. On 20 October 2015, during Mashujaa Day, he said; "As Kenyans we should continue praying. No judge has the power to order us to stop praying. We believe in God and we have the freedom of worship so we'll continue praying because we know the value of prayers."[29]

But who exactly was on trial? President Kenyatta and Deputy Ruto were describing their cases as "a personal matter." Yet the truth was, Kenyans within and without were on trial, a fact people like Prof Makau Mutua differed with suggesting that a presidency and a country are two different entities. In the *Sunday Nation*, Mutua told Attorney-General, Githu Muigai, to pause and search his conscience. "Besides, why do you act as though Kenya is on trial?" He asked. "You seem to believe that Mr Kenyatta is the Republic of Kenya, and the Republic of Kenya is Mr Kenyatta…You've deliberately conflated the interests of the two indictees (Kenyatta and Ruto) with that of the Republic of Kenya. This is my advice to you: read and ponder Mark 8:36."[30]

---

29   John Ngirachu, "Ignore ICC judges over Ruto prayer rallies, says Uhuru", *Daily Nation*, Tuesday, 20 October, 2015.

30   Makau Mutua, "Pause and search your conscience Mr Attorney-General", Funua, Sunday, 2 June 2013. Available at: http://concernedkenyan.blogspot.com/2013/06/pause-and-search-your-conscience-mr.html. Accessed on 2 June 2020.

Now, according to Chapter nine of the Constitution, President Kenyatta derives his authority from the people of Kenya, is the Head of State and Government, is the Commander-in-Chief of the Kenya Defence Force, is symbol of national unity and one who must safeguard the sovereignty of the Republic, among others. Deputy President William Ruto is his principal assistant. Thus, the authority and unity of the people were on trial. In a nutshell, Kenya was also on trial.

That being so, what was really disturbing was a truly possible scenario. Could you imagine President Kenyatta being locked up in a cell at The Hague and denied bail by the Court? (The *Nairobi Law Monthly* magazine March-April 2013 page 71 showed a picture of Kenyatta entering the ICC offices at The Hague through the revolving doors. The place looked exactly like prison!) Well, Deputy President Ruto would have immediately taken up his position in an acting capacity. (Kenyatta had himself said on 8 September, 2013, "It is not possible that I and Ruto be outside Kenya at the same time. If Ruto is out then I should be in the country running the government affairs." Maybe he was thinking of, "the worst can come".)

On 6 April 1994 the plane carrying Rwandan President Juvenal Habyarimana crashed. This air disaster triggered the 100-day genocide leading to the slaughter of close to one million people. Back on 28 June 1914, Archduke Franz Ferdinand, heir to the Austro-Hungarian throne was shot dead. Soon, World War I started. A leader takes his country along wholly in his wallet, for lack of better words. The safety of a country is directly proportional to the safety of its leaders.

Further, when Ivorian President, Laurent Gbagbo, was arrested by the ICC for crimes against humanity, soldiers later arrested his wife Simone, ripped her hair out by the roots and went dancing up and down the streets of Abidjan with her hair. Sometime earlier there was the dramatic arrest of Saddam Hussein by the US forces from a six-foot deep hole on 13 December 2003. One can imagine the safety of the spouses of President Kenyatta and Deputy Ruto in the circumstances. Even after a country acquiring sovereignty at independence, anything was possible from the Western powers. Perhaps this is the scenario Raila wished for; arrest and detention of either President Kenyatta or Deputy Ruto, insecurity of their spouses and families and collapse of the government for his benefit. Kenya knew; the whole world knew. That

Raila was the most prominent politician local sympathiser of the ICC process against UhuRuto. By any means he wanted them roasted at The Hague. He might not have been the genesis of indictment, but being the most senior opposition politician meant a great deal. The Agĩkũyũ say, *Gũtirĩ mũici na mũcũthĩrĩria* (the actual thief and the one who witness the theft without raising an alarm are both guilty). The ICC was a battle brewed from the ballot box.

While constantly defending himself, President Kenyatta accused Raila of the post-election violence (PEV) that was the basis of the trial. At The Hague in 2011, he declared: "… (But) he had political responsibility. If he did not hold press conferences using strong language in that period, if he followed due process and went to court and, lastly, had he used his political voice to tell supporters to stop violence, the level of violence would not have been what it was." The PEV resulted in 1,133 deaths, 3,561 injuries, 650,000 IDPs and 117,216 instances of property destruction.

At a rally in Sagana town on 3 September 2013 Deputy President Ruto added his voice: "*Mtashangaa na ile maneno itakuwa huko Hague* (You will be amazed by what will transpire at The Hague)… I know you have been seeking divine intervention, but I urge you not to give up… the ICC trials will not compromise our promise to deliver economic growth…If he (Raila) wants power, he should talk to the voters. He wants to try another way of ascending to power because we defeated him… I want to tell you that even if the Constitution is changed a hundred times, they (Raila's Cord Coalition) will not defeat us in any election."[31]

Raila never defended UhuRuto. He severally told them to carry their own cross; in fact, when the two were eventually freed and planned a thanksgiving rally at Afraha Stadium, Nakuru to mark the Court's ruling, Raila accused them of heading to dance on the graves of the post-election victims calling the exercise a *danse macabre*. And he called for the revival of the ICC cases (see Chapter Four).

They say politics is a dirty game, more so in Kenya. In the final analysis, person C could disagree with person A. Then he will like the

---

31   Quoted in "Ruto warns Raila in Central visit", Sahara Tribune, 14 September, 2013. Available at: http://saharatribune.com/ruto-warns-raila-in-central-visit/. Accessed on 2 June 2020.

speed of light proceed to person B and make a formidable coalition against person A. Then person A will be left a political orphan wailing and gnashing his teeth in frustration. That is how calculating and detrimental person C has always been. Beware the Ides of the Handshake, March 9, 2018.

Nairobi, early March 2018

Two men were locked in a room. One was the legally elected President of Kenya and the other illegally sworn People's President. The atmosphere was tense. Two "sitting" presidents of one country facing each other!

They were here to conceive the BBI. After 45 minutes of restlessness, doubts and each feeling superior to the other and taking many cups of tea and probably tots of expensive whisky, the work at hand commenced. For the 19 hours the meeting lasted (of course with some breaks), primarily it was not about the 47 million Kenyans. It was about me, you, and us. (Remember the song: One for Me, One for You… by La Bionda?) It was about plus, minus, multiplication, division and calculus, the mathematics of change, all focused to August 2022. Calculus of two individuals' power and wealth. Calculus of dynasties' rule. See, one president had excluded his deputy, the country's second in command, with whom they had been like *kidole na pete* for years and almost crucified at The Hague together. The other had evaded his three comrades in politics with whom they had attempted to go to the Kenyan moon aboard a NASA rocket.

Finally, 9 March,2018 the two gentlemen appeared outside Harambee House and did the infamous Handshake that birthed the BBI. Henceforth, *Tuko Pamoja*, *Kusema na Kutenda*, high fives, hugs, *gotta*, brother William, the Jubilee party supporters for one President, and Joshua taking his millions of people to Canaan for the other, were thrown into the dustbin of history.

NOW, HARD QUESTIONS MR. PRESIDENT, SIR

On 9 April 2013 Kenyans gave you the full mandate to take care of their affairs and chart their destiny, them fully behind you. And again they did it late 2017 (twice!) Their hearts and minds had agreed strongly and throughout about the Jubilee Promise. The words of your adviser on legal affairs, Abdikadir Mohammed, are among hundreds of thousands of others that confirm that Kenyans believed they had made the correct choice in voting in the Jubilee Party:

> He is a President who works hard. He is a workaholic and extremely sharp. He reports to his office early enough for 7am meetings and stays late. He likes documents and is keen to understand the inner workings of staff. He is extremely hands-on and absolutely determined to improve conditions. The President wants things done and fast…..whenever we sit, he is the most experienced around the table. The President is also very good with people and is willing to listen to any good idea regardless of whom it comes from.[32]

Your advisor wrote on:

> I have a lot of hope. I think Kenyans are too cynical. We should be more forgiving and celebrate ourselves whenever we do good…. I work for the President. He works very hard. I am glad that he is running this country at this particular time….. I know where his heart is about the future of this country.[33]

Now some questions, Sir:

1. Sir, with your God-given intellect, talents and drive, and a ruthlessly able deputy at hand, support of millions of Kenyans, were you not, collectively capable of completing the remaining Jubilee manifesto (covers nearly all BBI elements) pledges without the Handshake from one man who shouted the loudest, Crucify him! Crucify him! At the ICC? Here was a man, a Kenyan. Less than ten years ago he was passionately building bridges between Nairobi and The Hague to cross over the President and Deputy President of his own country to Golgotha for crucifixion by *wazungus* so that he can become President himself that you have picked as your best man. Unheard of, Sir.

   Author Nolifer Merchant noted: "The truth is this: The brand follows the work. Your brand is the exhaust created by the

---

32   Interview with former Mandera Central legislator Abdikadir Mohamed, published in *Saturday Nation*, 12 October, 2013.

33   Ibid.

engine of your life. It is a by-product of what happens as you share what you are creating, and with whom you are creating."[34] Especially during your first term Sir, you and your deputy transformed yourselves into a formidable brand. The completed and work-in-progress manifesto undertakings are the exhaust of your work. If you cannot kill the body, kill the soul, they say. Raila failed spectacularly to barbeque you at The Hague; he is presently determined to kill your brand.

See, you are answerable to 47 million Kenyans; since Raila broke NASA he has no sizeable genuine supporters, only some desperate sycophants. He is not answerable to anyone in case something terribly goes wrong with the BBI before 2022. You have a legacy to worry about; Raila does not care about legacies. Remember that story of the hare and the hyena. At midnight, when the hyena was beating up his wife, hare was hammering a drum. Sir, money or the box? Or rather, Raila or the legacy?

2. From the Holy Bible: Sir, you and your deputy were thrown into the hottest furnace (The Hague) like happened to Shadrack, Meshach and Abednego. Kenyans prayed to the living God. They refused to consult the Witchdoctor or side with the Western foreign gods. The African continent came to your rescue. Soon, you came out of the fire and brimstone, totally unhurt by the flames in Europe. Would you then come running to the waiting arms of the local King Nebuchadnezzar and embrace him with a kiss? Very odd, this.

3. Like yourself and Deputy Ruto, Moses and his partner Joshua had walked together in a most difficult journey en route to the Promised Land. Supposing, upon sighting Canaan, Moses made an abrupt U-turn, rushed back to Egypt, and did a handshake with Pharaoh to conspire to take the children of Israel back to slavery thereby leaving Joshua suspended in the wilderness like a pendulum? The history of the Israelites' final liberation would have been half-done, and so is your legacy.

---

34 Nolifer Merchant, "Your Brand is Exhaust Fume, not the Engine", Nolifer Merchant, 25 September, 2013. Available at: https://nilofermerchant.com/2013/09/25/your-brand-is-exhaust-fume-not-the-engine/. Accessed on 2 June 2020.

4. Mr. President, when the ICC summoned you to The Hague, you left Deputy William Ruto in charge. After the Handshake and BBI launch, whom can you trust the most? Can you leave Raila in charge of the country to attend to foreign duties like Mandela did to opposition leader Mangosuthu Buthelezi over 20 times, the Kenya constitution notwithstanding? The answer: you can't. Deep inside, you know that Raila cannot be trusted. Then what is the real meaning of the BBI deal to the country without your deputy?

5. The Handshake identified Raila rightly as the principal cause of violence at every electoral cycle and converted him into a "loser take something home." The Handshake portrayed Raila's supporters wrongly as violent and bloodthirsty, tainted their names and integrity and will end up as "losers take nothing home." The Handshake has been tragically unfair to the community you come from. The country is regretting: "We told you. The Agikuyu are notoriously power-hungry and money-hungry and can even shake the Devil's hands to get them. They are hypocrites, untrustworthy, bridges-breakers folks." Sir, will the people ever again take your word to the bank?

6. Here was a man who is disintegrating the ruling party Jubilee's political covalent bonds – the strongest bonds that hold atoms chemically together – as well as those of his NASA movement, a political blow to almost the whole country so that he can become the President or Prime Minister.

    Here was a man whose DNA was comparable to that of:

    (a) Julius Caesar – as described by Wikipedia and Adrian Goldsworthy,

    (b) Judas Iscariot – with a financial reward, he became a traitor to the world's Executive President and God's plan for mankind, and

    (c) Rawson Macharia – with a promise of a job, he became a traitor to the future first President of Kenya and almost messed the independence of the country.

Wonders of wonders: And this is the man you have brought forth to help build bridges between 47 million people with a view to building heaven in Kenya. Wonders will never cease. Does a great leader dismantle to unite? Does a master builder destroy to build? Betrayal. With all due respect, millions of people in Kenya and the African continent feel a painful act of betrayal in the whole Handshake and BBI drama. While the handshake was hailed as a peacemaker, the damage it will cause will take years to recover.

OR IS KENYA'S DAMASCUS MOMENT REAL?

Is Raila being judged too harshly? History bearing witness of his dark past and considering that just the other day he tried to make Kenya a "One Country, Two Presidents" Republic, could he have experienced a true Road to Damascus moment on the road to the Handshake like that of Saul of Tarsus, underwent an evolution from a persecutor to a patriot overnight and moved successfully to drive the BBI to its nationalistic conclusion? Or will he, sometime before 2022, ask the world like, Nicodemus from Jesus, "How on earth can a grown-up man re-enter his mother's womb and be born again?"

Ask again: Can Raila truly do a candid Road to Damascus instant for Kenya?

Majority of people are doubtful Thomases, in particular about Raila's ultimate motive in the BBI, whether national or for self-interest. Yet Kenyans know nothing is impossible and the Lord truly works in mysterious ways in this part of the world. They believe, like in Isaiah 2:18, that… "No matter how deep the stain of your sins, I can take it out and make you as clear as fleshly fallen snow. Even if you are stained as red as crimson, I can make you white as wool".

But, all said, the only time Kenyans will believe that the BBI drive is a patriotic calling and not for personal political ambition will be an occasion similar to this – no more no less: Raila sits one day sometimes before 2022 with President Kenyatta and Deputy Ruto (assuming the latter two's relationship will not have gone South absolutely then). Being a Christian, he decides to go the biblical way: "Gentlemen, in this world it is more blessed to give than to receive … the time has come for my departure. I finally have fought a good fight, I have finished the race, and I have kept the faith." A big shocker for the duo; they find no words.

Raila makes the final statement: "The BBI was my farewell gift to Kenyans after 40 years on the road. At 77 years, I am an old man. Remember when the President urged me to go home to Bondo and promised that he will be bringing me some *uji*. I have seriously thought about quitting and decided that I will not contest for any political position now, or ever."

"Mr. Odinga, are you sure you don't want to be President or Prime Minister or leader of official opposition?" Kenyatta and Ruto ask in unison. "Be honest Agwambo, come out clean. Can you swear by the gods of Kibra, Bondo or Lake Victoria that you are dead serious about retirement?" They push him further. "Absolutely." he assures them. *Ciaigana ni ciaigana* (Enough is enough). "With best wishes, kindly proceed with your Jubilee government endeavours. As for my community, *akina* James Orengo and the rest can take over. Adios amigo Kenyan politics."

That particular day Kenya will tell Paul wherever up he is that he or the Palestine nation of old had no monopoly on the Road to Damascus miracle and shout, Hallelujah and Amen. Yes we can in Kenya.

A Witch Doctor and UhuRuto
at *Danse Macabre*

Zig, zig, zig, Death in cadence,
Striking with his heel a tomb,
Death at midnight plays a dance-tune,
Zig, zig, zig, on his violin.

The winter wind blows and the night is dark,
Moans are heard in the linden-trees,
Through the gloom, white skeletons pass,
Running and leaping in their shrouds.

Zig, zig, zig, each one is frisking,
The bones of the dancers are heard to crack-
But hist! Of a sudden they quit the round,
They push forward, they fly; the cock has crowed.

Henri Cazalis, French physician,
Danse Macabre

*   *   *

Emperor, your sword won't help you out,
Sceptre and crown are worthless here,
I've taken you by the hand,
For you must come to my dance.

Bernt Notke, German artist,
Danse Macabre

Bridge building logo: Is there a concealed mamba snake?

The coming of the railway line in Kenya was prophesied by several prominent Seers of the land years before it happened. Koitalel arap Samoei, Orkoiyot or supreme chief of the Nandi people of Kenya, warned that "a black snake would tear through Nandi land spitting fire and would make its way into the people's lives". For his part Mugo wa Kibiru (or Chege wa Kibiru), a sage from the Agĩkũyũ, revealed that "an iron snake with many legs that spit fires would come and stretch from the big water in the east to another big water in the west of the Gĩkũyũ country." And it came to pass. Initially known as the Uganda Railway, Kenya Railway's first tracks were laid in Mombasa in May 1896 and reached Kisumu in December 1901, a project of the British Government.

Right from conception, the railway idea had been resisted by many. Some British Members of Parliament termed it a gigantic folly, extravagant and ridiculous to the extent of being christened, "Lunatic Express". MP Henry Labouchère registered his opposition at best:

> What it will cost, no words can express;
> What is its object, no brain can suppose;
> Where it will start from, no one can guess;
> Where it is going to, nobody knows;
> What is the use of it, none can conjecture;
> What it will carry, there's none can define…
> It clearly is naught, but a lunatic line…

The social, economic and political benefits of the Lunatic Express, whatever they were, are a story for a different day. What history demonstrates however is that the railway and subsequent European occupation faced a lot of resistance, even locally, in addition to bringing thousands of deaths. On the human toll, around 2,500 people died during the construction, including 28 Indians killed in 1898 by a pair of maneless lions at the Tsavo River Bridge. The big cats were believed to be the spirits of the deceased chiefs determined to stop the work. Fearing for their lives some labourers took a supply train and fled to the Coast. They told Lt Col John Patterson, the supervisor: "We will remain at Tsavo no longer for anything or anybody. We have come from India on an agreement to work for the government, not to supply food for either lions or devils."[1]

Two other memorable incidents: at Kedong, a large caravan of workers was attacked by Maasai who claimed that two of their girls had been raped. They killed 500 of them. Additionally, the Nandi resistance resulted in the killing of their leader Koitalel arap Samoei by Richard Meinertzhagen in 1905. Thus, on completion, the Lunatic Express crawled across the country for a century changing people's lives for better or worse and emitting poisonous fumes of carbon monoxide. Its story was described as one of mystery, intrigue, death and romance. Today, the Nairobi Railway Museum is home to the only surviving steam engine in the world, now a tourist attraction.

Though old is gold, the Standard Gauge Railway (SGR), recently build to replace the analogue transport system (with the digital), was a welcome venture. What is the relevance of this story to today's Kenyan politics of BBI? Plenty.

A few months after the Jubilee government was sworn in on 4 April 2013 Raila Odinga started laying down a new political railway line tracks. The people of Kenya had told him categorically through the IEBC that his old political transport system was incapable of carrying the country forward. Ditto the Supreme Court. Being a hard nut to crack, he had to go down in style as ever, never to surrender, and remain relevant. Why not in the name of the Opposition give the government a payback time? Give UhuRuto sleepless nights and make the country ungovernable? Raila sat down and began to write a book titled, "How the Opposition Underdeveloped Kenya".

SEER, WITCH DOCTOR, *DANSE MACABRE*

Oftentimes, prophets are not recognised in their homelands. Early enough, one modern Seer saw Raila's train coming with its newly minted manifesto. Like the Lunatic Express, this human train was to crisscross the country, siren blaring loudly as it spat blood, tears, and destruction from its compartments in every station of people's lives terribly poisoning the political atmosphere. This has been Raila's mode of operation since the August 1982 failed coup.

---

1   John H. Patterson and Frederick C. Selous, *The Man Eaters of Tsavo: And Other East African Adventures* (New York: Cosimo, 2010), p. 31.

I.   A prophet speaks

The Supreme Mullah, Ahmednasir Abdullahi, proclaimed his prophesy concerning Raila's Lunatic Express under construction and its imminent dangers:

> …So what role will he play and how should the government treat him? President Uhuru Kenyatta and his Deputy William Ruto should brace themselves and be prepared to deal with Raila the agitator because it is in this role that the former Prime Minister is in his element. Uhuru and Ruto should be under no illusion on the mechanization of Raila as an agitator. They will face all kinds of provocation, undermining, agitating, propaganda and riots.[2]

The Seer wrote on:

> Since he has no real job and too much time on his hands, Raila will be a thorn in the flesh of the new administration. An idle mind is the devil's workshop, goes the saying. Raila has enough time on his hands to ferment one problem after another for the administration. Only a well thought-out strategy that takes the fight to him will give the new government breathing space…

> Raila is providing divisive and wounded leadership, and that is a great disservice to the country. And because he is still in the denial that he lost the presidential election, Raila has continued to hold the country hostage through this personal brand of leadership… It serves no purpose for him to constantly put the country in an agitated state. He must give space to those leaders who were elected by the people...[3]

Very unfortunate, UhuRuto never heeded the Grand Mullah's caution. They did not take the fight to his doorstep; they waited for him to lay his tracks marking his time and ignite his Express. Hadn't Raila previously raised a great deal of hell on President Kibaki's government? Isn't his style of dangerous politics in black and white for all to see?

UhuRuto thought Raila would just fade away. How wrong they were! Had they just listened they should have donned tough gloves for constantly punching him hard in an endeavour to comfortably stay him

---

2   Ahmednasir Abdullahi, "Idle Odinga spells trouble for UhuRuto" *Sunday Nation*, 28 July 2013.

3   Ibid.

out of the ring; surely the "Rumble in the Jungle" seemed unstoppable and as it goes, the kicks of a dying horse are the deadliest. And looking forward to the General Election of 9 August 2022 it could turn out to be terribly messy.

Very quickly Raila's train hit the rails. Now and then the diesel combustion engine emitted poisonous fumes in various forms: Saba Saba, Okoa Kenya, Pesa Mashinani, Uhuru Must Go, We Will Occupy Harambee Avenue. Injuries, deaths, destruction. Investors and tourist got scared. The economy went to the dogs. The masses became tired and restless. But nothing worked according to Raila's expectations. Then Raila hit a Eureka! I have found it! Why not just get a Bible, a lawyer, a handful of supporters and goons, invite the media for maximum publicity and just get sworn pronto as the People's President? How simple it is with or without my NASA co-principals?

No, Sir. It was a bad dream. Raila thought he would wake up in the morning at Nairobi State House with outriders – *pikipiki*, Mercedes Benz limousines, flashes, sirens and all outside waiting to take him to Harambee House for the day's work. State House is serious business. Raila should have learned this in August 1982. Again he became president only by his imagination. The government reminded him of the word "treason".

After a brief sabbatical, another Eureka! visited Raila. Railway tracks resembles a bridge. Why not conceive another baby and name it Building Bridges? And for good effect invite President Kenyatta as the co-principal? He made it and the President agreed to shake hands to set the ball rolling. Whether this was his own initiative or pressure from Western nations effectively banning him from visiting their countries and financial problems as revealed by Amani National Congress leader Musalia Mudavadi in *Soaring Above the Storms of Passion*, Raila performed a beautiful hare's trick.

The BBI, or Raila's train, is a brilliant idea, but for the driver. Supposing the BBI is a vehicle minted fresh from an assembly line that must speed to meet the country's desired visions. Would you entrust a person close to 80 years old to drive it? A person who failed driving tests severally during the analogue age and caused many accidents, can he successfully drive one meant for the digital electronic era?

The BBI may be largely a duplication of the previous national master plan documents. Its parts are old, reconditioned, probably imported from the US or Britain. Again, going by the previous statistics, no Kenyan would wish to risk his life under an unqualified driver's navigation. They say, "*Ndongoria ĩngĩthua itikinyagĩra nyeki*" (when the leading animal limps, the rest do not reach the pastures). Qualifications or not, history has shown that all Raila's trains/buses had only one motive: to take him to State House and not reach millions of Kenyans to their destinations.

Kenya is a democracy. Like planet earth, people are already divided by the political equator into Northern and Southern Hemispheres BBI-wise. But it is important to trend very carefully knowing Raila. Like Venezuela that lacked a qualified leadership to manage the jackpot that was oil, so is Kenya in Raila.

Nevertheless, all is not lost. Even with the anticipated poisoned political atmosphere due to Raila's comeback to the high table of leadership, Kenyans must separate the wheat and the chaff wisely, reject in totality all Raila's machinations and believe in Providence as in the words of British poet, William Cowper:

> God moves in mysterious ways. His wonders to perform…
> His purpose will ripen fast, unfolding every hour.
> The bud may have a bitter taste, but sweet will be the flower.
> Blind unbelief is sure to err, and scar his work in vain,
> God is his own interpreter, and he will make it plain.[4]

This brings the story to some major questions majority of Kenyans have been struggling with about President Kenyatta. He is the son of Jomo Kenyatta the Total Man, *Mũthamaki*, *Mũtongoria Njamba*. Through his manifesto with Deputy William Ruto he campaigns for President. Kenyans give him full mandate to lead them. Confidently, he lifts the Bible up and invokes God. The whole world now gets to see the new President and Commander-in-Chief of the Republic of Kenya.

Then soon the unbelievable unfolds. The President invites to his bedroom the very person who tried all tricks to overthrow him. He makes him a co-principal. This political marriage scatters to the four corners of the earth his principal partner appointed by Kenyans and millions

---

4   "God moves in a mysterious way", retrieved from: https://www.hymnal.net/en/hymn/h/675

who elected him, *"Thuraku thuraku"* and have been the backbone of the completion of his election pledges and baby Big Four Agenda. Has there been some witchcraft, a *kamũtĩ* involved in this stranger than fiction drama as has be claimed? Wasn't there a better option of a man to build bridges with if Ruto was not qualified enough?

Are the witch doctor's tools of trade powerful enough to break apart a strong, ambitious political partnership and thereby threaten to drive out light and bring in darkness into a country? These are reasonable questions to ask.

The Europeans who were bringing railway lines to Africa were not confined to Kenya. In the Belgian Congo there was another Lunatic Express from Matadi to Stanley Pool. This hired workers from various regions in the world, among them the Chinese. Like in the Kenyan case, the working environment was not conducive for human safety.

According to *King Leopold's Ghost* by Adam Hochschild, among the 540 Chinese brought in 1892, 300 died on the job or fled into the bush. Most of the latter were never seen again, although several were later found more than 500 miles in the interior trying to reach Africa's east coast and then home. The coming of the Europeans and the opposition from local communities thereof in the Congo provides an example of how witchcraft can frustrate the light and encourage the darkness. Even in countries like Kenya.

> There's not a thing in this world hides as good as a green mamba snake. They're just the same colour as what they lay up against, and they don't move a muscle. You could be right by one and not know it...[5]

And:

> I know what it is: It's a green mamba snake way up in the tree.... They lie so still on the tree branch; they are the same everything as the tree. You could be right next to one and not even know....[6]

The above extracts are from a novel, *The Poisonwood Bible* by Barbara Kingsolver. In the preview, the *Los Angeles Times* called it "A powerful new epic.... She has with infinitely steady hands worked the prickly threads of religion, politics, race, sin and redemption into

---

5   Barbara Kingsolver, *The Poisonwood Bible* (London: Faber & Faber, 4 Sep 2008), p. 30.

6   Ibid. p. 82.

a thing of a terrible beauty". The *USA Today* termed it, "Tragic and remarkable….. A novel that blends outlandish experience with Old Testament rhythms of prophesy and doom".

The story begins in 1959, exactly 60 years ago. An American preacher heads to Congo, the country Joseph Conrad referred to as the "Heart of Darkness". On landing at Kilanga village airstrip Reverend Nathan Price declares, "Heavenly Father please make me a powerful instrument of Thy perfect will here in the Belgium Congo". Price has been sent by the Baptist Mission to spread Christianity among the locals. He is here with his wife and four daughters.

In Kilanga, grown-up men are called Tata, meaning Baba. Women are Mama so and so. Tata Ndu is the Chief. He is a huge man with a big bald forehead. He wears a tall hat made of sisal fibres, and large black glasses which bear no lenses and has a flywhisk as a sign of authority. The Chief has six wives and later on will want to marry Price's first-born daughter.

Then there is Tata Kavulundu with six toes on one of his feet. He is the village's witch doctor, a priest of the traditions called Nganga (like *mganga* in Kiswahili). Kavulundu help barren wives get children, throw children bones into a calabash bowl to bring down the rain, and could make live people dead and dead people come back to life. Above all, he sanctifies which bushes to use away from the rivers, for purposes of defecation to protect people from contracting *kakakaka* (cholera).

Like many African societies then, the Kilanga village wants to hear nothing of the new religion and white man's way of life. But Rev. Price is a fierce, fanatical missionary. He says that the Kilangas "are living in darkness. Broken in body and soul, and don't even see how they would be healed".[7] In fact, one day Tata Ndu orders an election in the Church to prove to the Reverend that his Jesus is not popular among the locals: For and against Jesus Christ, where the voting is done by pebbles. Once counted, Jesus Christ has lost, 11 to 56.

> … A small blunt head emerged and swiveled to face us. Very slowly
> it split itself wide, showing the bright blue inside of its mouth, two
> bare fangs. A tongue, delicately licking the air…. Green mamba,
> mistress of camouflage, agility, aggressiveness and speed. In this

---

7   Ibid. p. 14.

serpent the diabolic genius of nature has attained the highest degree of perfection.[8]

The climax of this cold war between good and evil, the beginning of the end, comes one night. Vodooman Tata Kavulundu puts a green mamba snake in a basket at night and plants it in the Reverend's chicken house. In the morning and out of curiosity, the four Price's girls and a boy servant decides to check the chicken coop. In the process the youngest, aged about six is bitten by the deadly snake. She dies.

The untimely death triggers a chain of events. The Reverend's wife hurriedly picks her three remaining children in protest and walks away, never to return. Left alone now, the Reverend continues with his preaching. Years later, he is chased away by the villagers. He climbs on a coffee field's abandoned watchtower. They set it on fire. Now ablaze, Reverend Price jumps off. He soon dies.

On 27 November 2019 President Kenyatta officially inaugurated the BBI Report at the Bomas of Kenya. Since its conception, many have hailed the idea as the wonder drug; a panacea for social-economic and political problems in the country. Very well. They say all is well that ends well.

II. Raila is Tata Kavulundu

Very fine. From the surface, BBI is a fantastic idea, almost, word for word, that is. But reading between the lines, something stinks to high heavens. Kenyans bears the genes of prophets and with relative accuracy they somehow can predict its final port of call. They can smell the elephant in the room light years away. History repeats itself, and what goes always comes around. You see, Raila Odinga is the chief navigator. But Job 34:13 asks: "Can one who hates right govern?"

Tata (Baba) Kavulundu's green mamba killed the missionaries' dream of bringing God's light into the Congo, just like the revolutionary snake in the Garden of Eden shredded into pieces and turned God's manifesto upside down. The green mamba is known to smile/laugh, perhaps as a disguise for the deadly poison within its fangs. It has a ruthless attitude of invisibility and wait-and-see. There is no hurry in Africa.

____

8   Ibid. p. 97.

Kenya is not the "Heart of Darkness" like Congo was deemed years ago. However, the country has no shortage of darkness that needs urgent fixing. Since 1982, Raila has fronted himself as Kenya's the Chosen One, the Messiah, with an express mandate from the Above to liberate it and its people. But always, his *dawa* prescription has been nothing but pure poison. Like Tata Kavulundu, his bag containing the BBI could as well be concealing a political green mamba snake that will poison Kenya Vision 2030, the Jubilee Manifesto, the Big Four Agenda and dreams of 47 million citizens.

Notwithstanding, is being a witch doctor such a terrible thing? This is a person who is thought to have magic powers which can be used to heal people, according to the *Collins English Dictionary*. Your dictionary defines him as one supposed to have the power of curing disease, warding off evil, etc. through the use of sorcery, incantations etc. And the *Merriam-Webster Dictionary* calls him a professional worker of magic usually in a primitive society who often works to cure sickness.

Raila has been called a witch doctor many times. In September 2017, during a campaign trail, Deputy President Ruto said:

> *Wakati Uhuru Kenyatta anapanga tujenge daraja ya urafiki na undugu na umoja wa Wakenya anasema tuko pamoja, hali yule mganga anasema, Tialala ati sijui Tibim, sasa mtu ya uganga na uchawi atashindana na mtu ya Mungu namna gani.* (When Uhuru Kenyatta is planning bridges of friendship and brotherhood and unity among Kenyans he say we are together, while that witchdoctor says *Tialala* I don't know *Tibim*. So how will a witch doctor compete with a God-fearing person?)

In May 2019, Raila hit back: "I am not a witch doctor and I have never been one. Whether you abuse Raila using derogatory words or not, it will add no value to your political discourse. Some people like calling me a witch and say I use a lot of proverbs while talking. Yes, I am a doctor because President Kenyatta and I are trying to heal what has been ailing this country." Raila went on: "Witch doctors are there in society. No one has been denied the chance to visit them. What is the farce about?"[9]

---

9   John Wanjohi , "I am Not a 'Mganga', Raila Says", Mwakilishi, Saturday, 05 November 2019. Retrieved from: https://www.mwakilishi.com/article/kenya-news/2019-05-11/i-am-not-a-mganga-raila-says

But wait. The story of magician Raila did not start with Ruto. Dr David Ndii, the former Chief Strategist at NASA, takes the reader back to the 1980s after Raila's prison years following his alleged participation in the abortive military coup. In a lengthy online article titled "From the Handshake to the BBI Report, Hope and Disillusionment: My Side of the Story" published on 13 December 2019, the text recalls:

> One of my early childhood memories is when Raila Odinga was released from detention in 1988. As a child, I was fascinated by my grandfather's surprise that Raila did not die in prison. Most people, having known how ruthless Moi's regime was, had expected Raila not to survive jail. I could sense massive euphoric relief when Raila walked out of detention alive. My grandfather regaled me with tales of how Raila's magical powers saved him. How he could turn into a fly on a wall in State House and listen to plans to assassinate him. They said he would then fly back to prison and surprise his killers with his knowledge of their plans beforehand, throwing them into total confusion.[10]

> Then there was the swearing-in ceremony of 2018, and the lack of charges against Raila when others like Miguna Miguna continue to be forcefully exiled. Was this also due to Raila's magical powers?...[11]

Even those who do not believe in the magic business still harbour unanswered questions. How did Raila escape the hangman after his treason trial due to the coup? Why didn't the ICC touch him following the 2007-2008 post-election violence? And more recently, why was he not put on trial for treason on the account of swearing himself the People's President?

Here was a man who had called President Kenyatta's election win computer-generated results (*vifaranga vya kompyuta*). A man who had called for secession and economic boycott. He is now literally the President's chief advisor. He has been in charge of the BBI rallies across the country with all due privileges accorded to him.

---

10 "From the Handshake to the BBI Report, Hope to Disillusionment: My Side of the Story", The Elephant, 13 December, 2019, p. 27. Retrieved from: https://www.theelephant.info/topic/the-handshake/?print=pdf-search. Accessed on 20 June 2020.

11 Norbert Odero, "Accept and Move On: The Handshake's Hollow Cure for Decades of Communal Loss and Grief", The Elephant-Speaking truth to power, 8 March, 2019. Retrieved at: https://www.theelephant.info/reflections/2019/03/08/accept-and-move-on-the-handshakes-hollow-cure-for-decades-of-communal-loss-and-grief/

Senior government officials run to him for advice and directions. He is at liberty to announce what the government shall, or shall not do. This unelected leader constantly finds huge courage to throw mud at the elected Deputy President Ruto. They laughed at him when he proclaimed himself People's President. And now they say that if an election is held today, Raila will beat Uhuru so comfortably. If this man is not a witch doctor, a true *mganga*, then what is he?

Witch doctors have existed since time immemorial. They have been part and parcel of societies and paying them a visit was no big deal. The big deal was the motive of the visit and what one brought from there.

The BBI has been called the greatest magic. Kenyans would mind less if Raila could perform all his *Tialala Tibim*; all the mumbo jumbos and abracadabra he wishes to if only his stories since August 1982 will not repeat themselves. In others words, healing the country through his celebrated political magic is what the BBI should be about.

Back to the British MP who had reservations about the Lunatic Express. Having known Raila's carbon monoxide-infested political train for years, some questions are unavoidable: What will be the BBI's cost, objective, Estimated Time of Departure (ETD), Estimated Time of Arrival (ETA), its use and carriage? Would it be too pessimistic to conclude it is a Lunatic Express?

The captain and co-pilot (also called Second Pilot or First Officer) of an aircraft are perhaps the best partners on earth. Their own lives and those of passengers while airborne are absolutely in their own hands either singly, or both. If you eject the First Officer from the cockpit, bring in a *jua kali* pilot instead and the captain becomes incapacitated, what happens? The aircraft will assume auto-pilot mode and soon plunge into some oceans. The BBI threw out First Officer Ruto from Boeing Kenya and brought in a fake pilot in Raila. Kenyatta went for leave. The passengers were left in a panicky mood.

III. UhuRuto performs *danse macabre*

On 16 April 2016, President Kenyatta and Deputy Ruto held a thanksgiving prayer meeting at Afraha Stadium, Nakuru, to mark the end of the ICC cases. On 5th April, the court had ruled that Ruto and Joshua arap Sang cases lacked evidentiary proof to sustain them and would therefore not proceed to full trial. This marked the release of all the original six suspects.

President Kenyatta had declared that Kenya will not allow any of its citizens ever to be tried by a foreign court, ICC included. *"Sisi hiyo chapta tumefunga,"* he said and added, *"Hakuna pahali pengine tunaenda na hakuna mtu mwingine tutaruhusu apelekwe pahali popote."* (We have closed that chapter, we are going nowhere else and we will not allow any other person to be taken anywhere).[12]

On the termination of the case by the Trial Chamber V(a) of the ICC, President Kenyatta welcomed the decision and reaffirmed his conviction right from the beginning about the innocence of Deputy Ruto at the same time committing to support judicial systems. "Over the last six years," he observed, "my Deputy President, together with a number of other Kenyans, including myself, have endured a painful journey with the ICC... and my Deputy has, at the same time, also borne the heavy responsibilities of leadership, while attending the hearing at The Hague...

> The decision brings to a close what has been a nightmare for my nation... For my Deputy and I, this focuses us fully on the affairs of running the State, a mandate given to us by the people of Kenya ... As a nation, we recognize our duty to, and respect for, international law and institutions. We will therefore continue to pursue ways to improve the delivery of international justice, uphold the rule of law and promote a just and fair global order ..."[13]

Ahead of the mammoth rally on 15th, Raila Odinga sent a statement to the newsrooms terming the planned Nakuru function a mockery to the 2007/2008 post-election victims. He had written it from Paris, he informed, where he had attended a meeting whose theme was, "Striving for a Just, Prosperous and Harmonious Global Community". Hereunder is a portion of the statement:

> While in Paris, I learnt of a medieval dance that originated in France called the *danse macabre*, which is French for 'the dance of death'.

---

12   Oliver Mathenge, "Why new ICC ruling is bad for Uhuru, Ruto", *The Star*, 22 October 2016.

13   "The President's Statement following the termination of ICC cases against the Deputy President and Mr. Joshua Arap Sang", Kenya High Commission in Ottawa, 6 April, 2016. Retrieved from: https://kenyahighcommission.ca/presidential-statement/#

It started in the mid-14th century and involved a procession which people danced to the graves of the dead in their community in celebration of death. As I thought about this perverse type of custom and traditions, I could not help but compare this with what President Uhuru Kenyatta and Deputy President William Ruto have planned to do at Afraha Stadium tomorrow, April 16, 2016.[14]

President Kenyatta, Deputy Ruto and thousands of Kenyans who intended to attend the prayer meeting celebrating the deaths of 1,133 people who perished during the 2007-2008 violence? Good gracious! Raila's message went on,

> … we must admit that," "the collapse of the ICC engagement with the Kenya situation denied this country the only chance it had to end the culture of impunity that has condemned us to an orgy of violence with every election … Clearly, as a nation, there is nothing to celebrate about. Instead, we have to reflect on the many critical decisions that we need to make…In light of these circumstances, it amounts to mocking the dead and the surviving victims of post-election violence for the President and his Deputy to assemble their political supporters at Afraha Stadium to celebrate the end of the pursuit of justice over the atrocities of the mayhem in 2007/2008. The only picture that comes to mind is that of the President and his Deputy leading a procession of Jubilee followers performing the *danse macabre* over the graves of their fellow countrymen …[15]

Celebrating that they are dead and gone. What reasons would these leaders have to rejoice over a thousand deaths of their citizens? The ICC erred terribly! Hang the two little devils! Dispatch them to political Siberia until Jesus come!

The statement continued:

> What Uhuru and Ruto should be doing is keeping their jubilation in check and thinking of the pain that abounds in the country… Kenya does not need a self-absorbed jamboree hosted by the Presidency but a genuine engagement to pursue truth, justice and reconciliation…

> Uhuru and Ruto must cease this continued mockery of the victims of the post-election violence and lead this nation towards the truth and

---

14   Kenfrey Kiberenge, "Raila: Uhuru and Ruto must stop mocking victims of PEV", Nairobi News, 15 April, 2016.

15   Ibid.

reconciliation that will save us from what is quickly becoming an irreversible descent towards another orgy of violence. We need truth and reconciliation in our Presidency… The President should open up the envelope and let people deal with the ICC ghosts and exorcise them from their national psyche…[16]

As Kenyans, we have a duty to believe and agree on some historical matters which are as clear as the daylight.

Kenya became free from 70 years of British domination on 12 December 1963. A year later, the country became a republic. We became a sovereign nation. During that dark era, Kenyans shouted with one voice, like Dedan Kimathi in the play, *The Trial of Dedan Kimathi* co-authored by Ngũgĩ wa Thiong'o and Mĩcere Mũgo: "… Break these chains/unchain my heart/my soul!/unchain four centuries of chains!"

The term sovereignty refers to an authority over a geographical area, such as a territory. It is the supreme, absolute, uncontrollable power by which any independent state is governed. It is the power to exercise supreme political (e.g. Executive, Legislative and/or Judicial) over a geographical region or group of people. Independence is the exercise of self-governance and self-determination without owing allegiance in any way to any other state. This is what Kenyans sought to achieve during the struggle.

On two Madaraka Day anniversaries, President Jomo Kenyatta was defending the newly acquired sovereignty:

> June 1, 1965: "… But let me say it quite plainly today that Kenya shall not exchange one master for a new one. We intend to remain our own masters forever… we may be underdeveloped, and our people may walk barefoot, but we are a proud people; proud of our heritage, our traditions and ancestry. What is more, we will not betray our children."

> June 1, 1966: "Some nations do not seem to have understood our determination to manage our affairs. In these past few months, we have seen positive signs of neo-colonialism… these nations have supported some individuals who have been rejected by the people of Kenya …we refuse to exchange one form of colonialism for a new one…"

---

16 Ibid.

Another point of consensus is our institutions, in particular the Judiciary and the National Police Service. Kenya's judges and magistrates are among the best in the world; our lawyers represent the best of brains. The police officers and investigators have been hailed as experts, in a class close to that of the US's FBI or the Scotland Yard of UK (here, you must allow for the few rotten individuals, political ineptitude and interference, corruption and disregard for human rights).

Soon after independence, Kenya became a member of the global community. It joined the United Nations and later the Organisation of African Unity (OAU), today the African Union. The country signed various conventions and protocols. Then fast forward it ratified the Rome Statute. Not long after, the ICC came for the "Ocampo six."

Okay, Kenya is not an island and has obligations to respect the agreements it signed with international institutions. But did subscribing to the ICC mean the Kenya Judiciary and investigative institutions had to go on a sabbatical once in a while? Whose court was this really? Was our sovereignty being respected?

Writing in the *New African* magazine March 2012, Dr David Hoile gave an insight on what the ICC really was. That over 70 per cent of the world population was outside the Court's jurisdiction, its members representing only 27 per cent. Secondly, among those who were involved in its formation were the Western NGOs.

Up to July 2007, the European Union member states provided 75.6 per cent of the Court's resources, besides more funding from international corporations, individuals and other entities. As of 20 April 2009, European states provided 59.6 per cent of the Court's employees. Dr Hoile observed: "The Court is primarily European-run yet those it judges are not from Europe; they are usually taken from their countries and shipped to Europe to sit in a European prison."[17]

Additionally, Dr Hoile raised the credibility of some of the eight judges of the Court. He gave two instances to support his point. Japanese Fumiko Saiga (had since died) had no legal training or judicial experience and his replacement, Prof. Kuniko Ozaki, had no experience as a judge and added : "These are the same people who are tasked with

---

17 Quoted in "Europe, masters behind the ICC: the power of the ICC remains with its big four funders", by David Hoile, Questia. Retrieved from: https://www.questia.com/magazine/1G1-283751283/europe-masters-behind-the-icc-the-power-of-the-icc

making complex decisions about some of the most complex situations in the world, which quite literally affect life and death in Africa."[18]

True, the Kenya of 2007-2008 could have been described by the words in Chinua Achebe's book, *Arrow of God*: "The lunatics might be outnumbered, but they own the place." Even so, was Kenya or Africa being particularly crucified? Dr Hoile explained:

> As of July 2009, the Prosecutor had received over 8,137 communications (informations of crimes) from more than 130 countries. Yet, despite all these complaints, the ICC has started the investigations into just seven countries all of them Africa, and indicted 27 people, all of them Africans again.[19]

This discriminative "justice" provoked Philip Ochieng to pen an article: "… When you allow all your ideas of justice to be defined by the states that have only yesterday reduced you to sub-humans and your highest edifice of justice to be based in those same states you reduce your 'sovereignty' to absurdity. When those states can subject your President and his Deputy to every form of indignity – while they remain silent about George Bush, Tony Blair, etc. - All Kenyans should find it intolerable for Europeans to order our UhuRuto about like common criminals".[20] Why only Africa?

Behold this. By May 2009, an estimated 40,000 civilians were killed in Sri Lanka in the final stages of the war when Tamil Tiger rebels were routed. Then mid-November 2013 in the capital Colombo, Britain Prime Minister, David Cameron, said soon after visiting the former war zone:

> The Sri Lankan government needs to go further and faster on human rights and reconciliation. I am hugely optimistic about the country's future. The message I have is that this issue will not go away and needs to be pursued vigorously. …Let me be very clear, if an investigation is not completed by March then I will use our position on the UN Human Rights Commission and call for a full, credible and independent international inquiry.[21]

---

18 Ibid.

19 Ibid.

20 Philip Ochieng, "The indignity of trying Uhuru and Ruto in The Hague", *Sunday Nation*, 16 February, 2014.

21 AFP, "David Cameron says Sri Lanka need to go 'further and faster' in answering human rights concerns", *The Telegraph*, 16 November 2013.

Had the ICC migrated to planet Mars in this instance?

Why was Kenya not given, for instance, by its former colonial master and other Western powers time to fast-track on human rights issues and reconciliation like in Sri Lanka? The UN Office of the High Commissioner on Human Rights (OHCHR) has an office in Kenya. Why was the country not subjected to the human rights arm of the UN instead of the ICC? *You reduce your sovereignty to absurdity*, Philip Ochieng warned...

The Sri Lankan government had a very straight answer to Cameron's 'threats'. That Colombo would 'definitely' not allow international investigations to conduct a probe on its soil. "Why should we have an international inquiry?" Wondered Basil, Minister for Economic Development and President Mahinda Rajapakse's brother. "Definitely, we are not going to allow it."

Elsewhere, the European Union (EU), Britain and the United States had imposed sanctions on Zimbabwe after the violent 2002 presidential election, citing breakdown of law and order and human rights violations. Afterwards, the visiting EU delegation was kicked out of the country. Much later, some Western countries observers wanted to monitor the polls. The Foreign Affairs Minister, Simbarashe Mumbengengui, barred them, reasoning that Zimbabwe had never been invited to observe elections in Western countries, and by the same token, it was not extending an invitation.

Probably, it was right for Africa to be ruled from Europe or America after the Scramble for Africa Berlin conference. But it was not logical after African countries got independence for the foreigners to force themselves on the continent as their prince, judge, brother's keeper or policeman. This sad state of things made Rwandan President, Paul Kagame, pose in the *Time* magazine, October 2007: "How Africa does accepts that its affairs are run by NGOs and other groups from outside? It is really something that needs to be corrected. This and that department, the World Bank, human rights blah blah blah, over and over, it becomes boring."

WIVES, HUSBANDS, FROGS' LEGS

Certainly, Kenya became hopelessly unstable during the 2007-2008 post-election period. But pray tell, what would have happened if it were one of the European countries?

Take Belgium, for instance, a tiny country that can fit into Kenya 20 times. Its capital, Brussels, is the de facto capital of the EU, an economic and political union of 27 member states (here, ignore Brexit).

The country has had a history of economic disparities and ethnic spats, especially between the seven million Dutch-speaking and five million French-speaking citizens, sometimes triggering the question of a break-up to have one part of it becoming part of the French Republic. By year 2013, Belgium has had 45 governments in 67 years. In June 2010, it held a federal election but did not get a government until December 2011, when socialist Elio di Rupo – the world's first male openly gay head of government – was sworn in as Prime Minister.

The 541 days under a caretaker administration, the negotiations and formation broke the world record of a country's longest period without a government, previously held by Iraq at 249 days. The election had produced a very fragmented political landscape where none of the eleven political parties won more than 20 per cent of the seats. This resulted in major differences, especially between the parties allied to the Dutch-speaking and francophone resulting in social unrests and movements against some controversial austerity measures.

To capture this Belgian moment, the *New African* ran an article in July 2011 titled: "If Only the Tables Could Be Turned (When Your Master Is Your Enemy, You Are Doomed)". It read, in part:

> If this had happened in Africa, say Zimbambwe, all manner of Western journalists, their governments and ambassadors and non-governmental organizations and even 'non-governmental individuals' would have run for their high horses upon which they would have assailed the ears of poor Africa, daily, with homilies about the values of a central government, and how it provides bread and butter and wives and husbands for the citizenry, and so on and so forth!

The writer warned:

> The Europeans and Americans and Australians and Canadians and the sundry nations of European stock, who have made it their business to disrespect Africa and Africans and our wishes and sensibilities should take note: 'The day their ambassadors in our countries ever again try to use press conferences, non-governmental organizations

and non-governmental individuals to rush African countries to do things that we are not ready or prepared to do, we will escort the ambassadors to the border and banish them across the river, to let them find their way home to Europe by whichever way is convenient to them.'

The article was apparently quite annoyed. It concluded with a question directed to Africa:

> Why can't African ambassadors call press conferences in London, Paris or Washington and pronounce on some British, French and American domestic politics that our countries don't agree with, or even to tell Belgium that if it doesn't form a coalition government in the next three weeks, we will impose sanctions on it, and stop exporting our diamonds, bananas and frogs' legs to them or some such threats!

You reduce your sovereignty to absurdity, Phillip Ochieng said…

Year 2019 will be remembered as one of the Great BBI. It also marked the Golden Jubilee (50 years) of Tom Mboya's death. It pays to remember him, *Mũndũ wa Nyũmba*, to Raila Odinga. A brilliantly burning candle blown off by a bullet that 5 July 1969, Mboya was described by Keith Kyle, in his book *The Politics of the Independence of Kenya*, as "one of the most gifted leaders modern black Africa has yet produced".[22] Mboya is famous for starting the Airlift Africa Project, which assisted many African students to be flown to the USA for further studies through the African-American Students Foundation. He is also credited with the drafting of the *Sessional Paper No. 10 of 1965 on African Socialism and its Application to Planning in Kenya*. Mboya, also called one of the greatest political leaders of the 20th century in East Africa, was appointed Chairman of the All African People's Conference (AAPC) in Accra, Ghana, between 5th and 13th December 1958. The meeting was inspired by the Prime Minister, Kwame Nkrumah, and focused mainly on Africa's liberation from colonial rule and white supremacy. Its slogan was "Hands off Africa!"

The Berlin conference on the Scramble for Africa had marked the birth of colonialism in Africa. In his keynote address, the 28-year old

---

22   Keith Kyle, *The Politics of the Independence of Kenya* (New York, NY: Palgrave Macmillan, 1999), p. Reviewed by John Reader in *London Review of Books*, Vol. 22 No. 6 · 16 March 2000.

Kenyan stood up and mocked the genesis of the Europeans coming into the continent. He declared, "Whereas, 72 years ago the Scramble for Africa started, from Accra, we announce that these same powers must be told in a clear, firm and definite voice: 'Scram from Africa!'"[23]

The BBI is a people's conversation just like the one Mboya was having as he organised students' airlifts for further studies, when he urged the delegates at the AAPC to speed up the continent's decolonisation, to pack off from Africa, and when he made the Sessional Paper meant for the whole country.

Then here comes Raila, Mboya's brother from another mother. Is it remotely possible? That, his mind has been working round the clock to resurrect the ICC cases come 2020, airlift President Kenyatta and Deputy Ruto (especially) and the entire Jubilee Party members to The Hague, telling the Court: "Come, let's make an example for Africa now!" And in the name of re-colonisation, is he now urging the Western powers, Come Baby, Come, Miguna Miguna style?

Raila is on record saying that when elected president, he would make sure the ICC cases are brought back to Kenya. It is also known that when the government had gone to convince the UN Security Council over deferral, Raila's ODM wrote to say that it wasn't party to that decision.[24] Is it possible that hidden inside the BBI is a draft of Raila's "Sessional Paper No. 2022" on Kenya's under-development through his politics of mass destruction?

In many people's minds the verdict has been that Mboya was the best President Kenya never had. Is it possible that Raila will be remembered as the worst President Kenya never had? Irungu Thatiah, in the aforementioned book, wrote about Raila: "Here was the footnote to the gallant story of a man who had been unable to transform himself from a freedom fighter to a leader … Raila had spent his time making alliances with every party, every politician, and every former foe, but forgot the most important thing – developing Kenya!"[25]

Back to Raila's April 15 2016 statement from Paris. He had been attending a meeting themed, "Striving for a Just, Prosperous and Harmonious Global Community". The full statement revolved around

---

23 "GHANA: Scram!" *Time*, Monday, 22 December, 1958.

24 Irungu Thatiah, *Hard Tackle: The Life of Uhuru Kenyatta* (Nairobi: Rizzan Media, 2014).

25 Ibid, p.

the 2007-2008 post-election violence with such key words as violence, burned homes, rape of women, deaths, eviction and destruction of property. But no sooner had he left the French capital than he hit the streets in protests and demonstrations, June 2016 and during 2017 election, with similar consequences to what he was probably condemning at the Paris conference. Talk of justice, prosperity and harmony abroad; raise hell at home!

Raila's statement was an irony of ironies. For ages, he has conceived and thrived on crises. Then when things went south, he converted into a wolf in sheep's skin, became a false prophet. His culture has been that of preaching water and drinking wine, seeing other people's log in the eye as bigger; *Nyani haoni kundule, huona la mwenziwe*. His story has been a perfect photocopy of Delilah in the Scriptures, pampering Samson with *bae, sweetie, sweetheart*, while organising for the Philistines attack. You cannot do good 30 per cent and then throw a 70 per cent stinking vomit on it and call yourself a judge, a liberator.

On the sidelines of the Paris meeting, there is a high possibility of Raila having engaged President Alassane Dramane Ouattara of Côte d'Ivoire who was also in attendance. Ouattara had been accused of backing the 2002 attempted coup in his country and being a stooge of the former colonial power, France. A former Prime Minister, Ouattara became the 5th Head of State on the 2010 election.

Laurent Gbagbo, a veteran opposition leader, disputed the election and a violent standoff ensued where 3,000 people died. A former President, Gbagbo was arrested in April 2011 by the ICC on crimes against humanity (released January 2019) becoming the first former Head of State to stand trial at The Hague.

Raila might have posed to Ouattara: "Your Excellency, how did you manage to fix Gbagbo at the ICC, and keep him in prison for eight years? My attempt on UhuRuto failed completely." After a brief silence, Ouattara replies, "Sir, count yourself lucky, you were the one who was destined for The Hague Prison and not your two countrymen!"

THE REAL *DANSE MACABRES* ...

Indeed, the African continent could qualify for the Disco Capital of the World for the *danse macabre*. From the 6th through to the 19th century, the trans-Atlantic slave trade "airlifted" 12 million Africans to the

Americas to become slaves. Millions died. The Scramble for Africa, engineered by Henry Morton Stanley (John Rowlands Bastard) left over 15 million deaths in the period it lasted. The Europeans behind it called themselves the "International Society for the Suppression of Savage Customs".[26] Hot on the heels followed colonialism and the Cold War, each leaving several millions dead.

The participating nations in the three eras later danced on the graves of the millions of dead Africans for a reason. They had a covenant with God, they said, a divine mission to civilise the black heathens upwards and onwards. As James Walvin noted, "These poor creatures are slaves in a much poor state: they are slaves of ignorance, of sin and of Satan ..."

Late 1950s and early 1960s Africans got independence and started civilising themselves. Susan Cheever wrote about transformation, similar to this new state of affairs in the continent: "In the 50 years we have become a more democratized culture. In those days a cat could look at a king: now every cat is a king ... we have brought our gods down to earth these days ..."[27] No more dancing on our people's graves, so we thought.

Some 52 years after Kenya independence, Raila came along. He claimed that President Kenyatta and Deputy Ruto were going to dance on the graves of the 2007-2008 election violence victims. First, wasn't Raila, the now self-proclaimed Black Moses for the victims, not a more talented *ndombolo* dancer than the two – in campaign rallies? Also, who was a most celebrated dancer; the one who owns the machinery in a factory that manufactured deaths of people or the two whose government had gone to the Afraha Stadium in the names of God and people of Kenya?

Before Raila issued the war battle of *danse macabre*, President Kenyatta established a Kes 10 billion fund to assist the said victims. He also offered his and the government's apology for all past wrongs. As at February 2016, the government had spent Kes 17.5 billion in cash, bought land for 28,924 IDPs and 5,261 households settled. Home-made solutions for some home-made problems.

---

26 Joseph Conrad, *Heart of Darkness* (Claremont, CA: Coyote Canyon Press, 2007).

27 Susan Cheever, "Jackie Kennedy's Tapes: Susan Cheever Reflects", *NewsWeek*, 18 September, 2011.

Secondly, is there a greater dance than the one directed to the Almighty? Irrespective of who had been wronged, who was the best judge? The Kenya Judiciary was the better option. The ICC was the least good option. And God was the Court of the last resort, the best.

The true Afraha Stadium that day: The President, Deputy and other leaders were joined by thousands of Kenyans. Millions watched on TV screens or got proceedings from radios. Thousands read in the following day's newspapers. What the world saw and heard was a big dance punctuated with a lot of Amens, Yes Jesuses, Halleluyas, Bwana *Asifiwe*s and Jehovahs. To crown it all were the very moving words: unity, peace, forgiveness, reconciliation and thanksgiving. In other words, the Afraha Stadium was a dance of the country's renewal; *danse de la vie*, the dance of life. And this dance shall continue Raila *apende asipende*!

Kenya has one mighty prayer ahead of the 2022 General Election. The guilty are afraid; Raila has always been afraid. The passionate prayer is that he will not use the BBI to manufacture more deaths for him later to perform his *danse macabre* par excellence.

To be fair, Raila is the exact opposite of Tom Mboya and other nationalists. He is a replica of the departed colonialists who never danced a good dance for Kenya. The self-professed patriot has been operating out of this world. His inaugural *danse macabre* was after the 1982 failed coup. The *danse* felt good. The 2007-2008 poll violence gave him the Mother of all *Danse Macabres*. Other little ones came after. He still want some more.

When Kenyans celebrated and danced about their constitution, athletics, the Oscar, the Nobel Peace Prize, the Guinness Book of World Records entries, innovations, carnations, tea and coffee industries, Raila was focusing on the next General Election and working around the clock on ways to manufacture human deaths for his *danse macabre*. For the trip to the *danse macabre*, he incorporated thousands of youth. For the last 40 years, Raila cheated himself and others that he was the county's cockerel that announces the coming of a new day every dawn. But his crowing was an alarm that darkness was about to emerge. Darkness leading to his *danse macabre*.

Before closure, there is need to come right and straight about *Danse Macabre*. The dance originated in medieval Europe in the 13th or 14th century. It was a ceremonial procession where dancers wore costumes to resemble skeletons (death) who escorted living humans to their graves in a lively waltz. The dance was meant to remind people about the fragility of their lives and universality of death. A lesson of mortality that, the Grim Reaper is inevitable, you are dust, and to dust you shall return. And irrespective of one's station in life – wealth, achievements etc, death is all – conquering and the great leveller. The *Danse Macabre* has been represented in drama, music, paintings and poetry.

Truly, the power of death is the most powerful equaliser. In an online article, "A Brief History of the Danse Macabre", Bethany Gotschall describes how the *Danse* reflected for both the mighty and the lowly:

> The grinning, dancing skeletons mocked the living by poking fun at their dismay and, for those in positions of power, by making light of their high status. "Enjoy it now", the skeletons implied, "because it's not going to last." And, "Unlike the rich and powerful, for whom Death represents a loss of status and wealth, the peasants finds relief in dying after a life of hard labour and exploitation". [28]

There are God-made deaths and there are man-made deaths. How should the latter be related in terms of the *Danse Macabre*, that life is too short? What logic is propagated when thousands or even millions of people lose their life on account of people chasing power and glory?

Take the two Great Wars for instance. At the 11th hour on the 11th day of the 11th month of 1918, the World War I ended. The war was sparked by the assassination of Archduke Franz Ferdinand of Austria along with his wife Sophie by a Yugoslav national. It involved all the great powers of the world with 70 million military personnel mobilised over a period of four years. By the time the drums ceased beating, nine million combatants and eight million civilians had perished.

Some twenty years later on 1 September 1939, Germany invaded Poland, setting off the World War II. More than 100 million people served in military units during the six years it lasted until August 1945. This conflict has been described as the deadliest and largest armed confrontation in human history. It left 20 million soldiers and 40 million civilians dead. The two wars and, in particular the second, are what led

---

28 Bethany Corriveau Gotschall, ""A Brief History of the Danse Macabre", Atlas Obscura, 11 October, 2017. Retrieved from: https://www.atlasobscura.com/articles/danse-macabre-david-pumpkins-art-history

to the establishment of the League of Nation, later the United Nations, to bring to the world community a message why such barbaric events must never be repeated again.

Now, what did the world learn and say after burying 75 million innocent human beings in a span of 30 years whose deaths were precisely man-made? The Tyne Cot Commonwealth War Graves' Cemetery and Memorial to the Missing in Belgium is the largest cemetery for any war in the world. Holding 11,960 dead soldiers with 8,300 unidentified whose graves are marked with the words, "Known to God," the burial ground has rows upon rows of permanent concrete headstones.

On 11 May 1922, King George V of Britain visited the Tyne Cot graveyards. His feelings, in what is termed as the King's Pilgrimage poem, is thought-provoking today as it was 100 years ago: "We can truly say that the whole circuit of the Earth is girdled with the graves of our dead. In the course of my pilgrimage I have many times asked myself whether there can be more potent advocates of peace upon Earth through the years to come, than this massed multitude of silent witnesses of the desolation of war."[29]

The Commonwealth War Graves has 23,000 cemeteries holding 1.75 million graves spread throughout the world, including Kenya. In Kenya, the largest mass grave is situated in Lari, Kiambu County, in a three-quarter acre stretch and housing 10,995 Mau Mau fighters killed by the colonialists.[30]

People visit graveyards – tombstone tourism – for various reasons. Before making peace with the living through the Handshake and BBI, perhaps Raila could visit at least one grave of a Kenyan who died on account of his chasing political supremacy illegally, a symbolic gesture to reconcile with all the thousands dead. As a tombstone tourist, Raila will assure that representatives of the other victims that his swearing-in as People's President that could have brought more thousands of deaths was the "War to End All Wars" (as World War I was termed though it was soon followed by the second) and that the BBI will not turn out to be the "Peace to End Peace".

---

29   Quoted from Thomas McDonald, *Winged Warriors: Memoirs of a Canberra and Tornado Pilot* (Barnsley: Pen & Sword Aviation, 2012).

30   Marion Kanari and Farouk Mwabege, "Mass grave holds remains of Lari Massacre victims", *Daily Nation*, 5 April, 2016.

Coming face to face with the material evidence of death and performing symbolic handshake with the advocates of peace, the silent witnesses of the 1982 coup and all election violence is a sure way of telling the living that the BBI means well.

The President should open up the envelope and let the people deal with the ICC ghosts and exorcise them from their national psyche..., Raila wrote.

CHAPTER FIVE

Were These the Acts of God?

When tempted, no one should say, "God is tempting me." For God cannot be tempted by evil, nor does he tempt anyone; but each one is tempted when, by his own evil desire, he is dragged away and enticed. Then, after desire has conceived, it gives birth to sin; and sin, when fully-grown, gives birth to death.

James 1:13-15 (NIV)

*   *   *

Do not be deceived: God cannot be mocked. A man reaps what he sows. The one who sows to please his sinful nature, from that nature will reap destruction; the one who sows to please the Spirit, from the Spirit will reap eternal life… Not even those who are circumcised obey the law, yet they want you to be circumcised that they may boast about your flesh.

Galatians 6:7-13 (NIV)

Hands of God: God not General Election chief

That Kenyans have collectively resolved to be a nation that shall not witness violence, deaths and destruction of property again in the name of power competition every electoral cycle or any other period makes the BBI arguably the most important concept in the country's history. But moving ahead confidently demands a reflection of what that bad past constituted, in terms of human life and economic loss. The magnitude will serve as a catalyst to accelerate the implementation of this particular area of the BBI.

The outstanding periods of interest excludes the pre- and immediate post-independence Kenya. From August 1982 attempted coup to 2017 election violence, for instance, thousands of innocent human deaths and billions of shillings in economic loss…

GOD IN TIMES OF DISASTERS AND VIOLENCE

Whenever humanity is faced with challenges, manmade or natural, of monumental proportions the first reaction has been to take the war to God's doorstep. Questions come into quick succession: where is God in the midst of all this suffering? Where is God when the world is burning? Is God really in charge around here?

Sample some authors in different circumstances: William Young, *The Shack*, "Where is God in a world so filled with unspeakable pain?" James Ryle, *Hippo in the Garden*, "If God is all powerful and full of love, why doesn't he do something about the pain and suffering in our world?" Ngũgĩ wa Thiong'o, *Matigari*, "The Father in heaven, why did He create a world that was so upside down?"

Such questions come about from the belief that the Supreme Being is all merciful and all powerful in the whole universe. Philosopher Plato explained, "[When] speaking of divine perfection, we signify that God is just and true and loving, the author of order, not disorder, of good, not evil. We signify that he is justice, that he is truth, that he is love, that he is order, that he is the very progress of which we were speaking ...."[1]

---

1   Plato, *Plato: The Complete Works : From the greatest Greek philosopher, known for The Republic, Symposium, Apology, Phaedrus, Laws, Crito, Phaedo, Timaeus, Meno, Euthyphro, Gorgias, Parmenides, Protagoras, Statesman and Critias* (Amsterdam: e-artnow, 2015).

Another philosopher, Aristotle, noted, "… We say therefore that God is a living being, eternal, most good…"[2]

But why would an individual foment violence because of an election dispute, disrupt God's order, justice, truth and progress such that brothers and sisters start killing each other in thousands and destroy their country's economy then we start wondering where God was?

Let's stretch literary imagination to the limits and reconstruct the world's first ever post-election violence. In the beginning, supposing that God was the IEBC Chief and His food plate was a ballot box. Cain, the world's First Family's first-born brought some farm produce (remember the orange/banana symbols during the referendum?), and Abel the second born some *nyama choma* to His plate. Apparently, God was not a vegetarian. He chose the meat instead making Abel win the "election".

Dejected, very angry and face dark with fury, Cain lured Brother Abel to the bush and killed him violently. "Where is your brother? Where is Abel?" God enquired shortly afterwards. "How should I know?" retorted Cain. "Am I supposed to keep track of him wherever he goes?" A brother killing a brother during past periods and scenes of turmoil in Kenya bears parallel and raises many provoking questions like in Leo Tolstoy's, *War and Peace* in the 19th century Russia:

> Throughout this twenty-year period, a vast number of fields go un-ploughed, houses are burned down, trade flows in different directions, millions of men grow poor, get rich or migrate, and millions of good Christian folks who claim to love their neighbours go about murdering each other. What does it all mean? Why did it happen? What were the causes of these events? What force impelled men to act in this fashion?[3]

The Kenya or the BBI of the 21st century doesn't need to struggle for the answers to the four Tolstoy's questions. They are fairly simple. To all of them is the five-letter word, Power.

Going back to the First Family's 'general election' two lessons can be derived. One, God told Cain that "your brother's blood calls to me

---

2   Aristotle, *Metaphysics,* translated by John H. M'Mahon (London: Henry H. Bohn, 1857), Book XII, Chapter 7.

3   Leo Tolstoy, *War and Peace*, e-version, Planet PDF, p. 2796. Accessed at: https://planetpdf. com/planetpdf/pdfs/free_ebooks/War_and_Peace_NT.pdf

from the ground." To those who caused bloodshed over the last 40 years in Kenya, is there any likelihood that their victims' blood continues to cry to the Lord from the ground to date?

Definitely it does. And the murderers know it does. But like elsewhere in history, they excel in the politics of forgetting. They always cry the persecuted, the wronged, and the victim.

King Leopold II's reign in the Belgian Congo has been described as the most murderous part of the European Scramble for Africa and one of bloodshed on an industrial scale. Despite massive exploitation of natural resources and deaths of over 10 million people, King Leopold went to great lengths to try erasing any evidence of his evil rule in the country. In *King Leopold's Ghost*, Adam Hochschild writes about this deliberate culture of forgetting:

> Forgetting one's participation in mass murder is not something passive; it is an active deed… It is not a moment of erasure, but of turning things upside down, the strange reversal of the victimizer mentally converting himself to victim. *Sometimes I think it is I who had suffered most…* Throughout history, people with blood on their hands have used such rationalization.[4]

The second lesson from the First Family's 'general election' saga is still from what God told Cain. Following his constant grudging after the 'electoral defeat', God warned him: "Sin is waiting to attack you, longing to destroy you, but you can conquer it." After the murder, Cain was banished from the land and told: "No longer will it (the land) yield crops for you, even if you toil on it forever! From now on you will be a fugitive and a tramp upon the earth, wandering from place to place."

Now, does this sound familiar to Raila Odinga's political CV? First, a feeling of dejection and anger on losing several elections. Face blackening like charcoal. God's warning of his imminent destruction. (Mind you, there was no Supreme Court in existence and the IEBC Chief's word was final.) Deaths. Blood in hands. Yield-less political career. Wandering from this to that political house.

That was a long time back, probably 4,000 years ago. Even after God declaring that the murder of Abel was not his act and that humans

---

4   Adam Hochschild, *King Leopold's Ghost* (New York: First Mariner Books, 1999), p. 295.

will always carry blood of their killed victims on their hands, the world continues to force God to carry their own crosses.

It was on Saturday, 11 August 1945. Leo Szilard was one of the scientists who had developed the world's first atomic bomb. He took a taxi with a friend for the University of Chicago, USA. According to the book, *Genius in the Shadows*, by William Lanouette, Szilard had lately opposed the bomb's use at the same time demanding the Church to confront the morality of the atomic bomb itself. A few days earlier, the US had dropped two atomic bombs on the Japanese cities of Hiroshima and Nagasaki. Studies today show that both detonations killed around 300,000 people in total, first from the blast and afterwards radiations sickness. Approximately 160,000 were injured and much of the two cities were destroyed.

Disturbed by the now obvious dangers of the atomic energy, Szilard had described the bombings quoting words of his colleague, Samuel Allison thus: "Dropping the bomb on Hiroshima was a tragic mistake, dropping the bomb on Nagasaki was an atrocity."[5] The scientist had also predicted that, "the outbreak of a preventive war will then hang over the world as a constant threat."

At the University, Szilard requested the Catholic Chaplain to conduct special prayer services for the dead of the two cities and offered to transmit the prayers to the survivors. The Cardinal listened keenly to Szilard then told him: "God had locked up the energy in question so securely so that only after a thousand of years has it been unlocked. Surely, there was a reason for this delay."[6] Dear Cardinal, an act of God?

Szilard was terribly shocked by the Churchman's reaction. He asked the Cardinal: "What was the reason?" To surprise Szilard even more, he answered: "The Church will consider the matter and in due time will make a statement about it." End of the discussion, no prayers, and a mission flopped. Visibly disappointed, Szilard and his companion left in haste "probably wishing that the atom's energy had been locked up still more securely."

Szilard had called the use of the atomic bombs against Japan as "one of the greatest blunders in history." But it was not only he who

---

5   William Lanouette and Bela Silard, *Genius in the Shadows: A Biography of Leo Szilard, the Man Behind the Bomb* (New York: Skyhorse Publishing, 2013).

6   Ibid.

was shocked by the destructive potential of the new weapon. The whole world was devastated. Even the USA atomic bomb researchers commented that henceforth, they would leave the field of atomic energy and devote themselves to studying the colour of butterfly wings instead!

NGAI NDETHYA TRAIN TRAGEDY

Fast forward, approximately 50 year in Kenya. A Nairobi to Mombasa passenger train plunged into Ngai Ndethya River at Tsavo Bridge in 1993. Some 200 people lost their lives. Confronted to explain the possible cause of the accident, the Kenya Railways Chief Executive Officer replied: "It was an act of God!" An apparently dissatisfied and angry respondent protested, "But God is not in the business of construction of bridges and rails!"

As the BBI work to prevent future election violence and loss of innocent human lives, one question must be answered. An election or disputes thereof are not supposed to result in loss of human life. An election may have been stolen, officials could have been bribed. Does this amount to an express ticket to the grave for the voters? Are voters supposed to be the sacrificial lambs, to carry the sins of politicians or an electoral body?

When a voter dies due to violence, a funeral service will be arranged. The priest will comfort the bereaved that the dead were "called by God to rest." That it was "an act of God, His will. *Hii ni mambo ya Mungu.*" And we will all agree with him. With time tears will cease to flow, the flowers on the grave with wither and grass will grow on the fresh soil. Yet as the heartache and memories last on, someone, somewhere will remain guilty of the death, but definitely not God.

It is not rocket science. God has better ways of summoning a voter to the hereafter other than through demonstrations and violence. Consequently, He is not in the business of carrying rocks, clubs, knives, machetes and matchboxes. He is not in the business of stoning motorists, mugging pedestrians, burning vehicles (and his own churches), looting businesses, raping women or shedding human blood. In short, God is not in the business of conducting General Elections!

Another example of, "it's not an act of God". It is a story of Mackenzie Phillip. His young daughter is abducted and brutally murdered in a shack. Four years later, he receives an invitation through a letter "from God" to meet him in the same shack. Here, Mackenzie finds the Holy Trinity together. Their conversation is quite interesting. Below are few lines:

Mackenzie (to God): But, what about your wrath? … Weren't you always running around killing people in the Bible? … But if you are God, aren't you the one spilling out great bowls of wrath and throwing people into a burning lake of fire?

God: I am not who you think I am, Mackenzie. I don't need to punish people for sin. Sin is its own punishment, devouring you from the inside …

Mackenzie (to Holy Spirit): Isn't it helpful in keeping people from fighting endlessly or getting hurt?

Holy Spirit: Sometimes. But in a selfish world it is also used to inflict great harm.

Mackenzie: But don't you use it to restrain evil?

Holy Spirit: We carefully respect your choices… you see, broken humans centre their lives around things that seem good to them… You humans, so little in your own eyes. You are truly blind to your own place in the creation …

Jesus: … Humans, who have been given the task to lovingly steer the world instead plunder her, with no consideration other than immediate needs. And they give little thought to their own children, who will inherit their lack of love. So they use her and abuse her with little consideration, and when she shudders or blows her breath, they are offended and raise their fist to God.

Mackenzie (to Jesus): So, why don't you fix it? The earth, I mean?

Jesus: Because we gave it to you.

| Mackenzie: | Can't you take it back? |
| Jesus: | Of course we could, but then the story would end before it was consummated… |

This tête-à-tête, extracted from William Young's book, *The Shack*, delivers a valuable lesson for Kenyans, especially during the BBI time. Choices have consequences, but God respect them all the same. Actually, two systems lives within us, the good and evil. But it is wholly in our power to choose which one to use.

It is logical to carry our own crosses instead of pointing to God, dragging him along whenever people mess things up. President Kenyatta spared God of blame in any instance Kenyans put their country upside down. On 2 June 2016, he said:

> God gave us a way forward when he helped us put in place a new constitution. God has done his part, it is now us to do our part… God has more important things to do for us including to helping us deal with poverty, ignorance, unemployment and unity…[7]

Accordingly, we must set God free, exonerate Him from blame of the past murders and destruction. Then we must own up the mistakes. Bridges cannot be built successfully with people with blood in their hands not coming out in the open. We must start with the person who lit the first matchbox.

Raila Odinga is a special person in the BBI process. Conversely, and very sadly, first he is the perfect manifestation of Kenya's dark past. He has been there and done. He has presided over the 40 years of Hell in the Kenyan desert. For the immediate future, he is the BBI co-principal. He is the Kenyan Saul miraculously evolved into Paul. Now he stands on the other bank of the River Jordan guaranteeing Kenya of a safe crossing to Canaan. Could he be the best person for the job?

The world should not doubt him so strongly for the transformation. Doesn't God work in mysterious ways? "Born again!" We exclaim like the biblical Nicodemus. "What do you mean? How can an old man go back into his mother's womb and be born again?" But Raila convinces the nation in the words of Jesus to the disbelieving Nicodemus: "You

---

7   James Mbaka, "No dialogue over IEBC, Uhuru tells Raila at annual prayer meeting", *The Star*, 04 June 2016.

must be born of water and the Spirit … Just as you can hear the wind but can't tell where it comes from or where it will go next, so it is with the Spirit. We do not know on whom he will next bestow this life from heaven."

RAILA AND THE BBI IN THE LIGHT OF PAST VIOLENCE

In this world, some things are difficult to believe, though. Raila need to convince the universe that the patriotism – Holy Spirit – indeed descended on him before the handshake with the President. Kwendo Opanga hinted on how to go about it:

> …Mr. Odinga will be in the eye of the storm. More importantly, forever on the losing end of polls, and always heading for the barricades, for Mr. Odinga to emerge as a serious peacemaker, he must do the unthinkable… He should offer full disclosure of his role in dividing Kenyans at election time or for political gain. He should then own the pain of loss and dislocations caused by his agitation and apologise… To apologise one must state simply, clearly what error or mistake one made.

> Then one must say clearly the damage that was suffered because of one's error or mistake. One must follow this up by expressing ones' apology, without conditions, if or buts. And last, one must commit oneself not to repeat the mistake …

> If Mr. Odinga is going to unite Kenyans on the bright promise of the moment, he must come to grips with the truth hidden in the darkness of the past. Such truth does not unite, it divides. Moulding divisive truth into glue of cohesion would be Mr. Odinga's new responsibility as a peacemaker.[8]

In other words, Kenyans would celebrate to hear Raila read them deep from his heart two Bible (isn't the book awesome?) verses. "I co-birthed the BBI." he introduces, guaranteeing his audience of his firm commitment not to repeat his historical sins and then quotes: "But, forget all that, it is nothing compared to what I am going to do! For I am going to do a brand new thing. See, I have already begun! Don't you see

---

8   Kwendo Opanga, "To unite Kenyans, Raila must face the dark truths hidden in his past", *Sunday Nation*, 15 December, 2019.

it? I will make a road through the wilderness of the world for my people to go home, and create rivers for them in the desert! (Is 43:18-19)

Finally, Raila will read truthfully a revelation similar to what the patriotism spirit has shown him: "Then I saw a new earth and a new sky, for the present earth and sky had disappeared… It was a glorious sight, beautiful as a bride at her wedding … He will wipe away all tears from their eyes, and there shall be no more death, no sorrow, no crying, nor pain. All of that has gone forever… See, I am making all things new." (Rev 21:1-5)

The summary of this: Raila having somewhat joined the Jubilee Party will have to assimilate their slogan of "Kusema na Kutenda". The BBI must be backed by social deeds from his heart. But the backbone of Raila's success in the BBI will be an honest and loud admission, "I, Raila Odinga, bears the greatest responsibility for the suffering of Kenyans in the 40 years (1982-2018) en route to the Promised Land. The tragic results of my activities was not an act of God! It was my act. Never shall I propagate hate speech and violence in the name of electoral defeat or hunger for power. Vox Populi, Vox Dei."

Yet, Raila could not have messed the country all alone. He was just the Chief Executive Officer (CEO) of the deadly company with shareholders scattered across the country. The Truth, Justice and Reconciliation Commission (TJRC) released its 200-page report in 2013. It gave a detailed account on reconciliation and healing as a pre-requisite for peace, national unity and justice. The document was a radical surgery, a perfect diagnosis of what had been ailing the country for decades.

PAST VIOLENCE AND RECONCILIATION

Perusing the pages of the TJRC gives a sorry state of the country then. It was a sad narrative of blood, tears and fears. A history of political assassinations, extra-judicial killings, ethnic fighting and killings; torture, detentions without trial and forced exiles; torching of houses, livestock and farm produce; land grabbing and plundering of the economy. It was a bitter tale where institutions starting with the Executive itself, the Parliament, the Judiciary and other sectors like agriculture, health, education, infrastructure – all went down into the decline. Obviously, a combination of these events overshadowed the positive things that were taking place in the country. The pre-report period also saw the 2007/2008 electoral violence, and the post – its babies: 2016 violent demonstrations and 2017 General Election violence …

In the aftermath of the USA bombings of the two Japanese cities of Hiroshima and Nagasaki, the Japanese people made a national resolution. That henceforth, they would campaign religiously that the nuclear war must never, ever, happen again to any country in the world.

In the book, *The Bells of Nagasaki*, Takashi Nagai proclaims passionately: "Never again plan war! No more war! God grant that Nagasaki may be the last atomic wilderness in the history of the world."

About ten days after the bombings, at exactly 12:00 noon (Japan Standard Time) 15 August1945, Emperor Hirohito made a four-minute radio address: "… to strive for the common prosperity and happiness of all nations as well as the security… we have resolved to pave way for a grand peace for all the generations to come by enduring the endurable and suffering what is insufferable." This speech marked the end of World War II hostilities.

It is the same path the people of Kenya must follow. That never the evils contained in the TJRC and BBI must ever happen again, presently and in the generations to come. That the evils were not acts of God, but a collective national madness led by mad leaderships. That the four-letter word PEACE must rule Kenya's airwaves moving forward. In particular, Raila must be prepared to suffer from the painful fact that State House was designed to reject him eternally, not infect his suffering to people and all of us collectively halt crucifying God for our insane way of life.

However, is it possible for a people to eliminate evil completely from their midst? In the February 2009 *Readers Digest*, President Barack Obama was interviewed by Rick Warren on the subject of evil:

Rick Warren:	Does evil exist? And if it does, do we ignore it? Do we negotiate with it? Do we defeat it?
Barack:	Evil does exist. I think we see evil all the time… and it has to be confronted squarely. One of the things that I strongly believe is that, as individuals, we are not going to be able to

erase evil from the world. That is God's task. But we can be soldiers in that process and we can confront it when we see it.

There are four key words in Obama's debate to be upheld. Evil, whether by an individual or a group of people, should never be ignored, negotiated with, and must always be confronted. Individuals in the society are the best soldiers for the task. To wipe off evil from the face of the earth would be impossible since that would render Satan an IDP, in some other planet. This would probably be against God's plan.

Meanwhile, it could be a grave mistake to completely give custody of the BBI calendar to the politicians to crusade. In such a situation, who could be the choice partner?

RELIGIONS ARE PRIME MOVERS

A long, tedious and unpredictable journey, like of the BBI, can be described variously; it will not be a walk in the park, it will require many rivers to cross and will encounter difficult valleys and mountains. From the citizens' participation and subsequent thumbs-up and finally the implementation stage, partners with unshakable commitment and a country at heart will be a big asset.

As it stands, the majority of the BBI's drivers will be the politicians. For obvious reasons these cannot be fully trusted with such an enormous national project. It, therefore, consoles to know that there exists no other valuable partner who can be relied upon to deliver the Initiative's promise better than religions. It will pay to seize the opportunity and incorporate them as one big voice of the process.

There is a mighty difference between building bridges using politicians as compared to religions. Politicians started building bridges just the other day, their areas of operation is confined to the earth and the best they can cross a citizen to the Executive – for good governance, Parliament – for better laws and budget allocation – or Judiciary – for justice, but these fruits may not always be certain considering that most are inexperienced and selfish in this field, are slippery and don't establish meaningful relationships.

On the contrary, religions have been building bridges between individuals, societies, communities and nations since time immemorial.

Their bridges also cross between two places, the earth and the afterlife. Their relationship with those crossing is permanent. Once you cross, the destination is eternal and rewarding.

One area religions have performed marvellously is in trying to create heaven on earth. Besides preaching the gospel, they have been involved in building schools, children homes, dispensaries and hospitals and uplifting living standards of the poor. The politicians, with generous funding by the tax payers, scores definitely poorly in this area.

This is how building bridges with a politician is limited. Politicians have a notorious leadership cycle. Like a python or boa constrictor that schemes and hunts an antelope, finally crushing it into nothingness, swallowing it and eventually slithering into a cave until its vicious enzymes digest the prey, and then emerging from months of hibernation later for another hunting expedition, so is the way they operate. When campaigning for leadership positions or other gains, politicians will be ever present with the citizens, rolling out first class ideas. Once they strike their jackpot, they will go underground and leave the projects mid-air.

The Economist of 3 December 2011 wrote about the Myanmar leaders: "… the reform process is fragile and could yet be derailed. For a start, just as there are clear reformers in the regime, so there are hardliners too… one of the reform-minded minister is reported to have put it thus: 'there are 60 decision-makers in this country: 20 have seen the light, 20 are asleep and 20 are waiting to see which way to jump.'"This is one reason the BBI will require an honest, stable and reliable partner in religions to compensate the limitations of the politicians.

Kenya has an assortment of established religions, namely Christianity, Islam, Hinduism, Buddhism, Sikhism and Judaism. For the purpose of our discussion, Christianity, taking up some 82 per cent of the population, will suffice. No pecking order and all protocol observed. This does not imply Christianity is the best; for instance, all the reports gathered and compiled by the TJRC implicated the clergy in addition to politicians, businessmen, the media, the soldiers and the common man as having participated or stood on the fence during the 2007-2008 mayhem and other epochs of blackness. During this period, to quote American author, Mark Twain, "If Christ were here now there is one thing he would not be – Christian."

For many years, especially during the tyrannical KANU regime, the Church was at the forefront in the fight against the societal evils – crucifying the Devil on the Cross. The clergy used their pulpits, published books and pastoral letters, held conferences and meetings, went out into the town streets and rural areas and even took their message outside the country.

For their struggle for peace, justice and equality, some church leaders paid heavily. Rev. Timothy Njoya, for instance, was beaten up by police officers at a church and outside Parliament by hired KANU hooligans. Archbishop David Gitari had his house raided by a group of about 100 armed thugs. Bishop Alexander Muge was killed in a road accident in circumstances that pointed to the government involvement. What these brave and outspoken church leaders were doing was to tell the government to search its conscience and see the reality on the ground. They were also sending a strong message that their work was not limited to spiritual matters but also covered all spheres of human life.

Another eminent priest, Bishop Henry Okullu, summarised what he thought was the ideal quid pro quo between the government and its people. In the book, *The Church and Politics in East Africa*, he observed:

> The best system of government is one that is based on the principle of the constant exchange of ideas between the rulers and the ruled; a system which provides everyone with an opportunity to make his or her political contribution to do the best of his ability and knowledge.[9]

These men of God were outstanding Bridge Builders. However, in the midst there also existed the Bridge Breakers. There were those prosperity gospel preachers whose only concern was to accumulate wealth at the expense of their struggling followers. They had made the whole world believe that majority of Kenyans were demon-possessed and the condition was only healable through miracles which turned out to be fake.

The other group of Bridge Breaker priests consisted of sycophants of the KANU government, who termed it the Second Heaven. They considered Moi's government as the Kingdom of God on earth. To them, gross human rights abuses, corruption, tribalism, greed and bad governance that characterised the one-party Moi regime were a case

---

9   Henry Okullu, *Church and Politics in East Africa* (Nairobi: Uzima Publishing House, 1974), p. 74.

study of excellence for human existence. Hear Bishop Arthur Kitonga of the Redeemed Gospel Church in February 1991: "In heaven, it is just like in Kenya has been for many years. There is only one party, and God never makes a mistake … President Moi has been appointed by God to lead this country, and Kenyans should be grateful for the peace prevailing… We have freedom of worship; we can pray and sing in any way we want, what else do we need? That's all we need."[10]

So while some clergy were building bridges by preaching the true gospel of both heaven and earth, others were breaking them by propagating only a false gospel of the earth. As Ngũgĩ wa Thiong'o writes in *Devil on the Cross*:

> After three days, there came others dressed in suits and ties, who, keeping close to the wall of darkness, lifted the Devil down from the Cross. And they knelt before him and they prayed to him in loud voices, beseeching him to give them a portion of his robes of cunning…[11]

So Kenya became a battlefield between priest builders and breakers of bridges. While the former were persecuted by the state, the latter were protected and rewarded. The builders continued questioning how a Christian government could entertain so much evil in the land. They were reacting like, Augustine Karekezi, a Rwandan Jesuits who wondered how a country with so many Christians could allow nearly a million deaths of its citizens during the 1994 Genocide:

> My faith as a Christian has been affected seriously, in the sense that I cannot realize that such evil could happen in a country where so many people are Christians… What have we been doing as Christians and priests? How can we preach the love of God, the compassion of God, in this situation? All these questions arise from an experience of the deep mystery of evil, evil that is so consistent and so strong that its power is prevailing.[12]

Priest bridge builders are highly demanded for the BBI.

---

10 Quoted in Terence O. Ranger (ed), *Evangelical Christianity and Democracy in Africa* (Oxford: Oxford University Press, 2008), p. 82.

11 Ngũgĩ wa Thiong'o, *Devil on the Cross* (Oxford: Heinemann, 1982), p. 13.

12 Quoted from Aquiline Tarimo, *Ethnicity, Citizenship and State in Eastern Africa* (Mankon, CMR: Langaa RPCIG, 2011), p. 30.

President Mwai Kibaki's government made three wonderful documents, or better described as visions: Kenya Vision 2030, the *Constitution of Kenya 2010* and the TJRC. The latter more or less provided the conducive environment necessary for the other two to be realised. For without peace, justice and unity no master piece, however ambitious, can see the light of the day. The TJRC also highlighted healing and reconciliation among Kenyans as the other pillars for the country's development. Indeed, the five items are part and parcel of the BBI. Let's talk about the importance of reconciliation in the BBI process.

The Catholic Church celebrated the 2013 40-day Lenten campaign with a story titled, "United and Peaceful Kenya, the Change I Want to See", published in the January-February 2013 issue of *The National Mirror*:

> 'For any community that has gone through the kind of experience Kenya had during the 2007-2008 post-poll violence,' the Catholic Bishops had said in their May 2012 pastoral letter, "Reconciliation is key because the consequences of not reconciling can be disastrous. As Christians, we should implement a spirituality of forgiveness, which entails acknowledgment of sin, acceptance of the sinners, seeking forgiveness and receiving forgiveness and penance.

> Pope Benedict XVI in the apostolic exhortation of the Africae Munus (Hope of Africa) remarked that '… Reconciliation is a pre-political concept and a pre-political reality, and for this very reason it is of the greatest importance for the task of politics itself. Unless the power of reconciliation is created in people's heart, political commitment to peace lacks its inner premises.'

The newsletter continued:

> '…In the wake of conflict, reconciliation pursued and achieved quietly and without fanfare restores a union of hearts and serene co-existence. As a result, after long periods of war, nations are able to re-discover peace and societies deeply rent by civil war or genocide are able to rebuild their unity…

> 'Reconciliation overcomes crises, restores the dignity of individuals and opens up the path to development and lasting peace between peoples at every level," emphasized the Synod fathers. "… It is important for the present and for the future to purify memories, so as to build a better society where such tragedies are no longer repeated (Africae Munus, 21)…

> 'The TJRC will have to make clear its precise mandate and consider various modes of reparations the country can afford, whether these will be individual, communal or sympathy symbolic...

> 'With forgiveness, human beings can rise above the dark clouds that threaten their future and seize the opportunity to see light in their world... To forgive is to set yourself free, to acknowledge that it does no good to hate. Hate really destroys both the other person and yourself.'

Both the TJRC report and the Catholic Church's pastoral letter were released in 2013. In 2016 and 2017 the recurrence of violence and loss of human life were witnessed, the latter relating to an election. This is the reason the Commission and the Church's messages and vision are still relevant to the BBI.

While presenting the annual State of the Nation address in Parliament in March 2015, President Kenyatta established a Kshs 10 billion fund to assist the 2007- 2008 post-election violence victims. At the event, he reached out to Kenyans on the injustices they were forced to endure in the past:

> I stand before you today on my own behalf, that of my government and all past governments, to offer sincere apology of the Government of the Republic of Kenya to all our compatriots for all past wrongs. I seek your forgiveness and may God give us the grace to draw on the lessons of this history to unite as a people and together embrace our future as one people and one nation.[13]

This gesture was well-received and demonstrated that home-made problems can have home-made solutions.

It is common knowledge that through the handshake President Kenyatta and Raila Odinga forgave each other and reached reconciliation (we pray it was sincere, will last). It was loudly whispered that, reportedly, Raila was compensated with billions of shillings as 'reparation'. Will the government compensate the victims of the previous and subsequent violence? Will the BBI finally extend its tentacles to all the 47 million Kenyans in a reconciliation process?

---

13 Government of Kenya, "Speech by His Excellency Hon. Uhuru Kenyatta, C.G.H., President and Commander-in-Chief of the Defence Forces of the Republic of Kenya During the State of the Nation Address at Parliament Buildings, Nairobi on Thursday, 26th March, 2015", Executive Office of the President, 26 March, 2015, par. 85.

Even so, the Church must be very worried. They remember Raila Odinga doing a handshake with President Kibaki at the steps of Harambee House following the 2007-2008 violence. This political marriage was witnessed by the African Union Panel of Eminent African Personalities led by former UN Secretary General, Kofi Annan, and watched by the whole world. A baby called Reconciliation was conceived. But very fast it was aborted, courtesy of Raila. What makes us think the handshake with Kenyatta was special than that with Kibaki? What makes us think that come 2022 and Raila fails to get the executive portion of his pound of flesh will not abort the infant BBI he conceived with President Kenyatta?

Then the documents: Three of them – Kenya Vision 2030, the TJRC and the Constitution of Kenya 2010 – were released during the Grand Coalition government of which Raila was a co-principal. But again, they meant nothing to Raila. Fast forward to May 2016 and 2017 election period, he was back in the streets preaching the gospel of violence, in effect disowning the documents.

Why is the Church critically important in the BBI? If Raila could not heed the books made by human hands, would he, by good luck, obey the message inspired by God and written by His prophets in the Holy Bible?

It has been a long journey. This time around the Church must take the firmest stand and contribution to the BBI promise. Having a membership of over 80 per cent of Kenyans, it is a force to reckon with. It is more powerful than any political party. Like any other religion, the Church has a universal duty to advocate for love, peace and unity in the country, in addition to providing spiritual paths to political leaders. The Church lights up the society.

To the priest bridge breakers: Some priests of the Church have been known to sit on the fence, bury heads in the sand or side with the evil. Rev Martin Luther King Jr advised: "The hottest place in hell is reserved for those who remain neutral in times of great moral conflict."[14] Oscar Romero, the Catholic Archbishop of El Salvador, was a fierce critic of his government's administration and lukewarm priests. He used the word of God to defend the poor and promotion of justice. Before he was killed by an assassin's bullet in a church as he conducted Mass in March

---

14 John J. Ansbro, *Martin Luther King, Jr: The Making of a Mind* (Maryknoll, NY: Orbis Books, 1982), p. 259.

1980, he challenged the Church and its priests through the publication, *The Violence of Love*:

> A church that doesn't provoke any crises, a gospel that doesn't unsettle, a word of God that doesn't get under anyone's skin, a word of God that doesn't touch the real sin of the society in which is being proclaimed. What gospel is that? ... Those preachers who avoid every thorny matter so as not to be harassed, so as not to have conflict and difficulties, do not light up the world they live in... The gospel is courageous.[15]

In the interest of the BBI, and in particular year 2022, the Kenyan Church must be bold enough, unsettle and touch where the real sin is, because its priests were called to preach the gospel of Jesus Christ that is courageous. Most of them may not be politicians, scientists, economists or lawyers, but they are anointed by the Spirit from the Above. The church is powerful beyond measure. In fact, by now they should have written a pastoral personal letter to Raila Odinga (see Chapter Ten) as a precaution act.

Finally, the BBI will need a pledge from Kenyans. Many master plans had been drawn in the past only to be frustrated even before they began to crawl. The agent of killing a people's vision is a devil who must be rebuked once and for all!

> The Devil, who would lead us into the blindness of the heart and into the deafness of the mind, should be crucified, and care should be taken that his acolytes do not lift him down from the Cross to pursue the task of building Hell for the people on Earth...[16]

... And he (the Devil) should be reminded of his past fall from the grace, as in the book of prophet Isaiah: "Is this the man that made the earth to tremble, that did shake kingdoms; that made the world as a wilderness and destroyed the cities thereof; and would not let his captives go home?"

---

15 Oscar A. Romero, *The Violence of Love* (Farmington, PA: Plough Publishing House, 1988), p. 44.

16 Ngũgĩ, *Devil on the Cross*, op cit., p. 7

CHAPTER SIX

Is Raila Odinga the 'God' of War in Kenya?

Unholy passion for gain broke up this peaceful life… headlong wrath, and lust which sets men's hearts aflame. Next came cruel thirst for power; the weaker was made the stronger's prey, and might took the place of right. At first men fought with naked fists and turned stones and rough clubs to the use of arms… Warlike Mars (Ares) invented new modes of strive and a thousand forms of death. From this source streams of blood stained all lands and the sea grew red.

Roman tragedy about Mars,
god of war

*   *   *

Magnanimous, unconquered, boisterous Ares, in darts rejoicing, and in bloody wars, fierce and untamed, whose mighty power can make the strongest walls from their foundations shake: Mortel-destroying king, defiled with gore, pleased with war's dreadful and tumultuous roar. Thee human blood, and swords, and spears delight, and the dire ruin of mad savage fight. Stay furious contests, and avenging strife, whose works with woe embitter human life.

Orphic hymn to Ares,
Greek god of war

'Swearing in' ceremony, 30 January 2018: Treason I (1982); P/E Violence (2007); Treason II (2018)

In the General Election of 8 August, 2017, the electorate gave Uhuru Kenyatta and William Ruto the second-term mandate to govern Kenya. The competitor rejected the outcome and took the matter to the Supreme Court. The Court nullified the results and ordered a repeat of the Presidential election, which was held on 6 October 2017. Again the victory of the two was upheld by the voters.

On 30 January 2018, President Kenyatta watched in disbelief as the competitor swore himself the People's President. How on earth can a country have two Heads of State? He definitely wondered. Forceful seizure of a throne from any king or president is normally a painful anti-climax for the holder of the office and the people. Every market has its mad man, but the Kenyan case was a record of sorts, the President must have concluded. This is a declaration of war!

The President recounted Kenya's history of election-related violence since 1990s. In every violence, war, there is the invading army. The army has generals and its boss. Call him the warlord, the warmonger or the commander-in-chief, or the god of war. The chief architect of every electoral cycle violence had to be stopped on his tracks lest the country degenerated into civil war. He had to be pacified and greased.

RAILA, CHARACTER AND THE BBI

President Kenyatta did not pick any other political leader. He picked Raila Odinga as the source of conflict not only for the last 30 years, but also for 40 years. And on 9 March 2018, the Handshake was executed by both. Forthwith, the drums of war ceased and the war instruments returned to the strong room. Forever?

Meanwhile, and very swiftly, the Handshake birthed its first offspring: The BBI.

I. Raila christened planet Mars

By the time the American NASA was marking the 50th anniversary of landing the first man on the moon, July 2019, Raila Odinga had already abandoned his NASA political spaceship that was meant to get him to State House. In its place he had boarded the BBI that to him looked more promising. Besides the US NASA's journey to the lunar surface, its explorations have also included the planets in the Solar System.

There are eight planets in the Solar System and five other dwarf planets. They move around (orbits) the sun, the centre of the Solar System, at different speeds. The sun, heavier than the earth by 300,000 times (it holds about 99% of all the mass in the Solar System and gives most of the heat and light) exerts the strongest gravitational pull that keeps the planets in orbits.

Names of planets and their moons are governed by the International Astronomical Union (IAU) founded in 1919, an association of professional astronomers headquartered in Paris, France. Its mission is to promote and safeguard the science of astronomy in all its aspect through international co-operation. The IAU adopted names of these celestial bodies from Greek and Roman mythologies.

In ancient Greek and Roman mythologies, planets were named after their gods and goddesses and were called the Wanderers in the Sky. The name 'planet' is also similar to Greek *plazein* meaning "to make devious, repel, dissuade from the right path, bewilder." For instance, this is how the following planets derived their names: Mercury was the god of commerce, travel and thieving; Venus was the goddess of love and beauty; Jupiter was the king of the gods; Saturn was the god of agriculture; Uranus was the god of the sky; Neptune was the god of the sea; Pluto was the god of the underworld; and, Mars was the god of war. Earth is the only planet whose name was not derived from these mythologies.

The Greek named their god of war Ares who was also identified with Mars, the Roman god of war. The Babylonians named it Nergal, king of conflict. The Egyptians referred the planet to as Her Desher meaning the "red one" or Horus of the Red or Horus of the Horizon. Horus means "the far away one" and was their national god of the sky. The Chinese called this red mass the "fire stars", while in the Mayan culture it was presented as a long-nosed beast. Mars has two moons, Phobos and Deimos, both named after sons of Greek war gods, "fear" and "panic" respectively.

The name 'martial' for arts like judo and karate originated from Mars; martial arts began as the Arts of Mars. The term means warlike, inclined or disposed to war and in modern times it also relates to military organisations (as opposed to civil). The month of March got its name from Mars. It was known as the Month of War, when wars were often started or renewed. Mars was referred as to the Mars the Revenger. It is also the month when animals wake up from hibernation. In Kenya, March is the month Raila birthed the BBI.

Mars is the fourth planet from the Solar System. It is cold, barren, dusty, a windblown world of mysteries with a thin atmosphere. Its surface tells a story of destruction.

Besides desert plains, hills, ridges, valleys and craters, Mars is home to Olympus Mons, the tallest mountain in the entire Solar System at 27 km, three times Mount Everest. With a diameter of 600 km, its volcano is also the largest. Additionally, Mars boasts of Marineris (Valles Marineris), the deepest (10 km) and longest (4,000 km) valley.

The surface gravity on Mars is approximately 38 per cent that on earth. An object weighing 100 pounds on earth would weigh only 38 on Mars. One could jump three times higher on Mars than on earth (think of a politician dancing!) While the sun, moon and the stars rise in the East and set in the West, sometimes Mars appears to travel backwards, from West to East then resumes its normal path, a characteristic long associated with omens or astrological predictions.

They say the Red Planet is plagued by devils. Mars is more prone to massive dust storms than any other planet, blown up by violent winds travelling at over 300 km/h. These are known variously as dust devils/ satans/demons. The Agĩkũyũ call the Earth's one '*ngoma cia aka*' – the women's demons. The Mars dust devils rotate huge columns of dust and strong winds that blow on the surface of the planet and can reach over 20 km in height, sending massive dust in the atmosphere. Compared by scientists to super-tornadoes, they produce electric fields and can suddenly appear and disappear.

Planet Mars often dances! Explorer Insight Lander touched down on Mars in November 2018. In April 2019, the robot felt the ground beneath shake as strong winds like atmospheric tsunamis battered the planet's surface. The robot registered the strange humming, amid hundreds – more than 400 – of quakes, the Marsquakes. The mysterious loud and clear music was said to result from seismic activity. On 24 February,

2020, the *National Geographic* called the constant hums, "The Martian song that never ends". Another journalist wrote: "Mars is singing a song we can't quite hear."[1] April 2020 NASA's Reconnaissance Orbiter, orbiting Mars since 2006, send through its camera a spectacular image resembling a "Chinese dragon"....

What is the future for Mars exploration? NASA's next move in July 2020 is a USD 2.5 billion Rover mission scheduled to land on 18 February 2021. It is aimed to look for past signs of life on Mars and learn more about the planet's history, billions of years back in time.

To get the Robot's name, NASA organised an essay competition that attracted 28,000 entries. Nine finalists had forwarded their proposals: Endurance, Tenacity, Vision, Clarity, Courage, Fortitude, Promise, Ingenuity. The winning proposal, Perseverance, announced on 5 March 2020, came from a seventh-grader student, Alexander Mather. The victorious student said: "We are a species of explorers, and we will meet many setbacks on the way to Mars. However, we can persevere. We, not as a nation but as humans, will not give up."[2] And the days ahead? "I want to work at NASA as an engineer after getting a degree," Mather said. A NASA official, Thomas Zurbuchen also endorsed the Rover's name: "There has never been exploration" he said – "never, never been making history – without perseverance. Perseverance is a strong word. It's about making progress despite obstacles."[3]

Next, NASA invited space fans called the Explorers for their names to be part of the voyage. The March 2020 campaign dubbed "Send Your Name to Mars" collected 10.9 million names which were pasted on the Rover. (Like collecting signatures for a referendum to change the Constitution.)

Except the Earth, Mars is the most explored planet in the entire Solar System with observations dating 4,000 years ago. From the beginning, US NASA's voyages to the moon are far exceeded by explorations on Mars. It is the most popular, hospitable to life after earth. The planet has captured imaginations in stories, films, fiction books and songs –

---

1   Josh K. Elliott, "Mysterious 'hum' detected amid hundreds of quakes on Mars", *Global News*, 26 February, 2020.

2   Associated Press, "NASA's newest Mars rover gets a name: Perseverance", *Los Angeles Times*, 7 March, 2020.

3   Leah Crane, "NASA's next Mars rover is called Perseverance and will search for life", *New Scientist*, 5 March 2020

including of its inhabitants invading the Earth. In 1998, an American rock band named Misfits released a song, "Mars Attacks":

Chorus I:

See the fire in the skies,
See them devastate the land,
Mars attack!
The warlord chief commands,
See the human fight and die,
See our planet laid to waste,
Mars attacks!
Monster invade the Earth from space.

Chorus II:

See the Martian cities fall,
See the death of the warrior tribe,
Mars attacks!

Now their planet won't survive,
See their world turn into ash,
See the terror on their face,
Mars explodes!

Casts the rubble into space.

Can man terraform Mars (convert it from the cold, dry planet to one that would be habitable by humans)? It is still a long way to go, though British astronomer P.M. Ryves was quoted in *Time* saying, "Mars appears to be far from a dead world".[4] On exploration, about 60 per cent of all spacecraft missions have met misfortune. The high rate failure is called the Mars' Curse.

On 27 October 2016, Fraser Cain wrote about the Mars' Curse in *Universe Today*: "Mars eats spacecraft for breakfast. It's not picky. It'll eat orbiters, landers, even gentle and harmless flybys. Sometimes it kills them before they've even left Earth orbit."[5]

---

4   Alexandra Sifferlin, "A Brief History of the Search for Water on Mars", *Time*, 28 September, 2015.

5   Fraser Cain, "What is the Mars Curse?" *Universe Today*, 27 October, 2016.

When God created humans after the heavens, his mind most likely was still with the planets. Some people resemble planets. But think of the politicians as planets, The Wanderers. Every election time, they get attracted by the Voter's gravitational force and therefore keep on going around and around them. Like the Sun, the Voter carries more weight and light than any politician.

The Wanderer Raila

The BBI was established in 2019, the 100th anniversary of the IAU. Like IAU, can Kenyans borrow a leaf from the Medieval Greeks and Romans names and liken their supreme gods of politics to the planets, the Wanderers? Supposing Kenyans wish to classify their top politicians, The Wanderers relative to the planets and their characteristics. First, they would fit them into eight groups, the number of all planets. Then from each category they would rank them from first position in the most resembling to a certain planet – to the last. Raila would be crowned No. 1 as Mars synonym, as he seems to possess over 80 per cent of the heavenly body's traits.

Since Raila's political odyssey to State House in 1982 and subsequent several orbiting of the Voter for same purpose, he has been a mystery, the most researched politician in Kenya, steeped deeply in myth (like the solar system Mars). He has been the furthest from the Voter, the fourth (just like planet Mars from the Sun) from the Presidency, after Jomo Kenyatta, Daniel arap Moi, Mwai Kibaki and Uhuru Kenyatta. He is the coldest, barren politician best at dissuading the Voter from the right path. Throughout his search for State House job, he has been a god of bloody confrontations and wars.

In politics, Raila is a Mountain-man with the largest volcano that frequently spews hot lava. He manifests strongest the violent dust devils similar to tsunamis or super-tornadoes, here now, next gone. He issues tremors, Railaquakes, accompanied by music that never ends and that is incomprehensible to Kenyans' dreams. And in most of his political activities, he travels backwards, rather than forwards.

Raila is a case study of a persistent political explorer, obstacles notwithstanding. The BBI is his new 2022 Rover to State House. Having dismantled his political NASA, he could adopt the US NASA

Perseverance name to Mars mission and next form the Perseverance Democratic Party (PDP). But can the man be terraformed?

Raila is hospitable politically, but lacks essential elements to provide life to millions of Kenyans. All his political missions to State House having failed, he suffers from the Raila Curse.

Thus, Mars was the god of war, destruction and destabilisation. He was associated with anger, blood and death. "The Romans identified their god of war, Mars with the Greek's Ares… Mars represented securing peace of a nation through war… The Romans were well-known as a war-like people; therefore it is not strange that Mars became their patron god. They built temples for him and honoured him by many celebrations during the year… The word martial, pertaining to war, came from Mars, the god of war…"[6] "Ares was the Greek god of war identified with the Roman god, Mars. He always acted like a strong warrior and had a strong desire for violence. He enjoyed the great noise of battle and loved bloody warfare. Conflict and mindless killings was how he liked to spend the day."[7]

In the 40 years of Raila – a great Wanderer indeed – orbiting the Voter, he had never been on Cloud Nine like in 2018. On 30 January 2018, he lifted the Holy Bible up and declared and convinced himself that he was now the President of the Republic of Kenya:

> Mars was brighter in 2018 than all the stars… It was a blazing red dot of flame in our night sky for several months… more than any other bright planet… Mars in our night sky changes from year to year. Its dramatic swings in brightness are part of the reasons the early stargazers named Mars for their god of war; sometimes, the war god rests and sometimes he grows fierce! Last year, 2018, was a very, very special year for Mars, when the planet was brighter than it has been since 2003. Astronomers called it a perihelic opposition (or perihelic apparition) of Mars…"[8]

---

6   "Mars, Roman god of War (fourth planet from the Sun)", Wyzant Resources. Retrieved from: https://www.wyzant.com/resources/lessons/english/etymology/planets/mars

7   "Myths about Mars", Window to the Universe. Retrieved from: https://www.windows2universe.org/mythology/planets/Mars/mars.html

8   Deborah Byrd, "Why 2020 is an awesome year for Mars", Earthsky, 17 March 2020. Retrieved from: https://earthsky.org/astronomy-essentials/why-is-mars-sometimes-bright-and-sometimes-faint

In 1610, Italian scientist Galileo Galilei became the first person in history to observe Mars through a telescope. Some of his best quotes are: "All truths are easy to understand once they are discovered; the point is to discover them."[9] And: "In questions of science, the authority of a thousand is not worth the humble reasoning of a single individual."

The surface of Mars is said to experience strong dust storms (Raila's tsunamis?) blown up by violent winds travelling at over 300 km/h. In 2017, NASA-backed experiments, as with the International Potato Centre (IPC) in Lima, Peru, under Mars-like conditions confirmed that potatoes can grow on the Red Planet. Before this experiment, Matt Damon, in the film "Martian", had fertilised the Martian soil with his faeces, sliced up potatoes and planted the cuttings in the soil. The potatoes grew and gave him food to last hundreds of days.

Kenyans have now discovered the truth about their planet politician. They now understand him better. They are waiting with bated breath to see a miracle happening: The BBI making food grow on their Red Planet so that they will never suffer hunger again, ever.

II.   When devils left Hell for Kenya

Every story has a beginning. The month of August. On 30 August 2012, yours truly wrote a piece in *The Star* newspaper titled, "August, the Month of Tears, Terror and Torment".[10] The eighth month of the year and one of the seven with 31 days, was named after Augustus Caesar, the emperor of Rome. It has been called the jinxed month perhaps a time when the gods get extremely angry and let hell open its doors releasing all its tormentor occupants into planet earth.

The article sampled some of the history's saddest moments in Kenya and the world at large during that month. The deaths: President Jomo Kenyatta, Bishop Alexander Muge, Masinde Muliro, Father John Kaiser, Michael Wamalwa, Prime Minister Meles Zenawi (Ethiopia), Martin Shikuku, and Neil Armstrong, the first man to land on the moon. Others: World's first atomic bomb dropped in Japan (300,000 deaths),

---

9   Quoted from, Alex Caldon, *The Quest for Truth: On Finding the Grail...* (Coventry: Easterly Press, 2007), p. 38.

10   Mũthende Ndũũcũ, "August - the Month of Tears, Terror and Torment", *The Star*, 30 August 2012.

Africa's First World War in the DRC start date (5.4 million deaths), Nairobi US Embassy terrorist bomb attack (over 200 deaths), and August 1, 1982 attempted coup d'état in Kenya.

In Africa, once called, "The Dark Continent" or "The Heart of Darkness", the period between 1962 and 1970 was referred to as the "decade of coups". With over 200 military coups, 45 per cent successful, these primitive and evil ways of seizing power left thousands of civilians and soldiers dead and a sorry trail of economic destruction and instability. Kenya had its share of this cake, too. To launch his political odyssey, Raila Odinga & Co descended the country into the darkest heart of darkness, never witnessed in history. The Kenyan coup in 1982 became the genesis of one man's forty years of unleashing tears, terror and torment in his country.

Revelation 12:9, "And the great dragon was cast out, that old serpent, called the devil, and Satan, which deceiveth the whole world: he was cast out into the earth and his angels were cast out with him" (KJV). Many years later William Shakespeare wrote in *The Tempest*, "Hell is empty and all the devils are here" and in modern times author Hal Lindsay produced a book by the title, *Satan is Alive and Well on Planet Earth*.

On 16 May 1994, *Time* magazine exclaimed on its cover page: "There are no devils left in hell," the missionary said, "they are all in Rwanda."[11] On 1 August the same year, the publication followed up, "This is the beginning of the final days. This is the apocalypse".

Time was referring to the Rwandan Genocide that started on 7 April 1994. For the next 100 days, approximately one million Tutsis and moderate Hutus were murdered, mass slaughter undertaken by family members, friends, neighbours, soldiers, priests and teachers.

Kenya, 1 August 1982. During the 12 hours the failed military coup by some Kenya Air Force soldiers lasted, 5,000 people were killed and an estimated Kes 640 million in economic loss recorded. Kindly note some media reports hereunder:

Saturday Nation, 3 August 2013: "How the Odingas and I plotted the August 1982 Coup": "It was Kenya's most violent moment involving the military. Hundreds of men and women were killed, businesses looted and many careers destroyed and a weary country woke up to

---

11 Nancy Gibbs, "Why? the Killing Fields of Rwanda", *Time*, Monday, 16 May, 1994.

the harsh reality of the attempted coup on August 1, 1982… Once in his office I tried to explain to him about …… overthrowing the government…. It was while there that Odinga told me that the idea we had was not bad. He said that he had also been thinking about the same idea but he had not got anybody who came from the armed forces to tell that."

Saturday Nation, 3 August 2013: *Raila Odinga, an Enigma in Kenyan Politics* by Nigerian lawyer Babafemi Badejo: "Two other civilians associated with the coup plotters were Raila and Patrick Sumba…The night of July 31, 1982, was set as the date to strike. Raila had been tasked with the provision of a command post …"

Daily Nation, 24 February 2017: Mutuma Mathiu: "… Of our population of 47,615,739 this year, about 30 million were not born in 1982, when Mr. Odinga went into politics by trying to boot out Daniel arap Moi in a coup."

Sunday Nation, 30 April 2017: Kamau Ngotho, recalling an interview with Raila Odinga when he first met him August 1992: "At the time Mr. Odinga was a much feared name. He had been out of detention for seven out of 10 years between 1982 and 1992. He was the kind of person you met those days and the next day you were trailed, or even picked up by police for interrogation."

Mr. Kamau Ngotho: "Mr. Odinga, this is the 10th anniversary of the 1982 coup attempt. Did you play any role in the coup?"

Mr. Raila Odinga: "Well Kamau, lets pass that question for now. You know at this juncture I don't want to tell the truth or lie to you, so let's leave it."

Mr. Kamau Ngotho (July 2013 interview): "Were you satisfied with Supreme Court ruling that you lost the 2013 election?"

Mr. Raila Odinga: "No. It's only that I didn't want to be Shylock and demand my pound of flesh at whatever cost."

December 2019: *Soaring Above the Storms of Passion*, by Amani National Congress (ANC) leader Musalia Mudavadi: "We were told that a judge of the High Court and a section of the military were willing and ready to come to Uhuru Park to swear in Raila Odinga as president. I never got to know the name of this judge or who in the military had been contacted." In this book, Mudavadi revealed that he was among those opposed to the swearing in because Kenya would have erupted in civil war.

At his old age of over 70 years, Raila needs a lesson to the effect that the Kenya military was not made to overthrow governments and catapult a political leader to the Presidency. In particular, he needs to be lectured on the Constitution, Chapter 14,238(1) on what the National Security means: "Protection against internal and external threats to Kenya's territorial integrity and its sovereignty, its people, their rights, freedoms, property, peace, stability and prosperity and other national interests" – and not for political interests and well-being of an individual. For instance, when terrorist killed tens of people in Mandera late 2014, Raila who was a party to authorising the KDF entry into Somalia blamed the government for the troops' presence there, and the deaths. Come July 2017, Raila claimed that the government was deploying military officers to help President Kenyatta retain power in the August General Election.

Speaking at a campaign rally at Kapsabet showground in Nandi County, an angry Kenyatta responded, explaining the role of the military: "We have no experience of planning coups. Kenyans know the master of coups; those who have used the army before to try to get power. We respect our military and its mandate is well known." [12] Mr. Kenyatta went on: "We cannot allow the good name of our military whose image is well known all over the world to be tarnished because of politics. This is why we say to Mr. Odinga, shame on you!"[13]

Explaining the work of military as one of protection and not politics, Mr Kenyatta fired more on Raila. "Our security officers are the ones who are protecting our borders and even giving you security and then someone wants to drag them into his dirty politics. I say once again Mr. Odinga: Shame on you!"[14]

---

12 Elvis Ondieki, "Nasa allege rigging plot as Uhuru, Ruto defend military", *Daily Nation*, Friday, 28 July, 2017.

13 PSCU, "Voting will go ahead despite NASA threats, Uhuru and Ruto say", Capital News, 28 July 2017.

14 Roselyne Obala, "NASA alleges military plot to rig elections", *The Standard*, 29 July 2017.

Briefly return to the Kenya abortive coup and the genocide in Rwanda. Provoke the mind and imagine the former taking 100 days like the latter! Meanwhile, take a calculator for a simple math. Both tragedies translate into exactly the same rates of deaths at given times!

Rwandan genocide: one million people divide by100 days divide by 2,400 hours divide by 144,000 minutes =10,000 deaths per day, 417 an hour, and seven for every minute.

Kenyan attempted coup: 5,000 people divide by 0.5 days divide by 12 hours divide by 720 minutes =10,000 deaths per day, 417 an hour, and seven for every minute.

Isn't it time the term genocide was redefined? Raila & Company could have sparked off genocide as well. A country requires safe, trusted hands in its leadership.

Besides the deaths, looting and massive destruction of property and economy during the 1 August 1982 mayhem, a four-letter word stand out as a manifestation of the evil: Rape. In human beings, and perhaps in animals, there is nothing more painful and traumatising as rape, both to the victim, family and society. Death or economic loss would be somehow tolerable or preferable. Rape is evil at its best. The only instance in history parents allowed their women to be raped was during the biblical Lot's time. "Take my two daughters." Lot told the rapists, "but leave God's angels alone" (Gen 19:8). During this 12-hour period in Kenya, women and girls were raped in front of their husbands, fathers, mothers, sisters and brothers. Even internationally, the shockwaves were felt. The *New York Times* wrote: "At least 30 Asian women were raped either during the disorder on August 1 or later by government troops conducting house to house searches for rebels and looted property."[15] On 1 September, the paper further wrote: "It has never happened before," Asian businessman said. "And it is not something we will forget...more than 200 women who were said to have been raped, at least 20 were Asians. Six Asian women reportedly

---

15   Alan Cowell, "leader of Kenyan coup attempt said to have been a private", *New York Times*, 29 August, 1982, p. 20 (National Edition).

committed suicide. According to their religion, sexual assault bears eternal disgrace."[16]

This was the world of the 37-year old Raila Odinga & Company. Some 37 years later, he has "a military that is willing and ready to stage another coup d'état." It seems overthrowing legitimate governments by unconstitutional means is a trait permanently embedded in his DNA. Raila believes that Kenyans owes him a debt for not making him President.

By declining to be Shylock and demand his pound of flesh at whatever cost (July 2013 interview) he was referring to the fictional character in *The Merchant of Venice* play by William Shakespeare. Shylock was a Jewish money-lender who lent money to his Christian rival Antonio setting the security at a pound of Antonio's flesh. When a bankrupt Antonio defaulted on the loan, Shylock went ahead and demanded his pound of flesh. For Raila, the Presidency must be gotten, by hook or by crook, including co-opting the military. So to Raila, Chapter 14 of the Constitution is a document that belongs to the dustbin. If BBI will not favour him year 2022 will he start thinking of the military assistance again?

The United Nations celebrated the 40th anniversary of the Beijing 12 Platforms Action Plan on Women, the most ambitious global master plan for the human rights of women, in 2020. The world should now declare a caveat emptor (without a warranty the buyer takes the risk): No leader who has ever been remotely mentioned in, accused or involved directly or indirectly in a military coup or specifically abuse against women should ever qualify for public office in all UN member states. Further, the BBI will have little meaning when the human rights of women and girls are not defended and protected by top leaders.

III. Raila resembles a Uranium bomb

Students of chemistry recall their first lessons. An atom is the smallest unit of an element that retains all the properties of that element. An element is a substance that cannot be broken down by chemical means. Years later, the subject becomes more complex.

---

16 Alan Cowell, "A Fearful Reminder Lingers For Asians in Kenya." *New York Times*, 1 September, 1982, p. 2 (National Edition).

Elements are grouped in the Periodic Table in order of their increasing atomic number. Today there are 118 of them. Following is a brief political chemistry class, at least in a layman's language: elements are either stable or unstable. In the unstable ones, the binding energy is not strong enough to hold the nucleus together and thus they become unsteady, shake (dance *ndombolo*) until they begin to decay by releasing radioactive particles in the form of Alpha, Beta or Gamma rays. Ingestion of or contact with some of these particles are harmful to the human body and they may cause cancer. Elements have a half-life; that is, the time it takes for a given amount of substance to become reduced by half as a consequence of decay through an emission of radiation – giving off energy and matter. The mysterious process results into a stable product called the daughter element or radio-daughter.

The Uranium element was named after the Greek god of the sky, Uranus, also the seventh planet, the seventh Wanderer from the sun. Uranus was first discovered through a telescope on 13 March, 1781. (March, the month of the Handshake). According to the Greek mythology, Uranus was the ancestor of all Greek gods. He was a cruel husband who rejoiced in evil-doing including child abuse. His main goal was to rule the universe. Uranus was imagined as a gigantic, star-spangled man with long arms and legs, resting on all fours, with his finger-tips in the far east, his toes in the far west, and his arching body raised to form the dome of the sky. He was not subjected to age or earthly diseases and was to live forever unless killed.

Uranus and wife Gaea brought forth 18 children; 12 sons and six daughters. The father sky disliked and mistreated his children and considered them a threat to his power. This attitude angered Gaea and to revenge, one of his sons ambushed and castrated him and threw the removed body parts into the ocean. The god was dethroned.

Planet Uranus cannot support life and is the coldest in the entire Solar System. Unlike any other planet, (except Venus) it rotates on its side as it orbit the sun, in the opposite direction from East to West; that is, spinning in the wrong direction.

Element Uranium is the heaviest naturally occurring on earth. It is a silver-grey radioactive metal with a slow rate of decay and an explosive potential able to sustain a nuclear chain reaction and release massive amount of energy, its power source described as "practically infinite".

Its nucleus is unstable leaving it in a constant state of decay as it seeks a more stable arrangement. Weakly attracted by magnetic fields and a poor conductor of electricity, Uranium's powder can ignite spontaneously at room temperature. It is stretchable into a long wire and beatable into a thin sheet. The early miners nicknamed it *pechblende*, meaning "bad luck rock."

For long, the world knew the devastating power of atomic weapon. Yet in the 1940s, US scientists went on with experiments to harness its power in what was called "tickling the dragon tail." On 6 August 1945, at the tail end of World War II, the US detonated a 10-foot-long bomb christened Little Boy 1,670 ft above Hiroshima city. Containing 80 per cent of enriched Uranium-235 and total 64kg of Uranium, but which only 1.32 per cent was used, Little Boy had a blast power of 15 kilotons TNT. The bomb killed thousands, triggered an earthquake, destroying over 50,000 buildings, steel melted due to high temperatures, water turned black and river levels went up. Interestingly, a big percentage of the Uranium came from Africa, the Democratic Republic of Congo. It was the first ever atomic bomb used in war and marked the coming of the Atomic Age.

In 1946, scientist Albert Einstein who was among the leading bomb researchers remarked: "The splitting of the atom has changed everything save our mode of thinking, and therefore we drift toward unparalleled catastrophe. The solution to this problem lies in the heart of mankind. If only I had known, I should have become a watchmaker."[17]

Today, Uranium mining industry is not prosperous and promising as had been projected previously. In May 2016, Christopher Ecclestone, a mining strategist at Hallgarten & Company in the US observed that Uranium has "made fools and liars of many in recent years, including ourselves" and that "Uranium bulls know how Moses felt when he was destined to wander forty years in the desert and never get to see the Promised Land." He added that Uranium exploration "is for the birds'" because "the market won't fund it and investors won't give credit for whatever you find."[18]

---

17   Quoted in, Robert R. Johnson, *Romancing the Atom: Nuclear Infatuation from the Radium Girls to Fukushima* (Santa Barbara, CA: Praeger, 2012), p. xi.

18   Jim Green, "Uranium on the rocks", On Line Opinion, Tuesday, 17 May 2016. Retrieved from: https://www.onlineopinion.com.au/view.asp?article=18236

Bombs are not only confined to chemical elements; there can also be human bombs. The *Daily Nation* reported President Uhuru Kenyatta, while in Kisii County, saying: "Raila was at the centre of the 2007 chaos in which Kenyans fought but he blamed it on Ruto. *Alikuwa katikati ya vita. Yeye ndiye aliwasha moto*. (He was at the centre of violence. He is the one who ignited the flames) *Nani alikuwa na lugha ya* 40 against one?" (Who was propagating the call for 40 against one?)[19] The President was referring to the December 2007/January 2008 chaos around the General Election. The violence resulted in 1,133 deaths, thousands injured, 650,000 IDPs and cost the economy an estimated Kes 200 billion.

In the Hiroshima case, countries were at war with each other, the World War II. In Kenya, it was brothers and sisters at war. The proportion of the mayhem was not as big as the Rwanda's 1994 genocide. Nevertheless, one would have been reminded of *Time* magazine cover page relating to the Rwanda's, "There are no devils left in Hell, they are all here", or "this is an apocalypse."

Let us now borrow from chemistry and analyse Raila Odinga briefly. Raila is a child of two worlds. From 1 August 1982, he holds the record of the longest half-life as an opposition politician. On the other side of the scale he has been the most unstable politician, possessing a political nuclear that is terribly unstable and hence his constant state of "decay" as he looks for more stable, powerful arrangements for the State House ambition.

Today, Raila will be in political party A, then "decay," hop to B, "decay" hop on to C, and, given an opportunity jump to Z. Today, he and Company will be overthrowing Moi's "evil" government, then "decay," and tomorrow he will become a Cabinet Minister in the same government. Today Raila will be saying Kibaki Tosha for the presidency and tomorrow he will drop him like a hot potato. Here this minute, next minute evaporates. Only yesterday he was calling the Jubilee government Satanic, today he is practically in there courtesy of the BBI.

During these "decaying" moments, Raila will emit dangerous political radioactive rays. So is he a human bomb? Never underestimate

---

19   Emeka-Mayaka Gekara, "Uhuru Kenyatta blames Raila Odinga for 2007/08 poll chaos", *Daily Nation*, Wednesday, 23 March 2017.

a person –"*Njamba ti ikere*" (one cannot tell a champion by looking at muscle size). See the devastation the 64 kg bomb brought to Hiroshima. And all was not exhausted. When enriched like an element especially nearing the General Election, Raila houses a powerful destructive and fatal political bomb within.

The post-election violence and other election-related violence takes one back in time about three years before Japan was bombed by the US. Ann Frank, a 13- year old Jewish girl, poured her feelings about the World War II in Nazi Germany. *The Diary of Anne Frank* (book banned by KANU government) cites her cries and prayers:

> There is in people simply an urge to destroy, urge to kill, to murder and rage, and until all mankind, without exception, undergoes a great change, wars will be waged, everything that has been built up, cultivated and grown will be destroyed and disfigured, after which mankind will have to begin all over again...

> Families are torn apart, the men, women and children are being separated, children coming home from school to find that their parents have disappeared, women return from shopping to find their homes shut up and their families gone... Ideals, dreams and cherished hopes rise within us, only to meet the horrible truth and be shattered... I simply can't build up my hopes on a foundation consisting of confusion, misery and death...[20]

Words touching as these uttered 75 years ago could have crossed the minds of children and adults alike in December 2007/January 2008. As the BBI takes shape and moves on they still do. Still, however good the BBI could be, if one of its drivers is a messenger of confusion, misery and death, there is no hope.

Kenya at 56 years is quite far from being an industrialised nation as envisaged by Kenya Vision 2030. It is light years away from the capacity to build and stockpile nuclear weapons like the USA, Britain, Israel and the rest. Then pray tell, why should the country tolerate an unstable political element or a human bomb in its midst, or correctly stated in Raila Odinga's leadership, ironically driving the building bridges?

---

20   Quoted in Ronald W. Jansen, *Anne Frank: A Memorial Tour in Current Images* (Frankfurt: R Jansen, 2009), p. 144.

IV. Prophets of Chaos

Kenyans could not have forgotten these Satanic verses:

(a) Politician Kihika Kimani instructions to the youth in 2002: "Even the illegal guns you have been hiding in banana plantations, you should go ahead and remove them. We can no longer watch as President Moi is insulted like an uncircumcised person."[21]

(b) William ole Ntimama added more fuel to the fire: "All the Igbos must lie low like antelope or suffer for their intransigence..."

(c) And much more: "If Karl Marx is the one who is teaching the students (University of Nairobi) bad things, why shouldn't he be arrested and locked up? Journalists are conceived by the roadside... The Third World War would begin should some leaders continue insulting Moi..."

(d) And: "*Mpende msipende* (whether you like it or not) KANU will rule forever (*milele*)... People of the milk to cut grass. The mongoose has come and stolen our chicken. This is war, we will start the war. We will divide Kenya. Those uncircumcised fellows... People of *madoadoa* (spots)..."

This was Kenya of yesteryears when the country had really gone bonkers, in 1992, 1997 and 2002 during tribal clashes. The same trend was repeated around December 2007/January 2008 post-election violence. These speeches of hate and incitement brought untold suffering to the people with thousands maimed, dead, IDPs and destruction beyond description. Hard questions follows: Who triggered these tragic events? Who blew the first whistle, made the first move, and fired the first shot? In fact, who lit the first matchstick that started the fire?

Some were Moi's sycophants and *vinyangarika* (useless fellows) whose only motive was to sing the master's tune and get declared more loyal (KANU *damu*) or secure a government position (promotion or some other favour). Others were more "sensible" leaders whose agenda was to scale to the pinnacle of power.

---

21 Quoted from Mugambi Kiai, "Kenya: Ending Political Intolerance", *The Star*, 12 November 2011.

Fast forward and hear this: "*Nataka wakenya wote kutoka Mandera, Isiolo, Samburu, Kajiado na pande zote za Kenya, wajihami na mikuki, mishale, na silaha zote twende huko Nairobi na tutoe hiyo kamati ya Hassan kwenye office.*"[22] Good gracious. This was former Prime Minister Raila Odinga calling Kenyans from all corners to arms for the IEBC removal. And surely, there came violence, deaths and destruction of property in 2017 election. This is the leader who swore in 2007 and 2017 that Kenyans had given him mandate to be their president, but his victories were stolen by Presidents Kibaki and Uhuru Kenyatta, respectively. This is the leader who swore himself as the People's President on 30 January, 2018.

Twice, Koigi wa Wamwere, former Subukia MP and Raila's comrade-in arms during the Second Liberation, advised him to discover the voice of reason and realise the "gravity of hate speech whose consequences has been war, genocide and holocaust."

The practitioners of hate speech, otherwise called the Prophets of Chaos according to author Federico Picinali, are "often intellectuals and skilled orators familiar with the present and past of their target audience, its social and economic difficulties, its concerns and its grievances. They are, therefore, in possession of the appropriate tools with which to mould 'inflammatory' speeches capable of creating a breach in the hearts and minds of their listeners and, consequently, of pushing the latter into committing acts of crime…"[23]

From inflammatory speeches and whipping up racial and tribal animosities through statements, the next stage was the acquisition of crude arms: machetes, stones, bows and arrows, spears, clubs, knives and match boxes. Then the hunting expedition began as citizens of one country killed and maimed each other; burned houses, vehicles, farms and livestock; looted businesses and raped women. Beside all these acts, thousands of refugees and IDPs were created…

In June 2016, eight leaders from different communities and political parties were arrested for alleged uttering of hate words. Raila Odinga threatened to go to the streets if all were not released. "These members

---

22   Brian Moseti and John Ngirachu, "Raila won't be arrested for 'toxic' talk, Kiraithe says", *Saturday Nation*, 7 October 2016.

23   Federico Picinali, "Can the Crime of "Persecution" Encompass Hate Speech?" *Anuario Mexicano de Derecho Internacional*, No. 10 (January 2010), pp. 415-454.

must be released without charge within the next 24 hours and if that does not happen..." he threatened. Eventually, they were set free and Raila invited them for a fish and *ugali* lunch at a Nairobi restaurant. Well, here was a president-in-waiting protecting and feeding accused war-mongers!

Hatred brews hate speech. Hatred on account of a tribe, religious or political affiliation is poison to a country's development. In a nation like Kenya with many communities of various leanings, this diversity should be an asset rather than a liability as stressed by former Vice-President, Michael Wamalwa, back in 2002: "Many tribes and many religions and many cultures are not a weakness but the strength of this Republic."[24]

There are many lessons on the dangers of hate speech and incitement and call to violence. The tongue is a little, boastful organ that is a fire, "It defiles the whole body and sets on fire the course of nature; and it is set on fire of hell... It is unruly evil, full of deadly poison! (James 3:5-8) "Whether there is neither Greek nor Jew, circumcised of uncircumcised, barbarian, Scythian, bond or free." (Col 3:11) "Circumcise therefore the foreskin of your hearts, and be no more stiff-necked..." (Deuteronomy 10:16)

Haruki Murakami, the celebrated Japanese writer and several times nominee of the Nobel Prize in literature describes the danger of hatred to both the hater and the hated in the best of words, in the book, *The Wind-up Bird Chronicle*: "Hatred is like a long, dark shadow... It is like a two-edged sword. When you cut the other person, you cut yourself. The most violently you hack at the other person; the most violently you hack at yourself... please be careful... It is very dangerous. Once it has taken root in your heart, hatred is the most difficult think in the world to shake off."[25]

Hatred and hate words from a leader often precipitates violence and war. Raila is perfected in this sector making the voter always hit back.

---

24 Michael Wamalwa Kijana, "Speech on the State Opening of the national Constitutional Conference on 30 April 2003", in Peter L. Onalo (ed), *Constitution-making in Kenya* (Nairobi: Transafrica Press, 2004), p. 5.

25 Quoted from Teja A. Jaensch, *The Ledger of Good and Evil: A Manual for Humanity* (Ishpeming, MI: BookVenture Publishing, 2014), p. 74.

V. Slow mouth, thick tongue

"My Lord, I have never been able to speak well, not yesterday, not the day before, and certainly not now… I have a slow mouth and a thick tongue". This was Moses in the book of Genesis after God ordered him to go and liberate the Israelites from the 430 years old Egyptian bondage. But God assured him, "I will certainly be with you."

Moses knew about his poor oratory skills. He also knew that to deliver God's message to Pharaoh and negotiate wisely, where it was necessary, required a person of eloquence. Then there were his people, the Israelites, who had to be explained properly about the journey ahead. And above all, both sides had to be convinced about who this God was.

Good communication skills in leadership are a prerequisite to development. Powerful orators like Winston Churchill, Rev. Martin Luther King Jr, Presidents Fidel Castro and Barak Obama made memorable speeches, high quality ones, with or without notes.

President Uhuru Kenyatta and Deputy William Ruto are master speakers. Speaking for hours non-stop without notes, every word, every sentence, clear and audible, they give inspiring speeches straight from the mind and heart. They propagate Kenya's agenda at 360 degrees as if their heads carries the entire Kenyan website.

Great speeches were described by Brett and Kay McKay thus: "These speeches lifted hearts in dark times, gave hope in despair, refined the character of men, inspired brave feats, gave courage to the weary, honored the dead and changed the course of history…"[26] Churchill observed, "of all the talents bestowed on men, none is so precious as the gift of oratory."[27]

To propagate satisfactorily the high-profile national agenda like the Kenya Vision 2030, Big Four Agenda, and now the BBI demand intelligent speeches, not jungle stories from a president. To project the country's international image and represent it in such important arenas like the United Nations or the African Union similarly requires

---

26 Brett McKay and Kate McKay, "The 35 Greatest Speeches in History", Art of Manliness (AOM), 4 May, 2019. Retrieved from: https://www.artofmanliness.com/articles/the-35-greatest-speeches-in-history/

27 Winston S. Churchill, *Churchill by Himself: In His Own Words* (New Yourk: RosettaBooks, 2013).

an eloquent president. Raila Odinga does not fit the bill on both. His speeches involves omitting or jumping words fillings the blank spaces with sighs, *hayaaa*, and gestures; jumping from one theme to another completely going off the track.

Sometimes you have to connect the dots or study Raila's body language to have an idea of what he was talking about or where the speech is headed to. Roman Marcus Cicero, one of the world greatest orators noted: "It is not by muscle, speed, or physical dexterity that great things are achieved, but by reflection, force of character, and judgment."[28] And they lack substance, say economy, peace and unity in the country. In many instances Raila's speeches are loaded with threats, intimidation, a call to war.

VI. 40 Years in the desert, irritable

August 1982, when Raila Odinga & Company attempted to overthrow the government of President Daniel arap Moi to August 2022 when in all probability he will be on the ballot box for President, totals exactly 40 years. For Raila, it has been a long, long walk to State House, perhaps the biggest in modern times. Along this journey, the story of Exodus in the Bible has been his greatest rallying call. He even nicknamed himself Joshua.

The journey started with Moses when he was told by God "I have seen the deep sorrows of my people in Egypt, and have heard their pleas for freedom..." The journey was long, 40 years to be precise. It was supposed to take 40 days, but numerous setbacks prevailed. People complained constantly, insulted Moses, revolted against God and worshipped idols. On occasions, they even wished Egypt's slavery was better than the road to the liberation promise. But Moses was a firm, encouraging leader who believed in God's word.

Here is the huge difference between Moses's and Raila's Exoduses. A good leader does not tire his followers. He does not put too much pressure on them. He does not look helpless every day. He is expected to work for them, not them for him. That's the trouble with Raila. Simply

---

28 Quoted from Sandra Evans and Jane Garner (eds), *Talking Over the Years: A Handbook of Dynamic Psychotherapy with Older Adults* (Hove, East Sussex: Brunner-Routledge, 2004), p. 78.

put, Raila is a black Moses who got a golden chance to lead Kenya to the Promised Land, but due to his political DNA, gods conspired against him.

For close to 40 years Raila has been opposing anything in Kenya there is to oppose, criticising everything under the sun. By doing so, he gives his supporters burdens and other assignments away from their everyday work: protests and demonstrations. He reports to his supporters: Kenyan courts are Kangaroo courts; the Judiciary has nothing to boast about; the military helped steal election; police officers are not good enough; KDF's presence in Somalia was a grave mistake; burning tonnes of ivory and rhino horns for conservation was a crude idea; President Kenyatta issuing title deeds to the landless was a clerical job; President Kenyatta is a drunkard; the Jubilee Party is satanic. Pray tell, what are the supporters supposed to do, begin leading the leader?

And by insulting the President in front of his supporters (including boycotting his inauguration and instead travelling to South Africa), the symbol of national unity, what does that amount to? It is the same as disrespecting the 47 million Kenyans, the government, the Defence Forces, national unity and the country's sovereignty. Smart, isn't it coming from a person racing to State House? Unfortunately, the climax of these series of complaining and criticising often involve loss of innocent lives and economic instability.

VII. The Nazareth Connection

Scene one: Somewhere in Palestine

> Some 2,030 years back in time. Two men meet along a village path. One tells the other: "We have found him, of whom Moses in the law, and the prophets, did write, Jesus of Nazareth..." The other responds, sarcastically. "Can there any good thing come out of Nazareth?" Then the first man urges him on with a smile, saying: "Come and see."

> For ages, the Israelites had encountered extremely bad times. From 430 years of slavery in Egypt, another 70 of captivity in Babylon, among others. And presently they were under the Roman colonial rule. To make matters worse they had eons ago been called God's nation and even promised the Messiah.

Generations after generations had come and gone. Feeling utterly hopeless, the Israelites felt that better times would never come and all promises and prophesies were nothing but white lies. This was the reason the man on the village path was disinterested in this reportedly newcomer Jesus. Today, about four billion people out of the seven world population can testify about the greatness of this man of Nazareth.

Scene two: Kenya

Throughout the world many have been awed by God's craftsmanship when he created Kenya. The map itself, although drawn up by the European colonialists at the Berlin Conference sometimes between 15 November 1884 and 26 February 1885, resembles a heart, the symbol of love. Behold the beaches, the savannah, forests, mountains, rivers, lakes… and the weather. Be amazed by the international brands God has created in the people. Great people. The Oscar, Nobel Peace Prize, Guinness Book of World Records. Uncountable prestigious victories in sports and the marvellous work of Kenyan hands. Tea and coffee industries, innovations, first class institutions, democratic transformation, peace and stability, the economy…

But things have not been this rosy from Independence Day. Kenyans pulled up their socks and got down to work. This, together with the blessings from the Above are what have made the nation a valuable asset for Kenyans to be proud of and become a darling of the global community. Yet Kenya has had no shortage of Nathanaels (can any good thing come out of Kenya?) who have lived in moles' hole for ages. Even in daytime they see only darkness.

In the Internet, there is a cartoon by Mike Waters titled, "Mole Hole". The mole is being urged to leave its pit and come out to see that there is something good on the outside.

Mole: "I just can't understand this sunlight you keep telling me about! I have lived underground for my entire life."

Other: "Just come and see light of God's love."

Apparently Raila Odinga has never appreciated the good work of creation in Kenya or work of Kenyans' hands. To him, Kenya has been a wasteland, a failed state, a Fourth World nation destined for the Armageddon! Its people are a hopeless lot. Seemingly, there is nothing good that will be about Kenya unless, and until he occupies the State House.

The Psalmist (115:5-8 – KJV) had seen Raila's lot:

> They have mouths, but they speak not;
> Eyes have they, but they see not;
> They have ears, but they hear not;
> Noses have they, but they will smell not;
> They have hands, but they handle not;
> Feet have they, but they walk not;
> Neither speak they through their throat.
> Those who make them will be like them;
> And so will all who trust in them.

Stretch imagination beyond borders to get what Raila sees whether when awake or dreaming in sleep. See the peak of Mt Kenya, he imagine himself on top surveying his vast kingdom of Kenya, and like Kisoi Munyao, proclaims, "light is shining all over the land." Sights of an aeroplane overhead and motorcycles brings pictures of a presidential jet and presidential escort respectively. Soldiers brings a guard of honour parade; a document and microphone, a presidential speech; a meeting hall is a Cabinet meeting chaired by himself at Harambee House; the vicinity of Serena Hotel or Uhuru Park takes his mind to State House.

When Raila sees the youth, an image of Saddam Hussein and Weapons of Mass Destruction (WMD) flashes across. Strong, tall feet of the youth are best for escaping from policemen during riots and huge biceps and triceps are an asset in throwing stones. A mineral water bottle reminds him of its use in cleaning tear gas fumes from the eyes.

You can only make, refine and develop something you love and if nothing is good about Kenya, or its people, why care about them? It is the reason Raila is never remorseful when his political activities results in bloodshed, death and destruction.

VIII. Raila's blood and monetary liability

President Idi Amin's eight-year rule in Uganda is a case study of political and economic insanity. Amin butchered close to 500,000 of his fellow citizens – approximately 4.5 per cent of the population then – and expelled 90,000 Asians from the country. The beast of a president had no regard for international borders. He invaded Tanzania and annexed the Kagera region in addition to claiming a huge part of Kenya.

General Amin did not have respect for other Heads of State. At the height of the Kagera war, he telegraphed President Julius Nyerere: "I want to assure you that 1 love you very much and if you had been a woman I would have considered marrying you although your head is full of gray hairs. But as you are a man, that possibility does not arise".[29]

In an atmosphere of this kind a county's economy can hardly grow. *The Washington Post* quoted a civil servant describing Amin's government: "During his rule, Amin started and completed only one project- the colour television system. All others were planned, the foundation stone laid and that was the end of them".[30] A report in the same paper concluded that "eight years of sustained mismanagement and gross mal- administration of Uganda have ruined virtually every economic and social sector in the country". And a school teacher recalled," all civil servants went into business. They were never in their offices. The government standards went very low".[31]

The barbaric reign of the Butcher of Uganda brought the country Winston Churchill called the Pearl of Africa in 1908 to its knees. It took years of grand plans and hard work from President Yoweri Museveni's administration to recover. How did Ugandans subsequently remember dictator Amin at the helm of the nation's leadership especially in respect of abuse of human rights?

In Flame and Song: A Memoir, for instance, Philippa Namutabi recalled: "For many, the horror of what happened in those times could not be put into words. Some did not talk about it for years, others remained silent, some vowed to fight this evil, either from within or from outside."[32]

---

29 Ross Petras and Kathryn Petras, *The Stupidest Things Ever Said by Politicians* (New York: Pocket Books, 1999), p. 15.

30 Martha Honey and David B. Ottaway, "Idi Amin Squandered the Wealth of Uganda", *The Washington Post*, 29 May, 1979.

31 Ibid.

32 Philippa Namutebi Kabali-Kagwa, *Flame and Song: A Memoir* (Cape Town: Modjaji Books, 2016), p. 68.

Coming back to Kenya, we meet Raila Odinga, apparently transformed to a Bridges Builder from a Bridges Breaker, through the BBI. What memory do Kenyans have about him say, from 1982?

In 2017, President Kenyatta regretted how Raila's brand of politics had under-developed Kenya for years. "Without him, Kenya would be miles away in development", he said, and added: "We will not allow him to destabilize the country. We want no Kenyan to be left behind in our journey of transformation and economic uplifting."[33]

Ever wondered how Kenya was bypassed by the Asian Tigers – Hong Kong, Taiwan, Singapore and South Korea – in development, while it was at par economically with them at independence? These are countries that experienced rapid industrialisation and economic growth between 1960s and 1990s. There are various reasons why Kenya was left dragging her feet, which includes mismanagement of resources and lack of proper planning. Some says that the best presidents Kenya never had, like Tom Mboya, would have made the country the African Tiger. And others say that the worst presidents Kenya never had like Raila frustrated this vision. "If Raila had not appeared in the political scene", to paraphrase President Kenyatta, "Kenya would in all likelihood be in the league of the Asian nations or very close by". That is, if Raila had opted to use his mechanical engineering course in his future career instead of focusing on being President. For those years, he would have fitted properly in the motor vehicle assembly lines, chasing tenders (and offering the 10% kickbacks?) to do government jobs or in recent times consult for the Standard Gauge Railway (SGR) construction.

Raila has been the Chief Executive Officer of a company incorporated on 1 August 1982. Call it Canaan Viewpoint Limited. A quick perusal of its performance and state of affairs (consolidated Profit and Loss Account and Balance Sheet) every financial year since reveals a shocking scenario that relevant authorities ought to have declared it insolvent ages ago. What the External Auditors find constitute massive losses and liabilities, year after year, as summarised hereunder.

---

33   Nation Team, "We will not allow Raila to destabilise the country – Uhuru", *Saturday Nation*, 3 June 2017.

Liability table

		No. of Human lives lost	Economic Loss (Kes)
1	August 1982 abortive coup	5,000	640 Million
2	December 2007-January 2008 Post -Election Violence	1,133	200 billion
3	May 2016: Protests and demonstrations	5	120 million
4	2017 General Election, nullification election by Supreme court	37	
(a)	Investors lost Kes 90 billion in paper value after shares were eroded with market capitalisation		90 billion
(b)	Economy lost Kes 21.3 billion due to wait-and see attitude among investors, low money circulation & missed business opportunities (*Source: Kenya National Chamber of Commerce & Industries – KNCCI*)		21.3 billion
	Total	**6,175**	**312.1 Billion**
	Estimated total, 2020	**7,000**	**500 Billion**

From the table, some questions come to mind. Can Raila afford to pay the Kes 500 billion debt him & Company owe Kenyans? It is a tall order unless the Western countries, who have funded his past political campaigns and other activities, come to his rescue. Can they help compensate for the loss of innocent human lives occasioned by his political activities?

Human blood is not measurable in monetary terms, unless we talk of the slave trade bygone era. Even medical practitioners do not price the blood donated in hospitals, or to the Red Cross. Shed human blood is priceless. But don't be mistaken. Even though it dries on the ground, it never expires. And it possesses the eyes. Forever, it looks from the soil upwards to the heavens, crying for justice. Thus, this becomes an extremely difficult riddle to crack because it is only God who keeps the barometer for human blood to tell how much it cost.

Meanwhile, the Holy Scripture is particularly strong on this subject. Proverbs 28:17 warns: "A man who is laden with the guilt of human blood will be a fugitive until death; let no one support him."

The problem with humans is their perennial shortage of shame, guilty and disregard for the life-sustaining liquid that is blood. Some after causing its shedding go back to the people with promises of making their lives and country better as if the blood that was spilt was mineral water or alcohol from a bottle. How can a father's actions lead to deaths of several thousands of his children in order for him to save the millions left?

For Raila, it feels better to gain the whole world of Kenya and lose his soul. From his mind he probably quotes to the departed, Ezekiel 37:5,12: "…I will cause breath to enter into you, and ye shall live: I will lay sinews upon you, and will bring up flesh upon you, and cover you with skin, and put breath in you, and ye shall live… I will open your graves, and cause you to come up out of your graves, and bring you into the land" (KJV)

That being so, things become terribly messy for Raila if only he can genuinely reflect on how a big liability he has been to Kenya. Sadly, Kenyans have not posted in their financial statements an entry called "bad debt ridden off." They remind him, borrowing from Kwame Nkrumah's words, "We can no longer afford the luxury of delay, the debt has not been paid; the accounts have not been settled".[34]

Question: How many years will it take for Kenya to recover economically from the loss associated with Raila's politics in the last 40 years? The Kes 500 billion owed to Kenya is enough to build one Standard Gauge Railway and keep change or 15 Thika Superhighways. That is the painful truth.

IX. The Raila's ugali revolution

"A human being is primarily a bag for putting food into". Wrote Arthur Eric Blair (George Orwell), famous for the classic *Animal Farm*, in *The Road to Wigan Pier*. "The other functions and faculties may be more godlike but in point of time, they come afterwards. A man dies and is buried, and all his words and actions are forgotten, but the food he has eaten lives after him in the sound or rotten bones of his children…"[35]

We eat to live rather than live to eat. However, every year, millions of Kenyans and livestock are in need of urgent food assistance. This also

---

34   Dudley Thompson, "The Debt Has Not Been Paid, the Accounts Have Not Been Settled", *African Studies Quarterly*, Vol 2, Issue 4 (1999), pp. 19-25.

35   George Orwell, *The Road to Wigan Pier* (New York: Harcourt, Bruce & Co., 1958), p. 91.

happens to various other world countries. The major cause, experts tell, is climate change, which brings about drought, among other disasters.

According to records, year 2016's global drought was the worst in 100 years. In Kenya, this resulted in maize production dropping from 43 million bags in 2015 to 37 million. Hence, the law of supply and demand took effect and the prices of food, more so *ugali,* went up in 2017.

In view of this, the Jubilee government had put in place tremendous efforts to see that Kenyans and their livestock had full stomachs and were healthy. Dams and irrigation projects, fertiliser subsidies, maize importation, import tax waiver on maize, removal of VAT on bread and maize flour, and livestock insurance, were just some of the measures that were put in place.

Raila Odinga thrives on crises. He celebrates when there are problems especially when the masses are suffering. He takes advantage of the *wanyonge* in order to portray the government in power as incompetent. Thus, he came out guns blazing in May 2017 pretending to speak for the starving: "The economy is in turmoil," he lamented. "The cost of living is beyond reach for millions of our citizens. From price of *unga*, bread and milk, to bus fare to rent and paraffin. We must stand together and liberate ourselves from such kind of life".[36]

Raila was blaming the government, accusing it of poor food policy. If he were truly "a man of the people," he would have offered workable solutions. Jubilee, do A, B and C instead of or in addition to what you have done already. But Raila's main agenda was possibly to capitalise on the hungry to ignite a rebellion against the government. He had used the youth several times before. A man knowledgeable with world history, Raila's mind was probably feasting on the story of the French Revolution in 1789 caused primarily by food shortages and high prices. In particular, lack of bread was exploited as a weapon of the uprising that resulted in the overthrow of the Monarch and execution of both the King and Queen.

Some people move faster that the speed of light. They told Raila how poor food ambassador he was. Can people produce enough maize in an atmosphere of violence, bloodbath and death? Can people forcibly made IDPs produce food crops?

---

36 Dennis Odunga, "Uhuru fights to push food prices off polls agenda", *Daily Nation*, 8 May 2017.

Archbishop Martin Kivuva, Kenya Conference of Catholic Bishops (KCCB) contributed his wisdom. "With the ongoing confusion on maize and other basic commodities, it is very sad that our leaders have made this situation a political campaign tool while Kenyans continue to suffer and die of hunger. People are hungry and they don't want to know how maize was imported; how it came into the country. The most important thing is that food should be made available to all".[37]

You were the Prime Minister of Kenya in 2008-2013, someone reminded Raila. Do you remember the pictures from Turkana during the 2011 famine? Women, children and the elderly migrating with their animals to look for greener pastures. Children with sunken eyes due to dehydration swarming with flies. Their dry hair and protruding stomachs. All shoe-less in the burning hot desert. Dust rising above barren cracked earth with skeletons and carcasses of dead animals scattered all over. A child suckling a dead mother's breast. Another suckling mother goat's teats. People dying. And did you hear that people actually ate cats, dogs, donkeys, pythons and wild roots?

Another reminder followed closely, that of the Maize Scandal that came to light in January 2009 when Raila was still the Prime Minister. Raila (and his family) was accused of involvement in the Kes 2 billion maize scam. In this saga, Wikileaks claimed, US Ambassador Michael Ranneberger sent secret cables to Washington. "We have credible reports that members of Odinga family, presumably with his knowledge and involvement, were involved in the Maize Scandal," he said.

Describing Raila as being increasingly perceived as "unable or unwilling to govern effectively and move forward the reform agenda," Wikileaks alleged that by suspending Agriculture Minister William Ruto, the Prime Minister was attempting to divert attention from his family's involvement in the scandal.

Now, Raila holds a presumably VIP document in his hands, the BBI. No point asking him where he was or what he did during the 2018 and 2019 food shortages in the country. Or moving backwards, the Turkana famine or the Maize Scandal. The crucial lesson here is that, *tumbo mbele* (stomach first).

---

37   Silas Apollo and Linet Wafula, "Bishops tell NASA to keep politics out of maize row", *Daily Nation*, 25 May 2017.

Kenyans needs information as to how the BBI *italeta sufuria ngapi za ugali*? Real *ugali* on people's tables. You cannot run around finding ways to create top political positions when millions of citizens sleep with empty stomachs, day in day out. Building bridges must begin from filling the stomachs first. Starvation breeds crime, violence and instability, the best prescription Raila would wish for a government he is NOT leading.

This chapter opened with a quote from George Orwell, from *The Road to Wigan Pier*. It closes with it. "….I think it could be plausibly argued that changes of diet are more important than changes of dynasty or even religion… Yet it is curious how seldom the all importance of food is recognized. You see statues everywhere to politicians, poets, bishops, but none to cooks or bacon curers or market gardeners".[38]

Question: Kes 500 billion in the Raila's liability table in the previous part: How many kilograms of *unga* can the amount buy to feed how many Kenyans for how many days?

X. Bel and the dragon: The true position

The Babylonians worshiped an idol called Bel. Bel was their national god. Every day, Bel "demanded" 12 big bales of *unga*, 40 fattened Dorper sheep and six drums of expertly brewed *mũratina* (local brew). These offerings were taken to the temple by his priests. To feed this one hungry god, people struggled to pay taxes, held *harambee* fundraisers or did the Panda Mbegu (plant the seed). Interestingly, Bel did not like breakfast or lunch. The sacred meal was for supper only. And the feeding programme went on and on until …

Scene I

The Babylonian King had a close companion, a Jew named Daniel. One day he called him and a brief conversation ensued.

King:	My friend Daniel, why dost not thou worship Bel?
Daniel:	Your Excellency, I cannot worship an idol made by human hands, but the living God only.

---

38 Orwell, *The Road to Wigan Pier*, p. 92.

King:	Don't you think that Bel is a living god? Don't you see how much he eats and drinks every day?
Daniel (*laughing*):	Do not be deceived, Your Excellency. This thing is only clay inside and bronze outside. It can never eat or drink anything."

The King called Bel's priests. Visibly angry, he challenged them to reveal who had been consuming the offerings. Either them or Daniel, death by the firing squad was waiting, depending on who was telling lies. The priests insisted innocence. They told the King to have the offerings delivered as usual but this time the King was to lock the door using his own padlock. He agreed and it was done.

Unknown to all, Daniel was a detective par excellence. He could have given Kenya's Directorate of Criminal Investigation a run for their money. During his numerous rounds, he had discovered that the priests had erected a secret entrance to the Temple. The moment everyone retired to bed at night, Bel's 70 priests usually collected their wives and children and sneaked into the Temple. Throughout the night, they partied big-heaps of *ugali*, *nyama choma*, *chemsha* or fry with *kachumbari* drowned with lots of *kanywaji*. They danced wild *ndombolo* until *chee*. Just before dawn, the weary thieves tiptoed back to their bunkers.

This time around, Daniel got an opportunity to prove that the whole population had been worshiping a false god. Just before the King padlocked the Temple, Daniel and his servants had scattered ashes all over the floor.

What did the three parties find come the following morning? As ever, everything had been consumed. And, lo, on the floor, behold, the footprints of the nocturnal criminals were clearly unmistakable… They were caught red-handed…

Scene II

Another day, the King summoned Daniel for another round of small talk. The subject matter now was the dragon, a living animal, not a statue like Bel.

King:	Daniel, you cannot deny that this is a living god? Worship him!

Daniel:	I only worship the living God, Your Excellency. Kindly give me permission to demonstrate without using a sword or club that he is not immortal. The dragon will die, to prove that it is a false god. Allowed, Daniel baked some *mandazis* which were unfit for animal consumption and fed them to the dragon. It exploded and burst open dead, apparently from indigestion…

Scene III

From 1982, the Kenyan Presidency allowed Raila Odinga to thrive like a political god. Many times over, he demanded and got blood, flesh and lives offerings of Kenyans in the name of taking the country to Canaan. Every time he was given, he asked for more. *Ngoma itũrĩkaga nĩ gũthĩnjĩrwo* (demons become arrogant when you continue slaughtering an animal for them) goes the Agĩkũyũ saying. But every time, the ballot box, in form of Daniel in Babylon, killed his ambitions by failing him in elections. Lucky him, he always introduced a secret entrance to come back to demand for more.

In 2019, through the Handshake, the BBI became yet another hidden staircase for Raila, like in the Babylonian Temple. The Presidency had resurrected Raila. "See, the dragon is alive, not a statue like Bel." Kenyans were told. "This time is for real. He is a true god, worship him! Give him your votes 2022!"

The Year of our Lord Twenty Twenty Two shall be the D-day for Kenyans. In their utmost interest, a cover to cover perusal, a radical surgery of the political dragon shall be a matter of life and death. For the truth is, Raila has never been a political god, but a Bel, a dragon, or more appropriately the god of war in Kenya.

CHAPTER SEVEN

Of Lilliputians, Dynasties and Hustlers

For man, when perfected, is the best of animals, but, when separated from law and justice, he is the worst of all; since armed injustice is more dangerous, and he is equipped at birth with the arms of intelligence and with moral qualities which he may use for the worst ends. Whereof, if he have no virtue, he is the most unholy and the most savage of animals, and the most full of lust and gluttony. But justice is the bond of men in states, and the administration of justice, which is the determination of what is just, is the principle of order in political society.

Aristotle, Greek philosopher

*   *   *

The Eagle should permit the small birds to sing and care not wherefore they sang.

Winston Churchill to Soviet leader Joseph Stalin, 4 February, 1945, meaning even small powers – *The Hustlers* – are important

*   *   *

When the war of the giants is over the wars of the pygmies will begin. There will be a torn, ragged and hungry world to help to its feet.

– British Prime Minister Winston Churchill telegram to US President Franklin Roosevelt, 18 March, 1945

*　　　　　*　　　　　*

So you must be the first that gives this sentence /And he that suffers /O! It is excellent / To have a giant's strength, but it is tyrannous / To use it like a giant.

William Shakespeare,
Measure for Measure

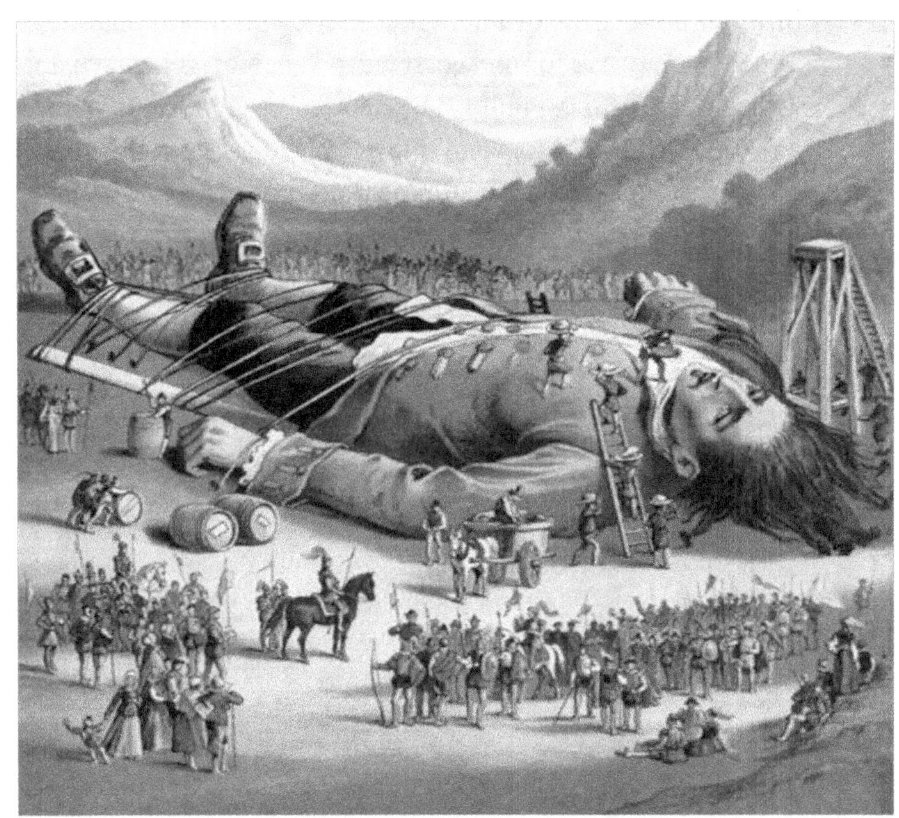

Lemuel Gulliver in Lilliput: BBI politics parallels Lilliputian drama

On 17 January 2020, Khagendra Magar passed on at the age 27 years following a battle with pneumonia. Standing at just 2ft 2.41in tall and weighing 6 kg, Magar was the shortest living mobile man on the planet, according to the Guinness World Records (GWR). "He was so tiny when he was born", his father had told the GWR, "that he could fit in the palm of your hand, and it was very hard to bath him because he was so small."[1]

Coming from home to the world's highest mountain, Everest, Magar travelled to more than a dozen countries and made many television appearances. He was also appointed the Nepalese Goodwill Ambassador for Tourism.

As he was being recognised by the GWR during his 18th birthday in 2010, Magar explained: "I don't consider myself to be a small man. I'm a big man. I hope that having this title enables me to prove it, and get a proper house for me and my family." Following his death, the GWR paid him a tribute thus: "He didn't let his small size stop him from getting the most out of his life."[2]

A human mind is really incredible. Research shows that the brain is capable of generating 50,000 thoughts a day, where more than 100,000 chemical reactions per second take place, and a memory that can store the entire Internet. The news of Magar's demise provoked the artist mind to revisit a book relating to a fictional island called Lilliput.

LILLIPUTIANS

Jonathan Swift, a prominent Irish Anglican Minister, historian, political commentator and patriot published *Gulliver's Travels* in 1726. Its original title was, *Travels into Several Remote Nations of the World*, and contained four different adventures.

Considered Swift's *Magnum Opus* (masterpiece), *Gulliver's Travels* has inspired readers and authors alike for more than three centuries.

---

1   GWR, "World's shortest man Khagendra Thapa Magar dies aged 27", Guinness World Records, 17 January 2020. Retrieved from: https://www.guinnessworldrecords.com/news/2020/1/worlds-shortest-man-khagendra-thapa-magar-dies-at-age-27-606518/

2   Ibid.

George Orwell – of the *Animal Farm* fame – claimed it to be among the six most indispensable books in world literature. Allan Boom, a literary critic observed that Swift was able to recreate "that world in a form which teaches where arguments fails and which satisfies all while misleading none." In 2013, *The Guardian* rated the book third best among the 100 novels written in English language. "It is universally read," remarked Alexander Pope when the book was first published, "from the Cabinet Council to the nursery."[3] Though regarded as an adventure children's book, *Gulliver's Travels* also targeted adults as well as it mocked the customs, society, politics and the English government of the day thereby calling for reformation.

Swift hoped that his work would convince people change their behaviour. His aim, he said, was "to vex the world rather than divert it." It was Swift who gave the English language new words such as Yahoo – meaning uneducated, ruffian, crude and brutish; Lilliputians (trivial, very small), Brobdingnagian (gigantic).

The Year of Our Lord Twenty Nineteen brought the BBI to Kenyans. It also marked the 320th anniversary since Dr Lemuel Gulliver, a surgeon and captain of several ships in the book, set sail for the high seas 4 May, 1699, on board *The Antelope*, a merchant ship headed for Lilliput.

The BBI revolves around two players; political leaders – President Uhuru Kenyatta, Deputy William Ruto and Raila Odinga – and Kenyans. Are there parallels or lessons which can be drawn from *Gulliver's Travels,* especially the first voyage where Gulliver encountered a sea accident then found himself in a land of extremely small people, between Lilliput and Kenya at the BBI?

I. Tanga Tanga

Lilliput

Dr Gulliver was a skilled navigator thanks to his several sea voyages. He had a taste for travelling, new countries and new planets where he enjoyed the adventures, gained more experience and returned home unhurt, immediately to plan for another trip.

---

3 Alexander Pope, *The Works of Alexander Pope, Volume 10* (London: J. M'Creery, 1824), p. 162.

Kenya

Deputy President Ruto knows Kenya like the palm of his hands. As the Principal Assistant to the President, he travels to the interiors of the country to touch base with the people and initiate development projects. Otherwise, how do you aspire to be President if you don't know the people and their problems?

President Kenyatta confirmed this fact someday in June 2018: "*Huyu kijana anaitwa Ruto kila wikendi anatangatanga kila mahali. Atakuwa akipitia hizi machochoro akiona kuna kitu gani inaenda kona kona mumwambie. Si ndiyo? Si namna hiyo? Tuhakikishe kazi ya mwananchi inafanyika*".[4]

The President was simply telling Kenyans to tell Ruto where things have gone wrong as he moved around the country every weekend since public service must be delivered.

Raila is different. He is an adventurer who visits specific areas in Kenya when he needs to release his political steam or when seeking votes. As a *mtalii* par excellence, he will arrive at a venue, entertain crowds with dances, riddles and stories and occasionally insult where the political tourism attraction does not fit his bill. No development matters except leisure and the mysterious Canaan heaven that will never come.

II. Setting sail

Lilliput

On his very first trip of discovery, Dr Gulliver was aboard *The Antelope*. Somewhere, a terrible storm happened and the passengers were shipwrecked. Gulliver was the only survivor. He swam up ashore and exhausted, slept for nine hours…

Kenya

On his very first serious voyage to State House, Dr Ruto boarded the Jubilee Party ship in March 2013. Then came period 2018/2019. Raila unleashed a deadly tsunami concealed in the Handshake and BBI.

---

4   Elvis Ondieki, "William Ruto's trips baffle even President Uhuru Kenyatta, *Sunday Nation*, 3 June, 2018.

The ship was temporarily destroyed, but did not sink. The sea winds drifted it away for some distance where it stopped near the shore. Dr Ruto survived…

III. Awakening, in captivity

Lilliput

When he regained consciousness, Dr Gulliver realised that he was in a kingdom inhabited by small miniature human beings. He found himself tied down by a hundred tiny threads. The people here were less than six inches tall, one-twelve his height. They discharged little arrows that pricked his body like needles.

Everything around looked proportionally small, he discovered later. The tallest horses and oxen were between four and five inches in height. A sheep was an inch and a half. And the tallest tree was seven feet high.

Dr Gulliver was to discover also: 500 carpenters and engineers were to build his carriage to town; 900 strongest men to lift him to the carriage; 1,500 Emperor's horses and 500 guards for the drive; 600 ordinary beds to make his own; 300 tailors for his clothes, and 300 cooks for his food. Once, he put five soldiers in his coat pocket and another time found boys and girls playing hide and seek in his hair!

Kenya

He was like in a dream, but awake all the same. Dr Ruto was in an unfamiliar territory. He could not believe his eyes or ears. Little-tiny people numbering not more than a hundred surrounded him including Raila who held the BBI high in the air swearing himself not for one position, but two: President and Prime Minister. Raila was not sure which one he wanted most.

The little-tiny people were working around the clock like ants. The little tiny- people had tied him down using a fishnet made of little-tiny sisal fibres. The little-tiny people were discharging little-tiny arrows like needles to his body. The Lake Man was beside himself seeing that he had made him a captive.

The little-tiny people were hurriedly deleting texts about the work-in-progress in the Jubilee Party Manifesto, Big Four Agenda and Kenya

Vision 2030. The little-tiny people also erased the "Kusema na Kutenda" and Ndugu William bonds.

The little-tiny people were heaping little-tiny stones and burning little-tiny tyres in the little-tiny streets to block Dr Ruto's access to the Jubilee House and State House. The little-tiny people had blocked his mobile phone to prevent him reaching the Boss. The little-tiny people claimed helping build houses of worship amounted to corruption. The little-tiny people were really keen to kill "10 for me, ten for you" covenant with his Boss. The little-tiny people were busy building their little-tiny Tower of Babel to reach them to a little-tiny State House.

The little-tiny people worked in haste to build a little-tiny carriage in form of the Jubilee Party sycophants and ODM fanatics to dispatch Dr Ruto to a little-tiny political Siberia by declaring him a persona non grata and an IDP from top politics. In fact, the little-tiny people were trying to revive the ICC case against him.

The little-tiny people placed Dr Ruto on a little-tiny Mt. Kenya and mocked him: Worship us and we shall give you this entire kingdom called Kenya. The little-tiny people put him on a little-tiny Cross and told him: You boasted to have the power to save others; now save yourself!

Dr Ruto did not move. The little-tiny people were blowing vuvuzelas, dancing on top of little-tiny platforms, singing and declaring *Veni, Vidi, Vici.*(Latin: I came, I saw, I conquered – a swift conclusive victory) Behold the Canaan!

Dr Ruto looked around. He could not trace his Boss. The Handshake had mutated into a Heartache and a Brain-ache. But in a moment, his eyes opened wide. Alas, these were just little-tiny people having their little-tiny fun, he discovered. And beyond this little-tiny kingdom of little-tiny people were millions of Kenyans who had been his supporters for years, waiting.

IV. Nuclear bomb!

Lilliput

Later, Dr Gulliver was taken to the capital and kept in chains in a large abandoned temple. The Emperor ordered him inspected to ensure he carried no dangerous weapons. His pockets were emptied and the pistol, sword and other items taken away. An inventory of them was made.

With time, the Emperor and his people discovered that Dr Gulliver was a compassionate, merciful and civilised person. They were impressed with his gentle, good behaviour despite being powerful enough to bring down the whole empire. "He is obviously a friendly giant", the Emperor observed, "there's nothing to fear". He was soon untied and made to swear to keep peace with the Emperor and the Kingdom.

Kenya

Since 2013, Dr Ruto has been a political giant in Kenya. Considered a co-President by then the state of affairs, he was obviously a heart-beat from the top seat. Until the Handshake and the BBI came calling.

A number of Kenyan Lilliputians started to view him now as the most dangerous politician. They thought that at his Sugoi and Karen homes he had stockpiled nuclear weapons or Weapons of Mass Destruction (WMD) like Saddam Hussein. The President-in-Waiting had to be cut down to his size lest the hidden agenda in the BBI fall like a pack of cards.

That Dr Ruto started to appear dejected, powerless and desperate is what the calm section of the ocean behaves like. Having net-worked with millions of Kenyans and global political leaders for years, having learned the best political paths arithmetic to State House, Dr Ruto was a sleeping, friendly giant, but not one to be taken for granted. Biographer Irungu Thatiah noted in *Hard Tackle: The Life of Uhuru Kenyatta*: "Ruto is religious as a Cardinal but also vicious as a honey badger".[5]

V. Urine in the Palace

Lilliput

One midnight, Dr Gulliver was summoned by hundreds of the crying little-tiny people. The Palace had caught fire on account of a careless house maid, and the Emperor wanted him there urgently. People were trying to put out the fire with little buckets of water, but the flames were very violent. Despite the fact that urinating within the precincts of the

---

5   Irungu Thatiah, *Hard Tackle: The Life of Uhuru Kenyatta* (Nairobi: Rizzan Media, 2014).

Palace was a capital offence, Dr Gulliver abandoned the water rescue and directed jets of his own urine to the raging flames. Within three minutes, the fire was extinguished.

Kenya

This book is not a project of doom. History knows that Raila is a master political arsonist. His jacket pockets have never missed a match box since August 1982. Will he use the BBI to burn the country like the woman in Lilliput sometimes before August 2022 and however hard people will try to extinguish the fire will turn out futile? Will a desperate President Kenyatta search for Dr Ruto as a matter of urgency to help douse the fierce fire by whatever means possible, including political urine?

VI. Thanksgiving

Lilliput

In theory, people held that ingratitude was a capital offence punishable by death. Those who made ill returns to their benefactors were considered enemies of mankind. But in practice, this was not always the case. After Dr Gulliver extinguished the Palace fire by pee-ing (high treason), the administration deliberated on getting 20,000 men with poisoned arrows to kill him. They also feared that next time he may drown the whole Palace with urine. Poisoning his drinking juice was also discussed.

Another alternative was to reduce his allowances so that he could eventually die, where between 5,000 to 6,000 men would cut his body into pieces and take them to a distant land to prevent stench and infection. Finally, it was decided to spare his life and instead 20 surgeons were put on standby to pluck out his two eyes.

Kenya

In the past, Dr Ruto has put off many fires in the country (not with urine!) He was instrumental in bringing lasting peace between two largest communities from Mt Kenya and Rift Valley after the 2007/2008 post-election violence. As the President's *"Mtu wa mkono"*, he has deputised in using about Kes 20 trillion (Kenya's budget since 2013) to quench various fires – in education, agriculture, infrastructure, health, etc. And he helped Raila and Kenyatta to become Prime Minister and President, respectively thereby quenching some political fires.[6]

Politics is a dirty, thankless game and oftentimes good is repaid with evil. From the moment the Handshake and BBI knocked the door, short memories took charge. Dr Ruto's putting off of past raging fires was forgotten. He now qualified for high treason like Dr Gulliver.

Some Kenyan Lilliputians led by Raila started collecting thousands of tiny poisoned arrows, brewed poisoned *mursik*, catalysed the slashing of Dr Ruto's state privileges then decided to remove his eyes, Samson style. They wanted him dead, in theory or practice. Yet they were mistaken. They were ignorant to the fact that the stone that builders rejected could be in the near future turn out the country's cornerstone. Ignorant that the Jubilee ship, though on its deathbed, was an UhuRuto project; it can be brought back to life or another one built.

VII. God's guidance

Lilliput

Men who were not believers in Divine Providence were treated as incapable of holding any public office. The Lilliputians deemed the Kings as deputies of Providence. They also trusted that Providence never intended to make management of public affairs a mystery to be comprehended by a few persons of sublime genius. To them, employment was never to be put into dangerous hands.

Kenya

Dr Ruto is a constant seeker of Divine guidance in his life and work. He is a good student of the Bible. From the first book of Genesis where God advised man to hit the Serpent on the head in order to kill it, to the tribulations of the holy man in Job, to giving God his due in Malachi, to being a good Samaritan in Luke to the New Jerusalem in the last book Revelation, Dr Ruto is solidly at home. Crown this with his forever "prayers is not a ritual, it is serious business" maxim and you get a man much more dependent on the Above.

---

6   Charles Wanyoro, "Ruto woos Kalonzo in search for new allies", *Sunday Nation*, 19 January, 2020.

To Raila, the Bible is like a dictionary or an encyclopaedia, not a spiritual life companion; you only need them when you want to search an item. Potentially, his only book of interest is the Exodus, which excites him greatly due to the Canaan journey. Even after being baptised by Prophet David Awuor in May 2009, the Holy Spirit apparently remained non-existent. In true politics he is not a genius, but merely dangerous hands.

VIII. Leadership qualification

Lilliput

To qualify for a high position in the government, a competition was held. Men seeking political office demonstrated their skills in rope dancing. The higher and skilfully a candidate danced upon a rope without falling determined his tenure in office. It was all about impressing the Emperor rather than ability to offer substantial leadership contribution.

Kenya

No one exactly knows or might ever know the reason why President Kenyatta gave Raila the job of steering the BBI ship. If the criteria were the expertise in dancing *ndombolo* and telling riddles and stories on political platforms, Kenyans would not have a problem with that. In the absence of this thought, to appoint a person with the worst history of building bridges to build bridges in the 21st century Kenya was like an electric shock to Kenyans.

IX. Nusu Mkate

Lilliput

One day, the Emperor's great-grandfather was opening a boiled egg on the big rounded end. By accident, he sliced his hand. Henceforth, it was decreed in the law books that eggs should be broken only on the convenient end, the smaller end, when cracking them. This became a religion for all true believers. From then on, those devoted to breaking their eggs on the big end offered themselves as martyrs and were banned from political office and their literature was censored.

Kenya

When pressure became too much to bear, President Mwai Kibaki decided to divide the national power from the big end; the middle. This resulted in the Grand Coalition or the "Nusu Mkate", one half for himself and the other for Raila. In the process, he and Kenyans cut their hands badly.

The experience taught them one vital lesson. Any power partnership incorporating Raila is a dangerous venture for the people and country. Raila's BBI is a path to make President Kenyatta create a Nusu Mkate, at worst. Will the President slice his hands, sooner or later?

X. Height of shoes

Lilliput

The Kingdom was divided between two great political affiliations: those men who wore high-heeled shoes and those who wore low-heels. The Emperor and his party wore low-heels and the opposition the high ones. His son, the heir-apparent put on one high- and one low-heel shoe making him walk unevenly. No one knew where he stood.

The Emperor appointed the low-heels to official positions regardless of the abilities and qualifications of the high-heels despite the fact that they were exceeded by the high-heels in numbers. There were constant quarrels between the two sides over the egg-dominated history and culture. They could neither eat, drink nor speak to each other. The conflict resulted in six rebellions where 11,000 people died and 40 ships were lost.

Kenya

It is the reverse of Lilliput. The BBI is a contest between the high-heels who are the majority and open-minded on one hand, and the low-heels, the minority who are averse to change and would like to hold on to the traditional status quo of recycling old leaders, on the other.

Raila is the Crown Prince the heir-apparent to President Kenyatta in the event the BBI succeeds, who wears one high-heel and the other low: see how he wobbles when he walks. He is not sure whether he wants to be President or Prime Minister. The rebellions, deaths and sinking ships over how to divide an egg was a story confined to Lilliput, hopefully.

XI. Law is an Ass

Lilliput

Justice was more disposed to reward than to punishment in this country. The law held that whoever can bring in sufficient proof that he has strictly observed the laws for 73 moons was rewarded with certain privileges including cash and a title was added to his name.

Kenya

In Charles Dickens' *Oliver Twist*, Mr. Bumble calls the law "a ass—a idiot" and suggests that its "eye may be opened by experience— by experience."[7] In the case of the *State vs Frank Sandstrom (1980)* Attorney-General James Karugu also admitted that the Kenyan law was an ass. Justice L.G. Harris had sentenced the 19-year old US marine to sign a bond to pay Kes 500 after he confessed killing Monica Njeri on 4 August 1980 in Mombasa!

Raila does not qualify for rewards for strictly observing Kenyan laws, the Lilliputians way. Instead, he deserves heavy punishment having broken the laws uncountable times since 1982. If he were not a son of the giant politician, Jaramogi Odinga, or the Kenyan laws not an ass, he would have faced the hangman or life imprisonment soon after the 1982 attempted coup. Ditto for swearing himself as People's President in 2018: Attorney-General Githu Muigai was burning to charge him with treason.

XII. Goliath, titans and arrogance

We are talking about giants and dwarfs. Jonathan Swift's story of the tiny race of people in Lilliput symbolised politics, religion and social affairs of Great Britain of the day.

The small size of Lilliputians signified low morality. They were mean and nasty, arrogant, greedy, untrustworthy, manipulative, dangerous with a high sense of self-importance.

To understand this race, Swift gave a hint: "Take a strict view of their excrements, and, from the colour, the odour, the taste, the consistence, the crudeness or maturity of digestion, from a judgment of their thoughts

---

7   Charles Dickens, *Oliver Twist*, Vol II (New York: James G. Gregory Publisher, 1861), p. 277.

and designs; because men are never so serious, thoughtful, and intent, as when they are at stool…"

Notwithstanding its more than 300 years since publication, *Gulliver's Travels* portrays an almost accurate picture of what is found in today's world, including Kenya. Every day, Raila presents himself as the greatest political giant in Kenya. Today, holding the BBI proudly, he deceives himself that truly he is the one and only giant, the Brobdingnagian, while others are just Lilliputians. But the outcome of his battle with Dr Ruto could prove him wrong. Rewind to around 1012 BC.

David was a humble, harp-playing shepherd youngster when he challenged giant Goliath to a battle armed with nothing but five smooth stones and a sling. Goliath, standing over three metres tall had a bronze helmet on his head and wore a coat of amour that had scales like a fish. It was made of bronze and weighed about 57 kg. His legs were protected by bronze. He had a javelin tied on his back. His spear shaft was like a weaver's rod, and its iron point weighed around seven kilograms.

David challenged the giant who was now menacingly mocking him. He told Goliath: "You come against me with sword and spear and javelin, but I come against you in the name of the Lord Almighty…"

Despite the heavy armoury, all it took David was to reaching into his bag, taking out a single stone, slinging it, and striking the Philistine on the forehead. The stone sank and the giant fell down on the ground, dead.

When Raila started harbouring political ambitions in 1982, Dr Ruto was only 16 years old, a shoeless teenager perhaps then learning to sell chickens in his village. In later years, while Raila spent most of his time in the streets with the youth and fighting the IEBC and Supreme Court, Dr Ruto was walking up the political ladder, gradually, studying the tricks of the game.

At one time, Dr Ruto was Raila's junior, a Cabinet Minister, when he was the Prime Minister, then bypassed him. With over 28 continuous years in politics, he is Deputy Leader of the Jubilee Party, the largest political formation in Kenya's history. Secondly, he is the second in command in the mighty Kenya. At one time, he was in charge of the country when President Kenyatta had travelled to The Hague. Raila has been in and out of government, has no un-interrupted experience. Who among the two is a political giant? The difference is like day and night.

Arrogance like that of Goliath or Raila is expensive and can sink a promising career. Relating to the sinking of the Titanic ship, James Cameron, the director of a film by the same name (1998) noted that not only was the ship destroyed by an iceberg, a state of mind also played part: arrogance. He also noted, "that life is uncertain, the future is unknowable… the unthinkable possible."[8] The Titanic tragedy provides a lesson to Raila who believes that he is the Alpha and Omega of Kenyan politics.

On 15 April 1912, RMS Titanic, then the largest and most luxurious British liner, collided with an iceberg in the North Atlantic Ocean. It carried 2,224 passengers and crew. Due to its size and technological advancements in its structure, it was considered unsinkable.

At the beginning of its maiden voyage, one of the deck hands was asked whether the ship was really unsinkable. He replied, "God himself could not sink the ship." Its captain was warned repeatedly about the ice fields ahead, but he ignored. Later, Phillip Frankline, the Vice-President of the company that owned the ship emphasised on the safety of Titanic, "We place absolute confidence in the Titanic," he stated. "We believe the boat is unsinkable." But at that very moment, the "ship of dreams" was already on the ocean floor, having sunk within a space of two- and-half hours after it struck an iceberg. Some 1,500 people perished, 70 per cent of its human cargo.

Raila lies to himself that he is unsinkable that possibly even God cannot drown him. But we have seen in the past several times voters sinking his ambitions by rejecting him. The victorious giant Kenyans desires through the BBI contest is not like Samson of the old: anointed by God to deliver Israelites from the Philistines, he developed arrogance and a taste for foreign wives, against God's will. When his downfall came calling, he refused to go alone. He died with 3,000 people. Or not like boxer Mike Tyson refusing to play by the rule of the game and instead biting a chunk of his opponent's ear and spitting the pieces to the canvas. This sound like Raila's character.

---

8   Quoted in John Meakin, "Titanic Arrogance", *Vision* (Spring 2002).

Kenyans will admire a political giant who will toe to the rules and prescribe to the great Muhammad Ali's motto: "Service to others is the rent you pay for your room here on earth."[9] One of the best of Muhammad Ali's quotes goes: "I've wrested with alligators. I've tussled with a whale. I done handcuffed lightning. And throw thunder in jail."[10] Raila must never take Ruto for granted.

Back to Lilliput: Dr Ruto has fought many local and international battles including with the ICC and won. As he amused himself watching the little-tiny people brought to fame by the BBI dancing on his feet, the body and the head; as he heard the little-tiny people singing their little-tiny jubilations songs with their little-tiny voices-he knew the 100 little-tiny people were nothing but a passing cloud, and by 2022, Raila will have returned to his favourite bedroom.

The BBI will need a giant, a Brobdingnagian, the name *Gulliver's Travels* used for them, to free Kenyans from the numerous challenges facing them. Both Raila and Ruto are Brobdingnagians, but each very different. While the former possess hands full of violence that passes the virus to his followers, the latter is a preacher of peace whom his supporters imitate. That is the main difference between the two giants.

The BBI booted out giant Ruto from President Kenyatta's compound. But in due course, giant Raila shall know that he doesn't know – *Atajua hajui*. A scenario like the one below could well come to happen:

> When Dictator King Saul banished David from his presence, the most unlikely happened. Thousands of warriors from all over Israel even those from Saul's tribe defected to David's camp. The Bible describe them as armed with bows and were able to shoot arrows or to sling stones right-handed or left-handed. They were brave warriors, ready for battle and able to handle the shield and spear. Their faces were the faces of lions, and they were as swift as gazelles in the mountains.
>
> Yet despite the warriors being giants in their field, David demanded one requirement: Peace and loyalty. David told them as he welcomed them: "If you have come to me in peace to help me, I am ready for

---

9 Ann Oliver and Paul Simpson, *A Rough Guide to Muhammad Ali* (London: Rough Guides, 2004), p. 230.

10 Michael Gaffney, *The Champ: My Year with Muhammad Ali* (New York: Diversion Books, 2012).

you to join me. But if you have come to betray me to my enemies when my hands are free from violence, may the God of our ancestors see it and judge you."

Their leader assured him:

> We are yours, David!
> We are with you, son of Jesse!
> Success, success to you,
> and success to those who help you,
> for your God will help you. (1 Chronicles 12:18)

The Bible informs that day after day men came to help David, until he had a great army, like the army of God. All came determined to make David King of all Israel. And "there was joy in Israel."

One day King Saul was desperate about the future as things were turning from bad to worse. "Find me a woman who can talk to the spirits of the dead. I'll go to her and find out what's going to happen." (1 Samuel 28:7) When giant Ruto peaceful and loyal warriors come marching, even giant Raila consulting with the witchdoctors or dead ancestors will not help the situation. The true giant will have won the battle.

DYNASTIES AND HUSTLERS

When loud whispers started circulating that the BBI will eventually make President Kenyatta Prime Minister and Raila Odinga President, people knowledgeable in world political affairs nicknamed the move, The Putin-Medvedev Agenda in Russia (The P-M Agenda).

In August 1999, Vladimir Putin was appointed acting Prime Minister of Russia by President Boris Yeltsin. In December the same year, Putin was made acting President; March 2000, he won first presidential election, and March 2004, the second term. In May 2008, Putin became Prime Minister due to the constitutional limits on him serving more than two consecutive terms. Dmitry Medvedev became President. In 2012, the presidential term was extended from four to six years and Putin won re-election. And May 2018, he won again and got a mandate to stay in power until 2024. A total of 25 years in power! Power interchanging hands several times between two persons as if they owned the country.

From the BBI's P-M Agenda, students of history recall the Russian Bolshevik Revolution of 1917 by peasants and workers led by Vladimir Lenin. The Revolution was against a Czarist regime of Nicholas II. Then there was the accession to power of Dictator Joseph Stalin after Lenin's death. Kindly read on. Three stories from Russia (Soviet Union) bear some interesting relation to the politics of the BBI.

Ivan Pavlov won the Nobel Peace Prize in physiology or medicine in 1904. He was the first Russian Nobel laureate. During his experiments that birthed what is known as Classical Conditioning (learning process), he discovered that dogs developed a hard-wired reflex in relation to feeding.

That, dogs became conditioned with time such that whenever they heard footsteps or saw the white lab coats of those who fed them, they began to salivate. In fact, when a bell was rang enough times before giving a dog a plate of food – it started to salivate at the sound of the bell rather than the sight of the food – salivating even before food was actually delivered!

Another memorable story was about Gregory Rasputin, nicknamed the Mad Monk, but who never took vows to become a monk. A self-proclaimed holy man, Rasputin claimed to help people resolve their spiritual crises although some believed he was an emissary from Satan. He also pretended to have some magical healing power and even took credit for the recovery of Tsar's son from a haemophilic condition.

Rasputin had found way to the Palace and became Csar's most trusted adviser to the extent of making recommendations for ministerial appointments. He was blamed for rapid economic decline in the country. Rasputin was once appointed the lamplighter charged with keeping the lamps that burned in front of religious icons in the Palace. He was assassinated by a group of officials opposed to his influence over the Csar.

The third story from the land of Vodka relates to space exploration. Majority of people know about the US National Aeronautics and Space Administration (NASA) programmes – foremost landing the first man on the moon, but few ever heard that the Russians actually were the one who sent the first person – Yuri Gagarin – in space. Not surprisingly, they also sent the first animal to orbit the earth, a dog! On the evening of 3 November, 1957, Sputnik 2, a Russian spaceship, blasted into space.

On board was a 3-year old stray female dog named Laika, plucked from a Moscow street and quickly trained for the trip. The animal rights defenders, including the British Society for Happy Dogs, had opposed the launch. Others called the mission monstrous, horrible and ethically wrong. Dispatched with one meal and only a seven-day oxygen supply to the excessive temperature in the spaceship, a frightened Laika died five hours into the flight.

Why did they opt for a female instead of a male dog? Or a stray rather than a domestic dog? Someone could have asked. On the 60th anniversary of Laika's death, her 90-year old biologist trainer told AFP News Agency: "We chose bitches because they don't have to raise a leg to urinate which means they need less space than the males. And we chose stray dogs because they are more resourceful and less demanding."[11]

Now, the assumed P-M Agenda between President Kenyatta and Raila aforementioned triple stories provides some lessons for the BBI era and conclude with a touch of the dynasties and rustlers issues. Every story, real or created has a moral story; and specifically the teachings go the BBI co-Principal, Raila.

Scientist Ivan Pavlov

In the past, when some Kenyans saw and heard Raila's footsteps as he climbed on a platform for a rally or danced to the *ndombolo*, they saw him wearing his trademark Nigerian attire, a god-father hat and a flywhisk in tow; heard the sound of his vuvuzela blown from his Kibra bedroom announcing a new round of "Mapambano" – they came out running like cheetahs to him, salivating for the supposed *sufuria za ugali* (political, economic and social benefits) like Pavlov's dogs only to be inducted into violence and death. Times have changed. Year 2022, the political Classical Conditioning will not work.

The Mad Monk

For long, Raila's supporters believed he was a larger than life person. They had no doubts that he held magical or spiritual healing powers like the Russians did to Rasputin. He changed names several times to

---

11   "Touching story of Laika the stray dog which became the world's first cosmonaut", *The Economic Times*, 04 November 2017.

showcase a transformation to higher political glory. (Gregory Rasputin changed his to Rasputin-Novyi, meaning New Rasputin.) Now Kenyans know better, going by the 40 years of hopeless experience. Their self-proclaimed healer has never attended any medical or theological institution, perhaps a medicine-man's lecture.

Dog Laika

Raila's political ambition had always been driven by experimenting, otherwise he would have become President since 1982. It has been a *pata potea* game. He treated his supporters like guinea pigs in a laboratory for his political experiments. He plucked young, hungry, jobless and less demanding men and women from the streets and put them in his political imaginary NASA spaceship heading for an imaginary Canaan. In Laika's case, animal rights groups protested her mistreatment in the name of scientific experiments. Today, Kenyans and more so the human rights advocates tell Raila in no uncertain terms that the helpless youth are not material for political space exploration.

The dynasties

Kenyans' deliberations on the subject of the P-M Agenda come 2022 mutated into something bigger. The BBI's main aim was to make Kenya a dynasty nation, it was becoming apparent. A country whose government would continue rotating between the Kenyatta-Odinga-Moi families' rule.

How did we find ourselves here? Kenya gained independence under the stewardship of Jomo Kenyatta. He was the country's first Prime Minister, one year later becoming President until his death in August 1978. From him was an interlude of 35 years of President Daniel Moi and Mwai Kibaki – before his son Uhuru assumed presidency on 9 March, 2013. Now Kenyatta II, completing his constitutional two-term tenure in August 2022 wanted to be the Prime Minister through the BBI door, the grapevine went.

Jaramogi Odinga became KANU Vice-President in 1960 and, at independence, was appointed Kenya first Vice-President. In 1966 he resigned the Vice-Presidency and from KANU to form the Kenya Peoples' Union (KPU). Fast forward, following the 1982 coup attempt, he was expelled from KANU (he had re-joined) and placed under house arrest.

In 1992, Jaramogi co-founded and became Chairman of the Forum for the Restoration of Democracy (FORD) and when it split into two, he formed Ford-Kenya on whose ticket he vied for the Presidency. He finished fourth. Jaramogi died in January 1994, having been in the opposition for considerable part of his life.

Jaramogi's son Raila was propelled to the limelight after the August 1982 coup attempt. He was arrested and detained. Except for the periods he was a Cabinet Minister, then Prime Minister, the rest of his political life has been out of the government. But having contested and failed the presidency several times, Raila now had manufactured his last bullet to make him President, the stories made rounds. The BBI was it.

Daniel arap Moi was Kenya's third Vice-President and thereafter President for 24 years from 1978 to 2002. Now his son Gideon wanted to be President.

"God moves in mysterious ways, his wonders to perform," so goes a hymn composed by William Cowper, a British poet who struggled throughout his life with depression, doubts and fears. President Kenyatta, Raila and Moi II may not have gone through much tribulations like most children of the hustlers, them having been brought up in 'high-class' families. However, the possibility of any of them being President /Prime Minister/Deputy President render Cowper's words truly prophetic in this particular case, at least.

Away for a moment from The P-M Agenda and to a study case of Cowper's statement come true. At 18, Ngina the daughter of Chief Muhoho wa Gatheca married Jomo Kenyatta, 57, as the third wife. At independence in 1963, she earned the title of 'Mama', denoting "Mother of the Nation." She bore four children, among them Uhuru Kenyatta in 1961. In the book, *Walking in Kenyatta's Struggles*, Duncan Ndegwa, former Central Bank of Kenya Governor writes of her: "Mama Ngina had literally gone from the village to State House ... Ngina's learning curve-into a lady of culture and elegance was steep, but we admired her resolve ... In the fullness of time, Mama Ngina's image blossomed in the eyes of the public as Mzee became Prime Minister and then President ..."[12]

---

12 Duncan Ndegwa, *Walking in Kenyatta's Struggles: My Story* (Nairobi: Kenya Leadership Institute, 2006).

Revisit from 1 June 1963 (first Madaraka Day), six months before the first Jamhuri to date. Ngina watched her husband being sworn in as the country's first Prime Minister. On 12 December, she became Kenya's ever first First Lady as Kenyatta became the first President.

On 9 April 2013, nine months before the 50th Jamhuri, Mama Ngina watched her son Uhuru being sworn-in as Kenya's fourth president. She literally returned to State House after 34 years, having previously occupied it for 15 years between 1963 and 1978. And on 12 December, 2013 (Kenya's Golden Jubilee) she witnessed the new President hoist the national flag on the same spot at Uhuru Gardens and plant a tree next to the one planted – 50 years ago – by the Republic's first President, his father. The First Mother, also described by *Forbes* magazine as one of the richest women in Africa, also watched as her son was inaugurated for his second term as President on 28 November 2017.

Well, some events in history defy the mind. For Mama Ngina, it has not been a politician making plans and campaigning for votes to be big. When blessings come knocking on the door, you don't start chasing them away with rocks. However, probably having no hand in The P-M Agenda, will she be a witness to Prime Minister/President Kenyatta's swearing-in late 2022?

Back to the BBI's much talked-about The P-M Agenda of dynasties. A dynasty is described by *Cambridge Dictionary* as a series of rulers or leaders who are all from the same family or a period where a country is ruled by them. Dictionary.com defines it as a sequence of rulers from the same family, stock, or group.

The Nehru family in India is perhaps the best example of those families who 'won big' in politics. The family was in charge of the country for 40 of the 60 years of independence, a total of five generations. Motilal Nehru was a prominent leader of Indian independence movement. His son, Jawaharlal Nehru, became the country's first Prime Minister. His only child Indira Gandhi became the third Prime Minister. Sonia Gandhi, wife of Rajiv Gandhi, Indira's eldest son, was elected the President of India National Congress. And Rahul Gandhi, the only son of Rajiv and Sonia, became the Vice-President and General-Secretary of the Congress. Elsewhere, there is the Kennedy and Bush family in the USA, the Marcos in the Philippines, among others who dominated the running of their respective countries at one time or another.

The picture of dynasties resembles a merry-go-round where a revolving machine on a continuous cycle loads and unloads, loads and unloads relatives to top leadership positions. The Kenyan case can be summarised thus: First President Jomo Kenyatta ruled for 15 years as Prime Minister and President; his son Uhuru was a Deputy Prime Minister for five years and President headed for 10 years. Jaramongi Odinga was the county's first Vice-President. His son Raila Odinga was Prime Minister for five years. Daniel arap Moi, Kenya's third Vice-President then President for 24 years and his son Gideon was Member of Parliament (MP) for ten years and now Senator. These three sons, 60 years after Kenya's independence are gravitating around the country's political pot to dish amongst themselves positions of President, Deputy President and Prime Minister. The fathers did their patriotic job to free Kenya from the colonial yoke; Jomo Kenyatta was detained. These personalities formed political parties and attended the Lancaster talks for independence, among others initiatives. But why always their sons and not the rest of us?

The Kenyatta II-Odinga II-Moi II trinity is all about consolidating the dynasties and ensuring their long-term capture of the Kenyan people. To achieve this, a plan to exclude Deputy President William Ruto from the succession race was cleverly executed. The result was the 9-letter word, Handshake, on the 9th day of the third month of year Twenty Eighteen. Tom Mshindi, elaborated on this:

> …Jomo died in power and his trusted assistant Daniel arap Moi took over. A man of modest means in 1978 when he became President, he died fabulously wealthy. He used his office to build a Moi dynasty that had vast resources and which had the largesse to buy the loyalty of the wider Kalenjin nation because he knew that in Kenya, political power must rest on tribal loyalty.

> But he also knew that he needed the pillar of support of another key tribe and he chose to repay Jomo Kenyatta's confidence by protecting the latter family and actively grooming a successor from the Kikuyu tribe. Uhuru Kenyatta confessed as much in his moving homage to the retired President, saying that the Kenyatta's owe their riches, and him his political career, to the late Moi.

> So, Jomo Kenyatta allowed the Odinga dynasty to thrive because they supported him in those early days. Moi nurtured the Kenyattas

because he owed his presidency to Mzee. Now Uhuru and Raila must pay back and give Gideon Moi the support he requires to consolidate the Moi dynasty.

And they will give it to him. No so much because of himself but because they need him to boost their arsenal against Deputy President William Ruto.

The Odinga and Kenyatta dynasties do not want Dr Ruto to ascend to the throne because he will be re-writing a script that they do not want interfered with. Gideon Moi fits the bill because he is of the right pedigree. Brought up rich and in power, he is amenable to cut deals that allow the bourgeoisie to consolidate power won and kept on the tyranny of the numbers of the dominant tribes.

Which is why a lot of resources – yes State resources – will be used to ensure that Gideon Moi upsets the William Ruto dominance in the Rift Valley. Any pretender to the throne, like the Deputy President, must be made to understand that unless you are an insider in the dynasties, you can only serve at their pleasure. That is what the Uhuru-Raila handshake consolidated.[13]

To many world citizens, the subject about dynasties always converges into a subject of the class. The governor and the governed; the chosen few and the un-chosen; lucky and unlucky; children of God and those of the lesser gods, liars and the lied to; the elite and hoi polloi. Thus, you find from the same family a political or power chain.

Starting from the bottom of the ladder there is the Mzee wa Nyumba Kumi, village chief, then an MCA, company CEO/Director, Principal Secretary, Ambassador, Cabinet Secretary, Senator, Governor, and Prime Minister or President, not necessarily in that order of seniority. And they get to interchange these positions amongst themselves regularly. And when they organise a get-together in the countryside, it is like a clan government, another seat of power. Here discussions will rotate around who among the citizens qualifies for appointment, transfer or firing from the government, who will get tenders, and so forth. At the venue you would think a Mercedes or Toyota showroom has shifted base to their rural homes.

---

13 Tom Mshindi, "Gideon Moi now a powerful mover in Kenya's dynasties", *Sunday Nation*, 16 February, 2020.

Why do some people effortlessly always find themselves in top leadership positions? Were they conceived through super-sperms and super-ova? Is it because of their level of education, through the peoples' will or by God's design? Or are the hustlers, the supposed children of the lesser gods condemned eternally to the very bottom of the leadership ladder?

In the event that The P-M Agenda is real, what choices shall Kenyans have? First, there is President Kenyatta. He promised Deputy Ruto support for 2022 and the world is witness to this. Fathers of nations are not known to backtrack on their promises. And we are urged, "Above all, my brothers, do not swear – not by heaven or by earth or by anything else. Let your 'Yes' be yes and your 'No', no, or you will condemn" (James 5:2. In case President Kenyatta decide to stick to the Premier position desire and keep his words about supporting Ruto, perhaps his better option will be to resurrect the UhuRuto bromance of "Kusema na Kutenda", Brother William, and maybe spray a dose of Mudavadi-Kalonzo-Wetangula-Moi II. This axis could work. That leaves Raila.

Unfortunately, any scenario where Raila will be part and parcel and whoever else is brought on board, the situation will best be described using US President George W. Bush's terminology in his State of the Union address on 29 January 2002: An Axis of Evil. There could be a way, though. Close to six times, Raila has claimed that his election victory was stolen through rigging. This time, the BBI made him the man on top of the game. What shall make him not rig in 2022 with all the power on his hands?

> …As an individual, I am totally fed up with this narrative of rigging. This country's instability is closely tied to supposed electoral injustices perpetrated on Mr. Odinga. In 1992, 1997, 2007 and 2013 Mr. Odinga claims to have had his personal victory, or that of the party he represented, stolen. Why these tricks are successfully played on him, election cycle after election cycle? "And as a matter of extreme exasperation, why doesn't he also rig, if that is the only way a Kenyan election is won?
>
> And if every time he runs for office he is unsuccessful because of rigging, why can't he find an alternative way to serve his country? Has he considered the possibility that his famed political skills notwithstanding that he is probably not good at winning elections –

maybe because he does not know how to protect them from rigging – and that perhaps his talent could be more productively utilized in other endeavours?

In Mr. Odinga's team are some of Kenya's heaviest brains. If they can't find a way to get him elected, including preventing rigging, then he will probably never be elected. I am so tired of this whining, which has gone on all my life, that if Mr Odinga complains one more time that he has been rigged, I should be among the people who will be throwing stones at him…[14]

It would pay for the BBI to touch base properly and get people's feelings about The P-M Agenda. Meanwhile, some verses attributed to Benjamin Franklin in *The Way to Wealth in the 14th Century* will inspire, because for the unwanted want, the BBI could lose the country:

> For want of a nail the shoe was lost.
> For want of a shoe the horse was lost.
> For want of a horse the rider was lost.
> For want of a rider the battle was lost.
> For want of a battle the kingdom was lost.
> And all for the want of a horse-shoe nail.

Finally, Kenya is headed for very trying times. Instead of being told that the BBI is what they have been waiting for, what Kenyans are reading between the lines is that The P-M Agenda is the long awaited Messiah. Instead of been told that they are about to make history through the BBI, what is apparent is that the Agenda is what is being pushed to be historic.

The P-M Agenda opened a battlefront between the hustlers and non-hustlers. But sadly, leaders are the last to know what the people want. Who believed that Barack Obama could win the US presidential race? On 4 November 2008, Obama defeated the Republican candidate Senator John McCain, eventually becoming the first African-American President in the history of USA. The following day, 5 November, Nancy Gibbs wrote in *Time* about the victory:

> Barack Hussein Obama did not win because of the colour of his skin.
> Nor did he win in spite of it. He won because at a very dangerous

---

14 Mutuma Mathiu, "Creating uncertainty and fear ahead of elections unforgivable", *Daily Nation*, 16 June, 2017.

moment in the life of a still young country, most people than have ever spoken before came together to try to save it. And that was a victory on its own.[15]

Gibbs wrote on: "Some princes are born in Palaces, some are born in mangers. But a few are born in the imagination, out of scraps of history and hope:"[16]

In December 2008, *Time's* Michael Elliot likened Obama win to the famous Butterfly of Chaos Theory. By all standards, The P-M Agenda looks like a recipe for a disaster. It might appear minute, but could explode like a bomb in due time. Tables can be overturned. The Agenda could precipitate the Butterfly of Chaos Theory effect whose beating wings can cause a storm thousands of miles away – a small change in initial condition can create significant outcomes. The Theory teaches people to expect surprises, the unpredictable, unexpected. Pick the key words in Gibbs' and Elliot's articles and construct a possible Kenya 2022: Born in a manger... From scraps of history and hope... dangerous moment ... people came together to save a young nation... Butterfly wings... and that was the victory. The Butterfly Theory could be a blessing in disguise for Deputy President William Ruto. His seemingly small, weak wings could cause a political storm across the country ahead of 2022.

---

15 Nancy Gibb, "How Obama Rewrote the Book'", *Time*, Wednesday, 05 November, 2008.

16   Ibid.

CHAPTER EIGHT

On Governance Credentials, Raila is Exceedingly Limited

Can people really know, for sure, how something started, where it started, why, what for, who by, Really know what was going on in the heart of the person who starts confusions, looks for them, or undoes or ruins conversations? Or is it impossible to grab on to the beginning of things in life, when you get to that beginning you see after all that same beginning was the end of another beginning and then, if you go on like this, backwards and forwards, you see that the thread of life can't be broken, even if it is rotten at some point, it always mends itself at another point, it grows, it strays, flees, advances, turns, stops, disappears, appears…

Jose Luandino Vieira,
Angolan writer in *Lumanda*

Dr Jekyll and Mr Hyde: Two extreme personalities in one

Immediately after the Harambee House handshake between President Uhuru Kenyatta and Raila Odinga on 9 March 2018, and the road to the BBI was paved, loud whispers started to emerge; that, the whole affair was largely manufactured to make Raila Odinga either Prime Minister or President. A pipe dream?

The saying that the sky is the limit is actually meant to motivate people to sweat more on their endeavours. Eliud Kipchoge told the world that *no human is limited* and went on to become the first human in history to conquer a marathon in less than two hours. Can he use the same catchphrase and determination, for instance, to run the same distance, say in one hour or a minute?

Humans are limited to some extent. In the land of Babylon, people unveiled their BBI, started building an ambitious tower reaching the skies. "This will weld us together," they proudly comforted themselves, "and keep us from scattering all over the world." At some point, God came around and said: "Look if they are able to accomplish all these when they have just begun to exploit their linguistic and political unity, just think of what they will do later!" So God scattered them all over the earth and henceforth stopped the Tower of Babel (confusion) project.

A beautiful chance comes once in a lifetime, they say. In 2008, Raila became Prime Minister when Mwai Kibaki was the President. Now, he was at the very heartbeat away from the presidency. Earlier he had declared, *Kibaki Tosha*! The whole country was behind him. Even the hitherto hostile region of Central Kenya welcomed him as a hero during visits. People there called him *Njamba*. But raw ambitions kill. He probably thought Kibaki was a weakling just like Charles Njonjo considered President Moi a passing cloud. Sir, not so fast. He became a thorn in the flesh of Kibaki's administration. He gave Kibaki restless night.

Raila had the guts to claim that, "even toddlers and mad men know that I was the one who won the presidential election" and also called Kibaki administration "Jua Kali and primitive," never mind that he was a member of the same government. The rest is history.

Now, is it remotely possible for Raila to be elevated either to Prime Minister or President from his current status, history and databank late

2022 courtesy of the BBI? The handshake and the BBI gave people an assignment to interrogate the person of Raila. How can a person suddenly resurrect from a political death and easily manage to mess the Jubilee Party and the government that was a darling of the people? No, this man died a real political death ages ago, it is his ghost that keeps on coming back. His is the Ghost who walks. Countless People's Assemblies and opinion polls experts sprouted across the country. Raila's name trended as No. 1 topic. In market places, workplaces, homes… even in dreams he became the most discussed and sighted personality.

Isn't the BBI the Tower of Confusion that its continued construction will force the voters, the voice of God to scatter its builders to the four corners of the wind sooner or later? Came out a top prediction.

Finally the people resolved that Raila carried numerous serious leadership constraints in his basket that it was by God's grace that he found himself in the National Assembly, as a Cabinet Minister, and wonders of wonders, a Prime Minister. However much they tried to change the meaning of the word impossible in the dictionary it remained just that: Impossible.

RAILA'S GOVERNANCE HANDICAP

Following is a journey through 16 selected leadership constraints which shall seal Raila's fate in the 2022 polls.

I. Dr Jekyll and Mr. Hyde

You will never meet God or Satan in physical form on earth or anywhere else. Yet both live within us. The trick lies in trying to choose or balance between the two. This fact was perfectly demonstrated by Scottish writer, Louis Stevenson, in *The Strange Case of Dr. Jekyll and Mr. Hyde*, first published in 1886.

Stevenson's novel is about the battle between good and evil; a split personality of moving from one extreme to another. Jekyll, 50-year old, was a highly respected doctor in London. He was sociable, attended church and would invite friends for a meal in his house. This was outwardly during the day. At night, he transformed into Mr. Hyde – a violent madman. A cruel and ruthless murderer even accused of killing an MP.

The 19th century story is strongly relevant to the BBI. Raila is a 2-in-1, double-hearted, double-faced person. While his one portion would be rated 30 per cent positive the other will score 70 per cent negative. It is a strange case that would interest theologians, medical practitioners, economists, patriots/nationalists and even PhD students.

II. Hell in Kenya

August 1-2, 1982 failed coup. Kenyans remember the injuries and deaths of both civilians and soldiers. Human blood. Orphaned children, widows and widowers. Women and girls raped in front of relatives. Broken marriages. Asian women committed suicide after rape. Business community's shops looted and destroyed. Some closed permanently or auctioned. Motorists stoned. Tourists and investors took off. Economy crumbled. Loss of youth jobs. Brand Kenya's name stained internationally.

Meanwhile, Raila & Company had made Head of State Moi hide in a bush like a wild animal during the failed coup. Henceforth, the attempt brought in the worst dictatorship in history under President Moi's government. Meanwhile, graves of the loved ones are still visible in home compounds and public cemeteries.

2007/08, June 2016, 2017 violence: More or less like in the above. Maimed and dead people. Human blood. Orphaned children, widows and widowers. Burned houses, farms and livestock. Women and girls raped. Broken marriages. HIV/AIDS infections. Business community's shops looted and destroyed. Some closed and auctioned. Motorists stoned. Pedestrians mugged and beaten. Tourists and investors left country. Lives of thousands of IDPs. Economy collapsed. Job losses. Secession threats and unconstitutional swearing in. Brand Kenya reputation soiled globally.

Raila succeeded in "overthrowing" President Moi on second attempt three dozen years at Kibaki Tosha. The vulture is indeed a patient bird. Raila also made history by becoming the first leader in Kenya ever accused of treason twice. Again, graves of loved ones are still visible in home compounds and public cemeteries. Nearly 40 years down the line many more horrible memories about these periods continue to haunt the country.

III. Children crying to their Jesus

Children don't vote in a general election, but they have the capacity to do so by "osmosis". They are ruthless influencers of the actual voters. Besides, they are the country's most valuable asset. We were all children once, weren't we? Baby-making also demonstrates the greatest partnership between God and humans. "With God's help, I have created a man." Exclaimed the world's first First Lady, Eve, after giving birth to her first born son." Eve did not even give credit to husband Adam.

Who would wish to hurt this partnership? Why would the thirst for winning an election and attaining power be a reason good enough to have children maimed, killed or orphaned? Or going hungry, being rained on or missing school while in IDP camps? Jesus called them the little angels and said that the Kingdom of Heaven is theirs and anyone who welcomes a little child welcomes Him. And when there is a danger don't you begin taking care of the children from the youngest up?

In the novel, *The Shack*, William P. Young vigorously defends the children and argues that even madmen will think twice before harming them:

> Something in the hearts of most human beings simply cannot abide pain inflicted on the innocent, especially children. Even broken men serving in the worst correctional facilities will often first take out their own rage on those who have caused suffering to children. Even in such a world of relative morality, causing harm to a child is still considered absolutely wrong. Period! (p. 55)

The book goes on to suggest that women as leaders would be superior custodians to children than men who supposedly have been the genesis of the much suffering in the world:

> I've always wondered why men have been in charge. Males seem to be the cause of so much of the pain in the world. They account for most of the crimes, and many of those are perpetrated against women and -children... The world in many ways would be a much calmer and gentler place if women ruled. There would have been far fewer children sacrificed to the gods of greed and power. (p. 157)

Yes, children don't go to the ballot box yet they have eyes and ears. They know a bad leader when they see one. And when the images of Raila's struggle for power come back to their mind, they raise their eyes up to their Jesus and do "A Child's Prayer" like the 13-year old Anne Frank in *The Diary of a Young Girl* (by Anne Frank) reflecting on the atrocities of World War II:

> … I see the world gradually being turned into wilderness. I hear the ever approaching thunder which will destroy us too, I can feel the sufferings of millions, and yet, if I look up into heavens, I think that it will all come right, that this cruelty too will end, and that peace and tranquillity will return again…[1]

Children know suffering cannot cease with Raila, peace cannot return when he is around doing politics.

Good. Children make up more than half of the country's population. Little, sweet, beautiful beings. Proudly growing up, loving their country with passion. Visions of a great future. Like eagles, waiting to soar above the clouds and beyond the skies. They are the custodians of the Kenyan Family Tree. Valuable treasures.

Year 2022, more than one million young people will flash back to September 2017. Then, they were just children, pupils and students in schools. Moi Girl's School fire tragedy had claimed the lives of nine students. At around the same time, Raila was calling for a delay in national exams involving 1.6 million learners in favour of repeat general election. "*Kwani watoto watakufa kama hawatafanya mtihani?*" (Shall the children die if they miss to sit their exams?) Raila roared to the shock of the nation. To Raila, the race to State House was more important and urgent than a traumatised country or the children's future. His reaction was the heartlessness of the highest order.

Behold! Come 2022, these very same beings will be over 18 years; adults in possession of voting cards. Raila will be pleading with them to vote in him President or Prime Minister. "*Kwani Raila atakufa kama hatakuwa Rais au Waziri Mkuu?*" (Shall Raila die – when we deny him votes – if he fails to become President or Prime Minister?) They will respond in unison recalling his statement exactly five years back; tit for tat.

---

1   Anne Frank, *The Diary of a Young Girl*, definitive ed. (London: Penguin Group, 1997), p. 330.

IV. The youth: "Jeshi ti ngenu"

"We refuse to believe that there are insufficient funds in the great vaults of opportunity of this nation." They echo Martin Luther King Jr.

Rev King Jr was concerned that 100 years after emancipation proclamation was signed, Americans particularly the blacks were not guaranteed the unalienable rights of life, liberty and pursuit of happiness. On that day 28 August, 1963, he and others organised the March on Washington "to dramatize a shameful condition."

Rev King told the American people that their country had given the Negro people a bad cheque, which has come back marked "insufficient funds". He said: "We've come to cash the cheque, a cheque that will give us upon demand the riches of freedom and the securities of justice". He talked of the fierce "urgency of now", in fact mentioning, "Now is the time" four times! Then he proclaimed, "I Have a Dream!"

Kenya is endowed with abundance of God's blessings and the marvellous work of *wananchi* yet six decades after attaining independence, one dark deep mighty forest still exist and growing … the forest of millions of educated, able and patriotic youth.

On 6 June, 1966, Robert F. Kennedy gave a story: A young monk began the Protestant Reformation, a young general extended an empire from Macedonia to the border of the earth, and a young woman reclaimed the territory of France. It was a young Italian explorer who discovered the New World and at 32 years old Thomas Jefferson proclaimed that all men are equal… "These persons moved the world, and so can we all…"

A young person in the paragraph appears five times. And we are told, they moved the world. The youth of Kenya who can move the country have been engulfed in a great swampy forest for long. This is where the 5th President of the Republic will have to shine his torch on most, to subdue the forest and rescue the youth, as a matter of priority.

One day Prof Muhammad Yunus of Bangladesh was in his university class. An economist, banker and civil society leader, he looked outside. Across the country, about 1.5 million people had died of famine. Disturbed, he questioned himself: "What is the use of teaching students elegant economic theories while people are dying in the village of hunger?" That was in 1974.

Prof Yunus went to the villagers. He learned their struggles at close range. Like the Greek Archimedes, he found his Eureka! Using his savings, he started lending to poor farmers. The banks always required collateral and termed the poor un-creditworthy, thus locking them out.

In October 1983, Prof Yunus opened Grameen Bank (Bank of Villages) to give micro credit without collateral condition. By 2007, the bank had issued USD 6.38 billion to 7.4 million borrowers, 97 per cent of them women, to help them start small businesses. By uplifting masses from the vicious cycle of poverty and hunger, the bank's microfinance model inspired similar efforts in more than 100 countries and was adapted by leading universities.

Besides diversifying from helping the poor in farming, bamboo furniture industry, fisheries and irrigation projects, Prof Yunus went on to knitwear, telephony and cyber sectors and additionally ventured into giving beggars small loans to hawk merchandise as well as loaning students for their studies. To date, Grameen Bank issues more than USD 1.5 billion new loans every year.

In 2006, jointly with the bank, Prof Yunus won the Nobel Peace Prize "for their efforts to create economic and social development from below." At the awarding ceremony on 13 October, the Norwegian Nobel Committee's citation also noted that: "…lasting peace cannot be achieved unless large population groups find ways in which to break out of poverty" and that, "Every single individual on earth has both the potential and the right to live a decent life".

The youth in Kenya, like Prof Yunus' students, do not want to hear about 'economic' theories from the politicians anymore. They have read the TJRC, Vision 2030, the Constitution, the Ndung'u Report, various campaign manifestos and now the BBI. To them, they did not elect leaders to write PhD thesis for them to mark.

Deep inside their hearts, the youth desire to see BBIs of opportunities. Even Angel Gabriel (leave alone Raila) becoming President or Prime Minister of Kenya (angels developed deep fear of cohabiting with humans since the day some youth fed with drugs and *kumi kumi* illicit brews threatened to rape them) will not quench their thirst in the absence of their emancipation. Remember, "It's the economy, stupid!" The bottom line is a wealthy country for their prosperity.

Vijana wamechanuka. Sometimes after the 2013 General Election, Susan Kariuki-Mwongera, CEO of the Youth Agenda, stated:

> We have stopped being used. A lot of young people aspired for positions of leadership in the last election and they were elected. Three Senators and one Governor are below 35. The National Assembly has 23 MPs who are also below 35 and 481 County Representatives…We have placed our hope and faith in them to deliver the youth agenda.[2]

The youth of Kenya have hit the Road to Enlightenment. They were not born to be stone throwers, looters, muggers, arsonists and battlers of police officers. Their career was not to be street protestors and demonstrators. They now want work in the public and private sectors. They want meaningful, genuine work in any sector. They want to be in charge of their country. Raila Odinga's DNA of using them like Saddam Hussein's Weapons of Mass Destruction (WMD) does not fit their aspirations.

Kenya is a youthful country. Data from the Kenya National Bureau of Statistics (KNBS) census 2019 showed that the youth – those aged between 18 and 35 years – stood at 35.7 million, which translates to 75 per cent of a population of 47.6 million people.

Youth unemployment stands at 39 per cent. Approximately one million youth enter the job market annually to compete for about 500,000 job opportunities mostly available in the formal sector. This is a dangerous time-bomb.

When empowered, youth are a country's gold mine. They become the strength, wealth creators and drivers of innovation in a nation. Failure to provide them with jobs results in a silent revolution that is brewing in Kenya. Tracy Chapman, American artist sang: "Don't you know? They're talkin" 'bout a revolution. It sounds like a whisper… poor people gonna rise up…" The Arab Spring (Jasmine Revolution) was triggered by the 26-year old Mohammed Bouaziz on 17 December, 2010, a *mkokoteni* pusher vegetable vendor when he set himself on fire protesting arrest by authorities for lack of a permit. This act became a catalyst for political upheavals that swept several countries in the

---

2   Emeka-Mayaka Gekara, Susan Kariuki: The SMS I'll never delete", *Daily Nation*, 13 August, 2013.

region, toppling several presidents in the process. In recent times the term, "*Jeshi ti ngenu* (in Gĩkũyũ language, the masses are discontented) has evolved to be the signature for the youth. The youth are unhappy. The Kenya Spring, the silent revolution that is gradually developing, is one where millions of youth are being swallowed into idleness, drugs, cheap banned alcohol, prostitution, petty and big-time crime and terrorism.

There is enough money and job opportunities for the Kenyan youth. Tame the corruption culture as a priority. As Prime Minister, Raila was the overall in charge of an ambitious World Bank multi-billion project, Kazi kwa Vijana (jobs for the youth). Initially, the Bank offered a grant of Kes 4.3 billion for the youth to get gainful employment, internship and training. Soon, an audit review revealed misappropriation of millions of shillings. The Bank cancelled the funding and asked for a refund of the amount spent so far.

Look out of the window. Millions of jobless, idling, hungry, angry youth on the verge of losing hope. If Prof Yunus can single-handedly uplift millions of women from poverty, how come a whole government cannot do the same for the youth? Raila frustrated a World Bank model that could have grown into Kenya's Grameen Bank. Now he is waiting for the 2022 General Election to ask the same desperate youth to vote for him. And when things turn upside down for him, he will urge them into the streets to do criminal acts. Mathew 18:6: "But if you cause one of these little ones who trusts in me to fall into sin, it would be better for you to have a large millstone tied around your neck and be drowned in the depths of the sea." Raila's DNA is not fit for youth empowerment.

V. From women, we all came

First, a question: since the world began, how many people have been born on earth? Not easy to approximate. But according to estimates by the Population Reference Bureau (PRB), from the time *Homo sapiens* (modern man) walked the earth some 50,000 years ago, more than 108 billion members of our species have been born. (PRB forecast that by 2050 about 113 billion people will have ever lived on earth).

Another question: from where were all these human beings conceived and nurtured particularly in the early stages of development?

In women's wombs, these billions souls were manufactured and provided air, food and shelter for whole nine months. The women also breastfed the infants and care-gave them until they became of age. So, is mother more important than father in the entire business of creating a human being and seeing him to maturity? No. A father will say that he contributed 23 chromosomes, the same number the mother gave at fertilisation and also did a big job in child upbringing. (By 2050, 30 years ahead 5 billion beings will have passed through the women's bodies!)

Then comes the irony of all ironies. The same woman who is a major factor in the creation and growth of a human being, endowed with so much strength and stamina even to withstand labour pain – said to be the equivalent of fracturing 25 bones at the same time – for ages has been portrayed by man as inferior. But she has consistently been insisting: I am a man's equal. God meant me to be so.

Travel back in time, some 160 years: A shabbily-dressed, illiterate, six-foot black woman known for her fierce fight against slavery and support for women's rights stands up to address a convention 29 May, 1851, in the US. With a baritone voice, she proclaims that women can do the same tasks, if not better, as men. "Look at my arms!" She roars. "I have ploughed and planted and gathered into barns and no man could head me! Ain't I a woman?"

Apparently in anger, Sojourner Truth goes on to challenge the men: "…Den dat little man in black dar, he says women can't have as much rights as men 'cause Christ wasn't a woman! Whar did your Christ come from? Whar did your Christ come from? From God and a woman! Man had nothing to do with Him."

The now energised Women's Rights Defender explains her case further: "If de fust woman God ever made was strong to turn de world upside down all alone, dese women togedder ought to be able to turn it back, and get it right side up again! And now dey is asking to do it, de men better let 'em…"

At another gathering in 1858, the congregation accuses Truth of being a man due to her deep voice and amazing courage. They demand that she bare her breast to prove her sex. Truth abruptly rip open her blouse in front of the crowd and declare, "Here, then, see for yourselves!" This black American woman almost two centuries ago was fighting against a tradition that held women as inferior to men and therefore deserved lesser rights.

And in Kenya, fast forward, when the colonial government arrested freedom fighter Harry Thuku in Nairobi, 15 March, 1922, thousands of people demonstrated outside the police station demanding his release. During the stand-off, the men appeared to take a back seat. Then Mary Muthoni Nyanjiru stepped forward, admonishing men as faint-hearted. "You, take my dress and give me your trousers," she commanded them. "You men are cowards! What are you waiting for? Our leader is in there – let's go get him." Other women ululated and jeered at the seemingly men's helplessness. Nyanjiru stripped naked and walked towards the station. In the confrontation and bloodbath that ensued, more than 150 Kenyans were killed, Nyanjiru being the first. Nyanjiru was demonstrating to the world that in the face of foreign domination, even women had what it took to protect and defend their country.

Many years forward, times for women have changed. They have continued to prove that they can. Thanks to their own awakening, women movements on their rights and global initiatives like the UN Universal Declaration on Human Rights (UDHR) and UN Sustainable Development Goals (SDGs) 2030, women's rights and empowerment agenda is today an important component in all governments' plans. On 8 March, 2020, was the Silver Jubilee, the 25th commemoration of the Beijing Declaration and the Platform for Action unanimously adopted by world nations in 1995 – advancement of women and girls: Action for equality, development and peace. Meanwhile, the handshake in Kenya marked the 2nd anniversary the following day, 9 March. Back in 1975, the UN declared every March 8 as the International Women's Day.

In Kenya as elsewhere, the government has been keen in recognising women's potential, to quote Chinese leader Mao Zedong, "Time has changed, and today men and women are equal, and, women hold up half the sky." The Kenya Constitution, Vision 2030 and the BBI all have formulations on matters women.

At the Women Deliver Conference held on 3-6 June 2019 in Vancouver, Canada, President Kenyatta emphasised the government's position on the crucial role women play in national development and called for more room for their participation. "We need to make the society understand that women are as capable as men. We have to create an enabling environment and the opportunity for them to serve," he said. Earlier at the World Thinking Day, celebrated annually under the auspices of the World Association of Girl Guides and Girl Scouts, on 22 February 2019, President Kenyatta hoped that one day Kenya will have a female Head of State noting that "some of my best ministers are women."

Like other nations on earth, Kenya is on the run. Millions of her women are still dragging behind men on social, economic and political issues. They have been waiting long enough. Now they have roused. They want their rights respected, defended and promoted. They want to be equal partners with men in moving their country forward. To use Pope Francis' words spoken sometimes in 2018, the Kenyan women want a journey of "walking, working and praying together" with their men counterparts.

So what kind of a president and /or prime minster are the millions of Kenyans looking for from the 2022 election? They know that the polls will be a two-horse race between William Ruto and Raila. In their bags, the women already have Ruto's record and vision for them, a symbol of women progress who will help them accomplish dreams and destines. What about Raila? What is his scorecard?

First, women are not selfish. They don't put themselves first, but their children. There is nothing closer to a woman's heart than her children, there is something very special about the bond between them. So the women look at Raila's CV. There is nothing that breaks a woman's heart than the death of her child, particularly manmade. They remember all Raila's politics as death chambers for their children. Women are terribly frightened by the sight of human blood, especially of their children. To them, Raila's political activities have been butcheries for their children. Women are damn strong and courageous, but are stiff scared of violence. Raila's politics always brings violence around. Women are disturbed when their children sleep with empty stomachs. They recall the Maize Scandal where millions of shillings was embezzled and Raila was implicated. Women get sleepless nights when they see their children idling, doing drugs and alcohol, sell their bodies (girls), enter into crime and terrorism – because of lack of jobs which can be easily created. They flash back to Raila's hand in the collapse of the World Bank-funded Kazi kwa Vijana mega project. Remember to a mother, infants, teenagers, adults – are all her children, ages irrespective.

Like all women globally, Kenyan women loves a stable marriage. A person who helps break a marriage is like Judas Iscariot. Raila used the handshake and the BBI to break the hitherto unshakeable political marriage of President Kenyatta and Deputy Ruto at the Jubilee Party household. Women are happiest in a stable country, for their children's sake. They saw Raila almost bringing the country in the brink of civil war during the 2007-08 post-election violence and on 30 January, 2018, self-swearing of the People's President.

Women know themselves as having a monopoly of gossip, Raila is a master gossiper and hatemonger. More important, women are born deeply religious. They admire a leader of faith. Raila is definitely not. And finally, the women of Kenya are patriotic and committed to their country and children, are able, performers and deserves their human rights of women in full. They require space. Sojourner Truth could as well have been addressing Raila: "Den dat little man in black dar…" That is the gospel truth. Raila's DNA is unfit for emancipation of the Kenyan women, scorecard: *Ziii*.

VI. The elderly flash back

They are children of two worlds. They got a bitter taste of 70 years of British occupation. They witnessed the crossing of River Jordan to Independent Kenya. They are the country's library of wisdom and nationalism.

The elderly recall the independence struggle. In particular, the four-year resistance to the British where 20,000 Mau Mau members and 2,000 civilians died, 1,090 Africans hanged and 150,000 of them detained without trial in 150 concentration camps, at one time rounding up a million people in 804 villages. The Wazee saw violence, deaths, torture and destruction at their best! The thought traumatises them to date.

At almost 60 years into independence, the senior citizens wonder: Is Kenya Not Yet Uhuru (see Jaramongi Odinga's book)? Why all the violence, destruction, blood and deaths particularly of young people, untold evil associated with Raila Odinga's politics? *Kwani Raila ni nani?* By nature, the young are supposed to bury the old, but in Raila's world the old have been burying their young ones in thousands. *Wa kwanza kuzaliwa anakuwa wa mwisho kufa* and vice versa provides a sad state of affairs that is against the natural law.

VII. The abandoned Christians

They constantly recall one of Jesus' best parables, Mathew 25:42: "For I was hungry and you wouldn't feed me; thirsty and you wouldn't give me anything to drink; a stranger and you refused me hospitality; naked and you wouldn't cloth me; sick and in prison and you wouldn't visit me." During these instances, Raila was an MP, Minister or Prime Minister and he was unwilling or incapable to be a responsible leader. And Jesus replied: "I tell you the truth, whatever you did not do for one of the least of these, you did not do for me."

VIII. Supporters bite the dust!

Sometimes God can just sit back amused by how people choose their journeys blindly. He whispers to Raila's followers: "Choices have consequences" and "limited contact," or "keep political distance to avoid Covid-19" remember these words? But they tell him, "Wherever he goes we will go…his gods shall be our gods ".This has been Raila's political supporters' motto for the last 40 years, warnings notwithstanding.

The supporters now regret the failed Canaan's promise. After years of gruelling trek, suffering, sacrifice and hope, their leader abandoned them on 9 March 2018 just before crossing River Jordan and joined the Jubilee House through the Handshake. Why didn't they join KANU, TNA or Jubilee parties? They wonder now. They accuse themselves and recall their comrades in another continent thousands of years back: "Would to God we had died by the hand of the Lord in the land of Egypt… For ye have brought us forth into this wilderness, to kill the whole assembly with hunger" (Exodus 16:3).

With deep hurt, the supporters try to digest the biblical warning of "beware of the false prophets in sheep's clothing". Former President Moi's advice come into mind: "*Siasa mbaya, maisha mbaya*" (Bad politics, birth bad life), and "*Mtajikaanga na mafuta yenu wenyewe kama nguruwe*" (You will fry yourselves in your own oil like swine).

Turning to history the shocking truth reveals itself. In Hebrew language NASA means "to deceive greatly in plain sight for all to see; to lead astray, mentally delude; morally seduce; a primitive root". What a revelation!

Too bad. Raila's supporters must be remembering all the political vehicles their Baba had driven them in; happy optimistic passengers on board. FORD (Forum for the Restoration of Democracy), NDP (National Development Party), LDP (Liberal Democratic Party), CORD (Coalition for the Restoration of Democracy), ODM (Orange Democratic Movement) and a while ago NASA (National Super Alliance). Then he deserted NASA claiming that it was just meant for the 2017 General Election. His left leg was now back to ODM and the right one migrated to the Jubilee Party. Would he totally defect to the Jubilee Party? Well, some men's culture of polygamous political marriage was quite puzzling. The moment a woman fails to conceive, she is thrown out of the door and another one is brought into the homestead. And the game continues forever.

What is in a name? Raila supporters notes that the American NASA Apollo 11 landing on the moon was celebrating its 50th anniversary in 2019. The spaceship had brought back to earth 400 kg of moon rocks, pebbles, sand and dust. Afterwards the worst news came in. Following painstaking analysis of the loot in laboratories, no evidence of human life was found on the moon, past or present. Like the NASA moons voyage, Raila's NASA brought nothing back of interest to his supporter's well-being, for now or the future. In Kiswahili, the word "*naswa*" means to get nabbed, trapped, like an antelope in a snare waiting to become meat for family dinner. Raila has been truly a spine-chilling liability to his supporters.

IX. Scaring power hunger

Raila is one person who can never be satisfied with whatever position or achievement. He will always want to reach the sky like the Babylonians and maybe from there, attempt to enter God's bedroom! He will always ask for more like Oliver Twist in Charles Dickens' book, *Oliver Twist*. Give him the presidential post in Kenya; next morning as the Commander-in-Chief he will wake up looking for his military to overthrow himself. Still, he may start planning of how to become the President of the East African Community countries or look for Kamlesh Pattni (the elder) for tips on how to become the President of the African continent through the African Union.

In the post-President Uhuru Kenyatta 2022, the President/ Prime Minister of choice will be the one citizens have trust, faith and confidence in. One whose CV is not frightening; a leader who is safe, has stable hands. A leader whose interests are not divided by political equator into Northern and Southern Hemispheres. Who, like the moon, is not sometimes dark or bright? One that you will be able to tell whether is cup half-full or half-empty. Kenya will transfer their will to him on conditions that he will express their will. He will achieve responsible use of the power and that power will not corrupt him for fear of losing it.

X. Weak political bonds

By nature, Raila is incapable of building solid, lasting bridges, not even with an angel. If he was unable to do this with gentleman/ patriotic/ economist Kibaki, or his NASA partners, with whom can he succeed? He is a master breaker rather than a builder. In 2017, he was leading his group of heavyweight politicians – Musalia Mudavadi, Kalonzo Musyoka and Moses Wetangula. Riding on a powerful vehicle, NASA, and a massive people's following, Raila was destined to be President, but his weak, unstable molecular bonds could not hold properly their partnership together.

The media called NASA co-principals the Flower Girls escorting Raila Odinga to some new marriage with Kenyans. Raila knew this was true and his heart smiled. And just before he said "I do" to the bride, he abandoned them. Was this the 6th or the 7th marriage attempt Raila was entering into? Hard to tell. But divorcing the three was a costly mistake. We call them the three stones supporting a cooking pot. Raila was just a blower of air to keep the *uji* boiling; they were the cornerstones. He ejected them and the pot spilled.

Lest Raila forgets. In Kenya the citizens have been trying to be a tribe-less nation, a feat the Tanzanians succeeded in over 50 years ago at the Arusha Declaration. One cannot reach to the Cloud Nine of Kenyan politics without the full support of communities where Musalia

Mudavadi, Kalonzo Musyoka, Moses Wetangula and William Ruto (he has swallowed three quarters of Kenyatta's community and others) come from. It is simply not practicable.

XI. Deadly political tsunamis

People remember them all. Every moment Raila is about to take a step or speak, Kenyans become very afraid. What is about to hit us next? They ask. If Raila is not seen in public for a week, Kenyans get worried. What kind of poison is he brewing from his political pot this time around? If he is around all the time, they ready themselves for suffocated political airwaves.

XII. Akemewe na ashindwe!

Serious and honest bridge builders have one big thing in common. They condemn the dark past and preach the bright future. How many times has Raila Odinga been quoted rebuking the unholy trinity of violence, death and destruction since year 1982 to date? *Nakemea*! *Ashindwe*! "Be sober, be vigilant; because your adversary the devil, as a roaring lion, walketh about, seeking whom he may devour." (1 Peter 5:8). Rarely. Why? Because, the three words are part and parcel of his DNA. But try the same with President Kenyatta or Deputy Ruto. "Never again… Kenyans… Brothers… and sisters… Bloodshed… Election… power" have been a constant calling.

XIII. The agri-business community

They will travel down memory lane and see Raila studying in some university in the Soviet-occupied East Germany. Didn't they teach socialism or communist ideologies there? They would argue amongst themselves. Those people of the East led President Julius Nyerere to introduce "Siasa za Ujamaa" through the Arusha Declaration in 1967 – Azimio la Arusha. The Tanzanian economy collapsed, particularly in the agricultural sector. Raila will introduce "Azimio la Kibra 2022". Didn't you see him visit President Pombe Magufuli for an Ujamaa lesson? Magufuli told him he (the President) was a capitalist. Wakakosana. Raila will be worst for coffee, pyrethrum, flowers, tea and milk industries. Remember he was mentioned in the Maize Scandal when he was Prime Minister?

Raila could also have learned something or two about Dictator Adolf Hitler. Hitler believed that the Aryan was a master race, superior people. He exterminated six million Jews terming them genetically inferior, lest they breed with the Aryan. He called the genocide, "The Final Solution". Raila seems to have a natural hatred for the largest community in Kenya who also constitutes the biggest percentage of the agri-business community. His main target during protests and demonstrations include their shops-loot, destroy, close, go home!

Raila was born in 1945 when the Berlin Conference demarcation of Africa was marking its 60th anniversary (Diamond Jubilee). Then he travelled to Germany. Wouldn't he have mastered the art of sub-dividing countries? Between 1963 and 1967 the Shifas threatened to annex part of the Northern Kenya. In 1976, dictator Idi Amin wanted to take the whole of former Western and Nyanza Provinces and part of the Rift Valley and make them part of Uganda. A government led by a hardened socialist, racist, dictator and secessionist will collapse the entire Kenyan economy, built passionately for the last 60 years.

XIV. Kibra, Raila's beloved bedroom

For months now, Raila Odinga has been living in wonderfully good times. It has been a transformation like no other. From a life of a *ndombolo* dancer on platforms with supporters, telling them humorous stories of wildlife and wild Canaan; one of constantly engaging security officers in running battles in the streets, always criticising the government and hurling insults to the country's institutions, to the Attorney-General threatening to hand him to the hangman for swearing himself the People's President – the unthinkable happened.

Since Raila staged a coup d'état on Deputy President William Ruto at the Harambee House handshake and the subsequent BBI proclamation at the Bomas of Kenya, things have never felt sweeter. Considering himself the country's second in command presently and a heartbeat from the presidency was a promotion to the glory long eluded him. Thus, the birth of the BBI provided Raila more than a rise from the ashes like the Phoenix in Greek mythology. He stopped singing 'Mapambano' and 'Aluta Continua'. To touch his NASA comrades – Moses Wetangula, Musalia Mudavadi and Kalonzo Musyoka or his supporters with a ten-foot pole became anathema now.

Raila started to look composed and calm, walked and smiled like a true president-in-waiting rehearsing for the big day. But there was a big problem. By substituting Ruto with himself, he did the nation a huge disfavour. He had stepped into an unfamiliar territory of UhuRuto, men of "Kusema na Kutenda". Men patriotic to the core. Will President Kenyatta at some time feel orphaned due to Raila's poor work ethics? Put it another way, will Raila fit into Ruto's big shoes?

Ruto is a workaholic by nature. Every day you find him having serious engagements with farmers, pastoralists, industrialists, hawkers and *boda boda* operators, *jua kali* workers, women, the youth, students and people living with disabilities, to understand their problems. The country's First Officer will be launching and inspecting development projects across the country; schools, hospitals, infrastructure, environmental conservation and churches (we hear you, Sir, kindly read by heart Malachi 3:10), across the country, twenty-four-seven. Ruto will at times be in three counties in a day. He knows every inch of the country like the palm of his hands. They call it touching base. Can Raila bring this sort of ant-like, fast-paced work culture in the BBI?

Sir, we hear you again. Instead we ask you, "Baba, when Ruto was away developing the countryside what did you do for your country?"

During the Kibra by-election after the death of MP Kenneth Okoth, Raila made a grave political mistake. He repeatedly claimed that the Constituency was his bedroom. No vagabonds were allowed there, he warned. True, Kibra was his stepping stone, the launching pad to intelligent politics (not coups) where he failed spectacularly. But why shout the word "bedroom" as if the place was a case study of excellence rather than that of a hopeless work culture? The world was shocked.

Kibra is the largest urban slum in Africa occupying about 700 acres and hosting more than one million people. The 115- year old settlement is one of the most densely populated places on earth. It ranks high as an example of urban neglect and shame. Located some five kilometres southwest of Nairobi, it is an overcrowded sea of thousands of wooden, mud-walled, tin-roofed structures. The place is heavily polluted with garbage, has inadequate clean water supply, poor drainage, and shortage of electricity. With roughly 600 toilets or 1,300 people per toilet, a sizable population of people uses what is called the "flying toilets".

Nearly half of Kibra inhabitants live in abject poverty. These circumstances provide a breeding ground for unemployment, illicit brew, drugs, organised gangs, diseases and orphaned children. In short, Kibra is a place where the United Nation's SDGs 2030 targets – poverty and hunger, access to education, gender equity and women empowerment, child and maternal mortality, diseases and environmental sustainability are at their lowest levels.

In times of political agitation, Kibra has always been the epicentre of violence. Whenever Raila launched a platform to drive his personal agenda, Kibra was the place to source the "weapons of mass destruction". During Okoa Kenya, Pesa Mashinani, Uhuru Must Go, We will Occupy Harambee Avenue, Saba Saba and Mapambano, the youth would be reportedly bribed, offered drugs and alcohol and dispatched to the Nairobi Central Business District (CBD) with firm instructions: loot businesses, stone motor vehicles, beat and mug pedestrians, and hurl rocks to the police officers. Meanwhile, the youth would go home hungry and others injured; turn up in police cells or dead in mortuaries. Why was the world shocked on Raila's proud claim of Kibra bedroom ownership?

The BBI is now known globally. It is a concept of gigantic magnitude covering Kenya's 580,000 square kilometres and revolving around 47 million citizens from 44 ethnic communities. It is supposed to be the Mother of all the country's previous master plans.

Unfortunately, the BBI requires serious sympathy and prayers. Here was a man who could not put his Kibra bedroom in order, a mere 12 square kilometres even after being its MP for 21 years and later Cabinet Minister and the country's Prime Minister (charity begins at home) for a total of nine years! Here was a man who fought several ugly battles with the IEBC and Supreme Court due to a supposedly stolen presidency and eventually sworn himself as one and who could not develop a mere bedroom for decades. Here is the man now co-piloting the BBI vision. This is why the global community laughed at the idea of Raila piloting the building bridges project for a whole monumental country like Kenya.

A number of world leaders visited Kibra time back. What could have been their assessments or conclusions? Barak Obama as a Senator saw a perfect example of poor leadership, USA Secretary of State Hillary Clinton heard about abuse of human rights of women 24/7, UN

Secretary-General Ban Ki-Moon witnessed the worst let-down of UN-Habitat and UNEP aspirations, and Britain Prime Minister Gordon Brown would have recalled King Baudouin's passionate call for performance as he officially granted the Congo its independence: "It's now up to you gentlemen, to show that you are worthy of our confidence".

On matters clean environment, Rainer Nolvak organised the "Let's do it" movement in Estonia, a small country in northern Europe, in 2008. This was designed to bring thousands of people to get rid of rubbish from roadsides, towns and forests. Later the initiative incorporated the World Waste Map. Nolvak said, "We are going to clean up the Planet, together with communities around the world... What we are cleaning is not just the garbage but the waste inside the heads of people." The "Let's do it" intended to bring 50,000 people to get rid of 10,000 tonnes of rubbish. It was done successfully in just five hours.

The Kibra shameful story would provide writers awesome material for masterpieces. If a "People's President" bedroom can remain so wasted and neglected in modern age, this is stranger than fiction. Joseph Conrad wrote *The Heart of Darkness*, Frank Fanon *The Wretched of the Earth*, Allan Paton *Cry My Beloved Country,* and Victor Hugo *Les Miserable*. It is time a book, detailing the dirtiest, most neglected, promise-less political base in the world titled, "The President-in-Waiting's Bedroom of Kibra", rolled off from the press.

XV. No respect for sovereignty

In July 2015, Raila & Company requested President Obama to push the Jubilee government on matters of the IEBC reforms, KDF soldiers exit from Somalia and corruption. Obama called them turncoat politicians and reminded them that there was a legitimate government in Kenya that was on the right path. Philip Ochieng told them, "But I can hardly mean that Barack Obama has a superpower right to order our own president about..."[3] And why were these leaders (Raila & Company) on the side of Western powers during the ICC cases? And have they ever received foreign funding to destabilise the government? Did Raila's discussion with President John Magufuli of Tanzania in 2016 revolve around undermining the Jubilee government?

---

3   Philip Ochieng, "Barack Obama should feel obliged to steer the war on intolerance", *Sunday Nation*, 19 July, 2015.

XVI.   Who is William Ruto?

This is not a secret. For long Raila Odinga has had a deep dislike for Deputy President William Ruto. Once, he sacked him as Minister for Agriculture, but President Kibaki reinstated him in a moment. And neither is it a secret that Raila wished Ruto's crucifixion on the Cross at The Hague. The August 2022 General Election will be a race of two horses incorporating the two men. Who can say no to the fact that Raila's greatest ambition using his last bullet is reserved for finishing Ruto politically once and for all? The BBI is the rifle housing the bullet, the third attempted coup d'état on Ruto.

To his benefit, Raila deserve a little philosophical advice on who Ruto really is. "*Ukiona vyaelea vimeundwa*" (when you see a top brand, it has taken a lot to build). First, Raila boast being a master in political tsunamis, but is no match to Ruto. While Raila will be sitting comfortably in a canoe and whistling some *ndombolo* tunes trapping fish in a lake, Ruto, coming from a community of marathoners, will be applying the speed talent, networking with millions of Kenyans and developing the country. Behold how steeply Shares-Ruto's value has continued to rise by the day at the Political Securities Exchange. Simply put, Ruto possesses no toughness of steel, but of diamond, a political genius at best.

In 2022, DP Ruto will have clocked ten years of seeing, hearing and feeling the State House. Raila had five as Prime Minister. As the country's First Officer or second-in-command, Ruto learnt an important lesson from President Moi, the self-proclaimed professor of politics: respecting the boss always pays handsomely. And whatever the Head of State or President means in the Constitution, Ruto is the Deputy, the One-in-Waiting. While Raila has one last bullet left, Ruto has several, the most potent described in the words of David as he faced Goliath: "You come against me with sword, spear and javelin, but I come against you in the name of the Lord."

Next comes the biggest part. By good chance, Raila will have noted, while using non-jealous eyes, the label millions of Kenyans have pasted on the back of Ruto's jacket, to borrow from Chinua Achebe's book: "A Man of the People".

CONCLUSION

Proverbs (*methali*) are easier to comprehend than riddles (*vitendawili*). Some in Kiswahili are particularly relevant here: *Kikulacho ki nguoni mwako*; *Usipoziba ufa utajenga ukuta*; and, *Lisemwalo lipo na kama halipo linakuja*. Loosely translated, respectively, as "the enemy is within"; "if you don't repair a crack in the wall, you will eventually be forced to rebuilt the whole wall"; and, "what is being whispered is there and if not present at the moment, it will definitely come". In other words, Raila has been the problem in Kenya and the people have resolved to have William Ruto instead, as the better option.

US President Lyndon Johnson had disturbing doubts about retaining his dangerous rival FBI Chief, Edgar Hoover. Eventually, he had to decide and then reported: "Well, it's probably better to have him inside the tent pissing out, than outside the tent pissing in". Raila Odinga is a live political electric wire – *thitima* – history can surely attest to this. From 2022 moving forward, in the interest of the 47 million Kenyans it will be better to have him outside the government peeing in than inside the government peeing out. Outside the government as the Official Leader of Opposition and his full *serikali* – supposedly in – waiting to eternity will give Raila the feeling of a president. This is his ideal bedroom, going by the sentiments of the minds of Kenyans in this chapter.

CHAPTER NINE

This is the True Truth, Mr Odinga

It is the nature of all hypocrites and false prophets to create a conscience where there is none, and to cause conscience to disappear where it does exist.

Martin Luther

*   *   *

Beware of false prophets, who come to you in sheep's clothing, but inwardly they are ravenous wolves. You will know them by their fruits. Do men gather grapes from thornbushes or figs from thistles? … Every tree that does not bear good fruits is cut down and thrown into the fire. Therefore by their fruits you will know them.

Mathew 7:15-20 (NKJV)

*   *   *

To return to higher standards of living we must abandon the false prophets and seek new leaders of our own choosing.

Franklin Roosevelt,
US President

*　　　　*　　　　*

There's a lot of false prophets around and that's the trouble. People say they think they know what's right and other people get people to follow them because they have a certain type of charisma, and there's always people willing to take over. People want a leader. And there will be more and more of them.

Bob Dylan,
Nobel Prize for Literature winner 2016

Word of God: Where to find the True Truth

You can fool all the people some of the time (Raila fooled all Kenyans especially during election times) and some of the people all the time (he fooled his supporters 24/7), but you cannot fool all the people all the time (he cannot continue to fool all Kenyans for 40 years). This is an adaptation of the quote attributed to US President Abraham Lincoln, years back.

But the person whom Raila managed to fool wholly and throughout was his own heart. He told it countless times that he was the best material sculptured from heaven dust to rule Kenya. However, he cautioned the heart: "In Africa there is no hurry, matters of rising to the pinnacle of power takes time. *Mambo ni mos mos katika Afrika.* Rest easy, one day we shall reside at State House and all this suffering will end", he offered comfort. The heart believed in him. They say a lie told a thousand times become the truth.

RAILA'S DELUSION

For four decades Raila's heart has remained in serious bondage inflicted by its own master. After much soul-searching recently it discovered the bitter truth. The whole business of State House was nothing, but day-dreaming. The heart is now freed. Next it wants its master to be rescued from his self-bound chains. Somebody, somewhere help him see the truth. The truth will set him free. From the Scriptures and renowned philosophers, therein lies the true truth.

I.   Raila likened himself to Jesus

"When you see Raila," he was quoted by a local daily sometimes July 2007, "you see a leader who stands for the truth. I can be compared to Mandela, Galileo Galilei or Jesus."

The law does not forbid a person to acquire or equate themselves to any names they feel like; a tree, a mountain or river. Indeed, many people have names, which have been borrowed from animals, but these do not change them into beasts. Raila Odinga has the right to call himself Jesus like the Spanish footballer Jesus Navas or Brazilian Gabriel Jesus, and others. Even appropriately, he is even free to rename himself Judas Iscariot if he can gather enough courage for it. But his "standing for truth" is not the one contained in any world dictionary. Yet to compare his character with those of the big two men, and even go further to liken himself to the Son of God is the height of blasphemy, like the difference between heaven and earth.

Nelson Mandela's story is pretty recent and still fresh in people's minds. The Jesus one is in the domain of 85 per cent of Kenyans. The two's traits require no elaboration and in few words, one statement closes the matter: Jesus Christ is history's greatest manifestation of truth, while Mandela is Africa's best.

It is close to 400 years since Galileo walked the earth. He was an Italian philosopher, astronomer and engineer. Without going to his complex scientific discoveries, a belief account of his similarities and differences with Raila, also an engineer, will give an approximate state of affairs.

Similarities: Galileo was an accomplished musician who excelled in playing the lute (*nyatiti?*); Raila is Kenya's most gifted politician dancer. Galileo left university without having obtained a degree and went on to teach in a university; so is Raila. Galileo collided with the Church due to his discoveries, was sentenced to life imprisonment, but because of age and poor health, the judgment was commuted to eight years under house arrest; Raila's unpatriotic activities saw him detained for slightly over eight years. In the recent past, Raila has been at logger head with the Kenyan Church because they receive offerings and tithes allegedly from corrupt persons.

One of Galileo's discoveries identified that anything thrown or fired on Earth, such as a rock or cannonball, flies along a curved path and that the shape of the curve is a parabola; Raila learned that rocks and other missiles thrown in a certain style during protests and demonstrations will always land on their targets: the police officers, motorists and business premises.

In 1939 Pope Pius XII described Galileo as being among the most audacious heroes of research… not afraid of the stumbling blocks and the risks on the way, nor fearful of the funereal monuments; Raila's political journey has been one of ambitious political experimentations, hail or shine, deaths, funeral and graveyards notwithstanding, his way or the highway always ruled.

And last but not least: Galileo died on 8 January 1642 aged 77, 377 years to the Handshake; Inshallah, Raila's political death could come in August 2022, at 77 years.

Three differences: Between 1589 and 1592, Galileo discovered the Law of Free Fall. It states that, in the *absence* of air resistance, all bodies fall with the same acceleration, independent of their mass. In 40 years of his political career, Raila has found that in the *presence* of voters' resistance, all politicians fall from grace to grass with the same speed irrespective of their political muscles.

Galileo became the first person in history to look at the moon through a telescope. He discovered that the moon was not smooth, but mountainous and rough, just like the Earth. Raila was the first person on earth to borrow American NASA name for his voyage to a political moon; his spaceship, many times over, did not manage to come out with any tangible results. And in 1835, everything Galileo had written was finally approved by the Church. To date, all manifestos Raila has composed have met the strongest resistance from Kenyans.

So, is Raila comparable to Mandela, Galileo, or Jesus? Go tell it to birds. However fabulous and great names might be, the real beauty lies in the inside. All these giants have no history of violence, undue appetite for power, shedding innocent human blood, property destruction, arrogance or dishonesty. Raila's inside is tainted and his past has all these. In a nutshell, these men were the world's greatest bridge builders, while Raila has been Kenya's biggest bridge breaker.

II. What Bible does Raila read?

Galileo Galilei once said: "I do not feel obliged to believe that the same God who has endowed us with sense, reason, and intellect has intended us to forego their use." In the course of his life Raila convinced himself that he was more appealing than other millions of people, discarded this God-given trinity and innovated his hate, incitement and violence. The Untruth seeks Truth, but cannot find true Truth because he himself is Untruth about the Truth. Want to find and be the Truth?

Out of the world population's 7.5 billion, the faithful account for 83 per cent segmented as follows: Christianity 32 per cent (2.4 billion), Islam 24 per cent (1.9 billion), Hindu 14 per cent (1.2 billion) and the fourth largest, Buddhism, 6.9 per cent (400 million). These religions are guided by sacred scriptures, which include the Bible, the Quran and the various texts such as Bhagavad Gita and Vedas, and, among the Buddhists, the Four Noble Truths is the most regarded.

In religious books is where the truth, but the whole truth, is to be found. Raila brags to stand for the truth like Jesus Christ. Jesus said, "I am the way, the truth and life". His Gospel is represented by the Bible. Galileo said that, "the Bible shows the way to go to heaven, not the way the heavens go." What way does Raila show his supporters?

Raila is a confessed Christian, in fact baptised a record two times. So, considering his messy history and claim to adhere to the truth, what Bible does he consult? Does he read the Bible upside down or from back to front? The people of Kenya want to know.

The Holy Bible is the most popular book ever created. With an estimated current total sales standing at over five billion copies and an annual sale of approximately 100 million, it is the global bestseller, ever. But there is no pure, perfect edition of the Bible in existence. Over centuries, numerous errors have been discovered in the book after thousands of copies were printed and distributed with printers fined heavily and the remaining copies recalled.

As recently as 2003, the late Prof. John Mbiti, Kenya's renowned theologian, author and Anglican priest, discovered 1,000 errors in the Kikamba edition of the New Testament. To correct the situation, Prof Mbiti embarked on a long 10-year journey of revision, word for word, and eventually became the first African scholar to translate the entire Christian New Testament from its original Hebrew and Greek versions to Kikamba language. The new text titled, *The Kikamba Bible* – "Utianiyo Mweu wa Mwiyai Yesu Kristo" (The New Testament of the Lord Jesus Christ) was launched in Nairobi in December 2014.

In particular, Bibles of the old were famous for misprints. Their peculiar translations led them to get special names. A brief journey of biblical terminologies drama:

- The Breeches Bible had Adam and Eve making themselves "breeches" instead of "aprons" for clothing (Gen 3:7)

- Place-Makers Bible said blessed are the "place-makers" for "peace-makers" (Matt 5:9)

- Fool Bible presented, the fool hath said in his heart "there is God" in place of "no god" (Ps 14:1)

- Basketball Bible said, the "hoopes" of the pillar instead of "hookes" (Exod 38:11)

- Printers Bible said, "printers" have persecuted me, in place of "princes" (Ps119:161)

- Religious Bible: she hath been "religious" against me instead of "rebellious" (Jer 4:17)

- The Cannibals Bible (Deut 24:3): If the latter husband "ate her" instead of "hate her"

- Sin-on Bible: Jesus telling someone to "sin on more" instead of "sin no more" (John 5:14)

- Vinegar Bible: The title appears as The Parable of the "Vinegar" instead of "Vineyard" (Luke 20)

- Child Killer Bible: Let children first be "killed" instead of "filled" (Mark 7:27)

- Murderers Bible: There were "murderers," in place of murmurers (Jude 16)

- Lions Bible: The murderer shall surely be "put together" in place of "put to death." (Num 35:18), and out of the "lions" appeared instead of out of the "loins" (Kings 8:19)

- The Owl Husband Bible: Being in subjection to their "owl" husbands came out instead of "own" (1 Pet 3:5)

- Pay for Peace Bible: Brought out "pay" for peace in place of "pray" for peace (Ps 122:6)

- The Affinity Bible: Had a chart indicating that "a man may not marry his grandmother's wife"

- Camels Bible: And Rebecca arose and "her camels" instead of her "damsels," (Ps 14:1), and

- He-Bible: Referred to Ruth as a "he" (Ruth 3:15).

The list of Bible translations with hilarious typographical errors or strange rendering is quite long. However, despite these and many other misprints in various editions of the Bible, the book was never distorted. The whole message is still intact, truthful and relevant.

Raila seeking for the truth would not be lost. Furthermore, one need not be a Christian or a follower of a major religion in order to be a person of the truth. One can still be a serious adherent of Judaism, Sikhism, Jainism, Shintoism, Confucianism, Zoroastrianism, Baha'ism, traditional African religions, or even an atheist, a non-believer in existence of deities, and still be a disciple of the truth.

Immediately after the birth of the BBI, Raila adopted reggae as a vehicle to drive the concept home. Globally, reggae music is associated with the Rastafarian religion. A Judo-Christianity, it originated from Jamaica in the 1930s and believes in a single God, Jah, a shortened form of Jehovah. Rastafaris believe former Emperor of Ethiopia, Haile Selassie, to be a direct descendant of Jesus Christ.

Some of the well-known signatures of these faithful include wearing of long beard and dreadlocks, use of red, black, green and gold colours, and smoking of cannabis, which they call variously as "the holy herb," " the weed' or "the grass." They claim the herb has spiritual and healing properties and defend its consumption based on Genesis 1:29, Psalms 18:8 and Revelation 22:2. One of the passage of a common Rasta prayer, according to Wikipedia goes: "…Thou God of divine majesty, thy spirit come within our hearts to dwell in the path of righteousness. That the hungry be fed, the sick nourished, the aged protected, and the infant cared for. Teach us love and loyalty as it is in Zion."

The most prominent symbols of the Rastafarian movement has been the propagation of resistance to the slavery and oppression of Africans by the white man. The today's close to one million members view this domination as akin to the Israelites captivity in Babylon for 70 years.

Supposing now Raila has converted from whatever religion to a devoted Rastafarian. Right from independence, Raila's father, Jaramogi Odinga, held that Kenya was "Not Yet Uhuru" under the first President Jomo Kenyatta. Like father, like son; Ras Raila has constantly maintained that Kenyans have been in an African Babylon under second President Daniel arap Moi, to President Mwai Kibaki and, presently, President Uhuru Kenyatta. And for nearly 40 years, he has presented himself like the sole God's messenger (all other leaders are conmen!), like Prophet Jeremiah who delivered the liberation promise to the exiled Israelites:

> Yes, this is what the Lord Almighty, the God of Israel, says: 'do not let the prophets and diviners among you deceive you. Do not listen

to the dreams you encourage them to have…When seventy years are completed for Babylon, I will come to you and fulfill my gracious promise to bring you back to this place. For I know the plans I have for you….plans to prosper you and not to harm you, plans to give you hope and future.

However, since the August 1982 abortive coup where Raila was charged for treason, his liberation theory has been very wanting. Like the Israelites who were required to sing a song by their captors while they sat by the Rivers of Babylon, Raila has been urging Kenyans to sing a fake National Anthem. The Israelites replied to their captors: "How shall we sing the Lord's song in a strange land?" Kenyans have been responding the same to him. Can he deliver Kenyans from their bondage through the BBI spiced up with Rasta religion?

Sample some personalities in the Second Liberation: Ngũgĩ wa Thiong'o, Maina wa Kinyati, Edward Oyugi, George Anyona, James Orengo, Willy Mutunga, Mĩcere Mũgo, Al Amin Mazrui and Koigi wa Wamwere; and religious leaders in the movement, namely Timothy Njoya, Alexander Muge, Ndingi Mwana a Nzeki and Henry Okullu. There are most recent top political leaders who would be included in the list, namely Musalia Mudavadi, Kalonzo Musyoka, Peter Kenneth, Martha Karua and Moses Wetangula. All these Human Rights Defenders have one thing in common: in the course of their emancipation undertakings, they did not hurt even a single fly, let alone a human being. And their protestations did not end up destroying property. These people are examples of genuine reformers.

But for Ras Raila it has been terribly different. His supposed liberation journey has left a frightening trail of bloodbath, IDPs and economic ruin unseen since the departure of the colonialist in 1963. For sure, scattered across the country are thousands of graves littered with invisible epitaphs that cry aloud:

HERE LIES XYZ, AN INNOCENT KENYAN WHO PERISHED DUE TO RAILA ODINGA'S GREED TO BECOME PRESIDENT UNCONSTITUTIONALLY. MAY GOD GRANT THAT OUR LAND SHALL NEVER BRING FORTH SUCH A POLITICIAN AGAIN, EVER.

Knowing Ras Raila's political theatrics, he will convert his political rallies into the Rastafarian affair with appropriate colours and reggae songs at maximum. But the main worry is that Kenyans continue to keep their fingers crossed – *kushikilia matumbo* – not sure exactly what kind of baby Ras Raila will conceive from the BBI's womb by 2022. Can he adhere truthfully to the aforementioned portion of the Rasta prayer: Help the hungry, sick, aged and infants for instance?

History says an emphatic no! And going by the Israelites freedom from the Babylonian enslavement of 70 years, Ras Raila will reach Kenyans to Canaan (from 1963) in 2033. He will then be 88 years old. Joshua (the name he has adpted for himself) passed on at 110 years. Can Kenyans wait that long?

In conclusion, Ras Raila has never, does not, and will never stand for the truth.

III. Helping Raila cross River Jordan

The Preamble to the *Constitution of Kenya 2010* opens: "We, the people of Kenya – Acknowledging the supremacy of the Almighty God of all creation," and closes with "God bless Kenya." It means God in this part of the world is very serious business, the same reason this book has borrowed heavily from the Holy Scriptures in the name of building bridges.

One major prayer by Kenyans has been that Raila Odinga will this time around change his past attitude on patriotism; like in the Christian Bible see the light on the road to Damascus in order for the BBI, which he propels, to bear beneficial fruits to the whole country. Raila has declared many times that he stands for the truth and that he has suffered greatly by sacrificing to save Kenyans from bad governance.

Following is a brief session on truth and suffering from one of the world's oldest religion. It could change the man forever:

A man is trapped on one side of a fast-flowing river with great expanse of water heavily infested with crocodiles and hippos. Where he stands, there is great danger and uncertainty, but on the far side of the river, it is secure and free from risk. But there is no ferryboat or bridge for crossing to the other shore and he cannot swim. So the man gathers grass, twigs, branches and logs and bind them together to make a raft that is invisible to water beasts. Lying on the raft, he uses his hands and feet as paddles and thus moves from danger to safety…and abandons the raft.[1]

The above is a slight adaptation of what is known as Buddha's Raft Parable. The author noted: "The shore on which we are is the present, ego-related existence; the other shore is what we aspire to be, represents our goals and dreams. The raft helps us cross the waters, this is its function, but after, we have to abandon it." He described his prescription for the end of suffering; a set of eight principles called the Eightfold Path as a means to enlighten, like a raft crossing a river.

The BBI was designed to cross Kenyans from bondage to freedom. For close to 40 years, Raila, the BBI chief pilot, has supposedly been working ant-like to get Kenyans to the other bank of River Jordan. Though he has never explained how, when and by who we first crossed the 440,000 square kilometres Red Sea of Kenya only to fail a miserable river, crossing we must, some day.

Apparently, the Moses and Joshua story of the trek to Canaan or the three-and-half years of Jesus' mission on earth, and especially the book of Acts on the road to Damascus, have not provided Raila authoritative directions on how rivers are crossed successfully. But since a shepherd must learn to cross first before his sheep, a revisit on the subject of the truth dated approximately 1,000 years after Joshua took his people to the other shore will be a useful asset to Raila.

Siddhartha (means he who achieves his aim) Gautama was born around 480 BCE in Nepal, home to Mt. Everest. He was born of a warrior caste and royal family. Predictions had it that he would become either a great king or a spiritual leader. Like Raila, he went on to acquire several names: Sakyamuni, Gautama, Buddha, Gautama Buddha, Sage of the Sakyas, Shaka, Shaka Nyorai and Tathagata. At 29 years of age, he abandoned the privileged surroundings of the palace after he discovered that life consisted of sad elements of old age, sickness and death. He became a wanderer studying the meaning of life, a seeker of truth.

After six years in the wild, Gautama became Buddha (the awakened one, having woken up to reality) after achieving the Enlightenment. He had found the Four Noble Truths, the backbone of his later teachings. The Buddha was to say later, "I teach suffering, its origin, cessation and

---

1   See Jack Kornfield (ed), *Teachings of the Buddha* (Boston: Shambhala, 2004), p. 92.

path. That's all I teach."[2] Has Raila suffered for Kenyans? No, he has suffered for himself. Buddha's first two Truths were: first, suffering, pain and miserly is part of life; and, second, suffering arises from attachment to desires (unfulfilled, unsatisfied, craving) that comes in three forms (The Three Roots of Evil or The Three Fires or The Three Poisons), namely (1) Greed and desire, represented in art by a rooster, (2) Ignorance or delusion, represented by a pig, and (3) Hatred and destructive urges, represented by a snake.

One day, this teacher, philosopher and spiritual leader addressed 1,000 monks in what he called "The Fire Sermon":

> Monks, all is burning. And what is the all that is burning? The eye is burning, forms are burning, eye-consciousness is burning, eye-contact is burning, and also whatever is felt as pleasant or painful or neither-painful-nor-pleasant that with eye-contact for its indispensable condition, that too is burning. Burning with what? Burning with the fire of lust, with the fire of hate, with the fire of delusion. I say it is burning with birth, aging and death, with sorrows, with lamentations, with pains, with grief, with despairs.[3]

The Third Truth by the Buddha was that suffering ceases when attachment to desires ceases. Liberating oneself from the desires was the cure to the suffering. And the Fourth Truth was that freedom from suffering – the prescription – is possible by practising the Eightfold Path (the Middle Way). The Buddha listed these as Right:

1. Understanding – accepting his teachings,

2. Intention – a commitment to cultivate the right attitudes,

3. Speech – speaking truthfully, avoiding slander, gossip and abusive speech,

4. Action – behaving peacefully and harmoniously; refraining from stealing, killing and overindulgence in sexual pleasure,

5. Livelihood – avoiding making a living in ways that cause harm, such as exploiting people or killing animals, or trading in intoxicants or weapons,

---

2   See Ajahn Sumedho, *The Mind and the Way: Buddhist Reflections on Life* (Boston: Wisdom Publications, 1995), p. 25.

3   See Lucien Stryk (ed), *World of the Buddha: An Introduction to Buddhist Literature* (New York: Grove Press, 1968), p. 53.

6.   Effort – cultivating positive states of mind; freeing oneself from evil and unwholesome states and preventing them arising in future,

7.   Mindfulness – developing awareness of the body, sensations, feelings and state of mind, and

8.   Concentration – developing the mental focus necessary for this awareness.

The Four Noble Truths seems to have been designed for student Raila. Attaining Nirvana or Enlightenment, the Buddha noted, means extinguishing the three fires of greed, delusion and hatred, a state of profound spiritual joy, without negative emotions and fears; filled with compassion for all living things… what can be done is done, of this there is no more beyond.

One might be tempted to argue that the message from this sage, who lived 25 centuries ago, holds no water in the modern world. Yet one Anglican priest, Fredrick Donaldson, preached something similar to the Buddha's. In a church sermon in London on 20 March 1925 – the sermon was also published in a newspaper under the title, "Evils of World are Outlined - The 7 Cardinal Crimes of Modern Society" – Donaldson identified what he also called the Seven Deadly Social Sins as:

i)   Politics without principles,

ii)   Wealth without work,

iii) Pleasure without conscience,

iv)   Knowledge without character,

v)   Commerce and industry without morality,

vi)   Science without humanity, and

vii) Worship without sacrifice

Mohandas Gandhi, India's greatest bridge builder, saw the article and applauded its content. In one of his best quotes he had observed, "A person cannot do right in one department whilst attempting to do wrong in the other department. Life is one indivisible whole."[4]

---

4   Gandhi quotes: "Gandhi quotations", Volunteer in Africa and India, available at: https://cicd-volunteerinafrica.org/quotations/ghandi-quotations. Retrieved on 2 June 2020.

Regarding "politics without principles," Gandhi reasoned that having politics without truth(s) to justly dictate the action creates chaos, which ultimately leads to violence, and these missteps he called "passive violence" fuels the active violence of crime, rebellion and war.

In the BBI, Raila believes he has crossed the Rubicon and possesses a Midas touch for its content. However, he could be playing the Russian roulette. He must first be honest with himself, embrace the true truth in order to be prepared for the BBI's challenges. The Buddha advised, "It is better to conquer yourself than to win a thousand battles. The victory is yours. It cannot be taken from you, not by angels, or by demons, heaven or hell."[5] This then is the ultimate truth.

For four decades Kenyans gave Raila a raft to cross them the River Jordan. Then he swore himself as People's President and got rewarded with the BBI stewardship. Regrettably, he left his people on the other side of the shore. That was his Nirvana, the climax. He cannot climb the political ladder further. The universe will not allow. It seems the Buddha was addressing him. He needs the Truth. He has been the genesis of suffering to himself and to millions of Kenyans. Thus, Raila has only one option. Use the Buddha's truths, the teachings. Desist from clinging to the State House or Prime Minister dream. Leave the raft on the shore, it served its purpose. Look what lies beyond politics.

The Buddha taught for 45 years. Raila will be 40 years in 2022 with his political chalk and blackboard. "In the end," the Enlightened One advised: "Only three things matters: how much you loved, how gently you lived, and how gracefully you let go of things not meant for you." The State House was not intended for him.

And finally, Raila is a lover of wildlife stories. One bright, hot afternoon, a strolling fox came across ripe oranges hanging from a tree. Instantly, he longed to quench his thirst with their succulent juice and get vitamins too. He salivated at their sight and started licking his lips. One, two, three! He jumped trying to reach the fruits. After many attempts the fox got exhausted, gave up. What did he do next?

The clever fox did not commence complaining and destroying the whole forest. He just walked away with an assumed air of dignity,

---

5   See Aniello Grimaldi, *A Guide to Life: a Book of Wisdom and Truths: A Book of Wisdom and Truths* (Xlibris Corporation, 2010), p. 496.

whistling proudly and waging his tail. "What a fool I had been." He comforted himself. "The damn fruits look sour, and some are even rotten. After all, oranges permanently make me sick." The Buddha's doctrine to Raila: letting go of what you can't get.

IV. This is Raila's true bedroom

One of the most important proposals in the BBI relates to the Executive: The creation of leader of opposition who is the runner-up in the presidential contest. This leader will constitute a shadow cabinet to keep the government in check.

In the book, *The Poisonwood Bible* by Barbara Kingsolver, a congregation sits in a church listening to the preacher, American Baptist, Nathan Price. Suddenly, Chief Tata Ndu interrupts the sermon: "Now it is time for the people to have an election." He thunders. This election is on whether or not the villagers who have been resisting Christianity to accept Jesus Christ as the personal Saviour of Kilanga Village, in the Belgian Congo.

Nathan Price is shocked. He has never heard, in all his preaching life, of this kind of nonsense. He explains that "Jesus is exempt from popular elections." Nevertheless, the voting proceeds with casting of pebbles and a cross as a symbol of those for Christ and a bottle of palm wine for those that support the traditional religion.

Meanwhile, Tata Ndu is confused about the Western democracy of the "winners take all" and addresses the priest: "Our way was... to speak to each other until every person was satisfied..... White men tell us: vote, Bantu! They tell us: You do not all have to agree, *ce n'est pas necessaire*! If two men vote yes and one says no, the matter is finished. A' bu, even a child can see how that will end. It takes three stones in the fire to hold up the pot. Take one away; leave the other two, and what? The pot will spill into the fire."

Tata Ndu continues: "But that is the White man's law, *n'est-ce pas*? Two stones are enough. *Il nous faut seulement la majorité*."[6]

Finally, when the votes are counted Jesus Christ loses, eleven to fifty six (11:56). Tata Ndu turns to the priest and concludes, "Jesus is a White man, so he will understand the law of *la majorité*, Tata Price."

---

6   Barbara Kingsolver, *The Poisonwood Bible* (London: Faber & Faber, 2008), p. 96.

Majority or minority? It depends on what perspective you look from. But here, the "winners take all" has won the day.

First-century BC philosopher, Lucretius, described the myth of Sisyphus as personifying politicians aspiring for political office who are constantly defeated, with the quest of power, in itself an "empty thing" being likened to rolling the boulder up the hill.

In Greek mythology, Sisyphus was an iron-fisted king of Ephyra. He killed guests and travellers, planned to kill his brother and seduced his niece. For his self-aggrandising craftiness and deceitfulness, he was condemned to roll a huge rock up a steep mountain. However, every time he neared the summit, the boulder would slip from his grasp and roll back. He had no choice but start the process all over again, to eternity.

After these frustrating, unending efforts and many failed attempts, Sisyphus would have realised that his unending attempts was a mission impossible, quit the game altogether, said to hell with the condemnation, and concluded like the Teacher in Ecclesiastes 2:11: "Then I looked on all the works that my hands had wrought, and on the labour that I had laboured to do: And, behold, all was vanity and vexation of spirit, and there was no profit under the sun." (KJV)

When the BBI regrets about violence every electoral cycle, this correctly refers to the consequences of one Kenyan Sisyphus who never respect the law of *la majorité*, and want the business of the "winner takes all" done away with, Raila Odinga. First, a surgery on the man. Where do you begin writing about him and what do you write? A man who, had the military coup of August 1, 1982, of which he has been mentioned severally, succeeded, his would have become the biggest revolutionary act by a Kenyan in the then 20 years of independence. A man who gets detained arguably longest in the country's post-independence history. One who leaves his rural constituency for the city, contests and wins election numerous times.

Here is a man who excels in birthing and dismantling political parties as he tries to reach the higher scales of leadership. One who becomes the country's second Prime Minister since independence. One who vies for the presidency several times and despite his huge popularity never wins; always claiming the contests were not free and fair – leading to mass protests and public violence never witnessed. A man who almost single-handedly helped end decades of KANU's dictatorship by declaring "Kibaki Tosha!". Such a person would require thousands of pages for the story of his life and times to be adequately told. Simply put, the man is a prime mover in his own right.

In his hugely successful book, *You Can't be Neutral on a Moving Train: A Personal History of Our Times*, US historian and author, Howard Zinn, says of changes:

> ...Revolutionary change does not come as one cataclysmic moment (be aware of such moments!) but as an endless succession of surprises, moving zig-zag towards a decent society. We don't have to engage in grand, heroic actions to participate in the process of change. Small acts, when multiplied by millions of people, can transform the world.

> To be hopeful in bad times is not just foolishly romantic. It is based on the fact that human history is a history of not only of cruelty, but also of compassion, sacrifice, courage, kindness...The future is an infinite succession of presents, and to live now as we think human beings should live, in defiance of all that is bad around us, is itself marvelous victory.[7]

That is the world of Raila Odinga, son of Jaramogi Odinga, Kenya's first Vice-President and the face of Kenya's opposition for many years. His is a world of zig-zags, small acts and defiance. For the better part of his years in politics, Raila has fought hard for more respect of human rights, accountability and democratisation, changing the country's political direction many times over, than any other politician. Commenting on his biography, *Raila Odinga: An Enigma in Kenyan Politics*, the then Chief Justice Willy Mutunga said: "Raila Odinga is a poster-politician in Kenya and indeed, in any African country. Given the crisis of political leadership on the continent, Raila Odinga's biography provides an interesting case study that in part provides for serious thought on both issues."[8]

For his great work on this arena, Raila's status can aptly be described by Howard Zinn's words: "The power of a bold idea uttered publicly in defiance of dominant opinion cannot be easily measured.

---

7   Howard Zinn, *You Can't be Neutral on a Moving Train: A Personal History of Our Times* (Boston: Beacon Press, 2002), p. 208.

8   Babafemi A. Badejo, *Raila Odinga. An Enigma in Kenyan Politics* (Lagos: Yintab Books, 2006), p. vi.

Those who speak out in such a way as to shake up not only the self-assurance of their enemies, but the complacency of their friends, are precious catalysts for change."[9] Yet Raila's journey has not been short of controversies, drawing in disciples of likes and dislikes alike. But he more or less decided to believe, like in Italian's author Christine de Pizan's "The Poem of Joan of Arc" of 1429 that, "when someone finds himself quite unjustly attacked and hated on all sides, there is no need for such a person to feel dismayed by misfortune...."[10] This is not just Raila Odinga: he is a brand in Kenyan politics. In fact, he is The Raila. Until you meet his other side of the coin, treacherously explosive like a nuclear bomb, inhumanly dangerous! Eventually, this gives him an unfortunate score: 30 per cent good, 70 per cent bad.

That said, credit must be given where due. We were all meant to be something. Different talents. Different specialisation. Try hammer in a human medicine lesson to a mind made to assimilate engineering or an architectural one to a theologian-made being, the results in all likelihood would come to naught. Raila Odinga was born an oppositionist. That is the genuine make-up of his DNA. Not for a presidency or premiership. His specialisation is that of a Mr. Check and Balance; Mr. Whistleblower. Politician William Ntimama once remarked, "I don't see any one who can step in Raila's shoes. The whole area (opposition) is empty."[11] However, for his oppositionist genius to help the country fully, he requires to inject a strong dose of patriotism in his work.

Thus, the recommendation by the BBI to create the position of Official Leader of Opposition is a welcome move. Raila Odinga is the man. This is his perfect bedroom. Here, he will leave a true legacy on his decades' struggle against poor governance. In *Lord of Light*, American novelist, Roger Zelazny, offers: "An army, great in space, may offer opposition in a brief span of time. One man, brief in space, must spread his opposition across a period of many years if he is to have a chance of succeeding."[12]

---

9   Zinn, *You Can't be Neutral on a Moving Train*, op cit, p. 33.

10 Christine de Pisan, *Ditié de Jehanne D'Arc*, edited by Angus J. Kennedy and Kenneth Varty (Oxford: Society for the Study of Mediaeval Language and Literature, 1977), p. 42.

11 Mayaka Gekara and Julius Sigei, "Ole Ntimama's Most Candid Interview Ever: Kalonzo Cannot Lead, Kibaki is Selfish and Saitoti Owned Half of Lavington", Nairobi Wire, Monday, 15 July 2013.

12 Roger Zelazny, *Lord of Light* (Harper Voyager, 2010), p. 134.

A BETTER OFFICIAL OPPOSITION

Can a world completely free of resistance or pressure really exist? Apostle Paul told the Romans, "there is none righteous, no, not one". Once *The Economist* ran a story that ended thus, "Even angels sometimes need the help of demons". This is a world of symbiotic relationship, balancing between good and bad. And so, a government in power needs a strong opposition to constantly inject a dose of adrenaline in its systems.

Opposition is a vital component of any government. It is a partner of the government, an alternative government also called a government in waiting. That is why it appoints its own government known as the Shadow Cabinet. Its role is to challenge those policies it views as not beneficial to the nation and hold the government in power accountable to the public.

Opposition to governments has been around since the world began. Even God knew the necessity of resistance. He chose Satan to be leader of the Opposition to his administration, to keep his people in check. Of course Satan's is not the government in waiting! In *The Cedar Post*, American writer, Jack Rose, describes the importance of the opposition: "Opposition can be your friend; opposition can be the fire that tempers the better sword, as well as the ice that cools a fiery temper. Don't ever run from it, learn from it."[13]

Since independence the Opposition has been the voice of the people in the darkest of times. During the tyrannical KANU regime, for instance, the opposition led the Second Liberation; thus, today Kenya has no detainees, no torture chambers and many reforms have taken place in prisons, the Judiciary and the Police Service. Until recently when it was "killed" by the handshake and the BBI, the Opposition has been at the forefront in fighting against corruption and abuse of human rights, and promoting democracy.

But the official opposition that will be delivered by the BBI in 2022 will need to rebrand. Times have changed. It will be a better voice of reason, pulling in the same direction with the country and not an enemy to the government in a bull fight or Cold War. It will be a formidable, responsible outfit, acceptable by both the people and the government.

---

13   Jack R. Rose, *The Cedar Post: The Pristine American Dream, Vol 1* (Heber, UT: American Dream Makers, 2012), p. 136.

The country will demand an opposition that writes plans, addressing the problematic areas with recommendations and improvements and present them to the government. And when work is done well it will be courageous enough to congratulate the government and the people.

A clever opposition will work as a catalyst for positive change, a voice for reconstruction and development and not one of destruction and underdevelopment so that in the event it assumes power, there will be a secure, peaceful and prosperous country to inherit and not a failed fragmented one. Spitting fire and brimstone at the government at every opportunity will not move the country forward. In other words, the Opposition must work to expectation.

A special team of experts, for instance, assessed the opposition Cord coalition and its leaders since the March 2013 General Election. The *Sunday Nation* of 22 September reported that the Opposition had, "performed poorly on the front of its ideology… luxury spending at the expense of development programmes … taken away too long to realize the crucial role it has as the official opposition … lack of 'confluence of ideological thinking and ideas' … looks very weak on the common strategy on national and international issues that are considered a priority and worthy of the coalition's is attention …"[14]

After the General Election, a political party that is defeated should not consider the outcome as a declaration of war. It simply means one get the job of doing things and the other ensuring the job was done well and advise accordingly. US President Dwight Eisenhower noted, "If a political party does not have its foundation in the determination to advance a cause that is right and that is moral, then it is not a political party; it is merely a conspiracy to seize power."[15] Thus, a political party should not excel in defying authority, always imagining itself as the Father of the Constitution, Alpha and Omega in politics. Challenges facing a country will only be resolved in a sober and mature manner.

Additionally, it will pay handsomely for the Opposition to appreciate that Kenya belongs to us all whatever the circumstances, must come

---

14   Nation Team, "You have failed, consultants tell Cord leaders", *Sunday Nation*, 22 September 2017.

15   Dwight D. Eisenhower, "Remarks at Fourth Annual Republican Women's National Conference", The American Presidency Project, March 06, 1956. Retrieved from: https://www.presidency.ucsb.edu/documents/remarks-fourth-annual-republican-women-s-national-conference

first at all times, and is a great country on a journey, a work in progress that cannot transform into heaven on earth overnight. This is close to what management experts Wale Akimenyi tried to explain in a *Daily Nation* article:

> ...Ordinary minds see final states. They look at a bottle and see it as an end... The truth, however, is that there is nothing today that has reached a final state. The world and life in general is in motion... People who see finality will always serve and be at the mercy of those who see progression. No matter how bad things may be, and no matter how good things may be, if all you see is what you are looking at, then you have reached stagnation... Closed minds see finality while progressive minds see stepping stones. It is a choice that no one can make for you...[16]

There is the other side of the equation: while both the government and president will facilitate the Opposition with adequate funding and conducive environment to operate from, they deserve reminders.

To a president: "The Opposition is indispensable. A good statesman, like any other sensible human being, always learns more from his opposition than from his fervent supporters (Walter Lippman)."[17]

To a government: "Once a government is committed to the principal of silencing the voice of opposition, it has only one way to go, and that is down the path of increasingly repressive measures until it becomes a source of terror to all its citizens and creates a country where everyone lives in fear (Harry S. Truman."[18]

To close up, once in a while, a nation thirsts for the blessings from the Above. But people are always expected to play their part. Raila Odinga delights in greatness. Yet, who is the greatest? A leader who consciously and consistently fight against evil in a government or one who presides in a government with occasional evil systems? Certainly it's the former.

---

16   Wale Akimenyi, "Try seeing beyond what you are looking at", *Daily Nation*, 1 August 2013.

17   See Clinton Rossiter and James Lare (eds), *The Essential Lippmann: A Political Philosophy for Liberal Democracy* (Cambridge, MASS: Harvard University Press, 1982), p. 233.

18   Harry S. Truman quoted in ReLeah Cossett Lent and Gloria Pipkin, *Keep Them Reading: An Anti-Censorship Handbook for Educators* (New York: Teachers College Press, 2013), p. 83.

Year 2022. Call it culture (*desturi*), wisdom or fate. Kenyans with BBI or not hold election. Raila becomes No. 2 and he accepts Leader of the Official Opposition post, his destined bedroom. He rebrands his opposition politics. With his explosive political atomic energy, oppositionist talent and courage, he helps make the government operations run straight like a railway track (like an SGR, not Lunatic Express). Hallelujah! Kenya becomes great. Raila becomes the greatest like Muhammad Ali in boxing. This is the nation's prayer.

In the meantime, Kenyans will permit him to tell all the *vitendawili*, *methali* and wildlife stories he wants, do the entire *ndombolo* dance he feels like, hold all the protests, demos and rallies he can, on conditions that he maintains PEACE. This mix of hot opposition politics, blended with peace and maturity, will be a great source of a block-buster movie: "East or West, Bedroom is The Best".

For patriotically agreeing to return to his favourite bedroom abandoned temporarily for the BBI, fully rebranded, Kenyans will give Raila a farewell gift in advance of retirement: "Lives of great men all remind us/We can make our lives sublime/ And, departing, leave behind us/Foot prints on the sands of time (Henry Longfellow, American poet 1807-1882).

A Pastoral Letter to Hon. Raila Odinga

I believe the purpose of all major religious traditions is not to construct big temples on the outside, but to create temples of goodness and compassion inside, in our hearts.

Tenzin Gyatso, 14th Dalai Lama

*   *   *

This is the true spirit of insolent dogmatism: We have proved to the satisfaction of every honest man, that we are right and that you are wrong; and therefore, if you are not convinced, it must be owing to your own perversity. When a man's shot is exhausted, he will try and terrify his adversary by firing off powder.

Julius Hare[1]

---

1   Julius Charles Hare, *The Mission of the Comforter, and Other Sermons*, Second Volume (London: Macmillan, 1846), p. 986.

The Cross: The Gospel of Redemption is courageous

Bishops of the Global Building Bridges
Church of Jesus Christ, Kenyan Chapter
P.O. Private Bag, GPO
Nairobi, Kenya

Sir, we are the Bishops of the Global Building Bridges Church of Jesus Christ, the Kenyan Chapter. Christianity is Kenya's most popular religion at 83 per cent. With Islam that comprises 11 per cent and recognises Jesus Christ as a Holy Prophet, our views therefore represents 94 per cent of the country's population.

The Church is Christ. We, the Bishops have been mandated to preach about the two Kingdoms: The Kingdom of mankind on Earth, strongly encompassing human rights and sustainable development for maximum fulfilment, and that of God in Heaven.

BROTHER RAILA, HIP-HIP- HOORAY!

Sir, from the onset, we need to offer our heartfelt congratulations. Truly, BBI is Baptism Beyond Imagination. In fact, some things are out of this world, stranger than fiction. That yourself and company you tried to overthrow the Government of Kenya way back in 1982; that several times you almost brought the country in the brink of civil war – and in those 40 years you were the biggest human wall that divided Kenyans (we cannot forget your struggles during the Second Liberation hereby assessed as 30 per cent good and 70 per cent bad.); that, you have decided to leave the nasty history behind; that you have seen the light on the Road to Damascus, that you are now the principal of a college with 47 million students all attentive to your audio-visual lesson: "How to Build Bridges in Kenya".

Cheers! Brother Raila. We, the Bishops, are fasting and praying that it comes to happen. If it does without a hitch by 2022, it will be the greatest miracle to have occurred in a developing country.

Prof. Wangari Maathai gave us the first Nobel Peace Prize in 2004; you could bring in the second. The "Out of Africa" film shot in Kenya bagged seven Oscars in 1985 followed by Lupita Nyong'o's in 2014.

Another Oscar could be on the way courtesy of BBI. Kimani Maruge and Eliud Kipchoge entered Kenya in the Guinness Book of World Records in education and marathon respectively; through you, the BBI could create another entry. Indeed, the United Nations Office of the High Commissioner for Human Rights could honour you since the BBI is basically about human rights. Additionally, we can request the government to set aside an annual day named after you.

For our part, your genuine success will compel the Church to do something perhaps never in history done for an individual. Come 2022, we shall hold a special national inter-denominational prayer day; an occasion to thank the Almighty for making your Road to Damascus real and also bless you for a good job done. The Church only does coalition prayers to an individual who is dead, not a living one. You can see how seriously we take the BBI's victory…

The BBI offers a momentous period in the history of our nation. But right from its conception, the project signalled destruction of some bridges constructed for many years and creation of a huge wall like the Berlin Wall, nicknamed the Wall of Death or the Strip of Death.

Sir, we could be partially, but not totally wrong. Our feeling is that you steering the BBI is a guaranteed path towards its Waterloo or at best a Pyrrhic victory.

As the anointed messengers of our Saviour Jesus Christ, and in the interest of our motherland Kenya, we feel strongly a fierce now to have a candid conversation with you Sir, through this letter. We therefore wish to address you, as a Christian and political leader, through important points about the BBI and the future of our country. We ask these crucial questions because you are not just a common *mwananchi*, a hustler, a *hoi holoi*, but a prominent politician. President Kenyatta having literally taken a back seat and leaving the BBI and 47 million Kenyans in your hands, experience command us not to trust you 100 per cent.

The BBI journey

We begin with a story that is immensely deep and close to your heart. The Exodus from Egypt by the Israelites and their arrival in Canaan. The journey took 40 years. The people were now on the eastern banks of River Jordan after crossing into Canaan, the land God promised to

Abraham five centuries earlier. Here, they encountered the first obstacle, the walled city of Jericho.

God instructed Joshua to have the army march towards the city with seven priests walking ahead carrying the Ark of the Covenant – the sacred chest containing tablets engraved with the Ten Commandments. At the appropriate time, they blew the trumpets as directed earlier. The walls came tumbling down. The power of the Ark brought victory to the Israelites and they took charge of the land flowing with milk and honey.

Sir, your political venture resembles Moses' and Joshua's in one way of the timespan. In August 1982, you commenced an adventure to supposedly deliver Kenyans from their political, economic and social bondage and land them into their Canaan. By 2022, the math gives exactly 40 years of this painful wandering.

By August 2017, you had 6.7 million followers (voters). Moses had left Egypt with 3 million Israelites, but majority never reached the destination. On 30 January, 2018, you swore yourself as People's President. However, the self-professed patriotism in you urged you to embrace all the 47 million Kenyans and consequently you and President Kenyatta carried out a deal known popularly and universally as the Handshake. How many Kenyans will eventually enter Canaan?

This new-found bond birthed the BBI that was unveiled at the Bomas of Kenya on 27 November, 2019. Kenyans and the BBI will cross River Jordan, the Referendum, no doubt about it. But already, there is an obstacle – it will be RESISTED VERY STRONGLY by Kenyans. Even before the BBI left the station, it started creating an enormous wall, a visible and tangible Berlin Wall separating the hearts and minds of Kenyans and the country as a whole. Kenyans are living in very exciting, but trying and unpredictable times. The BBI has been fronted as the Ark of the Covenant containing all the Commandments Kenyans have made for themselves in 60 years to make their country a better place among the world nations.

During the NTV interview on 26 January 2020 you informed the world that your People's President initiative was killed by the BBI and replaced by patriotism, but twice, you refused to confirm whether you aim for an executive position through it come 2022. But the world knows better. Kenya's biblical Jericho Wall is the 2022 General Election. Will the BBI evolve into a cursed Covenant and fail to bring down the Wall and therefore prevent Kenyans from entering their Canaan?

We need bridges, not walls

US President Ronald Reagan, Soviet leader Mikhail Gorbachev and Pope John Paul II have been credited as the prime movers who helped bring down the Berlin Wall on 9 November 1989. In an interview sometime in 1993, Pope John Paul II recollected: "I think the crucial role was played by Christianity itself; its content, its religious and moral message, its intrinsic defence of the human person..."[2]

The world celebrated wildly when the Wall came down. It brought a new era of respect and promotion of human rights. On the 25th anniversary of the fall, 9 November 2014, Pope Francis delivered a message to mankind. He asked for prayers that,

> ... the collaboration of all people of goodwill, there will spread even more a culture of encounter capable of bringing down all the walls still dividing the world...Where there is a wall, there is a closed heart. We need bridges, not walls![3]

The Pope was asking the people to commit "to build bridges of understanding and of dialogue, in order to make the whole world a family of peoples reconciled with each other, brotherly and harmonious".[4]

The Kenyan Wall dividing President Kenyatta and his Deputy Ruto and the whole country into two camps, brought about by the BBI, can be described by words of George Jahn, an AP correspondent, on the Berlin Wall as "Brooding, cold and gray. It was an ugly, intimidating structure".[5] However, it can be destroyed. During celebrations to mark the 25th anniversary of the fall of the Berlin Wall, German Chancellor, Angela Merkel, described the Wall as, "... [a] concrete-cast symbol of State despotism". She further remarked that: "Walls made of concrete and walls in our heads are surmountable when people come together and take their fate into their own hands... We have the strength to shape things from bad to good, that is the message of fall of the Wall".[6]

---

2 Quoted in Cindy Wooden, "Pope Hails Role of St. John Paul in Berlin Wall's Fall," *Catholic News Service*, 11 October 2014.

3 Ibid.

4 Gerard O'Connell, "Pope Francis: 'Build bridges, not walls'." *America: The Jesuit Review*, 31 March 2019.

5 Quoted in Jenny Hammerton, "Tying past events to today's stories", Insights [AP], 9 November 2015.

6 Philip Oltermann, "A city undivided: The fall of the Berlin Wall commemorated 25 years on", *The Guardian*, Sunday, 9 November 2014.

Sir, as the co-principal of the BBI, these are valuable lessons to all Kenyans and more so, to you. You are constructing walls, not bridges.

THE CHURCH'S BIG PUSH

In 1943, Paul Rosenstein-Rodan, an Austrian development economist, advanced the Big Push model. He argued that under-developed countries require large investments to embark on economic development from their present state of backwardness. This theory proposed that a "bit-by-bit" investment programme would not impact the process of growth as much as required in developing countries. Injections of small quantities of investments would merely lead to wastage of resources. He also quoted Massachusetts Institute of Technology (MIT): "There is a minimum level of resources that must be devoted to… a development programme if it is to have any chance of success".[7]

Sir, besides the Task Force, the BBI project is lacking a fundamental partner, a Third Force. When almost the entire space of the BBI is taken up by politicians, the bridges built will miss a solid foundation. You cannot get a better bridge builder than the Church. The Church is undoubtedly the only institution that can render the Big Push necessary to make the BBI bring forth the required fruits. Make the Church your foremost partner.

THE BRIDGE BUILDER'S WITNESSES

Jesus Christ is the world's best bridge builder in history. Before He ascended to heaven, He left His work to His disciples. They asked him: "Lord, are you at this time going to restore the Kingdom to Israel (independence from Roman rule)? "It is not for you to know the times or dates the Father has set by His own authority." He replied. "But you will receive power when the Holy Spirit comes on you; and you will be my Witnesses in Jerusalem, and in all Judea and Samaria, and to the end of the earth".[8] This was Jesus' last command: The sanctification and salvation of all mankind through his Church.

---

7 The study is titled "The Objectives of US Economic Assistance Programs", Center for International Studies, M.I.T., Special Committee to Study the Foreign Aid Program, Washington, D. C. (1957), p. 70.

8 Acts 1:8 (NIV)

With the Bishops, the Witnesses at the forefront, the BBI will proceed on the right footing to fulfil what prophet Isaiah demonstrated. "To bind up the brokenhearted, to proclaim freedom for the captives and release from darkness for the prisoners … They will rebuild the ancient ruins and restore the places long devastated; they will renew the ruined cities that have been devastated for generations."[9] As Jesus Christ's appointed Witnesses, the Bishops will help fulfil Isaiah's prophecy in Kenya.

CHURCH IN BBI NOT BOSS

Majority of politicians have wrongly projected the BBI to be a 2022 destination. Building bridges is a continuous process that shall be fully completed only by Jesus Himself on his Second Coming. But full participation of the Kenyan Church will make the BBI a way of life where past sins shall be owned, way of healing them determined and the salvation from repeating them achieved. The Church shall not be the boss, but an informed director.

To accomplish its mission in the BBI, the Church shall be, as ever, the one that Jesus Christ desired. To highlight its stand, the Bishops hereby elaborate on what a true Church means using statements of Archbishop Oscar Romero of El Salvador:

(a) Each one of you must be God's microphone; each one of you must be a messenger, a prophet.

(b) Authority in the Church is not command, but service…I am not a master. I am not a boss. I am not an authority that imposes itself. I want to be God's servant, and yours.

(c) A gospel that doesn't take into account the rights of human beings, a Christianity that doesn't make a positive contribution to the history of the world, is not the authentic doctrine of Christ, but rather simply an instrument for power.

(d) We… don't want to be a plaything of the worldly powers; rather we want to be the Church that carries the authentic, courageous gospel of our Lord Jesus Christ…

---

9   Isaiah 61:1-4 (NIV)

(e)   A preaching that does not point out sin is not the preaching of the gospel. A preaching that makes sinners feel good, so that they are secured in their sinful state, betrays the gospel's call.

Archbishop Romero was a fearless disciple, an example of love who persistently denounced injustice, challenged the status quo and fought for the poor and oppressed constantly emphasising that, "The shepherd must be where the suffering is". As he stood at the altar celebrating Mass on 24 March, 1980 (month of March, 40 years ago!), an assassin bullet went through his heart ending the illustrious life of one of the smartest bridge builders in recent times. In the BBI, we the Bishops intend to be a strong vessel to the fulfilment of what the Church stands for; we are in constant contact with where suffering is.

AGE IS NOT JUST A NUMBER

Sir, in 2022 when the BBI is set to mature for political harvest, you will be 77 years old (Saba Saba). This will be precisely 40 years since you launched the Canaan journey in 1982, and 30 years from the date you and comrades started the Second Liberation, the Saba Saba, 7 July 1990. We the Bishops have no problem with your continued State House drive. It is your constitutional right.

But we always turn to the Holy Scriptures for direction. "Seventy years are given to us!" The Psalmist wrote. "And some may even live to eighty. But even the best of these years are often emptiness and pain… Teach us to number our days and recognize how few they are; help us to spend them as we should."[10] Thus, the Bible talks about the human's productive age. For instance, the Catholic diocesan Bishops are required by the Code of Canon Law to submit their resignation to the Pope on reaching the age of 75 years; the Church of England Anglican Bishops retire at the age of 70 years, and the Kenya Chief Justice and Judges at 70 years. Sir, the oldest recorded person in the Bible, Methuselah died at 969 years old. Supposing this was the average death date for human beings in modern times.

Imagine great minds like the German-born American physicist Albert Einstein (died 76) credited with the Theory of Relativity or Stephen Hawkins (died 76), the British cosmologist famous for the black holes

---

10 Psalm 90:12.

study living for nine centuries like Methuselah. Or evil minds like Adolf Hitler (died 56) of Germany, Soviet Union's Joseph Stalin (died 74), Ugandan dictator Idi Amin (died 78) or Osama bin Laden (killed at 54) again clocking close to 1,000 years. Since humans are one-in-two, good and evil, a scenario like this could see each specialist side constructing its own real, physical, Standard Gauge Railway (SGR) from the earth: One to Heaven and the other to Hell. Humans are limited.

"There is a right time for everything." The Ecclesiastes commanded. "A time to destroy" that was Kenya of yesterday and "A time to rebuild" that is today's Kenya courtesy of the BBI. But every actor has a sell-by date. Sir, imagine if you were blessed with 1,000 years, and in every past century your politics were replicated! Kenya would be at the tail end of development and respect for human rights among the community of nations. "Think about all the time, brainpower, and social or political capital you continue to spend on some commitment only because you didn't like the idea of quitting." (Steve Levitt: Think Like a Freak- identifying the root cause of a problem, rather than attempting to build solutions that focus on obvious, though often incorrect, causes).

Sir, during an NTV interview on 26 January 2020, you implied that age is just a number and pointed out that even the British Parliament has MPs who are beyond 80 years. Remember that Britain started the First Industrial Revolution in the 18th century, participated in the Second from the 19th and the Third in the 1950s long before Kenya was born. Its 2019 GDP was USD 2.8 trillion compared to Kenya's USD 99 billion. Britain can do with octogenarian political leaders whose energy is almost exhausted, unlike Kenya. Nelson Mandela reasoned that "Quitting is leading too".

Remember also that despite retiring from His mission on earth at 33 years, Jesus has today billions of delegates congregating in His House seeking audience with Him. You too, if refined, can be an effective leader even after retiring from politics. Kindly desist from hiding behind the BBI, drop politics altogether.

OUT ON COURT BAIL

Sir, from a theological point of view, you have been on a heavenly court bond countless of times. Every moment a human being sins, he is literally arrested, entered in the Judgment book, bonded to await Jesus'

Second Coming. 1Timothy 5:24 says, "The sins of some are obvious, reaching the place of judgment ahead of them; the sins of others trail behind them" (NIV). And Romans 14: 11: "As surely as I live,' says the Lord, 'every knee will bow before me; every tongue will acknowledge God" (NIV).

Year 1982 moving forward, a basketful of sins was committed during events associated with your political activities. Innocent human blood was shed, bodies maimed, thousands of lives lost and economic loss to the country worth billions of shillings. Consequently, millions of people were left in tears, fears and untold suffering. In the age of the Building Bridges, what is the right thing to do?

The Bible has answers: Proverbs 28:13, "Whoever conceals their sins does not prosper, but the one who confesses and renounces them finds mercy"; Acts 3:19, "Repent, then, and turn to God, so that your sins may be wiped out, that times of refreshing may come from the Lord"; and, Mathew 18:18, "Truly, I say to you, whatever you bind on earth shall be bound on heaven, and whatever you loose on earth shall be loosed in heaven". To drive the BBI successfully, repentance of past misdoings is clearly vital to have your case withdrawn by the heavenly court and set free.

ANGER IS DEADLY, ANYWHERE

Sir, one of the characteristics that destroy a good leadership whether in church or politics is anger. The Bible is rich in warnings about harbouring anger. Proverbs 15: 18: "A hot-tempered person stirs up conflict, but the one who is patient calms a quarrel"; and, James 4:1-2, "What causes fights and quarrels among you? Don't they come from your desires that battle within you? You desire but do not have, so you kill. You covet but you cannot get what you want, so you quarrel and fight…" (NIV).

Sir, despite your outward appearance, deep inside seems to reside a very angry man. We understand that at your age you are going through a period Erik Erikson, the German-American developmental psychologist and psychoanalyst, called, in "The Eight Stages of Psychosocial Development", late adulthood – where one reflect on one's life and feel a sense of failure and a wasted life. Thus, you have constant feelings of bitterness, depression and despair mainly because of the inability to get to State House after 40 years of great trying. Because of this, you project the picture of a man forever angry, bitter and unappreciative with almost everything about the country you have for so long desired to lead.

Sir, you were born right here in Kenya as confirmed by your birth certificate. You grew up here, first schooled here and got a Kenyan passport. Your marriage certificate says you took a Kenyan woman for wife. You breathe, eat and drink from Kenya.

Sir, you are now the leader of the BBI. The ruthless, consistent hatred for your motherland must have evaporated, so it seems. The Church has a special request. To you, it is evident that Kenya has never had a good president since independence. From the Orange House, can you draw a sincere comprehensive master plan of how you can do things differently, better than the four presidents if 2022 turn out to be a blessing?

TWO BAPTISMS, NO HOLY SPIRIT?

Sir, it is not common for a person to be baptised twice. But it happened to you. First in the Anglican Church and for the second time by Prophet Edward Owuor of Holiness and Repentance Ministry.

You first met Reverend Owuor sometimes 2008 at a prayer meeting in Nakuru and declared the repentance of your sins and agreed to be saved; in other words to be born again in Christ. Later, and wearing a spotless white suit, you were fully immersed in a residential swimming pool on Riverside Drive, Nairobi on 5 May 2009. Reverend Owuor proclaimed: "What we are witnessing here today is not merely just a baptism but rather the healing of a nation and making of history. For a leader to lead his people back to the Lord, that is where the healing of this land lies. Through the healing of the land the nation will become cohesive because the peace of God surpasses human understanding."

This event of you apprently becoming a new man was captured and aired on both local and international media. The whole country ululated. Reverend Owuor explained further the meaning behind this auspicious occasion:

> The Honourable Prime Minister has come forth and followed the footprints of Jesus of Nazareth… when heavens open over his life tonight, it would have a ramification that will touch every fabric, every woman whether in a refugee camp, whether in village…

there will be open heaven for every citizen of this nation… Today is a major step, a major advancement towards peace in this country because Kenya is on the way out of the woods.

To cement the newfound relationship with Christ, the Reverend handed you the Holy Bible. "This is the word of God, it brings healing," were your acceptance words. You were also delighted by him for coming to your aid: "The Lord works in mysterious ways; his wonders to perform and I'm very happy that the man of God has received me and has blessed me."

What was the message to Kenyans as you emerged from the Holy Cleansing?

> The people of Kenya left Egypt, crossed the Red Sea, they have gone up the mountain and now we are at the banks of River Jordan. We do not want to go back to Egypt. Rather, what we want is to go to Canaan and the Lord will take us there. We shall cross River Jordan.

Very well, Sir. The Lord indeed works in mysterious ways. It is over 10 years back. Kenyans are still at the banks of River Jordan! Archbishop Oscar Romero of El Salvador noted that wherever there has been someone who has been baptised, that is where the church is. Have you been walking on the footprints of Christ ever since and have you been leading people to the Lord? Has the country, due to your seeing the light grown more cohesive and come out of the woods? Did the baptism open the heaven and bring peace? Were you truly healed? The Reverend's words seemed to indicate that you are exactly what has been ailing the country and your healing will consequently heal it. Kindly rethink the significance of a baptism.

AFTER BAPTISM, TEMPTATION

Immediately after baptism, Jesus was led by the Holy Spirit to various places where He was subjected to three awkward temptations to prove that He was the Son of God. The first was the wilderness, where he stayed for 40 days and 40 nights without food. Satan told him to turn stones to bread for Him to eat. Jesus responded: "Breads won't feed men's souls; only obedience to every God's word." Second was on the roof of the Jerusalem Temple. "Jump off, and the angels will prevent you from smashing on the rocks below." Jesus: "Don't put the Lord to a foolish test." And the third temptation, on the peak of a high mountain: "See all the nations of the earth; I will give them to you if you worship me." Jesus: "Get out of here, Satan. Worship and obey God only."

When the Europeans brought Christianity to Kenya, converts were baptised and given new foreign names. However, most of them did not grasp the actual meaning of the concept; what mattered most was the feeling-great of acquiring the *Wazungus'* names. Even today, baptism to majority Christians is just a name-giving ritual. And salvation is nothing more than Brother-in-Christ, *Bwana Asifiwe!* Sycophancy. Baptism is a rite of passage (like circumcision is a transition from boyhood to manhood in some communities). It begins with repentance for the forgiveness of sins, then salvation and immersion in water leading to purification and consecration. Baptism identifies the believer with the Holy Trinity and its end product is the acquisition of a brand new life.

Sir, you have undergone several meaningless political baptisms in the past where you got new names – Tinga, Agwambo, Nyundo, Jakom, Baba, among others. But when Reverend Owuor dipped you in water and proclaimed your salvation in the name of the Holy Trinity, it was not a joking matter. But what path did you follow thereafter? Was the occasion a publicity exercise?

Sir, you were the Official Leader of Opposition then, your usual bedroom, presiding over the Government-in-waiting. No problem about that. Even Satan is the chief opposition to God's kingdom although his is not the government that will come! Kindly note that we are not calling you the Devil. William Shakespeare advised us that any name can smell as sweet as the rose flower; even Lunga Lunga Member of Parliament, Hon. Khatib Abdalla Mwashetani, does not complain about his surname.

Sir, soon after your second baptism on River Jordan of Nairobi in 2009, the picture that emerged was the exact opposite of Jesus' following His baptism. After the River Jordan episode, the baptised became the tempted; while for the Riverside Drive, Nairobi, the baptised became the tempter. You took Kenya to a triple temptation adventure. You tempted the Judiciary and the IEBC institutions to the limit. You tempted the Kenya sovereignty – the secession and the fake swearing in business; you tempted the Kenyan people to the extent of driving them into a civil war: deaths, destruction, economic loss. All these because the country refused to make you president.

To Kenyans, the BBI is like a baptism – a movement from old bad days to good days ahead. Surprisingly, you, a person who does not understand the importance of rebirth is at its forefront. But instead of propagating its real issues, you have employed your same old brand of politics – *siasa za kujipiga kifua*; that this time around, nobody can stop you from entering the State House. They say that after the Canaan dream collapsed when you made yourself People's President you now want to take Kenyans to Jamaica, the home of reggae. The evolution of your *ndombolo* dance signature to Lucky Dube's reggae song tells it all:

> Reggae in bathroom/Reggae in the bedroom/Reggae everywhere/ Reggae in jail/Reggae in church/Everybody likes it/They tried to kill it/ many years ago/Killing the prophets of reggae/Destroying the prophets of reggae/… You can change the style/of playing reggae/ You can change the rhythm of playing reggae/But never ever/Change the message/Every time I play it a Babylon/ I wish me fe dead …/ Nobody can stop reggae/Nobody can stop reggae…

The reggae genre is recognised by UNESCO as one of the world's intangible cultural heritages valuable for tourism. For long, the music has served as a voice for the marginalised and the oppressed, drawing heavily on the Jews' story of 70 years of captivity in Babylon, a kind of religion that promotes the sacramental use of marijuana.

Sir, what is the message here? The BBI is not a revolution or the NASA reloaded; it is a rebirth of the country. Your reggae is unstoppable, has no breaks and therefore the BBI will have no destination. Very true, we recall, like in your other previous campaign slogans. But a vehicle without breaks oftentimes causes accidents. Kenyans are tired of political drama. They want serious work.

You frustrated other previous rebirths: the independence, the constitution, Kenya Vision 2030. You ignored the Holy Spirit's call during your own baptism. If you must lead the BBI, and for its success, then you need an alternative fierce baptism: One of the Fire and Holy Spirit of Patriotism.

'DEAD' SON COME BACK TO LIFE

Sir, there is one little matter that has disturbed the Church greatly. The Handshake, and more so the BBI conceived a huge barrier between President Kenyatta and Deputy Ruto – leaders who have walked and worked together in absolute harmony for years. Listen to President Kenyatta some moons ago: "I am doing 10 years, then Ruto will also do another 10. Let him (Odinga) stop being a nuisance and retire… will also benefit from the Social Protection Fund we give to the elderly…"

The BBI has now somewhat sidelined Deputy Ruto, forcing him into an immature road to retirement. Considering that the President and Deputy started building bridges from 2013, we find destroying them to make new ones very odd and a betrayal of the highest order. The idea looks like a Breaking Bridges Initiative (BBI).

Ahadi ni deni, a promise is a debt. Since the days of Judas Iscariot, the Church learned a bitter lesson and always tries to dissociate itself with traitors and betrayers. The Church, together with millions of Kenyans, both in the Jubilee Party and NASA (ODM) are deeply disturbed by this turn of events. However, we could be missing the point. Probably President Kenyatta was right to have you lead in building bridges, in other words, welcoming you back home, the Prodigal Son way: Luke 15: 11: A man has two sons. One demands his share of the estate. Father agrees and divides his wealth between the two. This son quickly packs his belongings and departs for a distant land where he squanders everything in partying and with prostitutes. All money gone, he starves almost to death. Then he gets hired by a local farmer to feed his pigs. He shares their food.

The Party man comes to his senses and returns home. The father notices him at a distance. Filled with pity, he runs to him, embraces and kiss him. "Father, I have sinned against heaven and earth, and I am not worthy being called your son. Kindly hire me as a *kibarua* person." Father puts him finest robe and expensive ring on his finger, best pair of shoes and slaughters the fattest bull. Eating, music and dancing take charge.

Meanwhile, the other son is in the field, working. When he comes back he hits the roof, considering all the hard work and obedience rendered for years while the brother was spending money with the prostitutes. "Look here, son." Father tells him. "You and I are very close, and everything I have is yours. But it is right to celebrate. For he is your brother; and he was dead and has come back to life! He was lost and is found."End of the Prodigal Son story.

The Bible does not go further to explain what happened next. Were the three men able to build their bridges? Was the sidelined son treated better? Did the loiterer son start a fight? Sir, you are a Kenyan Party man. History informs us that your rehabilitation has always been followed by growing of horns that eventually disintegrate the political households.

JONAH THE REBEL

Sir, when did the rain started beating you? Let us use this story. In the modern-day Iraq, a Hebrew prophet named Jonah was ordered by God to go to Nineveh city to tell inhabitants to put their house in order. Instead of obeying the instructions, Jonah fled to a seaport, boarded a ship and paid the fare. Destination: Tarshish. Soon, God made the sea angry. Heavy winds threatened to capsize the ship. Crew and passengers yelled for fright and flight. Jonah ran and hid in the deck. He fell into deep slumber.

Meanwhile, lots were cast to know the source of the evil. Jonah was found to be the source. He begged to be cast overboard in order to calm the sea. Once there, he was swallowed by a big fish. Three days and three nights he stayed inside its belly. While there, Jonah prayed:

> In my distress I called to the Lord,
> And he answered me…
> I said, I have been banished from your sight;
> Yet I will look again towards your holy temple.
> …Those who cling to worthless idols
> Forfeit the grace that could be theirs.

Eventually, he was vomited on the shore….

Sir, replicate Jonah's dramatic events in political Kenya. Fate threw you into politics and a voice dictated that you preach and help implement genuine reforms in the country. But along the way, like Jonah, you became arrogant and selfish. You took flight from the calling and boarded a vessel, MV Hunger for Power. Expectedly, this vessel collided several times with MV Patriotism.

Sir, this prediction is not far-fetched. Under your leadership, the BBI could be a tsunami that could rock ship Kenya violently come 2022. However, the people will cast their lots and could throw you out to be swallowed by a shark that will not let you go, ever again. We, the Bishops are not being harsh, but bold and honest.

BRIDGES, PRESIDENT MOI AND CHARITY

Sir, building bridges among communities and peoples of the world is a phenomenon that is as old as humankind. And in one of those sad moments in history, the world pauses to bid goodbye to an architect of this important concept. Julius Kabarage Nyerere (middle name means "the spirit which gives rain" in Kizanaki language) ruled Tanzania for 24 years (just like Daniel arap Moi Kenya's 24). The Arusha Declaration of 1967, his biggest blueprint for social development and nationalism focusing on rural development, though well-intentioned, failed miserably leading to a collapsing economy and systematic corruption. Nyerere admitted his mistakes, but still defended the vision. "There is a time for planting and a time for harvesting," he said. "For us, it is still a time for planting."

But President Nyerere became known globally as one of Africa's best bridge builders. In addition to fighting for his country's independence, he managed to promote and consolidate unity and cohesion among the 120 ethnic groups in the country. Today, Tanzania is one identity, one brand, a tribeless nation. Away from home, Nyerere gave support and residence to liberation struggle movements from other countries in the continent. Back in 1959 he had declared, "We cannot, unlike other countries, send rockets to the moon, but we can send rockets of love and hope to all our fellow men wherever they may be…"[11]

Nyerere died of leukaemia in October 1999, and in 2006, the Catholic Church in Tanzania made him a candidate for the sainthood, a process that leads to canonisation. On 5 December 2013, former South African President, Nelson Mandela, died aged 95 (same age as Moi). The first black Head of State of a multiracial South Africa had been imprisoned for 27 years for fighting against apartheid system, introduced in 1948. When he left jail on 11 February, 1990, Mandela emerged pumping his fist in the air, all-smiling. And instead of being a bitter and explosive person, he forgave the lords of racial segregation and reconciled the blacks and the whites. The Handshake with President Fredrick de Klerk thus broke the walls of the colour-bar and established a country that would guarantee racial harmony and freedom for all, where people of

---

11 Godfrey Mwakikagile, *Nyerere and Africa: End of an Era* (Pretoria: New Africa Press, 2007), p. 567.

all colours would co-exist in peace and harmony. The two earned the Nobel Peace Prize in 1993.

Today, Mandela remains a global icon in building bridges. Two days after he passed on, the *Saturday Nation* of 7 December 2013, dedicated 52 pages to his legacy; 100 world leaders attended his burial. Radio Africa's Maina Kageni and Mwalimu King'ang'i celebrated his heroism. That, if on a queue towards the Pearl Gates you spotted Nelson Mandela amongst yourselves, then you had to be absolutely sure that yours was headed to heaven!

Sir, on 4 February, 2020, Kenya and the world lost yet another great bridges builder in former President Daniel Kapkorios (means "welcome home the cattle") arap Moi. When he took over after President Jomo Kenyatta's death in August 1978, he soon crafted his BBI: a trinity of Peace, Love and Unity that he preached to Kenyans ruthlessly at every opportunity adding that people should be mindful of others' welfare. Moi, "a giraffe with a long neck that saw very far," as Jaramogi Odinga had described him years earlier or the Professor of Politics as he called himself, ascended to power with a high rating and goodwill from Kenyans. It was like a dream come true to the country.

The first four years of his reign were very promising. But Moi, like Nyerere, Mandela and others before him, was not a saint or Angel Gabriel or even Jesus. He was made of flesh and blood. This soon became evident when on 1 August 1982, a number of Kenya Air Force soldiers and you, Sir, reportedly part of the plan, staged a coup d'état. Henceforth, another different Moi was born. Matters would never be the same again…

Put yourself in Moi's shoes. As a Vice-President who would not hurt a fly, Moi had been insulted, humiliated and physically assaulted by high-ranking officials in President Jomo Kenyatta's government. The so-called Mount Kenya Mafia had worked around the clock to prevent him from succeeding the elderly Kenyatta. But against great odds he managed just that. Then, some Agĩkũyũ leaders called him a "passing cloud". And exactly 1,440 days, a Luo-led coup. A whole President Moi hid in a bush overnight near his Kabarak home for fear of his life. The incident left him frightened and traumatised and probably felt shame for not seeing it coming early enough despite the huge intelligence in place. You were charged with treason.

Sir, Moi had seen countless military coups elsewhere in Africa and their deadly consequences. Now under his watch 5,000 people lay dead, the highest number since the colonialists left the country. Kes 640 million in economic loss was staring the land.

Jomo Kenyatta was like a Moses to Kenya and Moi had come in as Joshua to complete the country's journey to Canaan. Yet instantly, the failed coup metamorphosed the latter from a humble sheep to a fierce lion; he made a hasty U-turn and began to lead Kenyans back to Egypt.

So for the next 20 years, his administration presided over a country of gross human rights violations – including political assassinations, ethnic clashes, detentions without trial, corruption and a broken economy. It also fought the same Church Moi was so devoted to. Frankly speaking, Moi could forgive, but not forget Raila & Company; so do Kenyans.

Nevertheless, Moi's weaknesses and failures during the quarter-century rule apart, one thing remained solidly permanent in his heart, mind and acts. The humble and God-fearing man who could have won the Guinness Book of World Records entry as the most church-going president in the world, from as early as 1930s, Moi was consistent in one gospel that he practised with enormous zeal until his last days: Charity to the Church.

Briefly, a flashback. "Are you going to restore the Kingdom of Israel?" The disciples asked Jesus before His ascension to heaven. Centuries back from 1700 BC, the Israelites were enslaved by Egyptians for 430 years; 586 BC as free people, they were invaded by Babylonians, exiled and placed under captivity for 70 years; and in 63 BC the Romans colonised them when General Pompey took over Jerusalem. With the long prophesied Messiah's arrival, a mere three decades dwelling on earth and now imminent departure, the disciples were genuinely concerned about their future.

But Jesus' Messianic mission was different. His was not only about political emancipation of Jews, but total liberation of the human person throughout the world using His gospel. And this gospel was to be spread to all corners of the earth through His Church.

Sir, the houses of worship are built from resources provided by the people. "Is it time for you, yourselves, to dwell in your panelled houses, and his temple to lie in ruins?" The Lord asked through Prophet Haggai.

"Go up into the mountains and bring down timber and build my house, so that I may take pleasure in it and be honoured." And Ephesians 4:11-12: "So Christ himself gave the apostles, the prophets, the evangelists, the pastors and teachers, to equip his people for works of service, so that the body of Christ may be built up." (NIV).

St Francis of Assisi, a 13th century Italian came from a wealthy merchant family. One day while praying in a neglected church, he heard a voice: "Francis, go and repair my house, which you see is falling down." Francis sold a load of cloth from his father's shop and his horse to raise funds for building the church. Today, he is one of the most venerated and inspirational figures in the Catholic Church's history.

This is what President Moi was at best in. Besides never missing a Sunday service, he built and developed the Church across the country. In turn, the Church build schools, homes for the elderly, hospitals and other small-scale charitable projects to uplift the human dignity – on top of its core work of evangelisation. What is better for being a Witness of Christ?

Sir, you have been against tithing and offerings to the Church. You have been calling leaders who give charity to the Church thieves and corrupt. Despite all his human shortcomings, the Church is grateful to President Moi for emulating the Good Samaritan and being a case study of promotion of the Church of Christ. Like you have painted Deputy President Ruto severally for his charitable work corrupt, was President Moi also a thief and corrupt person? You heaped praises on him during his funeral. Had the words thief and corrupt suddenly disappeared from your vocabulary? Where do you draw a line between genuine personal earnings and stolen wealth?

Building the Church requires goodwill and monetary contributions from the faithful. The Church does not own De La Rue, a currency-minting factory. It depends on tithes and offerings from its adherents as directed by the Holy Scriptures: "Take from among you an offering to the Lord; everyone who has the impulse in his heart, let him give his offering to the Lord; gold, and silver and brass" (Exodus 35:5).

Sir, how do you expect the Church to survive without finances, or would you wish it close shop? Would you wish for a situation where the priests of the Church walk naked, sleep hungry, sick and shelterless because of a church unable to provide for her servants? Or where people worship under trees and in shacks?

In an interview with a local TV early 2020, you mentioned that you are worth Kes 2 billion. Every year your party ODM receives billions of shillings from the government, which you are in total control. For years, what charitable work have you done for the Church, you, a white as wool Christian? Or for schools, hospitals, children homes, street children in Kibera or even a simple fish pond in Bondo? Don't the suffering of less privileged in the society disturb your heart? And being a very rare species in the Church, how do you spend your time on Sundays? Lest we forget, how do you expect Christians to elect you president when you do not support their Church?

Sir, some 39 million Kenyans are Christians. Imagine the Church demanding that they fill Wealth Declaration Forms to determine whether their tithes and offerings are proceeds from corruption or not. The Church does not condone corruption or other evils. But it is the place that calls and welcomes the sinners to repent their sins for onward salvation and becoming the people God desired. This is the institution you have been at war with, truth be spoken.

And, finally: "… there was a man named Cornelius, a centurion who gave alms generously to the people and prayed continuously to God… a vision of an angel of God came and told him: 'Cornelius, your prayers and your alms have ascended as a memorial before God." (Acts 10:1-4) All the millions who worship in the Church at every opportunity and contribute a portion of their harvest to the Church cannot be wrong; and in return, abundant blessings come their way.

Sir, former President Moi, Deputy President Ruto and other believers from the four winds will tell you this is true.

EMULATE GOD, THE GREATEST MATHEMATICIAN

Sir, when the African Union (AU) Commission Chairperson, Moussa Mahamat, and President Kenyatta facilitated your appointment as High Representative for Infrastructure Development at the continental body on 20 October 2018, they were dead right. They had undoubtedly read your CV (curriculum vitae) very well. They knew where you belonged, especially bearing in mind your vast experience as Minister in charge of Energy, Roads, Public Works and Housing. The Communique from Addis Ababa expected you pay particular attention on Africa's underlying structures including dams, water and sewer systems, airports and harbours, railways and subways, roads and – bridges – towards Africa Agenda 2063.

Sir, you are a trained engineer. You studied mathematics – algebra, geometry, trigonometry, calculus, statistics and probability – a requisite subject and the foundation of science courses. The AU job fitted perfectly. But when the Communique added an extra assignment of promoting pan-African and Africa integration, as well as the pacification by the President through the Handshake months earlier so that he can govern in peace, a serious error was committed.

You were not born a politician, but an engineer. Politics betrayed you. Can one feed and care for a cow continuously for 40 years, with time and money and sometimes even risking life, and no milk is forthcoming? The cow has refused! Evidence is clear that from 37 years of age moving forward, you have consistently been breaking and burning social-economic-political bridges in Kenya. You were unable to encourage and strengthen bonds of solidarity between various communities in the country. And now at mid-70s…

All hope may not be lost, however. You can still successfully build bridges in your motherland. Emulate God. God is more of an engineer than a politician. And he learned ultimate mathematics when he was a child and later created the universe. Genesis 1:1 says, "In the beginning God created the heavens and earth." Creation was purely a work of love for mankind and engineering. See, the universe design is quite awesome. The Psalmist was amazed, "when I consider the heavens, the work of thy fingers, the moon and the stars which thou hast ordained…" (Psalms 8:3). Greek philosopher Plato had earlier recognised God's engineering expertise, purpose and origin when he said: "God ever geometrizes, and the highest form of pure thought is the mathematics." By applying your God-given talent in engineering, you can redeem your legacy.

Vern Poythress, an American professor with six academic degrees and PhD in Engineering, and another in Divinity, released a book in 2014 titled, *Chance and the Sovereignty of God: A God-Centered Approach to Probability and Random Events*. The publisher describes it as work intended to, helping Christians trust God in the midst of an unpredictable world… studying chance and probability, exploring implications for the fields of math and science.[12] An endorser called it a "work that is both mathematically adept and theologically deep."

Forbes magazine reviewed the book on 19 April 2016 and noted, "The standard modern culture – war revolves around God vs the mathematical science. Take your choice: Faith or Physics." *Forbes* went further: "The argument is that mathematical laws, in order to be properly relied upon, must have attributes which indicate an origin in God. They are true everywhere (omnipresent), true always (eternal) and cannot be defied or defeated (omnipotent), and are rational and have language characteristics (which make them personal)… Math is an expression of mind of God… Modern natural science was created by people who said that they were trying to "think God's thoughts after him"".[13]

In the same magazine, Prof Poythress was quoted on the relationship between God, mathematics and science. "That God and science are neither enemies nor partners," he observed, "but rather that God is the necessary foundation for mathematics and therefore of every science which uses it." He added that, "God shows his character in the things that he's made … and with most use of probability and statistics, what we're seeing is that everybody secretly relies on God; even the atheist does."[14]

On the same subject MIT physics professor and cosmologist, Max Tegmark, has contributed thus: "There is something very mathematical about our universe, and the more carefully we look, the more math we seem to find…everything in our world is purely mathematics –including you."[15]

Sir, without incorporating God in your math and engineering knowledge, no tangible results could be forthcoming either from the AU infrastructure job or the political BBI. Kenya is in the middle of an unpredictable atmosphere and in the absence of faith in God all leadership efforts are likely to come to naught. Faith is paramount.

---

12 Vern S. Poythress, *Chance and the Sovereignty of God: A God-Centered Approach to Probability and Random Events* (Wheaton, IL: Crossway, 2014), p. 11-17.

13   Jerry Bowyer, "God in Mathematics", *Forbes*, 19 April, 2016.

14 Ibid.

15 Max Tegmark, *Our Mathematical Universe: My Quest for the Ultimate Nature of Reality* (New York: Alfred A. Knopf, 2014), p. 263.

Politics should not limit you to improve Kenya. God's formula of creation and managing the universe spiced up with love and good thoughts will help build Kenya. Still, learn from Poythress who, despite having a chain of university degrees including a doctorate in mathematics, went on to become a professor of the New Testament.

BBI, A PANDORA BOX?

Sir, the Church is not a believer in mediaeval mythologies. The institution of Christ is not an island either; it sometimes draws lesson from history. In Greek legend, Hesiod wrote, in the 7th century BC epic poems including in *Works and Days,* where one Prometheus, a Titan god and a champion of mankind, stole fire from heaven to help humans. To avenge, Zeus, the god of gods caused a large earthenware jar delivered to a woman named Pandora. In those days jars were used as storage for wine, oil and grain. The moment Pandora opened the jar, all manner of troubles – hatred, war, pain, poverty, crime, hunger and such evils – were released into the world to afflict humankind for eternity. The only item that remained trapped inside the container was Elphis, Hope. This act ended the Golden Age of humankind. Humans learned a lesson.

Much later in the 15th century, humanist Erasmus wrote about the jar of trouble, nicknamed the Pandora box. He noted in Latin, *malo accepto stultus sapit*, translated as "from experiencing trouble a fool is made wise." In modern times, to open a Pandora box signifies to start or do something that will cause many unforeseen problems. In a more popular phrase, the circumstance is termed as "to open a can of worms".

As Bishops representing millions, this is our considered observation. You seem to have a despised trinity: The voter, the IEBC and the Supreme Court. Whenever you claim that the trio have stolen your political fire for State House, you open your Pandora box. Henceforth, your manifestos, which hitherto promised prosperity, stability and peace to the country, suddenly transform into a curse. Consequently, Kenyans suffer terribly from the poisonous contents from the box. They are left clinging only to Hope.

Sir, our humble opinion is that the populace have become more enlightened and want nothing to do with your fires and boxes. They are totally convinced that the BBI is another Pandora box that, when opened come 2022, all hell will break loose in the country.

THE CONCLUSION

Sir, past behaviour has a habit of repeating itself. It is not easy to change one's DNA irrespective of the pressure of prevailing political circumstances. A leopard cannot change its spots; and even when a snake sheds its old skin, the poison in the fangs remains. It is the reason Kenyans are rightly afraid about a Raila executive position. Our sheep ask: Can Raila truly change for the better?

American writer Mark Twain (Samuel Clemens) remarked, "History does not repeat itself but it does rhyme." The book of Ecclesiastes 1:9 summarises this more perfectly. "What has been is what will be, and what has been done is what will be done; and there is nothing new under the sun."(Qoheleth, Hebrew Bible); "History merely repeats itself. Nothing is truly new; it has all been done or said before. What can you point to that is new? How do you know it didn't exist long ages ago?" (The Living Bible).

Sir, look out of the window from your bedroom. Do you see a beautiful country with unlimited blessings and possibilities? Like any other country on earth, Kenya has an assortment of problems. But a patriotic leader looks not only on the dark, but also on the brighter side. An assurance from God who is nicknamed Papa to the main character in a fictional novel, *The Shack*, by WM Paul Young, emphasises this point: "…don't forget that in the midst of all your pain and heartache, you are surrounded by beauty, the wonder of creation, art, your music and culture, the sounds of laughter and love, of whispered hopes and celebrations, of new life and transformation, of reconciliation and forgiveness." Look at your political past in the mirror on the wall. What images do you see? The issue here is to admit, honestly, have your political endeavours been an asset or a liability to the country?

The Church's central idea of BBI is a country that will never again be like Prophet Ezekiel's valley of dry bones or where its women will never have to cry like Rachel mourning her children in Ramah – because of politics. But don't let grief overwhelm you due to perennial loss of the State House job. Grief follows five stages, namely denial, anger, bargaining, depression and acceptance. Forget the rest and embrace the fifth. Kenyans spoke in the past and they will speak again in 2022.

Angĩkorwo kĩrĩndĩ nĩkĩaremire Musa, we nĩwe ũũ? If the multitude could still defy Moses (on Canaan promise) who are you?

Sir, BBI is just a 150-page document. Both evil and good are housed in hearts of men. You unleash the one you choose. The BBI will not prevent you from rejecting the General Election result in 2022. A document cannot prevent you from calling supporters to the street to protest and demonstrate and destroy and kill. The BBI will not fly like a drone to the IEBC and the Supreme Court to urge them to rule in your favour. The main solution to the current problems in Kenya was not the BBI's entry, but your exit from the political scene.

In your position one would set to surprise the world. The Handshake took place in the month of March, when Easter, the foundation of Christian faith normally occurs. The festival is an annual commemoration of Jesus's death, burial and resurrection, also connected with the Passover in remembrance of the freedom and exodus of Israelites from bondage in Egypt. Easter symbolises conquest over sin also described as "a season of growing sun" or "a season of new birth."

Assuming that you were denied by your three NASA co-principals on the way to becoming People's President (like Peter denied Jesus three times) and earlier humiliated by the masses and authorities during election (an experience similar to Jesus') you would take BBI as a miraculous political resurrection from the tomb to overcome your past evils and feast on the triumph of love to your country – in honour and recognition of Easter. Unfortunately, your DNA is incapable of accommodating such a transformation.

Finally, Sir, the Holy Spirit of God commands us, the Bishops, the Witnesses to deliver this final message: In the interest of you, the country and its 47 million people, kindly desist from contesting or holding any political office in Kenya in the Year of Our Lord Twenty Twenty Two.

Yours in Christ,

The Bishops
Global Building Bridges Church of Jesus Christ

Dated this 9th day of March 2020 (second anniversary of the Handshake)

PS: We don't encourage a reply to this letter. The same shall be pasted on the church doors across the country. The content shall be read during all services (except Sunday School): Morning Glory, Main Service, Praise and Worship, Bible Study, Healing and Deliverance, Ushirika, Kesha, Weddings and Funerals. Sir, it is in your human rights domain either to heed to the message contained herein or just ignore it partly or in total.

CHAPTER ELEVEN

Is William Ruto the 'God' of Corruption in Kenya?

Oh rogue, deceiver, crafty in heart… I most surely believe that you have broken into many a well-built house and stripped more than one poor wretch bare this night, gathering his goods together all over the house without noise. You will plague many a lovely herdsman in mountain glades, when you come on herds and thick-fleeced sheep, and have a hankering after flesh… you comrade of dark night. Surely hereafter this shall be your title amongst the deathless gods, to be called the prince of robbers (arkhos pheleteon) continually.[1]

Apollo addresses the infant Hermes, the god of thievery

* * *

She (Maia) bear a son (Hermes), of many shifts, blandly cunning, a robber, a cattle rustler, a bringer of dreams, a watcher by night, a thief at the gates.

Hymn for Hermes' mother, Maia

---

1   Quoted in Timothy Jay Alexander, *A Beginner's Guide to Hellenismos* (Raleigh, NC: Lulu.com, 2007), p. 150.

Responsibility: You can't pass on the blame

One beautiful afternoon of November 2019 the BBI hit the road. Immediately, the term corruption became the elephant in the room in Kenya. Its lord was identified as Deputy President William Ruto. Following this proclamation, particularly from Raila Odinga, Ruto could then resemble planet Mercury (Hermes), the god of thieves and cheats in Greek and Roman mythologies.

In the Solar System, Mercury is the smallest planet, save for Pluto. It is one closest to the sun and the speediest of all planets at one and a half times the speed of earth.

The Babylonians called Mercury Nebo, the scribes of the gods whose main task was to write down the laws and edicts for Marduk, his father, who was the king of gods, and to communicate them to the people.

In Egypt, Mercury was Thoth, the messenger of the gods. The Sumerians named him Gud, the deity in charge of good rains, agricultural fertility and harvest abundance.

To the Romans, Mercury married Venus, the goddess of love and beauty and together they bore a son named Cupid, the god of love. Venus is the brightest planet in the Solar System and the third brightest object in the sky after the sun and moon. It has also be nicknamed the Evening Star and the Morning Star.

Mercury was considered as the winged god, god of winds because of his speed who served as a messenger for all other gods. He was represented wearing *talaria*, the winged sandals made of "imperishable gold which bore him swift as a breath of air over sea and earth." He also donned a broad-brimmed winged traveller's hat, the *petasos*. Both gave him advantage of speed for fast conveyance of messages. Mercury carried a special staff called *caduceus* that was used to reconcile conflicts. He was also the patron of circulation of people, goods and ideas.

Mercury was also the god of shopkeepers and merchants (especially of grains), and travellers and transporters. Oftentimes, he was portrayed holding a purse signifying his role as the god of riches, trade and good fortune. On May 15th annual festivals, merchants and seamen sprinkled themselves and their merchandise with holy water from Mercury's sacred well as they prayed for higher profits from their commercial transactions.

Normally, Mercury was accompanied by a cockerel and a ram or a goat, a symbol of a new day and fertility, respectively. He was generous, lord of dreams and visions, swift and conversant with major events fostering on foresight. Additionally, being the god of translators, interpreters, eloquence, manual arts, and athletes, he was held as the cleverest of the Olympian gods and extremely popular among the nations. Besides protecting gymnasiums, stadiums and youth, Mercury was the intermediary between the four elements of air, earth, fire and water.

But Mercury was also the god of thieves and tricksters. Barely five minutes after his birth, he stole a herd of cattle from his brother Apollo, the sun god and confused the trail by making the animals walk backwards. When he was discovered, he compensated the theft with a stringed musical instrument he had made from a tortoise shell. On yet another episode, he stole cattle and drove them into a nearby forest. A man who witnessed the stealing was sworn to secrecy. But when Mercury came back in disguise and the man unknowingly spilled the beans on the whereabouts of the loot, the god turned him into stone.

Mercury gave the world names such as Wednesday, merchandise, market, merchant and merciful. The American NASA designated its first manned space programme, Project Mercury. The programme aimed to put man into orbit around the planet and it ran from 1958 to 1963. The word mercurial in English refering to someone who is erratic, volatile and unstable – came from Mercury's swift flight...

Supposing William Ruto is the lord of theft in Kenya like Mercury in the Greek world: When and by whom did the stealing game originate?

ONE HUNDRED AND THIRTY (130) YEARS OF MASSIVE EXPLOITATION

The history of corruption in Kenya goes back to 1895 when the British Government declared it a Protectorate, and thereafter a colony in 1920, which continued until full independence on 12 December, 1963. These 70 years were occasioned by a brutal rule of human rights abuse and exploitation of the country's resources – the two prime issues that triggered the First Liberation movement.

With the power shifting from the 55,000 Europeans to 8.5 million Kenyans at independence, a bridge had moved Kenyans from an era of robbery by foreigners to one where everyone would be masters of their own sweat as well as harvest. Unlike in the past when the colonialists stripped all Kenyans of their fundamental rights and went scot free, now in a free country governed by its owners, justice was expected to prevail. That was the vision of the new nation.

The vision could not have been captured better than what Barack Muluka wrote 47 years after independence in *The Nairobi Law Monthly* magazine of November 2010:

> A people's vision… is the vision of a country in which everyone works for their keep, a country in which criminals are punished and made to pay their debt to society rather than being rewarded with trappings of good living. It is a society devoid of tribal kingpins and overnight billionaires with mysterious personal fortunes. It is a society founded in justice, humane nation that all can be truly proud of. Visions which cannot capture such a society are in the end irrelevant…

But alas, not all dreams ever come true. The new administration embarked on a stealing spree. No one was punished, instead thieves were given lucrative positions in government and companies. The newly-minted black exploiters accumulated more and more wealth at the expense of the common man. First President Jomo Kenyatta, shouted at Bildad Kaggia, his former comrade-in-arms at Kapenguria detention a few years back. "Hi Bwana, what have you done for yourself, do you want to remain a pauper forever?" But Kaggia warned that their illegal accumulation of riches would cripple the young economy and was against the spirit of nationalism.

Josiah Mwangi Kariuki, popularly known as JM, and one of the foremost critics of national coffers' invasion, also voiced his concerns:

> We fought for independence with sweat, blood and our lives… we must ask: What did we suffer for, and were we justified in that suffering?… Kenya has become a nation of 10 millionaires and 10 million beggars.[2]

---

2   Quoted from Dorothy Kweyu, "50 years on, the dream for equity is all but lost", *Daily Nation*, 11 October 2013.

JM was assassinated for his patriotism in March 1975. Today, even after the Second Liberation that ushered in important reforms in the country, mega thefts and corruption continue. Every person and community in the country has been critically affected by the demon of corruption. This is the base that was laid down by the 'makers of the nation' as explained by Hassan Omar Hassan, former Chairman of the Kenya National Commission on Human Rights (KNCHR):

> I now realise why we have been rendered to poverty, ethnicity and corruption. ... in the 1960s, independence 'hero' Jomo Kenyatta immersed the country into corruption and greed, transforming State resources into personal estate, built an ethnic State and eroded the foundations of good democratic governance..[3]

Thanks to the BBI. Apparently, in Raila, some scales have been removed from the eyes for better sight, most wax from ears melted for better hearing, and tapes unstripped from mouths for better shouting. Finally, the devastating effects of corruption can be beholden by Raila and the number one suspect is one William Ruto, so he preaches. But all along, hasn't the country been run by governments – Executive, Judiciary and Parliament – whose leaders were not away without official leave (AWOL) to some planet?

THE EXECUTIVE, WHERE THE BUCK STOPS

When the Kenya constitution affirm that the President is the Head of State and Government and Commander-in-Chief, it means serious business. He is the Chief Executive Officer of a company called Kenya with 47 million stakeholders. Harry Truman, the 33rd President of the United States, ordered a sign made, which was mailed to him on 22 October, 1945. Always on his desk in the Oval Office, it read; "The Buck Stops Here!" He meant that he could not pass the country's responsibility to someone else.

In his farewell address to the American people in January 1953, Truman revisited his concept very specifically in asserting that, "The

---

3   Hassan Omar Hassan, "Kenya needs transformational leadership like that of France", Standard Digital, 30th October, 2011.

President – whoever is – has to decide. He cannot pass the buck to anybody else. No one else can make decisions for him. That's his job".[4]

What does that mean in the Kenyan situation? The President is the foundation, the base that holds this pyramid called Kenya. He is the symbol of unity among the building blocks consisting of 47 million people in the Republic irrespective of their ethnicity, religious affiliation, political parties or economic status. He is the cement that binds together the blocks to protect the pyramid from natural and man-made catastrophes. The President provides the architectural expertise to help the masterpiece stand firm. Yet when a tsunami or earthquake threatens to shake it or bring it down, he cannot pass the blame to the Governors, MPs, Cabinet Secretaries or the MCAs. He is the Father of the Nation.

But there is a caveat, a proviso. The President will have a human brain and not one of a god; one heart and not three like an octopus; two eyes and not compound ones like the dragonfly; two arms and not four pairs like an octopus; and two legs and not 750 like a millipede. In short, the President cannot comprehend, feel, see, walk or travel every region in the country simultaneously. In this, President John F. Kennedy's book, *Profiles in Courage*, rescues the President:

> For in a democracy, every citizen, regardless of his interest in politics, 'holds office'; every one of us is in a position of responsibility; and, in the final analysis, the kind of government we get depends upon how we fulfill those responsibilities. We, the people, are the boss, and we will get the kind of political leadership, be it good or bad, that we demand or deserve.[5]

So we are all in this journey together. Kenyans have a patriotic duty to help to make their president an achiever's hero, a brand. You don't vote for someone and then cut his legs; you support him.

In his book, *In the Name of the Mother*, Ngũgĩ wa Thiong'o agrees with the citing of heroism in Alex La Guma's *In the Fog of the Season's End*:

> Heroism lies in the ordinary acts of ordinary men and women driven by the need and the commitment to change intolerable social

---

4   Harry S. Truman, "The President's Farewell Address to the American People", The American Presidency Project, 15 January, 1953. Available at: https://www.presidency.ucsb.edu/documents/the-presidents-farewell-address-the-american-people

5   John F. Kennedy, *Profiles in Courage*, Memorial Edition (London: Hamish Hamilton, 1964), p. 255

conditions. It consists of doing one's part in the link of chain of human struggle. The achievement, whatever it is, is not the result of the work of many hands and minds.[6]

Yet when the corruption tsunami keeps growing and growing all barbs are directed to the President. Why? Again, he is the boss. Kenyans elected him to show the way forward and act. Except God, he is the ultimate authority in the land.

Exactly two years into his office, President Uhuru Kenyatta dropped a bombshell. Some 175 public officials had been suspected of involvement in corruption, he revealed to a not-so-surprised nation on 27 March 2015. Through Cabinet Secretaries, Principal Secretaries, Governors, MPs, Senators, civil servants and parastatal chiefs, the country had lost hundreds of millions of shillings to dirty deals. The report was christened "The List of Shame".

Soon another report revealed that government ministries lost Kes 600 million every month to ghost workers and Kes 300 billion through corruption annually. In that year, Transparency International had ranked Kenya at position 145 out of 175 countries studied in the Corruption Perception Index. This was the highest thieving rate in Kenya's history.

Since then, the trend seems to have gathered even more momentum. The theft magnitude has increased. How much enough is enough? Kenyans pray earnestly. How much must one steal in order to say enough is enough? Must it reach to squeezing the last drop, milking dry the producer of wealth? And so to ask, how far can a thousand-shilling note in a billion, arranged side by side, reach from the ground? Planet Mars?

Economist David Ndii attempted to explain why those who plunder have trillions of shillings and yet steal more, don't tire, and it is never enough:

> Money and power buy social status, he wrote, and social status is a rat race. If you overtake me, I must overtake you. The goal is to be the number one rat... When, then, does plunder stop? It stops when it becomes more painful and more dangerous than labour...[7]

---

6   Ngugi wa Thiong'o, *In the Name of the Mother: Reflections on Writers & Empire* (Suffolk: James Currey, 2013), p. 50.

7   David Ndii, "Of plunderers and sexual predators, how bad can it get? Fight corruption", *Daily Nation*, 28 March, 2015.

Despite having governments in place for nearly six decades, thieving has remained more pleasurable and safer than honest production.

Since the fight commenced, no serious corruption convicts have emerged. Suspects, especially on the upper scale of the graft chain are always the untouchable. They are quickly arrested, the media are tipped for maximum publicity, rushed to court, released on bail, mentions of case spread over months, hearings adjourned and adjourned again, till Jesus comes. End of the story. Sometimes the anti-graft institutions are disbanded and new ones established. Business as usual.

But the begging questions will not die off. Can the President afford to disappoint the millions who put him in charge to protect their hard-earned money, among other duties? Can he put his tail behind hind-legs, surrender to the corruption barons and leave the country to sink? Is he scared to be eaten by the lords of theft? "Fighting corruption in our country is like holding the tiger by the tail." noted Farida Waziri, then Nigerian head of Economic and Financial Crimes Commission (EFCC). "If care is not taken, the tiger will devour you." Mumo Matemu, former Chairman of Ethics and Anti-Corruption Commission (EACC) contributed to this point: "Fighting corruption in Kenya is like fighting a war. Those animals that constitute grand corruption in Kenya can easily eat us…"[8] If a president is frightened by the graft cannibals, where does that leave the masses?

Kenyans believe in everyone doing their fair share of work and getting their fair share of rewards. And they believe that the Presidency is not a toothless dog to let the people's lives and national vaults to end up in the ICU due to corruption, when billions of shillings are allocated annually to fight the same menace. Have the fat cats hijacked the government?

Back in October 2011 in *Termites at Work*, Peter Grastrow warned about government institutions being taken hostage by corruption cartels. He said: "governments that lack the capacity or the political will to counter such penetration run the risk of becoming 'captured state' – state whose government structures have become captives of

---

8   Samwel Born Maina, "In war against corruption, one should be ready to be bruised", *Saturday Nation*, 28 September, 2014.

uncontrolled corruption."[9] After the state is captured, it has no remedy other than join the thieves' club. And when corruption becomes a way of life at the top, the poison trickles down and infects the masses as US Supreme Court Justice, Louis Brandeis, opined long back:

> The government is the potent omnipresent teacher. For good or ill it teaches the whole people by its example. Crime is contagious. If the government becomes a 'lawbreaker,' it breeds contempt for law; it invites every man to become a law unto himself, it invites anarchy.[10]

What about the law enforcement officers who include investigators, arrestors and prosecutors? One may ask: the Kenya Police Service is held in high esteem the world over, holds responsibilities of exceptional and absolute national importance, yet, curiously it has been ranked continuously as the most bribe-prone institution in Kenya. Bearing in mind the vital position the body occupies, two lessons will do. The first is from Liberia, where Kenyan doctors led the battle to eliminate the deadly Ebola virus, yet the corruption [virus] at home has grown impossible to handle.

In 2004, the UN had posted 15,000 peacekeepers to Liberia following a civil war that killed 200,000 people. With 700 officers, Mark Kroeker from United States was the UN Police Commissioner there. His assignment was to help transform the national police department that had mutated to an embodiment of state terror, corruption and ineptitude, to one which was in line with modernity. In an article in *Granta* magazine titled, "Policemen to the World", Daniel Bergner gives an insight of what transpired at the Police Academy.

> "Is anybody above the law?" Kroeker would ask, standing in front of a classroom of about 25 trainees.

> "No, Sah!" The students called out in unison.

> Kroeker gestured with his hands, encircling the room, "The law is above all of us. We don't enforce our opinions. We don't enforce our emotions. We don't enforce the will of politicians. We enforce the law… Our number one value is what?"

---

9   Peter Gastrow, *Termites at Work: A Report on Transnational Organized Crime and State Erosion in Kenya* (New York: International Peace Institute, 2011), p. 105.

10   Quoted in Joel K. Goldstein and Charles A. Miller, "Brandeis: The Legacy of a Justice", *Marquette Law Review*, Vol. 100, Issue 2 (Winter 2016), pp. 480-481.

"Compassion!" They replied.

"Number two?"

"Courage!... Respect!... Integrity!" They gave the series of answers.

"Yes. Yes." He agreed. "If you don't have integrity, you wander in an ocean, lost, not knowing what to do. You sacrifice your ideals for a few dollars on the street... Number five?"

"Excellence!"

"Number Six?"

"Service!"

"Yes. Yes. Every day for a policeman begins with compassion and ends with service."

And the training continued, in and outside the Academy. "The core value," Kroeker reminded them – "Compassion, Service," will be hammered in, hammered and hammered and hammered, because I am the boss.... and that's what will breathe a whole new air into the thing... You either believe that or you go home."

Apart from training, Kroeker who was more passionate about inculcating principles and remaking the soul of the department was also concerned about the welfare of the Force. Later he was appointed the head of all UN's police missions around the world, headquartered in New York.[11]

Lesson number two. 7 October, 1960, Kenya's Commissioner of Police, Sir Richard C. Catling was receiving gifts on behalf of the Force. In the acceptance speech he prompted the officers that they were responsible to the citizens and not the politicians. "Kenya policemen exercise their powers and responsibilities on behalf of the citizens of this country," he said. "...powers and responsibilities which in essence are shared by all citizens alike – and not as the agents of any higher authority...We are in changed circumstances now (towards independence) and the police have a part to play also. It is not merely

---

11   Daniel Bergner, "Policeman to the World", *Granta*, 96 (2005)

a matter of keeping the ring for the politicians or catching the 'baby' should they drop it..."[12]

Well, that is exactly 60 years ago. When the law enforcers demonstrate inefficiency in their work because they are pocketed by corrupt politicians and the mighty, they lack integrity and sense of service and finally they imitate the masters of theft. Never wonder again why it is practically impossible to tame corruption.

So after the looting race, the rats climb on the podium and reward themselves with medals. The celebration is accompanied by the Thieves' National Flag hoisting and Thieves' National Anthem singing and toasting by champagne as they recite their Mass, do covenants and beseech the god of graft to grant more wisdom and energy for tomorrow...

Meanwhile, the rats will present themselves to their families and country as the most intelligent, hardworking national builders and then embark on a maddening acquisition of vast tracks of land and shares at the national bourse.

THE JUDICIARY WHERE LAWS ARE AN ASS

Isn't it absolutely strange that for 20 years after independence, all the five Chief Justices in Kenya were white, except one Kitili Mwendwa? And according to many African lawyers the white judges were not wholly appropriate in serving the interests of an independent African government. One particular case brought this argument forward.

In the *State vs Frank Sundstrom* (1980) Justice L.G. Harris sentenced the 19-year old US Marine, Frank Sundstrom, to sign a bond to pay Kes 500 in case he failed to maintain good conduct for the next two years. The accused had confessed killing Monica Njeri, a commercial sex worker, on the morning of 4 August 1980 in Mombasa. The judgment triggered a countrywide uproar and demand for retrial.

The matter was brought on the floor of the House (in Parliament). Attorney-General, James Karugu, expressed the predicament and anxious moments he was in and said he was legally impotent to do anything. "Mr. Speaker Sir," he told the members, "that is why one

---

12 William R. Foran, *The Kenya Police, 1887-1960* (Londone: Robert Hale, 1962).

judge said that the law was an ass." Mr. Karugu was referring to the statement in Charles Dickens' book, *Oliver Twist* that, "…the law is an ass, an idiot" (a donkey has a reputation for abstinence and stupidity).

In the country then, there were 14 white judges out of 19 High Court judges, while the whites made less than one per cent of the 15 million population. In the Sundstrom case, the suspect was white, had been tried by a white British judge, prosecuted by a white Briton, and the Chief Justice was white. In addition, the accused defender was an Asian lawyer. Therefore, no black African participated in a case that involved the murder of a black. If a murderer could walk free out of court of law, how about a thief?

Irrespective of the skin colour, right from independence, the Judiciary was a proxy or an employee of State House, the Legislature and the powerful people. "Laws are like cobwebs, which may catch small flies but let wasps and hornets break through," observed Jonathan Swift, an Anglo-Irish poet.[13] "Laws. We know what they are, and what harm they are worth! They are spider webs for the rich and might, steel chains for the poor and weak, fishing nets in the hands of government," wrote Pierre Proudhon, French social theorist.[14] Thus, the country breathed a sigh of relief when Dr Willy Mutunga came in as Chief Justice. Kenyans saw in him integrity, professionalism and a committed human rights defender. There was an unprecedented optimism in the air.

After 120 days in office, Justice Mutunga presented the "Progress Report on the Transformation of the Judiciary" on 19 October 2011. He said he picked the day, "...tomorrow being the Mashujaa (Heroes) Day to remind us how an oppressive system of government can easily use courts to perpetuate a miscarriage of justice". He revealed that, he had inherited "an institution… so low on its confidence; so deficient in integrity; so weak in its public support that to have expected it to deliver justice was to be widely optimistic …a judiciary that was designed to fail." He added: "In sad moments in our history, courts have failed to uphold the rule of law to defend the rights of man and woman."[15]

---

13 Jonathan Swift, *The Prose Works of Jonathan Swift: A Tale of a Tub, and Other Early Works* (London: George Bell & sons, 1897), p. 295.

14 Pierre-Joseph Proudhon, *General Idea of the Revolution in the Nineteenth Century* (New York, NY: Cosimo, Inc., 2007), p. 133.

15   Quoted in Tom Maliti, "Kenyan Chief Justice outlines progress in judicial transformation, " *The International Justice Monitor*, 25 October, 2011.

Even with the infamous Radical Surgery on the Judiciary and the establishment of Judges and Magistrates Vetting Board to determine suitability to serve and restore the confidence in the institution, there seems a long way to go especially on the fight against corruption. In Kenya, the laws, repeat, on corruption, remain "an ass and idiot" and appropriately designed never to convict the rich and might. The victory in fighting corruption in Kenya is still very distant. This "war without spectators" as Ngũgĩ wa Thiong'o demonstrates in *Devil on the Cross* – between forces of the clan of the producers who symbolise the nature of God and forces of the clan of parasites, the nature of Satan – still continues, sadly at a snail's pace, the producers being the constant victims.

Thou shall not steal, warns the Eighth Commandment. Stealing from Kenyans does not make God hungry or suffer for shortage of cash for school fees, medical bills, clothing or shelter. He is self-sufficient. Perhaps the best He does is to write down the thieves' names in the black Book of Judgment.

Money does not mint itself or grow from the trees. All the money in the hands of Kenyans, in banks and the National Treasury comes from the sweat and blood of the wealth producers. In theft and robbery, those women who toil day in day out in tea, coffee, flower and pyrethrum plantations, young men in factories and *jua kali* (informal sector) etc, are the most sinned against. The working class, the prime agent of change in the society, feel the greatest pain even before God puts pen on His book. And when the Judiciary, the people's topmost rights defender, fail or became compromised in punishing the corrupt, the institution becomes their comrade-in-arms, guilty as the thieves.

Sixty years since independence, the freedom fighters must be spinning in their graves like some cosmic bodies. They fought for the abolition of the colonialist's robbery of African's labour, resources and land. Unfortunately, independence brought another form of robbery: from Africans by Africans.

If he were to resurrect, Kisoi Munyao would hike the fastest parachute back on top of Mt. Kenya and ask the nation: "Is this the light I told the whole world in broad daylight was shining across the land December 12, 1963?" Kisoi would take the war against corruption, an economic violence on people, to where it rightly belong; where its punishment is supposed to come from. He would take it to the priestly judges – wigs, robes, pretended nationalism, and all – with a lesson from a novel on how oppressed workers confronted injustices in a judiciary similar to what Dr Willy Mutunga found in Kenya.

The book, *The Mother*, by Maxim Gorky (Alexei Peshkov) published in 1906, centred on factory workers – poverty-ridden, oppressed and politically helpless who staged a demonstration on May Day 1902 celebrations. A handful of them were arrested and soon arraigned in a court of law. Their leader Pavel Vlasov addressed the court boldly thus:

> … We maintain that a society that regards man only as a tool for its enrichment is anti-human; it is hostile to us; we cannot be reconciled to its morality; its double-faced and lying cynicism. Its cruel relation to individuals is repugnant to us. We want to fight, and will fight, every form of the physical and moral enslavement of man by such a society; we will fight every measure calculated to disintegrate society for the gratification of interest of gain. We are workers – men by whose labour everything is created, from gigantic machines to childish toys, we are people devoid of the right to fight for our human dignity. Everyone strives to utilize us, and may utilizes us, as tools for the attainment of his ends…[16]

One could imagine the elderly, powerful, now restless Judges and those in attendance wondering where this mad young man had come from as Pavel continued courageously with the speech:

> We are against the society whose interests you judges have been ordered to defend; we are its un-compromising enemies, and yours too, and no reconciliation between us is possible until we have won our fight… As a matter of fact, all of you, our masters, are greater slaves than we. You are enslaved spiritually, we – only physically.
>
> You cannot withdraw from under the weight of your prejudices and habits, the weight which deadens you spiritually… The poisons with which you poison us are weaker than the antidote you unwittingly administer to our conscience… Your energy, the mechanical energy of the increase of gold, separates you, too, into groups destined to devour one another… Everything you do is criminal, for it is directed towards the enslavement of the people…

---

16 Quoted in Richard Freeborn, *The Russian Revolutionary Novel: Turgenev to Pasternak* (Cambridge University Press, 28 Feb 1985), p. 48.

Pavel was instinctively aware of having touched a live wire. In his conclusion, he added even more venom:

> …To insult you personally was not my desire; on the contrary, as an involuntary witness to this comedy which you call a court trial, I feel almost compassion for you, I may say. You are human beings after all; and it is saddening to see human beings even our enemies so shamefully debased in the service of violence, debased to such a degree that they lose consciousness of their human dignity.

In the end, the Court sentenced Pavel and his comrades to exile in Siberia. When his mother went to cyclostyle his court speech for distribution, she was beaten, chocked and arrested. She told the police officers, "Not even an ocean of blood can drown the truth." Can, in this 21st century of democracy and improved human rights, a Kenyan address a court using such powerful words as Pavel's? To agree with Pavel, when the Kenyan Judiciary sit on the fence in the midst of corruption growing in leaps and bounds they transform themselves into slaves, spiritual corpses and criminals.

THE PARLIAMENT: BATTERED CONSCIENCE FOR BRIBES

The Honourable members are the people's watchmen and watchwomen. One of their primary duties is to make laws to protect their subjects from among others, robbery without violence: corrupt elements. Some voices of reasons hereunder tell their story:

(a) On 7 June 1963: Humphrey Slade, the new Speaker of the House of Representatives concluded his maiden speech with his vision of the House: "This House will be a lighthouse. A lighthouse which will not only stand against all tumultuous seas but will hold out hope and guidance to all who sail on those seas, in Kenya, in East Africa, and throughout this great continent."

(b) On 2 November 1965: President Jomo Kenyatta, while opening the second phase of Parliament Buildings: "The conduct of this Parliament must also be a source of pride… This Parliament represents our Republic and the Republic is the people… The members of Parliament are in a position of trust."

(c)   On 6 August 2012: President Mwai Kibaki while opening the refurbished House. "It (the Parliament) is, therefore an institution for governing as well as defending the rights of Kenyans, particularly the unprivileged... we should set examples of hard work, integrity and national building to our fellow citizens."

(d)   On 27 April 2013: Prof Makau Mutua, writing in *Saturday Nation*, "The Legislature isn't a place where MPs make laws. No Sir. They come to the August House to 'make money.' That's why people lie, cheat and even kill to be elected. Being an MP in Kenya has always been an open cheque to the nation's Treasury... like bees to honey. That's why some of the most corrupt and seediest persons usually get elected to the Legislature..."[17]

(e)   On 12 March 2015: Mutuma Mathiu, writing in *Daily Nation*, "Parliament is corrupt and broken. The oversight function, and perhaps even the legislature one as well, has been sold for bribes by MPs whose greed, selfishness, and corruption appears beyond belief... Parliament is a critical institution. It is our protector, the custodian of our civilized way of life, guaranteed of democracy, the watchman who keeps watch of our money...They have betrayed the people ..."

That is a 60-years brief Parliament's journey. The legislators can pass whatever laws they feel like. They can threaten to paralyse government operations and disband the Salaries and Remuneration Commission unless their salaries and allowances are increased. They can laugh at the protestors demonstrating against their greed who bring a pig and six piglets outside Parliament Buildings (14 May, 2013) who scramble for blood brought in jerry cans. They can get amused by their new moniker of MPigs. But when billions of shillings belonging to the taxpayers are stolen every now and then under their real watch, it becomes a different matter altogether. Yet it may not be totally strange since majority of them belong to the category of looters. And if there are leaders who deserve to be sent home packing, look no far, you are home and dry.

____

17 Makau Mutua, "For Siding with Greedy MPs, Atwoli Should Go" *Saturday Nation*, 27 April, 2013.

The Kenyan legislators' conduct over the years provides a reminder of one parliament that constituted dishonourable members, failed the people and its dissolution became inevitable. Oliver Cromwell was an English statesman, a solider and the Lord Protector of the Commonwealth of England, Scotland and Ireland. After learning that Parliament was attempting to stay in session despite an agreement to dissolve, and having come up with a working constitution, his patience ran out. On 20 April 1653 he attended Parliament, listened attentively to the members' speeches and immediately called in a troop of soldiers and ordered the MPs to clear the chambers, thus dissolving the August House by force. He roared, "You are no Parliament, I say you are no Parliament; I will put an end to your sitting!" He then looked at the Speaker's mace and declared it a "fool's bauble." He ordered his officers, "here, carry it away!" Following is an extract of his speech in the Chambers during that historical day:

> It is high time for me to put an end to your sitting in this place, which you have dishonoured by your contempt of all virtue, and defiled by your practice of every vice. Ye are a factious crew, and enemies to all good government. Ye are a pack of mercenary wretches, and would like Esau sell your country for a mess of pottage, and like Judas betray your God for a few pieces of money.
>
> Is there a single virtue now remaining amongst you? Is there one vice you do not possess? Ye have no more religion than my horse. Gold is your God. Which of you have not battered your conscience for bribes? Is there a man amongst you that has the least care for the good of the Commonwealth?[18]

Today, more than 360 years since, one can visualise Cromwell literally sweating blood and shaking heavily in anger as he continued:

> Ye sordid prostitutes have you not defiled this sacred place, and turned the Lord's temple into a den of thieves, by your immoral principles and wicked practices? You are grown intolerably odious to the whole nation? You were deputed here by the people to get grievances redressed, are yourselves become the greatest grievances.

---

18 Quoted from, "A message from Oliver Cromwell Directed at the Sleazy Politicians of Today", Conservative Home, 11 April 2009.

> Your country therefore calls upon me to cleanse this Augean stable, by putting a final period to your iniquitous proceedings in this house; and which by God's help, and the strength he has given me, I am now come to do.[19]

And Cromwell made the final move to the Honourable members, like a charging elephant:

> I command ye, therefore, upon the peril of your lives, to depart immediately out of this place. Go, get out! Make haste! Ye venal slaves be gone! So! Take away that shinning bauble there, and lock up the doors. In the name of God, go![20]

After this nationalism endeavour, the Parliamentarians and other anti-reformists did neither forgive nor forget Cromwell's act that greatly humiliated them. In September 1653, he passed away after a period of illness. Three years later, the vengeful Parliament ordered the exhumation and posthumous execution of his corpse. On 30 January, 1661, his decomposed body was removed from the grave and dragged through the streets of London to the gallows where it was publicly hanged and the skull cut off. His headless corpse was then thrown into an unmarked grave and the skull put on a spiked pole and placed on display above the Westminster Hall where it remained for 20 years!

It is unfortunate Kenyans may not dissolve their Parliament easily and therefore remain helpless in the wake of lawmakers' unwillingness or inability to protect their wealth and other rights through effective laws.

SO, CRUCIFY WILLIAM RUTO FOR GRAFT NOW!

This then, is the bottom line. Kenya has evolved into a sea infested with corruption germ, its DNA deeply ingrained with the monster. In 2005, artist Eric Wainaina sang "Nchi ya Kitu Kidogo", a country of little bribes. Tanzanian President Julius Nyerere had previously called Kenya a "man-eat-man society" due to its culture of parasitism. This was the plain truth. Corruption has permeated all spheres of Kenyans' lives. Right from the top in the government, institutions, companies, NGOs, religious bodies, to the common person. Did the nutritionists

---

19 Ibid.

20 Ibid.

and dieticians prescribe human sweat and blood cocktail as the best balanced diet for the citizens?

The ropes of theft and robbery have been excelled such that qualification into crooks and embezzlers has made corruption domesticated as a national culture, a religion. The vice has been personalised (it's my time to eat), clan-lised (it's our clan's time to eat), tribe-lised (it's our tribe's time to eat) and nationalised (steal from each other). Consequently the country has been condemned to posting deficit in its Profit and Loss A/C and unhealthy Balance Sheet every financial year then rush with begging bowls to international lenders and donors. And the perpetrators have no conscience. They fear no one. What God? What government? President? Courts? Prison? They worship the money god and every waking morning is a mission to steal.

Year 2019 Transparency International Corruption Perception Index had Kenya at 144 out of the 175 countries surveyed, an improvement of just one position from 2015. Isn't it high time everyone threw hands up in defeat and admit the war lost and declare corruption a legal way of life, introduce it as a subject in school curricula and for PhD thesis scholars, as well as include it as a master plan for development and dismantle all anti-corruption institutions?

No, all is not lost. There is one option only. The BBI principals require an understanding that to win the war on corruption will require an invention of an anti-graft jab to inoculate not just one person, but the whole system. The search for vaccination will go hand in hand with that of novel coronavirus. Meanwhile, at the tail end of *Petals of Blood*, Ngũgĩ wa Thiong'o delivered a prophetic message on the current System:

> A system that bred hordes of round-bellied jiggers and bedbugs with parasitism and cannibalism as the highest goal in society... These parasites would always demand the sacrifice of blood from the working masses. These few who had prostituted the whole land turning it over to foreigners for thorough exploitation, would drink people's blood and say hypocritical prayers of devotion to skin oneness and to nationalism even as skeletons of bones walked to lonely graves.
>
> This system and its gods and its angels had to be fought consciously, consistently and resolutely... to overturn the system of all its preying

blood thirsty gods and gnomic angels, bringing to an end the reign of the few over the many and the era of drinking blood and feasting on human flesh… Then, only then, would the kingdom of man and woman really begin, joying and loving in creative labour…[21]

This chapter began with likening William Ruto to Mercury, the god of theft in ancient mythologies. The question has not yet been answered on the validity of this resemblance. But first, a lesson from the man who taught the world that pointing other people's speck in the eye while yours has a log is wrong, John 8:3-11:

> The Scribes and the Pharisees brought a woman who had been caught in adultery and placing her in the midst they said to him, "Teacher, this woman has been caught in the act of adultery. Now in the Law Moses commanded us to stone such women. So, what do you say?

> …Jesus bent down and wrote with his finger on the ground… He stood up and said to them, 'let him who is without sin among you be the first to throw a stone at her.' And once more he bent down and wrote on the ground. But when they heard it, they went away one by one, beginning with the older ones, and Jesus was left alone with the woman standing before him.

> Jesus stood up and said to her, 'woman, where are they? Has no one condemned you?' She said, 'No one, Lord.' And Jesus said, 'neither do I condemn you; go, and from now on sin no more.

Even before the BBI could start crawling, Raila exclaimed to his foot soldiers a phrase that had been eating his bowels for eons. Tolgo phonic! (Shoot the arrows! – In Jonathan Swift's book, *Gulliver's Travels,* little people's language). Raila & Company quickly approached Wanjiku (common person) dragging Ruto along. "*Wanjiku,*" Raila, heading the delegation commenced the lengthy accusation reporting:

> From January 30, 2018, I became the People's President, the ultimate representative of the masses. No one knows Kenya's economy better. In Kenya's history, no greater thief had been born by a woman. William Ruto is the symbol, a case study, centre of excellence in corruption, and Number 1 candidate for the Guinness Book of World Records on Theft in the country. He is at mid-50s and I at late 70s

---

21 Ngugi wa Thiong'o, *Petals of Blood* (Nairobi: East African Educational Publishers, 1977), p. 344.

yet my combined wealth is not even a quarter of his. In fact he is the richest politician after the President. From a chicken seller in a village to a multi-billionaire with unexplained sources of wealth he has refused to fill the Wealth Declaration Form. Every Sunday he heads to churches with bags of money to show off his philanthropy. I call it hogwash.

The money greed in this man must be tamed. His sticky fingers possess a huge currency magnetic field such that all coins and notes at the Central Bank of Kenya are at risk of being swallowed by him.

Raila was visibly excited by his imagined Messianic expose, swaying sideways like in a slow dance, and gesturing with hands to bring points home.

Remember Chief Wangombe wa Nderi who allegedly sold Mount Kenya to one John Boyes for a sum of four goats in 1920s. Remember also that Kenya lost Mount Kilimanjaro reportedly through the greed of Queen Victoria of England when she gifted the same to her grandson and therefore reverted it to Tanzania in 1886 that was under German rule.

Ruto is a money-slave individual who can dream (actually attempt!) to sell Mount Kenya to the lowest bidder; gather all wildlife in Maasai Mara, Tsavo and Amboseli National parks and sell them to European Zoos. He can contemplate packing every grain of sand in bags at Diani Beach and pass them off as sugar in the fashion of the ancient conman Abdul. Without these national heritages the tourism industry would collapse and the country would forget about foreign exchange earnings. Wanjiku, this man is money-hungry to the extent of envisioning packing all air in Kenya in bottles like mineral water for sale or even selling our girls and women in European brothels or our young men into slavery!

In fact Ruto is like the Lernaen hydra in Greek mythology, a serpent-like monster with many heads. You cut off one, two more grow back. The hydra had poisonous breath and blood so virulent that even its tracks were deadly. In the real world he is like a mosquito with a huge thrombosis for drinking Kenyans' blood. He can't get enough of money.

Recently, this man built a national prayer altar at his Karen home, borrowing from the biblical King David. Rumour mill has it that his every moment's prayer is, 'God, bless me with all world gold reserves in Central Banks and currencies-dollars, francs, pounds, yens, shillings, yuans, etc and then have them stamped: Property of WSR.' Failure to this, another gossip goes, he will set a chair and a pair of pointed sandals in front like Abdul of old and invite the 47 million Kenyans and international visitors to see an imaginary angel for a fee. In other words, convert the altar into a spiritual-based tourism attraction.

The problem with Ruto is his massive popularity. He is a man of the people. As a ruthlessly ambitious person, what would happen when he becomes the President of Kenya 2022? With his unquenchable thirst for wealth, will it be a wonder to see him pack whole of country Kenya in a suitcase and speed like lightning to the New York Stock Exchange – the world's largest – with a banner: A COUNTRY FOR SALE! The Scramble for Kenya. Wanjiku, the country will be doomed, its economy will go to the dogs unless something drastic is done pronto!

Wanjiku, the UN International Covenant on Civil and Political Rights prescribes the abolition of the death penalty in peacetime. Kenya is a signatory to this. But can there be peace when big thieves like Ruto prostitutes the country with abandon making citizens into walking corpses? They also say prisons are for such and their keys belong to the deep oceans.

Presently, Raila was sweating profusely. He was restless. He knew Wanjiku was the overall boss. Wanjiku had denied him enough votes severally to qualify to State House. With President Kenyatta's departure in 2022 Ruto was almost assured the presidential win. However, by unveiling the country's biggest thief he had fully captured Wanjiku's heart, at last.

To Raila, the whistle-blowing was impactful than "Nobody Can Stop Reggae" BBI campaign signature. Ruto was on his way to political Siberia. Elvis Presley's song, It's Now or Never was crossing his mind, for Wanjiku: It's now or never/Come hold me tight/Kiss me my darling /Be mine tonight/Tomorrow will be too late…

Wanjiku drew on the ground what seemed like a map of Kenya and a set of statistics. Then she raised her head and looked Raila in the eye. "Mr Hurgo," he addressed Raila (Hurgo means Great Lord in *Gulliver's Travels* Lilliputian people). "On matters of reviving death sentence forget it. You are lucky to have escaped the hangman unlike your co-conspirator in the 1982 abortive coup. I will respond to you in summary."

Raila & Company became very attentive. "For many years," Wanjiku began,

> ... the Auditor-Generals have raised queries on hundreds of suspected mega scandals –NSSF, Fertilizer, Water Dams, Uwezo Fund, Relief Food, Youth Fund, NHIF, Universities, KMC, Foreign Embassies, Saccos, Sports Ministry, Prisons... Let us pick at random a few from 1990s, with their respective estimated economic loss. Goldenberg (Kes 100 billion), Triton Petroleum (Kes 6.0 billion), Anglo Leasing (Kes 55 billion), Cemetery Land (Kes 283 million), NYS (Kes 791 million), Education Fund (Kes 4.2 billion) and Health Ministry (Kes 13.7 billion)...

Wanjiku paused for a moment.

> You were an MP for many years, a Prime Minister for five years, can you provide your performance card relating to these and other scandals? Number of convictions, punishment and amount recovered? It is terribly odd that a country loses approximately one trillion shillings annually to corruption, a third of its State budget, then spend billions of shillings pretending to investigate and prosecute and suddenly, the whole thing lands on a cul-de-sac: a point leading to nowhere. And lest I forget, in God's name what was your role in the Maize (Kes 23 billion) and Kazi kwa Vijana (Kes 4.3 billion) scandals where your name was mentioned adversely?

Raila and his foot soldiers kept mum as Wanjiku continued with interrogation.

> Mr Hurgo, let us be honest. From the first President of this country to the current fourth; from yourself to your NASA co-principals, you are all multi-billionaires. Swearing by the Holy Scriptures, sincerely can you pick just one from the list who have acquired their wealth genuinely without an element of corruption, 100 per cent? I repeat, 100 per cent means 100 over 100?"

And lastly Mr Hurgo. You suggest so strongly that Ruto is the biggest dragon of corruption. Isn't there a government in place? The investigators are not on leave. The doors of police stations, the courts and prisons are wide open. Kindly supply them with answers to these four W's: 'What has Ruto stolen? When? Whom from? What amount?' In a nutshell, uncover all Rutobergs and Rutogates with solid facts and inform the authorities. I am not an investigator, a prosecutor or a magistrate. My only weapon is the vote card. Bring concrete evidence of his theft and 2022 I will decline to elect him. Mr. Hurgo, we know you are not very fond of religion or the Bible. But try to read Romans 3:21-24 below. Chapter closed.

But now God has shown us a different way to heaven-not by being good enough and trying to keep his laws but by a new way…Now God says he will accept and acquit us – declare us 'not guilty'– if we trust Jesus Christ to take away our sins. And we all can be saved in the same way, by coming to Christ, no matter who we are or what we have been like.

"Yes, all have sinned; all fall short of God's glorious ideal; yet now God declares us 'not guilty' of offending him if we trust in Jesus Christ, who in his kindness freely takes away our sins.

CONCLUSION

Back to the Roman and Greek mythologies. Is William Ruto a manifestation of Mercury /Hermes in Kenya? A brief comparison. Ruto is a winged god of speed. With his several golden helicopters he is able to travel across the country with messages and ideas of development, politics (life is all about politics) and reconciliation. Like Mercury he symbolises closing of boundaries in his role as a guide. Planet (the Wanderer) Mercury is closest to the sun and circle it faster than all other planets. Ruto is closest to the Voter (the sun) and reaches to them fastest (Tanga Tanga) than any other politician.

As a god of merchants, he is in hospitality, agribusiness, insurance, real estate and other industries. Like Mercury, he always carries a pulse-loads of money – with cash for charity work. Mercury had a cockerel as constant companion. Ruto started selling chicken in the village. The birds followed him. Today he has one of the largest chicken farms in the country. And like god Mercury, he is eloquent, clever, visionary, skilled in diplomacy and popular.

Is Ruto then the god of thief like Mercury/Hermes? These mythologies had other great thieves. Autolycus, son of Hermes was gifted in thievery and always escaped detection as he changed form or colour of both the stolen property and himself. Prometheus (the wolf) raided a workshop on Mt. Olympus, stole fire and gave humanity for warming up and making metalwork as civilisation.

Thus, provisionary, Ruto is not a resemblance of Mercury/Hermes, Autolycus or Prometheus as far as corruption is concerned. Ngũgĩ wa Thiong'o advised: Overturn the System! Wanjiku concluded: Bring forth solid facts of corruption then crucify the little devil!

CHAPTER TWELVE

Vox Populi, Vox Dei: The People Decide (Vision 2022 – 2032)

Through history, it has been the inaction of those who could have acted; the indifference of those who should have known better; the silence of the voice of justice when it mattered most; that has made it possible for evil to triumph.

Haile Selassie,
Ethiopian Emperor

*   *   *

Your beliefs become your thoughts. Your thoughts become your words. Your words become your actions. Your actions become your habits. Your habits become your values. Your values become your destiny.

Mahtma Gandhi,
Indian Nationalist

Raila Odinga: DNA, blood group, heartbeat lacks leadership qualities

On 28 September 1978 Pope John Paul I (Albino Luciani), famously known as "The Smiling Pope" died at his residence. Soon after David Yallop, an investigative journalist, produced a shilling-shocker book titled, *In God's Name*. In it, Yallop analysed the circumstances surrounding the demise of the Holy See and concluded that the Pope was murdered, a revelation that was heavily criticised in some quarters. In a preview, the *Aberdeen Evening Express* described the shocking findings in the book as "Deeply disturbing … If only a small percentage of it is true, then the Vatican and the world has much to fear, for God appears far from home."

On his part, Yallop came out strongly to support his research and the facts in the book as credible. He said, "If the Vatican can prove me wrong on just two simple questions of facts … then I will donate every penny of my royalties from the sales of this book to cancer research." To date, to the best knowledge of the author(s) of this book, Yallop has not been disapproved.

This book has a mission similar to Yallop's; it has dwelt on the period when 'God was away from home' and attempted to find out Kenya's 'killer'. Extensive research has been done. Relevant authorities have contributed their thoughts. Then consciously and consistently, the story has been compiled, with a strong angle on historical perspective and Holy Scriptures narratives. And the credible facts have given way to the gospel truth…

Kenya has several established media houses strong on the print and electronic (TV and radio) segments, key among them the Nation Media Group, the Standard Group and the Royal Media Services. Can they do the country a great favour? Search in their libraries the number of times the words "protests", "demonstrations", "violence", "loss of life", "destruction of property" and "economy" have appeared say, in the last 40 years, in relation to Kenya? Then determine one single person who has been associated with them the most. Raila Odinga's name would come No. 1.

This book is about building genuine bridges in our country, with a strong dose of the 2022 General Election. Boldly and lacking bias, it has proclaimed the verdict: Raila Odinga has never been, is not, and will never be the right person to occupy the country's top seat. Simply put in few words, Raila's DNA is not capable of promoting peace; his blood composition is unfit for country's unity and heartbeat not fast enough to drive Kenya Vision 2030.

Is this a harsh conclusion? No, it's the history, stupid! Take those lines and ridges in the shape of loops and spirals on the palms, fingers and feet of humans. A 19th century English anthropologist and eugenicist, Sir Francis Galton, discovered that "chances of the two fingerprints or footprints being identical are as small as 64 billion in one". The BBI could be unlike any other document the Government of Kenya has ever made, remarkable indeed. But consider in 40 years the fingerprints Raila has left on various documents in form of signatures, consider the imprints he has left on people's palms in form of Handshakes and consider the footprints he has left in form of visits to different parts of the country, one word this: Dangerous – this point to a man who was never made and did not deserve to be Kenya's President, Prime Minister leave alone the BBI main propagator. His prints belong to another miserable world.

Fortunately, everything with a beginning has an end. Raila's reign is staring at sunset. The only fear is it could be tragic. Author Alex La Guma could have been talking about him in the book: *In the Fog of the Season's End*. "You are reaching the end of the road and going downhill towards a great darkness, so you must take a lot of people with you, because you are selfish and greedy and afraid of the coming darkness…" Yet Raila should consider himself a lucky person indeed. He should count himself awesomely blessed and thank the Almighty a great deal; that, four decades down the line Kenyans still afford to give him space to operate from, listen to him, reward him financially handsomely from their taxes is a big mystery by itself.

Literally, the book has been a trip spanning four decades across the country. Life is a journey. Some words from Dr Lemuel Gulliver, the main character in *Gulliver's Travels* are in order. After the fourth voyage of the adventures author Jonathan Swift wrote:

> I know very well, how little Reputation is to be got by Writings, which requires neither Genius nor Learning, nor indeed any other Talent, except a good Memory, or an exact *Journal*. I know likewise, that

Writers of Travels, like *Dictionary*-Makers, are sunk into Oblivion by the Weight and Bulk of those who come last, and therefore lie uppermost. And it is highly probable, that such Travellers, who shall hereafter visit the countries described in this Work of mine, may by detecting my Errors (if there may be) and adding many new Discoveries of their own, jostle me out of Vogue, and stand in my Place, making the World forget that I was ever an Author. This indeed would be too great a Mortification if I wrote for Fame. But, as my sole Intention was the Public Good, I cannot be altogether disappointed…

I am not a little pleased, that this work of mine can possibly meet with no censurers; for what objections can be made against a writer; who relates only plain facts… I meddle not the least with any party, but write without passion, prejudice, or ill- will against any man, or number of men, whatsoever. I write for the noblest end, to inform and instruct mankind over whom I may, without breach of modesty, pretend to some superiority, from the advantages I received by conversing so long among the most accomplished *Houyhnhms*.

I write without any view to profit or praise. I never suffer a word to pass that may look like reflection, or possibly give the least offence, even to those who are most ready to take it. So that I hope I may with justice pronounce myself an author perfectly blameless; against whom the tribes of Answerers, Considerers, Observers, Reflectors, Detectors, Remarkers, will never be able to find matters for exercising their talents. [1]

Article 33(1) of the constitution on Freedom of Expression gives every person this right, which includes:

(a)   Freedom to seek, receive or impact information or ideas;

(b)   Freedom of artistic creativity; and,

(c)   Academic freedom and freedom of scientific research.

Writers are important messengers in a nation. In a critical point of history such as the one rendered by BBI, they have an urgent duty

---

1   Jonathan Swift, *Gulliver's Travels*, Dover Thrift Study Ed. (Mineola, NY: Dover Publications Inc., 2011), p. 222.

to conceptualise two scenarios and inform the country appropriately: What if Raila Odinga becomes President or Prime Minister of Kenya in 2022? Alternatively, what if Deputy President William Ruto becomes the President? (Imagination is the supreme sovereign for it is not bound by time and space and authority. No authority can enforce a command: Don't imagine. Don't dream. In that sense even with an oppressive system the artist can still exercise the sovereignty of his imagination to dream of new worlds…[2]). Thus, using their artistic talents, the writers will help the nation to decide on the all-important matter of leadership from 2022. (My task which I am trying to achieve is by the power of the written word, to make you hear, to make you feel – it is, before all, to make you see. That – and no more, and it is everything – Joseph Conrad.) Let as many Kenyans access this book.

Michael Hart is considered the Father of the e-book and founder of Project Gutenburg. When he died on 6th September 2011, aged 64, *The Economist* wrote on his obituary:

> He was a musician who gave the music away for nothing because he believed it should be as freely available as the air you breathed or as the black berries and raspberries he used to gorge on. He came to apply that principle in books too: Everyone should have access to great works of the world, whether heavy or light. Everyone should have a free library of their own, the whole Congress if they wanted… a quadrillion books, just given away. As powerful as bomb, but beneficial.[3]

The Economist explained further how "… Printing had torn down the wall between haves and have-nots, literate and illiterate, rich and poor until the whole power structure toppled." Hart's mantra was: 'unlimited distribution,' give everyone everything! Break the bars of ignorance down!"

BBI is intended to bring down walls that have flourished in Kenya over time. It is a noble idea, but with a big question mark on leadership. More books on this subject in print or online version shall help the BBI in breaking these barriers and give readers different viewpoints.

---

2   Ngũgĩ wa Thiong'o, *In the Name of the Mother: Reflections on Writers & Empire* (Nairobi: East African Educational Publishers, 2013), p. 41.

3   "Michael Hart – Obituary", *The Economist,* 24 September, 2011.

But don't shoot the pianist as yet. Listen keenly to the message in the song. For Raila's fanatical followers could call this work, 'one from a Kenyan gone mad again, one that belong to a lunatic asylum'. They say we are all mad and only the degree of madness matters. But like David Yallop's critics on the truth behind his book, readers are hereby invited to proof this book wrong on one fact that Raila's leadership is totally unfit for human consumption not only in Kenya but in any modern country.

Martin Luther is known as the Father of Reformation. Before, he was called "a leper with a brain of brass and a nose of an iron" for writing the 95 Thesis in 1517 challenging the Church's authority. His work was termed as "idle chatter and inappropriate books… a plague and cancerous disease." Nevertheless, his efforts went on to change the history of the Church forever.

This book is a compressed version of two volumes, which were written in the pre-2017 General Election period as a campaign vehicle for the Jubilee Party. However, they were not able to reach the publishers due to time constraint. Then, the Handshake and the BBI were not born. Today, the message herein is basically the same and even more relevant and urgent.

The opening statement dwelt on an introduction about Kenya's Triple Heritage– a country, horizons and leadership. It argued that the real problem that has plagued Kenyans for ages is not the first or the second (including the BBI) but the third. Now, it reaches a time in the history of a nation when people come together as one, speak in one strong voice on a matter of national importance. Presently, the BBI is the one horizon that demands serious brainstorming and a sincere handling by the people.

FORTY VOICES FROM THE PAST

In this chapter there are forty (40) selected past voices symbolising Raila's four decades of trekking to Canaan and selected verses from Dr David Ndii's works. They were reproduced by local mainstream media houses. From the President of the Republic, the Deputy President, government and political leaders, the private sector, the clergy, scholars and common *mwananchi*, these voices declare that Raila Odinga is the most single dangerous person in any political movement, society, nation, state, government and the country. "The Voice of the People is the Voice of God", in Latin *"Vox Populi, Vox Dei"*.

1. Can Raila manage Vision 2030?

Raila Odinga is going for the number one post of President of the Republic of Kenya. Does he have what it takes? Global leadership guru and bestselling author of *The Monk Who Sold His Ferrari* series, Robin Sharma, says: "You cannot lead others until you have first learned to lead yourself...!" What can we learn from Raila?... Those who criticise his development record argue that he has squandered too many opportunities to transform his massive influence to ensure that his followers grow wealth and sustain livelihoods beyond the basic needs...

If Kibera (was MP for nearly two decades) is to be used as the microcosm of Raila's leadership and developmental capacities, one would be tempted to ask what he hopes to achieve at the national level...and expedite the achievement of Vision 2030? Let him tell us what he brings to the table.

Masika Wambilianga, *Saturday Nation*, 2017[4]

2. Can Raila be trusted with power?

August is here again...of great historical significance is the commemoration of the 35th anniversary of the August 1, 1982, coup attempt...Also implicated in that coup attempt were .... and ... Raila Amolo Odinga, who is today's Nasa's presidential candidate... was sent to detention after initially being charged with treason... The aftermath of August 1, 1982 remains one of the darkest and lowest moments in the history of Kenya... They even attempted at gunpoint to force some of their fighter pilot colleagues to bomb the State House, Nairobi... I always wonder what could have prompted anyone to want to overthrow the government in 1982. Mr. Moi... was busy trying to unite and heal

---

4   Masika Wambilianga, "A Leader Needs a Lot More than a Track Record", *Saturday Nation*, 5 August, 2017.

a country that had been torn apart by tribalism. The coup leaders and planners must have been driven only by greed and a raw desire for power… what the younger generation who form the bulk of his unquestioning followers might not know is that their leader's youthful improprieties included treason… a serious offence then and today…Raila Odinga has been a part of Kenya's turbulent history. Can the man heal the country's wounds? Can he be trusted with power?

Masika Wambilianga, *Daily Nation*, 2017[5] [6]

3. Asking for votes

While on a voter registration tour of the Nakuru County in preparation for the August 8 2017 General Election, President Uhuru Kenyatta said:

We are getting votes because we are going to war. But as Jubilee, we don't believe in the war of the spear; we don't believe in the war of throwing stones; we don't believe in the war of bloodshed. We believe in the war that will be won by votes that we shall have in our pockets. That is what will win for us. I am asking you for my last vote this year. I ask you respectively, help us, vote for us so that we can go back.

President Uhuru Kenyatta, *Sunday Nation*, 2017[7]

4. Raila's Canaan slim chance

Mr Odinga, the self-styled biblical Joshua leading his followers to Canaan, is fighting to ascend to the presidency that has eluded him three times in the past. This is his last chance and best bet. As he graphically puts it in his traditional figurative language; it is the last bullet. Time is running out for him. Currently aged 72,

5   Masika Wambilianga, "Lingering Questions on Coup Attempt", *Daily Nation*, 2 August, 2017.

6   Masika Wambilianga, "A Leader Needs a Lot More than a Track Record", *Saturday Nation*, 5 August, 2017.

7   Francis Mureithi, "Uhuru Criticises Raila over Itare Water Project", *Sunday Nation*, 12 February, 2017.

he may not have a chance in 2022, when he'll be 77 to contest. He will certainly be tired to mount any formidable campaign and his supporters would be fatigued having stood by him for two decades without success.

David Aduda, *Sunday Nation*, 2017[8]

5. Master in intimidation

Kenyans are supposed to be intimidated into submission and accept what ODM and Raila Odinga want if we are to buy some peace in the New Year… All in all, Kenyans have to decide at what point they would rather face up to this intimidation with minimum damage to the country…Do we face it… in the second week of August 2017? Because facing it we must, given the history and political styles of the players.

Raphael Tuju, *Saturday Nation*, 2016[9]

6. Nothing good about Kenya

Raila's job from morning to evening is to criticize my government. Such utterances cannot bring development. He does not see any positive thing to talk about this country. I wonder why he wants to lead a bad country.

President Uhuru Kenyatta, *The Standard*, 2016[10]

7. Visible transformation

There is a rapid counter-narrative being bandied… to the effect that the Jubilee administration has done nothing in its first term… Tens of millions of Kenyans can see for themselves… the transformation in their lives and communities… One thing is for sure: President

---

8   David Aduda, "Why Tuesday's Election is Hotly Contested Affair in Kenya History", *Sunday Nation*, 5 August, 2017.

9   Raphael Tuju, "Cord Should Listen to Reason on Elections", *Saturday Nation*, 31 December, 2016.

10   Grace Wekesa, "Uhuru Responds to Raila's Public Criticism of State", *The Standard*, 25 November, 2016.

Kenyatta has… added great software and transformed the development arena into a model of what enlightened and visionary statesmanship can achieve… There are none as blind as those who will not see…Opposition Chieftain Raila Odinga… should know numbers do not lie and are the emblems of victory in political contests – not idle heresies.

Raphael Tuju, Saturday Nation, 2017[11]

8. Road to genocide

….either Raila does not realize the gravity of hate speech whose consequences has been war, genocide and holocaust, is reckless in supporting hate speech or is willing, embracing the demon of negative ethnicity to get power.

Koigi wa Wamwere, The Star, 25 June, 2016[12]

9. Fake Messiah

People who should know better have been conned by willy demagogues that the Jubilee government is the worst they have ever had since independence, when this is not actually the case. As the saying goes, a lie often repeated becomes the truth… For how long will Kenyans be held in thrall by masters of propaganda with messiah complex?

Magesha Ngwiri, Saturday Nation, 2016[13]

10. No regard for institutions

There are not many opposition leaders in Africa who occupy the unique position that Mr Raila Odinga does. However, Mr Odinga has a 'my way or the highway' attitude when it comes to his viewpoint on the way the State should function. …This stance raises

---

11 Raphael Tuju, "All Those Who Can't See Jubilee Success are Wilfully Blind", *Saturday Nation*, 11 March, 2017.

12 Koigi wa Wamwere, *The Star*, 25-26 June, 2016.

13 Magesha Ngwiri, "Jubilee Losing Propaganda War to Cord Due to its Complacency", *Saturday Nation*, 4 June, 2016.

many questions. Does Mr Odinga believe in the rule of law at all? As an individual who has held one of the most powerful offices in the land, one wonders why Mr Odinga shows an extremely casual disregard for institutions and for due process. Any true democrat should not act in a way that courts a breakdown in the rule of law simply because they are out of the government.

Bagaka Obuya, lecturer, 2016[14]

11. Injuring, killing youth

….the youth of Kenya have a lot of trust in the Jubilee administration for its focus on their interests. The Opposition coalition has in the recent past mobilized young people to participate in demonstrations where some of them have been injured or killed. In contrast, the Jubilee administration has worked hard to ensure that young people are continuously engaged and it will do anything to protect this. The Opposition has had nothing to offer the youth of Kenya, in and out of parliament, and should therefore not be trying to convince the youth otherwise.

Machel Waikenda, political consultant,
The Star, 25 June, 2016[15]

12. Cool revolutions

The best revolutions are not affected by bloodthirsty and murderous hotheads, but by ordinary, low-headed people, each contributing to the changing of society in the best way they can by doing best that which they know best how to do.

Austin Bukenya, English language scholar,
Saturday Nation, 2016[16]

---

14 Bagaka Obuya, "Raila Wrong in Faulting EACC Investigation of Auditor-General's Office", *Saturday Nation*, 29 October, 2016.

15 Machel Waikenda, *The Star*, 25-26 June 2016.

16 Austin Bukenya, "Uhuru, Revolution and the Future Golden Time", *Saturday Nation*, 17 December, 2016.

13. Whistling jokers

How can Mr Odinga hold a government, unwilling to beholden to him, accountable? The answer is in two places. One, his troops in Parliament should wake up and report to duty. There has to be a semblance of opposition in the two houses of parliament. Forget the whistling jokers… The Opposition in Parliament, not outside it, is what the Constitution envisaged… Two, Mr Odinga must seriously look around him and decide if he is surrounded by the kind of strategic and tactical minds that can outmanoeuvre their plans in the government.

Dennis Mosota, Advocate,
Saturday Nation, 2016[17]

14. Baba, while you were away

If Opposition leaders had done their homework a little, they would have known that the mere concept of a foreign leader working with the opposition against a government in office is a red rag for Mr Obama. He was looking for them to articulate an alternative vision, to be statesmen, to suggest solutions, not just to report, expose, undermine, and play party politics… They wasted an important, rare opportunity to secure their country and win a powerful ally…

Mutuma Mathiu (on President Obama visit to Kenya),
Daily Nation, 2017[18]

15. Opinion polls

(a)   On the decided voters, President Kenyatta would lead at 54 per cent compared to Mr. Odinga's 35 per cent.

(b)   On the 2022 General Elections, 58 per cent polled that Deputy President Ruto would one day be president.

---

17   DBM Mosota, "How Raila Can be More Effective in Holding Government to Account", *Saturday Nation*, 23 April 2016.

18   Mutuma Mathiu, "Yes, it is time Kenyans said 'enough is enough'; did leaders get message?" *Daily Nation*, 31 July, 2015.

(c)   On political parties, 45 per cent said they supported Jubilee, while 34 per cent backed NASA.

Ipsos, *Daily Nation*, 2017[19]

16. NASA's short lifespan

Could NASA promise to last longer, at least? There is a lot of splitting and splitting, because everyone wants to be a leader. Sometimes you sit and wonder if this is Kenya. I hope NASA will still be there in 2022.

Provost, All Saints Cathedral,
Daily Nation, 2017[20]

17. Dangerous path

While seeking power through democratic means is proper, the temptation to use ethnic antagonism to acquire it is always tempting but dangerous… Mr. Odinga is entitled to seek power, but he must do so through democratic and legitimate means and never by pitting one people against another. He should exercise restraint because we know how dangerous this can be. Thus, the Bible asks, of what value is it, to win the whole world but lose your soul.

Koigi wa Wamwere, *Daily Nation*, 2017[21]

18. Overthrowing government

These people care nothing for you… They have threatened to make Kenya ungovernable. They have shouted insults in rallies and held the presidency – which belongs to all Kenyans – in contempt. They have even in the past threatened to march to the

---

19 Ipsos, "Kenya: 2017 Poll a Two-Horse Race", Ipsos, 9 and 16 January, 2017. Available at: https://www.ipsos.com/en/kenya-2017-poll-two-horse-race

20 Aggrey Mutambo and Patrick Lang'at, "We Know How We Will Secure 10m votes - Kalonzo", *Daily Nation*, 29 May, 2017.

21 Koigi wa Wamwere, "Raila Should Not Preach Ethnic Propaganda on Itare Water Dam", *Daily Nation*, 15 February, 2017.

Seat of Government and overthrow the government of the people. This is not opposition politics; this is disruption and undermining of a country. Elections come and go but Kenya and our families remain. Together, we are strong.

President Uhuru Kenyatta,
Nairobi News, 2017[22]

19. Kenya not banana republic

…Whether you look at this from bottom or top, NASA lost the election… it is not clear whether he (Raila Odinga) has the majority in Parliament to rule the country… Declaring yourself winner in an election is like grabbing the crown from the hands of the bishop and putting it on your own head… Secondly, we had a good election. It was complex but well-managed… observers were almost universally impressed by how we voted… The commission appears genuine and well-meaning and professional… NASA had raised objections on the basis of problems…

Kenyans would have paused and listened. But to disregard the legal process and demand to be sworn in and given power even before the votes are counted and on the basis of some tally you have done yourself is outright laughable… The winner will be declared by IEBC. If you don't like those results, go to court. Kenya is not a banana republic.

Mutuma Mathiu,
Daily Nation, 2017[23]

20. Mr. Odinga, Kenya first!

…According to international monitors, the electoral commission has conducted itself professionally and credibly… Raila Odinga alleges this (President Kenyatta's re-election) veneer of fairness is, in fact, foul, foggy and fishy… We no longer want or appreciate our

---

22 Isaac Ongiri, "My Agenda for Kenya in 2017 – Uhuru", *Nairobi News*, 2 January, 2017. Available at: https://nairobinews.nation.co.ke/news/agenda-kenya-2017-uhuru

23 Mutuma Mathiu, "Nasa's Premature Declaration of Victory in Poll is a False Step", *Daily Nation*, 10 August, 2017.

leaders fueling flames of ethnic discord…we are one of the fastest growing economies in the world… This is a new Kenya. A new generation, a youthful one that is inching towards transcending tribal loyalties and is united in its nationalistic endeavors. Mr. Odinga may have lost this election. But do not forget what he has done for Kenya. He has fought for human rights and democracy, and has endured torture, exile, and detention. He deserves respect. This was his last shot at the president…. Kenyans have spoken and, days after this election, their message is: Kenya First!

Zain Verjee, former CNN anchor,
Daily Nation, 2017[24]

21. Rigging prophesied

Why does the opposition National Super Alliance (NASA) spend so much energy attacking the institution that will preside over the election – the Independent Electoral and Boundaries Commission (IEBC)? So ferocious have the assaults on the electoral commission been that someone landing in Kenya today from outside the country would imagine that the electoral contest is a battle between NASA and the electoral commission rather than one between the opposition and the Jubilee Party…

These consistent hurdles placed in the path of poll preparations raise legitimate questions as to whether the opposition, in fact, want the election to go ahead as scheduled. More troubling have been the verbal missiles aimed at the electoral commission by the opposition leaders, particularly Raila Odinga. The message from the opposition leader is simple. He has told his supporters that there is a plot to rig him out during the elections. …This messaging is dangerous because it primes Odinga's supporters to believe a fallacy: That the Opposition can only lose the election if it is rigged out. This could then lay the grounds for a violent uprising in the event Odinga loses.

Obuya Bagaka, *Daily Nation*, 2017[25]

---

24 Zain Verjee, "Golden Milestone within Nation's Grasp", *Daily Nation*, 18 August, 2017.

25 Obuya Bagaka, "Raila should tell supporters poll can go either way", *Daily Nation*, 2 July, 2017.

22. Raila, respect will of God

… I simply cannot decipher why a political figure, who has sacrificed so much for the country, would want to erase all the dignity and honour by failing to acknowledge that Kenyans have made a choice… That this year's elections were largely incident-free and one of the most transparent ever in Africa should be enough reason for Mr. Odinga to respect the verdict. At his level of political maturity and his sacrifice, his desire to see a freer country governed by progressive democratic principles, winning an election or even assuming power should not be the only thing he should be prepared to die for. He is at a vantage position to demonstrate dignity in defeat that would leave his reputation, locally and internationally, intact… A people's choice ought to be respected as many equate it to the will of God…

Dr Njogu Barua, former MP,
Daily Nation, 2017[26]

23. Violent politics

Even in the midst of so much democracy, there are still those in the Orange Democratic Movement, who think that the only way you can be an MCA is by deploying thugs to unleash violence on those who disagree with you. ODM responds positively, it caves into violence … That is the kind of politics the party does.

Mutuma Mathiu, *Daily Nation*, 2017[27]

24. NASA, do not issue threats

The IEBC has put in place and has thus far followed a detailed process of paper ballot counting and security which, if followed through to the final steps, can give every Kenyan confidence that their vote was properly recorded and therefore this election can appropriately certify the outcome. We affirm with conviction that

---

26 Njogu Barua, "Conceding Defeat Can Bolster Peace", *Daily Nation*, 18 August, 2017.

27 Mutuma Mathiu, "What Violence in ODM Rank and File Says About Leadership", *Daily Nation*, 7 April, 2017.

the judicial process and the election laws of Kenya make full and adequate provisions for accountability in this election. The streets do not. Do not issue threats. If there is a legitimate complaint, there is a lawful process to deal with it. If there were hackers, were they able to change anything? ...

John Kerry, Head of Carter Center observer mission,
Daily Nation, 2017[28]

25. Cool heads needed

Kenya's opposition is now suggesting that the present government can never do anything good for society... It so polarises a country as to forge it to squander its extremely little political energy... opposition for opposition's sake is again beginning to characterise Mr Odinga's political army... The Opposition leader's task is to examine every government policy and to react to it publicly... with a cool head... Thus a country like ours... requires a keenly responsible-minded opposition. A mature opposition will speak in terms that do not insult anybody or cause mindless unrest... why not offer it to State House?

Philip Ochieng, *Sunday Nation*, 2016[29]

26. Clueless Opposition

An alternative government must, of necessity, take an alternative agenda to that of the government of the day. It should sell a competing vision of how the country should be governed. In other words, any opposition worth its name should at all times through a coherent narrative, articulate what it would do differently were it to be in power...

NASA... Their agenda is premised more on critiquing Jubilee than offering an alternative. Pointing out actual and perceived

---

28 Wanjohi Githae, "Go to Court If Aggrieved, Kerry and Other Observers Tell Nasa", *Daily Nation*, 11 August, 2017. John Kerry is former US Secretary of State and a one-time US Presidential Candidate.

29 Philip Ochieng, "Government and Opposition are Two Sides of Same Coin", *Sunday Nation*, 27 November, 2016.

negatives without offering solutions or hope… Their collective life in government runs into decades… can they demonstrate how they would be different…?

Ambrose Weda, lawyer,
Sunday Nation, 2017[30]

27. *Uji* to Bondo

Maybe it is his (Raila) age and that is why we are asking him to retire now that he is an old man. We will ensure he is treated well. Occasionally, I will bring him a bowl of *uji* in Bondo if he quits. Even he can see the good things we are doing, but he cannot point them out. It is a foolish way of conducting politics…

President Uhuru Kenyatta,
Daily Nation, 2016[31]

28. Doing worse job

Many Kenyans are simply not convinced that the Opposition would do a better job. For some, this is an issue of polices and approach… If they were in power, they might do an even worse job at managing the economy overall.

Gabrielle Lynch, Warwick University,
Saturday Nation, 2016[32]

29. Taking power by force criminal

When we connect homes with electricity, they ask how we can connect a grass-thatched house to power. Don't poor people deserve power? We must distinguish between a genuine and legitimate desire for change from its exploitation by short-sighted and cynical leaders who use us for their own selfish ends. We have

---

30 Ambrose Weda, "Why Nasa Agenda is Just about Power", *Sunday Nation*, 16 February, 2017.

31 Guchu Ndung'u, "It's Time to Hang Up Your Boots, Uhuru Now Tells Cord Leader", *Daily Nation*, 28 November, 2016.

32 Gabrielle Lynch, "Uhuru's re-election chances undented despite graft spiral", *Saturday Nation*, 12 November, 2016.

suffered attempts to take political power by force, resulting in the loss of life and property of great value. These actions were not just criminal but they betrayed our freedom fighters' sacrifice and sinned against our sacred nationhood....

Elections can no longer be about individuals but about people, agendas, transformations and not dividing our people and shedding blood... Our security apparatus will remain vigilant, ready to deal with acts of lawlessness and disorder. All I ask of you is that you reject the politics of division and conflict and that you vote in peace. That way no matter the outcome, we will all win.

President Uhuru Kenyatta,
Daily Nation, 2017[33]

30. Our time to eat

We vote for our own no matter what. The Opposition is not a government in waiting but other tribes lurking in the dark, longing to annihilate us.

David Ndii, Economist,
Saturday Nation, 2017[34]

31. Road to NASA

It is now clear to all that this is one person who is selfish and would only want to do things that will only benefit him. He wants to cheat people that he is leading them to NASA, which has no agenda for this country. While we in the Jubilee team are concentrating on bringing electricity, building roads, building the railway, creating employment for our people in the country...our competitors are regrouping to share power.

William Ruto, Deputy President,
Daily Nation, 2017[35]

---

33 Guchu Ndung'u, "Uhuru touts Jubilee's scorecard in Madaraka Day fete", *Daily Nation*, 2 June, 2017.

34 David Ndii, "A review of anomalies that doomed the year 2016", *Saturday Nation*, 31 December, 2017.

35 George Sayagie, "DP Ruto terms Bomet Governor Isaac Ruto's Nasa move as selfish", *Daily Nation*, 1 May, 2017.

32. Distrusted leadership

… It is also clear that his (Mr Odinga) leadership has a number of weaknesses. First his longevity and prominence within Kenyan politics means that… he is also distrusted in some pro-government parts of the country, with critics argue that there should have been an investigation into his alleged role in the 2007/2008 election violence… Second Mr Odinga, at 72, is getting older and has not always been in great health. Consequently, there is a question mark over whether he has the energy and ideas required to lead together an effective campaign in 2017. Even some Cord supporters and activists were disappointed with the 2013 effort…

Nic Cheeseman, University of Birmingham,
Sunday Nation, 2017[36]

33. Soul searching

To trip and fall is human. But to trip and fall at the same spot, over and over again is an indication that there is a problem. Are we going to sit back and wait to experience the same devastation in 2017 as we did in 2007, 2002 and 1992? If we do so, then indeed, we must question not just the quality of our leaders, but ourselves as a nation. We need to soul search and ask ourselves, is our loyalty to our ethnicity and kin, or is it to our country?

Bishop Anthony Muheria,
Daily Nation, 2016[37]

34. Majority vote counts, Mr Odinga

… One will be forgiven for wondering if NASA was fighting for an electoral system only free and fair if it gives them victory. Mr Odinga is a genuine Kenyan hero. He has fought a hard and a long battle for democracy, human rights and a just and equitable

---

36 Nic Cheeseman, "Who should lead the Kenyan opposition?" *Sunday Nation*, 2 April, 2017.

37 Anthony Muheria, "Of Kenyan elections and 'blood groups'", *Daily Nation*, 18 July, 2016.

society. He has withstood record stints in jail without trial, torture, exile and suffering, so that Kenya can be a better place for all its citizens… However, he would destroy his well-earned legacy if he continues working so hard to validate accusations by the Jubilee propaganda machine that he knew he couldn't win all along and was only set on provoking a crisis. His legitimate pursuit of the presidency must not ignore the simple democratic principle that ultimately it is the majority vote that counts. And no single-minded determination to clinch the prize should drive Kenya to the edge of precipice.

Macharia Gaitho,
Daily Nation, 2017[38]

35. Brothers, sisters

Hate speech is taking us back to a sleepy road. We can differ politically but remain peaceful… Although we are from different backgrounds we are all brothers and sisters… Our commitment as government and what we want and are asking from all those in leadership positions is to be watchful. Let us use language that bridges communities, religions and faiths so that we can create one stable, peaceful and united country…

William Ruto, Deputy President,
Sunday Nation, 2016[39]

36. Thrives on passionate hate

…He had been denied any chance to reward his own people and he was sharpening the knives, ready for battle. Raila evokes only two emotions in people: Passionate fanatical blind loyalty, on one hand, or passionate hate on the other. There is no middle way. The man seems to thrive on it and he is not fazed by it. Although the NARC

---

38 Macharia Gaitho, "Why Nasa claim on poll result is dead in the water", *Daily Nation*, 11 August, 2017.

39 Caroline Wafula, "DP Ruto warns leaders against divisive talk, protests", *Daily Nation*, 19 June, 2016.

Cabinet hit the ground running in 2003 and performed effectively, sibling type of infighting was the order of the day...

Moody Awori,
Riding on a Tiger[40]

37. Humble leaders are key

...when we choose humble, unassuming people as our leaders, the world around us becomes a better place. Humble leaders improve the performance of a company in the long run because they create more collaborative environments. They have a balanced view of themselves and a strong appreciation of other's strengths and contributions, while being open to new ideas and feedback. They help their believers build their self-esteem, go beyond their expectations and create a community that channels individual efforts into an organized group that works for the good of the collective... a leader's humility can be contagious. When leaders behave humbly, followers emulate their modest attitude and behaviour...

Margarita Mayo,
Daily Nation, 2017[41]

38. Raila litigates on his fears, hope

Mr Odinga never brings legal grievance to the courts. He didn't in 2013. He didn't in 2017. Mr Odinga always brings to court a sorrowful bundle of personal grievance informed by the zeal to have his way. This is further enveloped by a sense of entitlement to be president and four times near-misses. Mr Odinga doesn't litigate on facts or empirical evidence. He litigates on his fears, hope and state of mind. He has loyal and vociferous groups of myth makers in civil society who credit him with all historic milestones in Kenya and make excuses for all his failures. His complaints before the court were an omnibus full of fiction and wild fantasies... All

---

40 Moody Awori, *Riding on a Tiger* (Nairobi: Moran Publishers, 2017), p. 273.

41 Margarita Mayo, "Why we glorify leaders who exude charisma", *Daily Nation*, 12 April, 2017.

these allegations were false, and he knew it. The court found them false…

No doubt, Justice Maraga will be idolised and immortalised in the folklore of Mr Odinga's supporters. He will bask in the glory of nullifying a presidential election in an African country. But his gains are the losses of the Supreme Court of Kenya… Justice Maraga…threw the court to the political wolves, whom he invited to feast on the flesh and soul of the court.

Ahmednasir Abdullahi, Senior Counsel,
Daily Nation, 2017[42]

39. Never again

We shall never compete again in this country to the detriment of our people or cause bloodshed in our nation… We shall compete and compete healthily… never again should we shed blood because of political enmity. At one time, all of us will be out of this office. The only legacy that will matter is what we did during our time in office to make this country a better place…

President Uhuru Kenyatta,
Daily Nation, 2016[43]

40. Disorganised, unpatriotic opposition

In 2013, we ran as different parties. In 2017, we will face Kenyans as one people under a national party. In 2013, we faced a formidable team with half the government- a sitting prime minister and a sitting vice-president. In 2017, we are facing a clueless, rudderless, leaderless, plan-less and disorganized opposition.

William Ruto, Deputy President,
Daily Nation, 2017[44]

---

42 Ahmednasir Abdullahi, "Judges' decision signals end of Supreme Court's innocence and neutrality", *Daily Nation*, 21 September, 2017.

43 Pauline Kairu, "Uhuru and Raila promise to avert poll chaos", *Daily Nation*, 22 August, 2016.

44 Patrick Lang'at, "DP William Ruto's 5 reasons why Jubilee will win 2017 polls", *Daily Nation*, 13 January, 2017.

FROM THE MOUTH OF NASA'S CHIEF ADVISOR

"No man is an island entire of itself," wrote English poet, John Donne, in the 17th century. "Every man is a piece of the continent, a part of main…" The poet was likening people to countries urging them to cultivate their interconnectedness with God, adding that "I am involved in mankind." This doctrine of non-isolationism has been held vital since time immemorial, because from the highest to the lowest mortal, all belong.

Then and now, for instance, rulers appointed trusted confidants and advisors who formed *curia regis* – council of advisors and administrators. Considering that a ruler is judged by his achievements, members of the council drew manifestos to give directions to their master in order for him to reach desired targets for his subjects, win over the competition, remain in power or leave a lasting legacy.

With the eye on beating the Jubilee Party and hence becoming the government in power, the opposition, National Super Alliance (NASA), engaged wise men and women. In this *Curia Regis* was an economist David Ndii, a brilliant public intellectual, writer and researcher; Ndii was ranked 30th among the 100 most influential economists in the world by Richtopia, a digital platform. While at NASA, the chief strategist was a constant critic of the government, especially on the economic agenda accusing it of corruption and over-borrowing. He has since severed working relationship with NASA. In December 2019, he published online a length article titled, "From the Handshake to the BBI Report, Hope and Disillusionment: My Side of the Story".[45] In the 40-page document, Dr Ndii pours his heart out about the Handshake, BBI, Principals and Kenya tomorrow. The following is a bird's view of his story, in quotes form.

1. Better than BBI

Our preferred road map to a political settlement was a transition government (that) would have spearheaded the process of building a national consensus on political reforms that would have culminated

---

45   David Ndii, "From the Handshake to the BBI Report, Hope to Disillusionment: My Side of the Story", The Elephant", 13 December 2019. Retrieved at: from-the-handshake-to-the-bbi-report-hope-to-disillusionment-my-side-of-the-story. Accessed on 20 June 2020.

in what we hoped would be an uncontested constitutional amendment referendum, if one were required, followed by a free and fair election. We had also suggested that Uhuru and Raila commit publicly to retiring, so as to strengthen their hand as honest brokers and midwives of a new political dispensation, and by so doing, insulate the process from succession politics. This was a reasonable proposition since Uhuru would be retiring anyway, and Raila had signed a one-term deal with the NASA co-principals.

2. BBI's dangers

…The two leaders (Uhuru and Raila) have asked us to give them an opportunity to spearhead this process. We have been assured that this initiative will be about the people, will involve the people, and will be validated and owned by the people. But we are alive to the painful history of political betrayal. We know that once (crises) subside, leaders can get comfortable and allow the issues of the people to fade into the background. That is how we have ended up where we are.

3. Cutting DP Ruto to size

There were two other issues that I found troublesome. The first was anti-corruption crusade that was mounted immediately after the handshake. My concern was that corruption cartels were the last adversary that the BBI needed, especially as it appeared to be a one-sided assault on Deputy President Ruto's patronage network. Secondly, I was persuaded that the country was headed into an economic (crisis that is now unfolding). By embracing Uhuru Kenyatta, Raila Odinga was in essence sanitizing Jubilee's economic delinquency, and jumping into a sinking ship. In fact, I postulated that by the time of his departure from office, Uhuru Kenyatta would be more unpopular than Moi was in 2002.

4. Which way TJRC report?

If the TJRC report offers the residents of Kisumu an official amnesty for the 1969 massacre in exchange for the recognition of the years of economic marginalization which followed, then what will the BBI report yield? Will it offer restorative justice or compensation for lost life, limb and property to the recent victims of political violence? Who will foot the bill?... will it offer victims of past political evils or yet again endorse a tactic collective amnesia and unofficial amnesty for the perpetrators and principal beneficiaries of the past political evils? Who decides?

5. BBI gave Luos bad deal

Contrary to popular belief being peddled by 'Raila evangelists' that the Luos are now in government, nothing could be further than the truth. Luos aren't in the government and more than ever before, they are languishing in poverty. I fret every time I hear that Luos are now enjoying and I ask: which Luos are these? If there are any Luos in government, they must be Raila's friends or his relatives from Siaya County. The promises that Raila made after the Handshake, ostensibly to the Luo community, are nothing new. They are the same promises Raila has been making since 1997 when he merged his fledging National Development Party (NDP) with KANU. Since then, it is the Odinga family that has continually grown rich at the expense of the Luo people. Because of these Raila Handshakes, the Luo people are treated as the Odinga family's captives to be traded with politically any time the family wants to reap financially from the existing government. There are no deliverables, neither are there fruits to be harvested from the Handshake. All what we are hearing is what it intends to do, it is classical political brinkmanship. What the entire Handshake has done is to entrench even further retrogressive leadership in Luo Nyanza – quoting Steve Ochuodho, African history researcher.

6. Appetite for bloodshed

The Luo people were not ready for the Handshake. Because they were ready for war. The State's unceasing violence against the Luo people had created in them an appetite for unstoppable bloodshed. They were prepared to go the whole hog. For the first time in the history of post-independent Kenya, a people had successfully held back a state with all its militarized violence. From then on, the people decided there was no turning back and then the Handshake happened – quoting Mike Osilo, information technologist in Nairobi.

7. Youth sidelined

The youth are always ready to participate in protests, but where are they now? Some were killed and maimed, others were arrested and falsely accused of robbery with violence and are now languishing in jail, having been forgotten... Let us not kid ourselves – the Handshake has not worked for the youth: the *boda bodas* (motor cycle riders), street vendors and hawkers are still suffering – some lost their lives, others are today living with live bullets in their bodies. Nobody talks about their plight and President Uhuru and Raila have largely forgotten about them. The youth have been promised Canaan. Instead what they got was a Handshake between two political bigwigs who cared nothing as far as the youth were concerned... – quoting George Owuor, civil society leader.

8. Women hurting

Drunk with power by proxy, the party, it seems, is wasting its energy, distracted by chasing 'the rat that is escaping a burning house' rather than putting out the fire that is consuming the house... the ODM party leaders may have to work extra hard to keep women's support. Many women who support the party are hurting and hard done by tough economic times.

9. What birthed the Handshake?

The question that has been boggling many Kenyan minds is: What exactly led to President Uhuru Kenyatta and Raila Odinga, two of the bitterest of political rivals, who had left nothing to chance – as one fought to keep the coveted seat of the presidency to himself, while the other hoped to snatch it from the incumbent – to suddenly make peace? Was this a spontaneous reaction of two leaders who had suddenly been imbued with desire to save their country, which was on the verge of ethnic and geographical fragmentation?

10. Journey to Handshake

…I culled an array of information that suggested a presidency in crisis, trapped in a paradoxical pyrrhic victory and a withering state. Then there was a defeated opposition leader who for the very first time in his political career was caught between the devil and the deep blue sea, and was faced with the devil's alternative of either quitting politics altogether or re-engineering his ebbing political career. Add to this scenario a scheming deputy president who had already trained his guns on 2022 no sooner had his Jubilee Party won the presidential elections.

11. Economic boycott

The most potentially lethal of NASA's projects was the economic boycott, in which Kenyans of oppositional goodwill were asked to keep away from the Kenyatta family's business and any companies that were either associated with them, or had, in one way or another, presumed to have abetted President Uhuru's contested win… 'The boycott was a dangerously crippling idea as a political tool, because the Kenyatta's best-known flagship (Brookside Dairy) was going down the drain, right in front of their eyes…something had to be done very fast,' said my friend. 'Let us cut to the chase. Uhuru Kenyatta is not concerned with the Kenyan nation's legacy, but with the Kenyatta family's legacy.'

12. Raila is spent

Raila Amolo Odinga has paid a huge price for dabbling in national politics: He has been detained for close to a decade by the state. In the 2007 general elections, he saw his presidential victory snatched. In recent times, he has also experienced personal traumas… At 75, Raila is also no longer the youthful adrenaline-driven politician who could park public rallies and indoor meetings into 18 hours and still spare four hours of just enough sleep to see him through the next day's political onslaught.

13. President summons MPs

(a) 2014: A year after Uhuru and Ruto formed the Jubilee government, President Uhuru summoned all Kikuyu MPs to State House and told them that if they needed anything, they should go to the Deputy President. 'We must ensure our people trust the DP… you know our people are conservative…'

(b) August 2017: He met with newly elected Jubilee Party MPs. 'He was soaking drunk and he lectured us, as a headmaster would his pupils' said a first-time MP from North Rift. 'Rookie MPs who had never been to State House were excited to be called for the breakfast meeting. But when they were lectured by a drunk president, who was allegedly banging tables, cursing and swearing, they were dumbfounded.' He explained. 'Don't joke with a president who's not seeking a second term', President Uhuru is reported to have told the MPs,' 'I dare anyone who will not do as I say to walk through that door'; he hollered to the now cowed MPs. 'Why he was angry, we don't know. When he finished ranting, the MPs stood up and instead of heading to the laid out breakfast tables, they hastily walked to their waiting cars, and drove off in a huff.'

(c) September 1, 2017, after the Supreme Court nullified the election. '"You've seen what the Court has done to our win,' said a now mellow and pliant president. ' We need to put our heads together and strategize on how to win the presidential seat again'. He was now speaking to us in collegial terms – our win' – the insults and threats had gone; he wanted our help so badly… that's our President Uhuru.'

14. BBI is dynasties politics

'BBI is nothing but an entrenched political cabal's way of controlling national politics and state power so that they remain with the people who have always controlled the two. But more importantly, it is the cabal's way of ensuring the state power does not land in the 'wrong hands'', said a Jubilee MP, who is a friend to both President Uhuru and deputy. 'The Kenyatta family would like to have a political stranglehold, the way the Bongo family in Gabon has done.'

15. Meetings are dress rehearsals

'The emerging theme of these meetings has been – *punda amechoka… punguza mzigo* (The donkey is overloaded and therefore fatigued… – let's lessen its weight)…BBI's town hall meetings are supposed to culminate in a referendum and this is where the catch is – it'll not be by popular vote, but by delegates voting by acclamation', opined the Jubilee MP. 'These meetings are dress rehearsals that are supposed to dupe the people to believe that their voices matter. Carefully selected delegates from 24 counties will be assembled at the Bomas of Kenya for a convention in which they will all unanimously agree to pass the tabled resolutions. That's how it shall come to be'.

16. Come, referendum

'We welcome the referendum', said a North Rift Jubilee MP and one of the DP's close associates. 'We are not afraid of it. We are going to frame the question differently and better and we'll be asking Kenyans – *kama kweli punda amechoka,* (if truly the people are overwhelmed, hence, the demand for a reduction of the constitutional stipulated seats), why then expand the executive?'

17. Ruto, tough nut

'The MP observed that the machinations against Ruto by the so-called 'Kiambu Mafia' will not work. Ruto is a hardened and seasoned politician; he has passed through many political tribulations and overcome them. Even this one, he's going to overcome it.'

18. Jubilee on deathbed

'…Take it from me, the Jubilee Party, as currently constituted, will not be there in 2022', said the MP. '… The Mount Kenya MPs are not only privately accusing President Uhuru of political inaction, they are also nervous and suspicious of him,' continued the MP. 'They know President Uhuru, on his own, cannot out-think both Raila and Ruto. They therefore cannot hitch their wagon in his current party'.

19. The Ides of March?

March was a mostly interesting month for Kenya. Indeed in just one week a series of events combined to affirm a significant reversal in Kenya's economic sovereignty with far-reaching implications for our politics... On the 6th of March, Minister of Finance, Henry Rotich, made a surprise announcement that the government was broke… It is thus that the next day, March 7th, the IMF made its 'end of mission' statement pronouncement in Kenya's regard. Two days later, on the 9th of March, Uhuru Kenyatta and Raila Odinga stepped out of Harambee House to their now famous 'handshake' ….But just as in Moi's case in 1991, the handshake deal was fronted, not by the usual political or bureaucratic types, but by the men from the shadows who give advice on matters of national security and preservation of the regime.

20. Messy economy

…Kenyatta is attempting to manage his own succession with the economy in a mess; the politics polarized but opposition demobilized for now; and, in the midst of a looting spree that makes Goldenberg look like a minor hold-up in a corner shop. Behind it all one cannot help that feeling that, as they say, 'we just got owned!' Literally in our case as Kenyans.

Ndii's sample from social media

1. *Raila is naked*: How dare we question his magic? If we can't tell Raila he is naked, how different are we from UhuRuto toadies we rail against all day long. If this is a foretaste of President Raila – my way or the highway – how different is it from a Ruto one?...Raila abandoned his troops but Sifuna (ODM Secretary-General) and

company have no choice but to keep complimenting the emperor on his new clothes. Raila is not providing leadership, what we see is a follower clinging on a drunkard struggling from pillar to post, expecting the troops to follow blindly.

2. *Send Ruto to jail*: Ruto and his people are pigs (likening fight against corruption to the biblical casting of demons by Jesus into pigs before they were drowned). I am not saying that Ruto and his people have not done what they are accused of. A very close associate of Uhuru told me that his mother asked him why they cheated on Ruto (about supporting him), and he had no answer… They will destroy him if he runs and loses. They will bankrupt him and send him to jail. The dynasty is also scared that Ruto will also destroy them if he wins… He (Uhuru) is in there for his business, associates and not for Kenyans. It is pure personal interests.

3. *Use and dump*: I worry for my compatriots clinging to BBI like dear life when they wake up to reality that #handshake has not only outlived its usefulness, it's been overtaken by events. Uhuru has nothing to gain from fighting Raila's political battles. Use, dump, that's the name of the game.

4. *Mother of corruption*: The biggest mistake that Kenyans are making is to believe that William Ruto primitive procurement rackets is our biggest corruption problem. Nah. The mother of corruption is state capture by the crony capitalist cartels fronted by Uhuru Kenyatta.

5. *Eternal slavery*: Let me be clear. The imperative for progressive forces is to send both Ruto and the dynasties home. But if God forbid we must suffer one evil let us suffer Ruto – him we have a fighting chance. If we don't uproot the dynasties in 2022, they will enslave up to our grandchildren.

CONCLUSION

The foregoing voices are just a tip of an iceberg, a sample representation of millions of Kenyans who hold similar views on leadership. It is giving voice to silence. Since BBI is basically about reconciliation, reconstruction and opening of new horizons, people's voices matters a great deal. Despite the novel Coronavirus, for instance, forcing the world to cover their mouths with masks, people are still making use of them. Oftentimes, governments innovate mechanisms to suppress the people's constitutional right to thought and expression, but in the end, the people's voice prevail.

CHAPTER THIRTEEN

Like Diamond, Ruto is the Better Option for Vision 2022-2032

At 15, I set my heart on learning; at 30, I firmly took my stand; at 40, I had no delusion, at 50, I know my mandate of Heaven; at 60, my ear was attuned; at 70, I followed my heart's desire without overstepping the barriers of right.

Confucius, Chinese Philosopher

*   *   *

The true mark of a leader is the willingness to stick with a bold course of action – an unconventional business strategy, a unique product-development roadmap, a controversial marketing campaign–even as the rest of the world wonders why you're not matching in step with the status quo. In other words, real leaders are happy to zig while others zag. They understand that in an era of hyper-competition and non-stop disruption, the only way to stand out from the crowd is to stand for something special.

William Taylor, American author of
Simply Brilliant

Dr William Samoei Ruto: Kenya's Better Option President

Of all the foreign visitors to have graced Kenya during the Jubilee administration, two stand out: President Barak Obama in July 2015 and Pope Francis in November the same year. During their presence in the country Kenyans felt as if they were in the Seventh Heaven.

At State House on 25 November 2015, Pope Francis praised President Kenyatta's leadership calling it a model for the African continent and a country at the forefront of good governance in this part of the world.

> I am grateful for your warm welcome on this, my first visit to Africa….. Kenya is a young and vibrant nation, a richly diverse society which plays a significant role in the region. In many ways, your experience of shaping a democracy is one shared by many other African nations. Like Kenya, they too are walking to build, on the solid foundations of mutual respect, dialogue and cooperation, a multiethnic society which is truly harmonious, just and inclusive…". "…I thank you once more for your warm welcome and upon you and your families and all the beloved Kenyan people, I invoke the Lord's abundance blessings. *Mungu abariki* Kenya! God Bless Kenya![1]

INCUMBENT PRESIDENT

On President Obama, writers and analysts were quick to draw similarities between him and President Uhuru Kenyatta: that they are both left- handed, that they were born two months apart and two oceans apart, that both their fathers read economics at universities in foreign countries, that they served in the same government, that they went on to marry several wives, and that they became the 44th and 4th president respectively of some great countries – one leader of the wealthiest, most powerful country on earth and the other a young, small country that became a global brand. And that both men are humble, brilliant and eloquent.

---

1   Quoted from "Full text of the Pope's first speech in Kenya", Rome Reports, 25 November 2015. Available at: https://www.romereports.com/en/2015/11/25/full-text-of-the-pope-s-first-speech-in-kenya/

Besides pledging a generous financial package to Kenya from the US government, Obama heaped praises on the Jubilee government, the youth and the Kenyan innovation. At the same time he condemned sexual assault and domestic violence on women, media suppression, tribalism and terrorism.

Looking into the future, President Obama told Kenyans that, "you are poised for a big role in the world", but he regretted that the opposition led by Raila Odinga was frustrating this journey by constantly undermining the President. He admonished them: "Hoping that your president fails, is the same as hoping your country fails and it's not patriotism. Patriotism is supporting your commander-in-chief even if you don't agree with him on everything. It's what will make Kenya great, not complaining every time this nation tries to make progress."[2]

During this memorable visit Obama was 18 months to go to his presidency. Soon after he left Nairobi and landed in Addis Ababa, Ethiopia, he addressed the African Union on the subject of 'African strongmen and power': "I don't understand why people want to stay so long especially when they've got a lot of money." Obama wondered. "Yes, in our world, old thinking can be a stubborn thing. That's one of the reasons why we need term limits – old people think old ways and you can see my grey hair, I am getting old."(When he was delivering this speech Obama was 54 years old.) He continued:

> I am in my second term. It has been an extraordinary privilege for me to serve as President of the United States. I cannot imagine a greater honor or a more interesting job. I love my work but under our constitution, I cannot run again. I can't run again. I actually think I am a pretty good president – I think if I ran I could win. But I can't.

> So there's a lot that I'd like to do to keep America moving but the law is the law and no one is above the law. Not even the President. When a leader tries to change the rules in the middle of the game just to stay in office it risks instability and strife... And this is often just a first step down a perilous path.[3]

---

2   See Peter Kagwanja, "End of US 'opposition strategy' and future of power in Kenya", *Sunday Nation*, 2 August, 2015.

3   Steve Benen, "Obama says he 'could win' a theoretical third term", MSNBC, 28 July 2015. Available at: http://www.msnbc.com/rachel-maddow-show/obama-says-he-could-win-theoretical-third-term

There are other interesting similarities between Presidents Obama and Kenyatta, and their countries. The men are age-mates, born in 1961. By all standards, both have been performing presidents (Uhuru, more so in first term). Like the US, Kenya has two-terms presidential limit and both leaders are respecters of constitutions.

In Kenya the clock is ticking towards August 2022. President Kenyatta will leave office at 61years (Obama retired at 56 years) as he has declared severally, in accordance with the constitution. In the past, Uhuru has declared that his interest is to complete his ten year term then his Deputy William Ruto do another ten years.

Writing in March 2015 on the achievements made by the Jubilee government in its second year President Kenyatta noted:

> The work we have done so far has changed Kenya and touched every person. In another two years, the impact will be even greater….a fast- growing nation requires large-scale, institutional and systematic interactions to deliver services and generate opportunities…

> We are doing even more. Delivering each of our manifesto pledges in full remains our manifest commitment. We are working very hard, every day. We are making progress. The transformation is on. We now rank as the third fastest growing economy in the world. By the time we are done we will be the best and will be unbeatable.

During campaigns and inauguration on 9 April 2013, President Kenyatta, made various promises: of the growth of the economy; of job creation and industrialisation; of addressing insecurity and healthcare; of empowering youth and women; of promoting sports, tourism and education; of critically looking at the cost of living; and of having a government that is all inclusive, that promotes realisation of a nation; that is rich and at peace with itself. By the time we are done ….August 2022… some pledges will have remained undone.

The release of the BBI provoked a sleeping nation, for lack of better words. The mention of a new formula to create positions of President, Deputy President and Prime Minister trigged a nationwide debate. August 2022 looked like tomorrow. The BBI created a mini-General Election campaign. It is a healthy conversation enshrined in the constitution. Citizens have the right to discuss, brainstorm and forecast their most suitable leaders amongst the senior-most politicians on board.

The weatherman tells of the coming rain to prepare farmers for seed planting in good time. They informs when a tsunami, floods or drought are expected in order for the people to take appropriate actions. The same with an election that is months ahead.

From that moment of BBI, Kenyans commenced a serious separation between the wheat and the chaff; to make hay while the sun shines. Others say, "*Tene nĩ tene marigiti mbũga itanahoha* (a Gĩkũyũ phrase literally meaning "Go to the market early before the vegetables wither). In other words the journey to the government Kenyans want past August 2022 had taken off with a bang.

Why this fierce urgency to start thinking about Kenya's top leadership years beforehand? Precisely because the challenges Kenyans are facing – climatic change, unemployment, medical care, food shortages, insecurity, etc – are not the real problem. The problem is within the leadership. But what kind of leadership are Kenyans thirst and hungry for?

Maxim Gorky (Alexei Peshkov), a celebrated Soviet author, told a wonderful story on leadership. In the beautiful book titled, *Danko's Burning Heart*, we learn of the flaming heart of Danko:

> There are these people who have been driven by the attacking tribes to the depth of the forest. There, it is dark, for the sunlight cannot penetrate; swampy with water that is emitting poisonous vapour. They are getting sick and dead. Trapped, they get confused pondering on how to get out. A young man named Danko steps forward and volunteers to lead them. "…Arise!" He commands. "Let us go through the forest until we come out at the other end… Come! Let us set forth!"

The people embark on the challenging journey. Somewhere along, they become exhausted, losing hope. They start grumbling and abusing Danko for the seemingly failing liberation promise (remember Moses' story during the Exodus?) to the extent of wanting to kill him.

Suddenly Danko reaps open his breast and tear out his heart and hold it high above his head! "It shone like the sun, even brighter than the sun and the raging forest was subdued and lighted up by this torch, the torch of a grave love for the people, and the darkness retreated before it and plunged quivering into a yearning bark in the depth of the forest…" Kenyans are in a journey out of a dark impervious forest. The pace is disappointingly slow, though. They have started complaining. Who will bring forth the flaming torch to light the way?

On assuming power, President Mwai Kibaki saw a beautiful country Kenya: "I was woken up this morning by rays of sunlight … I looked far into the horizon and the beauty of what I saw around me stirred my soul… I said to myself, 'Oh, What a beautiful country!'"

On the same date, 30 December 2002, Kibaki saw an impenetrable forest that he called "a country that had been badly ravaged by years of misrule and ineptitude. "The President was referring to the 24 year-rule of President Daniel arap Moi. There had been a move by some politicians to bar Moi from ascending to power after President Kenyatta's death through the Change the Constitution movement: "*Bata no mũndũ ũyũ ehere*" (most important is for this man to go), and thereafter the consolation that "*Rĩĩrĩ no itu rĩrahĩtũka*" (this is just but a passing cloud). Is the BBI another "Change the Constitution" to prevent William Ruto become president?

President Kibaki came into this deep, dark swampy forest called Kenya in a wheelchair due to an earlier motor accident. His administration shone the light in the country like Danko's heart. During his second term, however, he went forward two steps, but Raila Odinga pulled him one step backward. Nevertheless Kibaki transformed Kenya into an enviable state. In five years the GDP rose from 0.6 to 7.1 per cent. He brought the constitution home. Many including his fiercest critic like Prof. Makau Mutua called him Kenya's greatest president. And Kenyans were described as the most optimistic people in the world.

August 2022 and moving forward from the day of President Kenyatta's exit, three scenarios will emerge, namely finished product, work-in- progress and un-started work. Kenyans are therefore presently brainstorming vigorously. Among the frontline politicians, who is the better option for the president to succeed Kenyatta in addition to successfully managing the country?

LOOKING FOR THE NEW PRESIDENT

The 5th President (the boss, not a toothless one) of the Republic of Kenya *wananchi* are praying for is one like Danko. Take the potential presidential candidates going by their previous desire for the top seat and their ages in years as in August 2022: William Ruto 56, Raila Odinga

77, Musalia Mudavadi 61, Moses Wetangula 66, Kalonzo Musyoka 69, Ekuru Aukot 50, Peter Kenneth 57, and Japheth Kayulu 54, *eight* of them. Among these, who is the better option?

Now let Kenyans be honest to themselves. Frankly, none of the mentioned leaders can satisfactorily (100%) pass Chapter Six of the Kenya Constitution on integrity or any other national requirement on leadership. Nevertheless, in addition to constitutional requirement of integrity, the most suitable candidate to be President will have to pass through a sieve consisting of various stages:

I.   Divine grace

Kenyans should make plans, counting on God to direct them (Prov. 16:9). Get all the advice you can and be wise the rest of your life. Man proposes, but God disposes. (Prov. 19:20-21)

While making reference of each of the *eight* leaders, a flashback in the event would suffice: The year was 1010 BC and Israelites want a king badly. The Lord orders Judge Samuel to head to Jesse's household to have his eight sons interviewed for the position. One by one seven fail the test. In one case, the Lord tells Samuel: "I have refused him: for the Lord seeth not as man seeth; for man looketh on the outward appearance, but the Lord looketh on the heart (1Sam 16:7 – KJV). Eventually, the eighth and the youngest son (shepherd) enteres the 'boardroom.' He is said to be 'goodly to look at.' "Arise, anoint him; for this is the one!" (1 Sam 16:12-KJV). Thus, came the greatest king of Israel, David. To date the Star of David has been the premier Jewish symbol in his honour and the country's flag bears the same at the centre. Who would God anoint from the Kenya's Big Eight?

David had one big enemy named King Saul. But in came a friend, Jonathan, who promised to stand by him all the time. David would never walk alone… Saul, the first King of Israel came from a wealthy and influential family. Surprisingly, he was anointed against his will and even went to hiding when (Prophet) Samuel had called to notify of his calling. During the early years Saul was a strong and courageous humane king whom God, the prophets, priests and people were on his side. But gradually he started making tragic errors in judgement and the Spirit of God in him was replaced by an evil spirit.

Young David was first a favourite of the King, especially due to the former's slaying of Goliath and the music entertainment he provided at the Palace. But David who had been anointed king at the age of 17 was becoming increasingly popular with the people, troubling the King greatly. Saul sought to eliminate him, throwing a spear at him on several occasions and hunting him all over the land. The more Saul tried to destroy him the more fame and strength he got. David respected authority and would not raise a hand against him.

With pride, fear, jealousy, violence and depression having become part and parcel of the King, he was finally abandoned by those who previously supported him and at one time went to seek help from a witch doctor… The love-hate relationship between Saul and David ended tragically for the former. During a battle where defeat was imminent Saul told his armour-bearer: "Draw your sword, and thrust me through with it, lest these uncircumcised men come and thrust me through and abuse me." Afraid, the armour-bearer refused. Then Saul took a sword and fell on it, ending his life. Soon after David was made king.

II. Leadership qualities

Kenyans are longing for a person who will be at the very forefront, possess grave love for their country, who can sacrifice, who can literally reap open his chest, tear out his heart and let it shine brighter than the sun; it will shine only "within our borders", but outside as well just like the Tanganyika Prime Minister, Julius Nyerere, predicted on 22 October 1959, that his country's "Mwenge wa Uhuru" would also "shine beyond our borders giving hope where there was despair, love where there was hate and dignity where before there was only humiliation." Kenyans should start ranking the candidates.

III. Action, work and results

"The harvest is great, but the workers are few…send more workers into his fields." (Mat 9:37 – NLT).

One evening in November 2019, Mr Buri Edward was interviewing Israel Deputy Ambassador to Kenya Eyal David on Hope TV. In between, the ambassador commented that what makes Israel a great nation is that the moment one steps in the Holy Land all they feel is "holiness in the air". Similarly in Kenya richness of the un-harvested fills the air waiting for the right commander to lead the soldiers.

In his address on the second Madaraka anniversary President Jomo Kenyatta warned: "…We knew and accepted that the aspirations of our people would be realised only through hard work and discipline. There is no room here for the lazy and idle; there is no room for those who wait for things to be given for nothing. There is no place for leaders who hope to build a nation of slogans." What Mzee Kenyatta was emphasising was his independence motto of "Uhuru na Kazi" and "Turudi Mashambani"; that this country will never be prosperous through a culture of slogans, theories and riddles. It is only through "Kusema na Kutenda (saying and doing)" that prosperity would be realised.

Kenya is a country of 580,000 square kilometres consisting of 47 Counties, hundreds of Wards in total hosting 47 million people from 44 different communities. The CVs Kenyans are perusing in readiness for August 2022 are about past and current performance of the leaders.

Among the listed leaders, who would Kenyans say has the most footsteps and greater visibility across the country (*Viongozi ni kuonana na wananchi*)? Which leader has shone the development torch most around the country – in hospitals, learning institutions, youth and women welfare, houses of worship, agribusinesses… and outside, Kenya's foreign policy? That would indisputably be William Ruto.

IV. Kenya's Diamond Age

Since independence, the four Kenyan Presidents have governed through several Jubilee ages, according to the hierarchy of years. First, President Jomo Kenyatta did not see any Jubilee since his reign ended before the country celebrated the 25th Anniversary. From 12 December, 1988 (Silver Jubilee) to 12 December, 2013 (Golden Jubilee – 50 years) was the Silver Jubilee Age when President Moi governed, followed by President Kibaki. The Golden Jubilee Age (10 years) will end on 12 December, 2023, to pave way for the Diamond Jubilee (60 years) whose age will then extend to Platinum Jubilee anniversary (12 December, 2033) when Kenya will be 70 years old. Do these Jubilees and ages have any bearing on the leadership? President Kenyatta's reign will have lasted almost the country's entire Golden Jubilee Age (2013-2023). Only his legacy will tell whether his was a golden period or not.

The Golden Age, according to classical Greek mythology, denoted a period of primordial peace, harmony, stability and prosperity. During this age, peace and harmony prevailed…the earth provided food in abundance. In *Works and Days*, Greek poet Hesiod said of this period: "Men lived like gods without sorrow of heart, remote and free from toil and grief: miserable age rested not on them; but with legs and arms never falling they made merry with feasting beyond the reach of all devils". Therefore, Kenya will celebrate its Diamond Jubilee on 12 December, 2023.

The Diamond Age (10 years) will extend to 12 December 2033. Among the listed contenders, whose Jubilee will coincide with the country's? William Ruto will mark his Diamond Anniversary (birthday) in December 2026, three years into the country's Diamond Age. Question: Will his government, *inshallah*, which will cover almost the whole of this period, reflect the characteristics of a diamond?

A diamond is the hardest known naturally occurring material. It is very strong and requires a lot of energy to break due to the strong chemical bonds binding its pure carbon atoms. It can withstand great crushing pressures, has high melting point and is one of the best conductors of heat. A diamond has few weaknesses, but much strength. Ancient Greeks called diamond *adama* meaning invincible, indestructible, unalterable, unconquerable, proper; it also means, "I tame", "I subdue". Records show that warriors wore diamonds to strengthen their muscles and bring invincibility.

So special is a diamond that it is described in dozens of words; it attracts and symbolises abundance, power, creativity, imagination, purity, harmony, faithfulness and innocence. A diamond embraces strength of character, ethics and faithfulness to oneself and others and encourages the aspect of truth and trust. A diamond symbolises excellent memory and all forces necessary for a healthy society – growth process and prosperity. It helps accomplish dreams and destinies. It is a stone of exceptional power, opens many spiritual doors – a stone of winners.

With its sheer beauty, a flawless diamond is extremely rare. For this reason it is presented as a special ultimate gift of pure love and relationship during engagement representing an unbreakable bond in marriage. A symbol of human progress. Diamond is the mark of the 60th anniversary of a marriage. And as the slogan goes, "Diamonds Are Forever".

The Tibetan culture has a philosophy called "The Diamond Way". In this, the people see diamonds as symbols of human progress. As a diamond moves from coal (carbon) to brilliant, long-lasting gem, a human can become refined even with humble beginnings. Thus, before and during the 2022 presidential campaigns, it will be upon Deputy President William Ruto to continue demonstrating to the voters, and Kenyans in general, that his heart, mind, body, patriotism and vision for the nation dynamically symbolises the diamond gemstone.

V.   Can human sweat, patriotism amount to naught?

From December 2007 to January 2008, some people had plotted to assassinate Mr. X. Later, Mr. Y, a God-fearing person who dearly love his people, got to hear of the plan. He reported the matter to the authorities. The plotters, including a Mr. Z were arrested, found guilty and sentenced to death in the court of people's minds. With time, the story was forgotten.

Meanwhile, Mr. Z was the Prime Minister. An evil man, he hatched a plot to kill Mr. Y and his people on account of dubious accusations. He even offered USD 20 million (Kes 200 billion) for the job and ordered the construction of a 75-foot high gallows for the mission. Then it was August 2022. Mr. X ordered for a set of historical records – the Book of Chronicles – and read the portion where Mr. Y had exposed the assassination plot on Mr. X. "What should I do to honour a man who truly pleases me?" Mr. X enquired. Mr. Z, thinking that he was the subject matter of honour recommended the best package. To his shock, Mr. X ordered: "Give the honour to Mr. Y" and then "take Mr. Z to the gallows he had built for Mr. Y!" Very soon, Mr. Y was made the new Prime Minister.

In this narrative, reconstructed from the Book of Esther in the Bible, Mr. X (King) is Kenya; Mr. Y (Mordecai) is Deputy President William Ruto and Mr. Z (Herman) Raila Odinga. For many years now, Kenyans have been perusing the historical records of performance by the current top political leaders with keen concentration, page by page. By August 2022, they will have read the last page and give credit where it is most deserved. God, and good people rewards genuine labour.

VI. It's the bedroom, stupid!

Baptism by the spirit of patriotism. Will the Jubilee Party survive the era of the Handshake?

Slightly before 9 March 2018, three men and two political parties changed gender and became women, good ones that is, and acquired new names. (William Shakespeare –That which we call a rose, but any other name would smell as sweet. As the Gĩkũyũ saying goes, "*Gũtirĩ rĩtakũria mwana*, a name cannot hinder the growth of a child".) And for the first time in the history of mankind, these men had conceived and birthed babies!

From then, Wairimu and Achieng slept in a king-sized bed with their infants, Ju-dy and Na-ncy, respectively. There, time had a habit of flying abnormally fast and 9 August 2022 was morning of the same night. During the night, Achieng had rolled on her baby and killed her. On discovering this, she switched her for Ju-dy. When Wairimu woke up to breastfeed her young one she was shocked to find herself next to a dead unfamiliar being whose physical features even did not match her own baby. An argument ensued and the two women headed to Wanjiku, the ultimate Judge. They explained their case as Wanjiku listened keenly…

Eventually, Wanjiku applied her Solomonic wisdom and issued the verdict: "You Achieng, your age-long appetite for invading other people's bedrooms, hijacking their babies and ejecting their parents is known globally. Not only that. You kill or abort your chain of children and then hijack others' for ransom. Look at Ju-dy's nose and ears. See her birth certificate. Ju-dy is a photocopy, the legitimate child of Wairimu and Chebet."

After a brief pause, Wanjiku closed the matter: "You must be contented with your 3 by 3 bedroom somewhere in the outskirts of Nairobi, Achieng. As for you Wairimu, take your baby; call Chebet and the three of you return to your bedroom."

This story is an adaptation of an event in 1 Kings in the Bible where King Solomon (Wanjiku) made one of the most celebrated judgments involving a dispute in which two women were claiming ownership of a baby. Raila (Achieng) invaded Uhuru (Wairimu) government and after killing his NASA (Na-ncy) Party claimed now Jubilee (Ju-dy) belonged to him. But Wanjiku, that is year 2022, told him, "No way", evicted him from the house and ordered Wairimu to summon Chebet (Ruto) to both take charge of their baby once again.

VII. Ruto, hustler nation and spirituals

What is so special about him? Ruto is specifically special because he dreamed the biggest dream about Kenya at the right place and time, convinced himself, "That we can", took the first courageous step of a thousand-mile journey, became ahead of the pack, believed in himself and the people of Kenya, took the Bible along his pilgrimage, and then Kenyans and God happened to be on his side. That is the reason he will end up in the House on the Hill; God's will be done (*inshallah*). In other words, some things were just meant to be. The sun rising or setting at a particular time. Rain seasons starting. It is just about time having arrived. The Scriptures talks about this: "For still the vision awaits its appointed time; it hastens to the end—it will not lie. If it seems slow, wait for it; it will surely come; it will not delay.." (Hab 2:3 – ESV) One does not need to meet a leader in person or interview him to know where his heart and mind lies about the future of a country. History – development projects, social activities and spoken word – would be a sufficient witness.

Rev. Martin Luther King Jr was an American evangelist and civil rights crusader. Employing both religion and human rights doctrines, Rev King became one of the most inspirational and influential leaders, a great voice of reason that today he is considered as one of the best bridge builders in history. His work of building bridges between blacks and whites in the US and fighting for justice and freedom earned him the Nobel Peace Prize in 1964 at a young age of 35 years.

On 28 August 1963, Rev. King organised a peaceful march known as March on Washington where he launched his famous address of "I Have a Dream". In commemorating Rev King's Golden Jubilee of the dream speech, on 29 August 2013, former US President Barack Obama said of him: "He offered a salvation path for oppressed and oppressors alike. His words belong to the ages, possessing a power and prophecy unmatched in our time..." Another former President, Bill Clinton, noted: "The choice remains as it was on that distance summer day 50 years ago. Co-operate and thrive or fight with each other and fall behind."

By relatively high standard Ruto – like Rev. King, an evangelist, political leader and a powerful orator – has what it takes to offer a salvation to the downtrodden than any other current leader. A son of peasant parents from humble background, who as a student sold peanuts and chickens along highways and across villages to supplement family income, Ruto has hands on experience on what toil means; for instance, when President Uhuru Kenyatta was born in 1961, his father Jomo was two years to becoming President. At birth in October 1963, Gideon Moi's father was four years to be Vice President. And slightly after age 18, Raila's father Jaramogi was appointed Vice President. These men's childhoods and backgrounds compared to Ruto's is like equating heaven and earth.

One cannot blame a child for being born in an aristocratic family where daily breakfast was eggs, bacon and sausages; getting school fees or money for medical or best clothing including several pairs of shoes was no big deal. But honestly, growing up, such a child will never appreciate the taste of poverty real-time. To qualify for a job, one is required to have so many years' experience; so is the case in leadership. The three men have not savoured poverty in their whole lives and therefore their motivation and abilities to eradicate the same adequately is terribly limited. Ruto is the opposite case.

A book written 160 years ago is a great friend of this story. Victor Hugo is one of the most celebrated French novelists and poets. His novel, *Les Miserables* (translated variously from French: The Miserable Ones, The Wretched, The Poor Ones, The Wretched Poor, The Victims) was first published in 1862. *Les Miserables* begins with Jean Valjean, a thin bare-footed young man dressed in mud-spattered clothes. The hustler was illiterate and came from a peasant family. A man of enormous strength and agility and orphaned at 25, fate eventually drove him to establishing a manufacturing enterprise that made him wealthy, brought his town prosperity and him onwards to be elected major of his town. (Years back Valjean had been convicted for stealing a loaf of bread to feed his starving sister and her family.)

A novel nearly 1,500 pages, *Les Miserables* has been described as an evergreen blockbuster, a book of wisdom, global phenomenon and a book of little people. It identifies with human struggle in the midst of persisting poverty, dwells on redemption, forgiveness, sacrifice and selflessness.

Valjean, the main character is generous and benevolent person who assist the needy and is dependent on God for strength and salvation.

Hugo said that this story of repression and redemption was "written for all nations" and desired its message to touch everybody, everywhere. In a letter to his Italian publisher, M. Daelli, he noted:

> Misery concerns us all... In every place where man is ignorant and despairing, in every place where woman is sold for bread, wherever the child suffers for lack of the book which should instruct him and of the hearth which should warm him, this book Les Miserables knocks at the door and says: 'Open to me, I come for you."[4]

Kenya was basically built by the millions of hustlers, right from the scratch. To date the same goes. But there is an urgent need to uplift their living standards.

As long as Kenya continue to witness millions of idle youth roaming the shopping centres and streets, lives of college and university graduates being wasted daily due to joblessness, masons, *jua kali* artisans, hawkers, *boda boda* operators, shoe shiners, barbers, small traders, *Mama mboga*, plantations workers – not being sufficiently empowered and afforded conducive atmosphere to operate from – leaders who started from the bottom of the ladder up, been there and overcame will continue to be in high demand in Kenya.

In the Preface to *Les Miserables*, Hugo observes:

> So long as there shall exist, by reason of law and custom, a social condemnation which, in the midst of civilization, artificially creates a hell on earth, and complicates with human fatality a destiny that is divine; so long as the three problems of the century – the degradation of man by the exploitation of his labour, the ruin of women by starvation and the atrophy of childhood by physical and spiritual might are not solved; so long as, in certain regions social asphyxia shall be possible; in other words and from a still broader point of view, so long as ignorance and misery remain on earth, there should be a need for books such as this.[5]

---

4   Victor Hugo, *Les Misérables*, "Letter to M. Daelli" (New York: Planet eBook, 2018), p. 2448-49.

5   Ibid, p. 4.

In this 21ˢᵗ century and ahead of the 2022 General Election, Victor Hugo is speaking to Kenyans. More than ever before, this country needs a leader whose agenda resonates powerfully with the hustlers. The country must come into terms with the condition of the hustler. Or perhaps it is the wearer who know where the shoe pinches as the adage goes. In their minds, the hustlers constantly hums a song about the leadership-inflicted slavery similar to the African-American spiritual published in 1867 titled, "Nobody Knows the Trouble I've Seen". Since then, the religious slave song has been done by dozens of other artists. When the Fisk Jubilee singers produced their version in 1872, Mark Twain, a celebrated American author, remarked: "I would walk seven miles to hear them sing again." W.E.B Du Bois, a black American historian and civil rights activist said the song "helps bridge the gap between Africans and African Americans." Of the Negro spirituals he said they are music "of an unhappy people, of the children of disappointment; they tell of the death and suffering and unvoiced longing toward a truer world, of misty wanderings and hidden ways."[6]

In the Sorrow Songs contained in the 1903 classic, *The Souls of Black Folk*, devoted to the Jubilee Singers, Du Bois observed that the blacks had given their all to their nation (like Kenyan hustlers have done) and was this not enough? "Our song, our toil, our cheer, and warming have been given to this nation in blood-brotherhood. Are not these gifts worth the giving? Is not this work and striving?"[7]

In the same chapter Du Bois gave probably one of his best paragraphs about love for one's country and sacrifice:

> They that walked in darkness sang songs in the older days-sorrow songs – for they were weary at heart… Then in after years… I saw the great temple builded of these songs towering over the pale city. To me Jubilee Hall seemed ever made of the songs themselves, and its bricks were red with the blood and the dust of toil. Out of them rose for one morning, noon, and night, bursts of wonderful melody, full of the voices of my brothers and sisters, full of the voices of the past.[8]

---

6   Edward J. Blum and Jason R. Young (eds), *The Souls of W.E.B. Du Bois: New Essays and Reflections* (Macon, GA: Mercer University Press, 2009), p. 126.

7   Quoted in ibid, p. 56.

8   W. E. B. Du Bois, *The Souls of Black Folk* (New York: Cosimo Classics, 1903), p. 155.

And now the song lyrics. Mahalia Jackson, an American gospel singer whose best hits include "You'll Never Walk Alone", "Move On Up a Little Higher" and "Wait Until My Change Comes", released her version:

> Nobody knows, Lord, the trouble I've seen
> Lordy, nobody knows my sorrow
> Yes, nobody knows the trouble I've seen
> But glory hallelujah!
>
> Sometimes I'm standing crying
> Tears running down my face
> I cry to the Lord have mercy
> Help me run this all race
>
> Oh Lord, I have so many trials
> So many pains and woes
> I'm asking for faith and comfort
> Lord, help me to carry this load
>
> Nobody knows the trouble I've seen
> Well, nobody knows but Jesus. Well, well
> No nobody knows, oh the trouble, the trouble, I've seen
> I'm singing glory, glory, glory hallelujah!
> No nobody knows, oh the trouble, the trouble, I've seen…

And yet another artist thought that this song of all times had better include the Devil who was relentlessly lurking somewhere, bringing all the troubles to mankind and only prayers could chase him away:

> Nobody knows the trouble I see, Lord
> Nobody knows the trouble I see
> Nobody knows the trouble I see, Lord
> Nobody knows like Jesus
>
> Brothers, will you pray for me? x 3
> And help me to drive old Satan away
>
> Nobody knows the trouble I see, Lord…
> Sisters, will you pray for me? x 3
> And help me to drive old Satan away
>
> Nobody knows the trouble I see, Lord ….
> Mothers, will you pray for me? x 3
> And help me to drive old Satan away

Nobody knows the trouble I see, Lord…
Preachers, will you pray for me? x 3
And help me to drive old Satan away

The kind of slavery under discussion in Kenya is none like the 16th to 19th centuries one where an estimated 12 million Africans were uprooted from their homes and shipped across the Atlantic, two million dying on the way, for sale in the Americas. There is no comparison whatsoever. In Kenya, no one is being kidnapped from their houses, no one is put on some auction block to be sold to some Master and no torture chambers or forced labour in the country.

Like the Du Bois' Jubilee Hall, modern Kenya was built by the bricks made of red blood and dust of toil of independence struggle fighters, majority of whom were hustlers, to free the country from 70 years of foreign domination. Colonialism was the worst experience of slavery in Kenya. Some 60 years of independence, the hustlers have been battling a new kind of slavery – a bondage inflicted by their own leaders such that they, the hustlers, cannot benefit fully from the fruits of freedom, which ironically are in great abundance beyond measure.

Today in Kenya, everyone is singing Sorrow Songs about the hard times. The multi-billionaires and the multi-millionaires and the leaders are shedding crocodile tears. The hustlers are pouring out God-made tears.

Those high up the evolutionary economic ladder have no slightest idea "The Trouble the Hustlers Have Seen". They cannot comprehend their sorrow, pain and woes. The hustlers' hearts are weary, limbs tired. Lord, have mercy. Things are elephant down around here. Give the hustlers faith and comfort to run the race and carry the heavy load. And Lord, help the hustlers drive the old political Satan away. Brothers, sisters, mothers, preachers: *Kemea kabisa, Ashindwe!*

They say religion catalysed the enslavement of blacks more and put them in their rightful place during the slave trade era and that it also nourished colonialism years later. But true, honest religion also breaks the chains of human bondage. The spirituality of those under bondage help bring them together and approach God collectively.

Faith. Indeed it was the deeply religious William Wilberforce who influenced most the abolition of slave trade particularly in the British Empire, in 1833. His Christian faith had prompted his interest in social reform. An evangelical Christian, Wilberforce was also the leader of the Association for the Better Observation of Sunday, philanthropist and an MP who never lost a parliamentary election.

Required like yesterday in Kenya: A leader who understands the transformation of human economic and spirituality to higher levels, will employ spirituality in governance, identify thoroughly with the hustlers, and wholly depend on the power from the Above! William Ruto fits the bill.

Back to Victor Hugo. In 1877, the genius of literally hustling wrote an essay titled, *"Histoire d'un Crime" – The History of a Crime*. It recorded the events of December 1852, which brought Napoleon III to power. It was in this piece that he penned one of the greatest lines about sticking to a vision in French: *On resiste a l'invasion des armees; on ne resiste pas a l'invasion de idees*, variously translated, "You can resist an invading army; you cannot resist an idea whose time has come," or "there is one thing stronger than all the armies in the world, and that is an idea whose time has come." Ruto's idea has come.

Supposing two suns exist in the Solar System, each with a term limit to shine the Earth. The first will rise in the East in the morning and will fade in the West in the evening; next, the number two will start its journey across the sky in the same fashion from the East and end in the West, both having done their jobs. You cannot stop them. Some things were just meant to be.

VIII. Age of the president

There is no remembrance of men of old, and even those are yet to come, will not be remembered, by those who follow (Eccl 1:11) No, we remembered them. We love them, our Wazee. We value them.

In the last paragraph of acknowledgment in the book, *Roots*, Alex Haley records "immense debts to the griots of Africa" who "symbolize how all humanity ancestry goes back to some place, and some time, where there was no writing." He says: "Then, the memories and the mouths of ancient elders was the only way that early histories of mankind got passed along …for all of us today to know who we are".[9]

---

9   Quoted in Elisa Bordin and Anna Scacchi (eds), *Transatlantic Memories of Slavery: Reimagining the Past, Changing the Future* (Amherst, NY: Cambria Press, 2015), p. 80.

The BBI is about both historical and a future government. The current elders made their contributions to the country and are the library on the past. Collectively making the Council of Elders, it is from them that wisdom should be drawn by the younger generation on how to run the country. It would not be logical for octogenarians with hearing aids, king-sized eye glasses and walking *mkongonjos* to traverse across Kenya seeking for votes while there are qualified youth and middle-aged people who are capabla, willing and ready to manage the affairs of the nation.

Erick Erickson was a German-born American developmental psychologist. He is credited with creating a theory known as "The Eight Stages of Psychosocial Development in Human Beings". The following is an analysis of the last two stages in relation to the aforementioned race to succeed President Kenyatta:

(a) *40 to 60 years old (middle age)* – A middle-aged person, according to Erickson, discovers a sense of contribution to the world and engages in meaningful and productive work, which contributes positively to the society. During the period, family and work oftentimes satisfy this desire. They are passionate about supporting and satisfying future generations. Their important event: parenting. Writing on the subject of middle age in a *Sunday Nation* article in December 2014, Dr Lukoye Atwoli, a consultant psychiatric, noted that this period, "Is a stage of middle adulthood where the main task is to shape the sort of legacy they shall leave behind when they age and eventually die." And, "middle age is when we tend to be occupied with creative and meaningful work and with issues surrounding our families. It is when we can expect to be 'in charge', the role we've longer envied."[10]

(b) *65 years to death* – During the late adulthood, a person reflects on life and may experience satisfaction or a sense of failure. In other words, he has expressions of Integrity or Despair and Distrust. Here a person harbours deep resentment, low self-esteem and is always complaining and irritable. He is closed to others. He feels angry at self, others, world and society. He feels anger at aging

____

10 Lukoye Atwoli, "Kenya on right track but leaders need to grow up", *Saturday Nation*, 13 December, 2014.

and feels cheated. This person feels nothing left, uselessness. He constantly focus on what 'would have', 'should have' and 'could have' and face end of his life with feelings of bitterness, depression and despair.

Analysis – William Ruto, Peter Kenneth, Ekuru Aukot and Japheth Kayulu fall under category (a), the best age for leadership, according to Erickson's theory, them being in the 40 to 60 years bracket. The rest would be automatic knockouts for the president's post.

But Erickson would go further and examine the four failures. He would pick Kalonzo Musyoka and Musalia Mudavadi as the next preferred presidential material despite the age factor having disqualified them. Reason? They are intelligent, humble, gentlemanly leaders only that they always associate themselves with the wrong company thus leaving their communities wandering in political desert for years. "You dine, walk and work with the losing guy; you get infected with losing genes". Erickson may also point out that Kalonzo would offer a soft and spiritual touch to the presidency, while Mudavadi would be an asset for an ailing economy. Erickson, however, will note one Kalonzo disadvantage. The man has inherited some "changing colour" genes from Raila. He has been nicknamed a watermelon and chameleon. A simple whistling from a new suitor will make him abandon with haste his political family without thinking twice. Once a trusted Vice-President, he was a heart-beat from the State House. Centuries ago, Moses was telling his three million followers: "We are almost there… we are almost there," only for the Israelites to discover that they had been circling some stupid mountain for 40 years! For Kalonzo, he has been urging them on: "*Andu Maitu,… No vaa, ovaa, ovaa,*" again going endlessly in circles.

That leaves Raila Odinga and Moses Wetangula in the contesting field. In all fairness Erickson would say a big no to the two. Note the key words in (b). For Odinga, in particular, another negative attribute would be that he has done a truly messy job of taking his supporters in hopeless treks in the political desert for close to 40 years.

Erickson would then have to make his final selection. Automatically the preferred presidential candidate would be William Ruto since he has, besides passing the age test, the longest, continuous experience, as MP and Minister and now Deputy President – a heartbeat from the presidency, which the other four lack. Added to this is the anointing from the Above.

But, no. Kenyans will be told that President Kenyatta performed the original handshake with William Ruto in 2012. Then he did phase two handshake with Raila Odinga in 2018. So the August 2022 election will be a two-horse race to determine which one will be more acceptable to the *mwananchi*. Kenyans will respond firmly: "but we have done a radical surgery of the two from the perspective of leadership quality, biblical, work ethics, and scientific models, and Ruto emerges the undisputable victor…"

In an ideal situation, Ruto would not have any problem beating Raila. "President Kenyatta promised ten for me, ten for you." To consolidate this fact Majority Leader in the National Assembly, Aden Duale, also assured the country: "With the permission of the Almighty God William Ruto will be on ballot paper come 2022. The leadership of President Kenyatta represents a transformational leadership that spans over 20 years and the President himself will be our coalition's chief campaign manager in 2022."[11]

Six months earlier, State House Senior Director for Public Communications, Munyori Buku, had repeated the President's commitment to support his deputy in his 2022 bid:

> The President has been categorical about the 2022 Jubilee party ticket. He has made it very clear that the party will fully back DP William Ruto. First, the President has explained that 10 years of his own term are not long enough to implement the grand plan Jubilee has for Kenya. He has pointed out this super plan needs about 20 years to implement.[12]

In an interview with the *Sunday Nation*, Duale responded to the various questions, including: "Do you think the President will support the DP's candidature in 2022?"

"I have not heard the President renounce the many pledges he made in public to support the DP … Those of us who are men of honour, integrity and fear God will stand with the DP to be the fifth President

---

11 "Ask your Question: Aden Duale", *Sunday Nation*, 22 January, 2017.

12 Quoted in Aggrey Mutambo "Ruto to carry Jubilee flag in 2022, says Uhuru", *Daily Nation*, 29 June, 2016.

of Kenya. He has all the necessary qualities despite the assembling of election losers and political rejects – who are owned and financed by taxpayers through the said government bureaucrats – against him."[13]

Wasted words? Water under a bridge? In all likelihood, Raila will be accorded state campaign machinery and support. Perhaps the Bible provides the ultimate verdict. A few days after resurrection, Jesus wanted to know whether "Peter the rock" loved him and was his friend. Peter replied in the affirmative. Jesus directed him to feed and take care of His sheep. Among the eight candidates in this article who has supported the gospel of Jesus Christ most?

In the book, *The Poisonwood Bible* by Barbara Kingsolver, Baptist preacher Nathan Price explains to her daughter Leah how God reciprocate on good work: "God created a world of work and rewards on a big balanced scale. Small works of goodness over here, small rewards over here. Great sacrifice, great rewards! God merely expects us to do our own share of the perspiring for life's bounty, Leah". And more critically, never underestimate a man who believes that "prayers is not a ritual, it is serious business."

No, this literary endorsement of William Ruto for president is not about 'our man, our tribe.' The era of tribalism "when most Kenyans still worked with older maps of identity, more ancient loyalties" (Barack Obama, *Dreams From my Father*) is fast fading away, especially among the younger generation, because Kenyans today appreciate that "politics that is based solely on tribalism is the politics that is doomed to tear the country apart."[14]

The Agĩkũyũ community is the most populous, arguably the wealthiest in the country. For the first time in Kenya's nearly 60 years of independence they have wholeheartedly, collectively and overwhelmingly started to gravitate around candidate William Ruto who is not one of their own in readiness for offering him unconditional support to becoming Kenya's fifth President from 2022 to 2032. This is Kenya of the 21st century!

---

13 Kipchumba Some, "Duale to Uhuru: Handshake is killing our party and destabilising country", *Sunday Nation*, 29 December, 2019,

14 Aggrey Mutambo, "Kenyans have to make tough choices so as to succeed, says President Barack Obama", *Sunday Nation*, 26 July 2015.

CHAPTER FOURTEEN

Building Genuine Bridges: Critical Lessons from Covid-19

I know, I know,
It threatens the common gestures of human bonding,
The handshake,
The hug,
The shoulders we give each other to cry on,
The neighbourliness we take for granted,
So much that we often beat our breasts,
Crowing about rugged individualism,
Disdaining nature, pissing poison on it even, while,
Claiming that property has all the legal rights of personhood,
Murmuring gratitude for our shares in the gods of capital.
Oh, how now I wish I could write poetry in English,
Or any and every language you speak,
So, I can share with you, words that,
Wanjikũ, my Gĩkũyũ mother, used to tell me:
Gũtirĩ ũtukũ ũtakĩa:
No night is so Dark that,
It will not end in Dawn,
Or simply put,
Every night ends with dawn.
Gũtirĩ ũtukũ ũtakĩa.
This darkness too will pass away,
We shall meet again and again
And talk about Darkness and Dawn,
Sing and laugh maybe even hug,
Nature and nurture locked in a green embrace,
Celebrating every pulsation of a common being,
Rediscovered and cherished for real,
In the light of the Darkness and the new Dawn.

Ngũgĩ wa Thiong'o,
Dawn of Darkness (23 March, 2020) on Covid-19

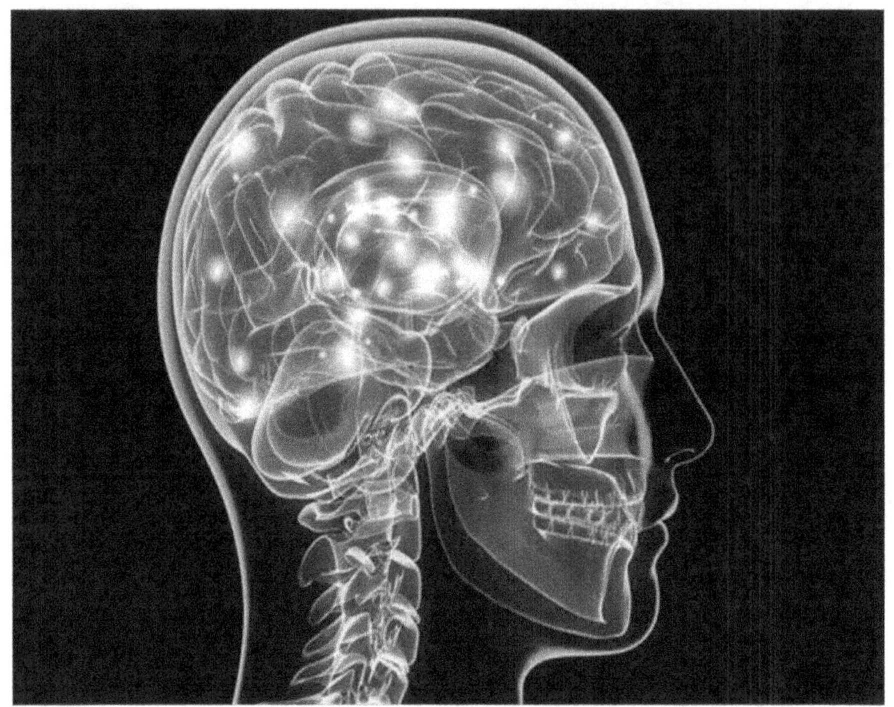

The human mind needs serous sanitising

Late 2019, no one saw it coming, but it did with a bang. Even the prophets of doom who normally predict end times were caught by surprise. And the same way most people ignored the prophecy of Europeans' coming is the same way they could have treated the coronavirus one. Supposing Kenyan true *seers* like Koitalel arap Samoei, Mũgo wa Kĩbirũ and Mepoho (Giriama prophetess) were living. A prophesy would have gone out thus:

> There shall come tiny-little organisms from the Kingdom of Dirt who will be wearing tinny, little spike-like hats. These uninvited visitors will 'coronaise' the whole world such that the British, Belgian and French colonialism in Africa would look like a kindergarten's play. And just like the *Wazungu* called Africans "savages," "barbaric" and "uncivilised" these 'coranaisers' will call every human being the same due to their insensitivity to Mother Nature.

On 17 November 2019, This Thing made its maiden visitation to *Homo sapiens*. People were scared to call the uninvited guest by its name. In some communities they call a leopard *the spotted one* and snake *the rope* lest the beasts come to devour you at night; hence, This Thing, *Hii Kitu*.

From the bowels of the earth, the ocean, forest, air, far-away planet or wherever This Thing had been locked up in since the beginning of times, its first port of call was the country of the Dragon. There, they name years after animals, and one of their best delicacies is the snake aka the Satan. The inhabitants of this land work like ants and once they built a huge wall that can be seen from the space even today. Theirs is the land of Bruce Lee of the Kung Fu fame and ancient philosophers like Confucius, Sun Tzu, Lao Tzu, Mencius and many others.

Like a newly-born baby, This Thing was given a 6-letter name, 'Corona', derived from Latin meaning a crown, headgear, garland or wreath because under a microscope its surface appeared to feature little crown-like spikes as if it was wearing some tinny hats. Rulers used to wear a crown as a symbol of sovereignty; hence; the term coronation. So This Thing wore minute godfather, cowboy or fedora hats like certain Congolese musicians. Fedora comes from Greek *theodoros* meaning the "gift of God".

But this Corona was not a gift of God, but one straight from the Devil himself. It was the most hideous virus to have come from the coronavirus family where common cold, pneumonia and other infections are manufactured and sojourn the man's household since the world was born. In the history of mankind where do you read a total global lockdown? Like the devil it was, the coronavirus carried a disease, Covid-19 – named after the year it appeared into the world – that came to steal, destroy and kill.

It moved with the speed of light, literally. In a short period of time coronavirus had made it to every continent on earth except Antarctica; *coronaisation* of the Earth, in other words, stamping its sovereignty over all human beings. On 30 January 2020, the World Health Organization (WHO) declared the Covid-19 outbreak a Public Health Emergency of international concern and, on 11 March 2020, a global pandemic – the worldwide spread of a new disease.

The world was desperate for answers to the hard questions. Was coronavirus Satan's only begotten son dispatched from Hell to tempt mankind for the very last time, Job-style? Surely, it could not have come from God. Was it a kind of *danse macabre*, the dance of death, to remind humanity of their limited time on earth and better they behave themselves? Where did the virus originate from?

Theories started to fly about: the virus accidentally escaped from a Chinese laboratory in Wuhan City and jumped to human population. It could have come from snakes, cats, bats or pangolins. It could have been transmitted by stray dogs, which had eaten bat meat. A battlefield was immediately formed between the US and China each blaming the other with the former's President, Donald Trump, calling the pandemic the Chinese Virus. The European Union called for an independent probe on the origin of the virus.

A VICIOUS, INVISIBLE ENEMY

World leaders appeared terribly helpless. The stockpiles of nuclear weapons, submarines, jetfighters, guns or mighty armies at their disposal or any available drug or vaccine could not help combat the monster. And the most powerful man on earth, US President Trump, embarked on displaying his craziest traits thinking that you could play with the virus the way you would with a grandmother. Meanwhile, think tanks and pharmaceutical companies began burning the midnight oil to find a medical solution to the problem. The whole earth was suffocated with prayers to God as the prosperity gospel priests, false prophets and witchdoctors went into hiding lest they be challenged to perform a miracle to eradicate Covid-19.

Thence, the coronation of suffering and death on earth by coronavirus forced people into a Maximum Remand Prison or into a State of Emergency in form of curfews and lockdowns. They became like an American NASA astronaut in the International Space Station doing orbits. For Covid-19 was the Great Leveller. It distinguished no race, ethnicity, creed, power, economic status or geographical locations. It knew no children or adults. It was speedy and unpredicable, destructive and dangerous. You could not plead or negotiate with the invisible enemy. But thank goodness, all countries came together as one to confront a common adversary.

From those endowed with much know-how, a list of dos and don'ts was innovated and released. The WHO issued guidelines for "protecting yourself and others from the spread of Covid-19": "Regularly and thoroughly clean your hands with an alcohol-based hand rub or wash them with soap and water. Maintain at least one metre (three feet) distance between yourself and others. Avoid going to crowded places. Avoid touching eyes, nose and mouth. Make sure you, and the people around you, follow good respiratory hygiene. This means covering your mouth and nose with your bent elbow or tissue when you cough or sneeze. Then dispose of the used tissue immediately and wash your hands."

The WHO was not done yet. "Stay home and self-isolate even with minor symptoms such as cough, headache, mild fever, until you recover. Have someone bring your supplies. If you need to leave your house, wear a mask to avoid infecting others. If you have a fever, cough or difficulty breathing, seek medical attention, but call by telephone in advance if possible and follow the directions of your local health authority. Keep up to date on the latest information from trusted sources, such as WHO or your local and national health authorities." And elsewhere, researchers at the UK's London School of Hygiene and Tropical Medicine received a £500,000 government funding to train dogs to screen and detect people of Covid-19. As a whole, this was the world's new normal.

History has numerous cases of diseases that have plagued humanity with devastating consequences. The Plague of Justinian (541-542) killed between 30 million and 50 million people. The Black Death (1347-1351) resulted in deaths of between 75 million and 200 million people, about half the entire population of Europe. Smallpox (1520-forward) 56 million deaths. The Spanish Flu (1918-1920), referred to as the mother of all pandemics, infected an estimated 500 million people resulting in 50 million deaths. Since 1980s HIV has claimed the lives of more than 30 million people. The H1N1 Swine Flu of 2009-2010 affected an estimated 60 million people and resultant deaths at 12,000. The world cannot take chances with Covid-19 that is caused by virus SARS-COV-2.

Covid-19 restrictions plunged countries into a new normal. In Kenya, doing the Handshake that had mutated into a political national brand courtesy of the BBI was like stepping onto the unholy grounds. The country's economic growth in 2020 was now projected to slow to 3 per cent or less from an earlier forecast of 6.1 per cent due to the effects of the novel coronavirus. President Uhuru Kenyatta unveiled a Kes 53.7 billion 8-point economic stimulus programme to cushion families and companies post-Covid-19.

Earlier, the World Food Programme (WFP) had warned of widespread famine "of biblical proportions" across the world because of coronavirus pandemic describing it as a hunger pandemic. At least 265 million people were being pushed to the brink of starvation by the Covid-19 crisis, the UN body revealed. At least 265 million people pushed to the brink of starvation…

On 19 October 1984, a shocking and shameful story emerged from Korem town in Northern Ethiopia. Mo Amin, a Kenyan photographer and cameraman together with two colleagues filmed what was termed as Biblical Famine. The famine threatened over seven million people with starvation. The tragic images of malnourished, dying and dead resonated around the world as the seven-minute clip got viewed by over 1.5 billion people. The international community swung to action. A group of eminent artists under the 'USA for Africa' joined hands and recorded "We Are the World" on 28 January 1985.[1] The song went on to raise USD 100 million for the starving populations.

On 17 November 2019, an extremely dreadful tale started from Wuhan City in China of coronavirus having made the city its epicentre. When it became evident that the visit actually meant *coronaisation* of the whole earth, the world awoken from its slumber and came together as one. Within a few months, the biggest question was getting the answer: The source of the pandemic was because Mother Nature has been made to look ugly by mankind and she was ailing and angry.

Nobody can afford to go round in circles any more. The truth is known. To avoid the destruction of the humanity, walls that have been built over the years to separate mankind and Mother Earth must be brought down. It is the only way to get the unlimited goodness within her. Destroying these barriers equals building better, stronger, genuine bridges for peace, prosperity, healthier lives and human survival.

"We Are the World" looks like it was composed for the Covid-19 pandemic. It resonates marvellously in today's Covid-19 circumstances. Listen to the voices of those great men and women singing. They haunt and humble. The song is just about the best signature fight against Covid-19. The pandemic has brought hunger in people's stomachs, hunger in pockets, hunger in minds, and hunger in memory of the loved dead. A big salute is in order for this 35-year old masterpiece sang by the 45 music prophets. And the biggest one to Kenya's Mo Amin, who started it all.

LEARNING FROM EXPERIENCES

The following is an account of lessons on building genuine bridges with a strong angle of love, derived from past, present and forecasted experiences of Covid-19 and which the world need more than ever before: (1) Respect for the Pale Blue Dot; (2) Interrogating leadership amidst Covid-19; (3) God's Cabinet, a belt around Earth; (4) Our children are very afraid; (5) Humans are diverse, yet they are the same; (6) Embrace God much more; (7) The Barrel of a Pen, and, (8) We shall sing and dance post-Covid-19.

---

1 USA for Africa. *We Are the World*. Michael Jackson and Lionel Richie. Columbia CBS. April 23, 1985. Audio Cassette/Compact Disc. Music video available at: https://www.youtube. com/watch?v=M9BNoNFKCBI. Accessed on 20 June 2020.

Respect for the Pale Blue Dot

One evening God called Abraham for a little chat. "Look up at the sky and count the stars, if indeed you can count them," he told him. "So shall be your offspring." You could imagine Abraham trying to count the heavenly bodies and thinking God's a big joke since at already 99 years he had no children to multiply the descendants as the stars. Yet soon he was blessed with a son, Isaac, who God again wanted to consume as a burnt offering on a certain mountain. But Abraham continued to gaze at the sky in an attempt to comprehend how numerous his offspring will be. If only Abraham could get the slightest idea of what the sky held in star numbers! Welcome to our universe.

According to Wikipedia, the universe "is all of time and space. This includes planets, stars, galaxies… and all matter and energy…" Like it or not the vastness of the universe renders it completely beyond human understanding. Scientist Albert Einstein described it thus:

> The human mind is not capable of grasping the universe. We are like a little child entering a huge library. The walls are covered to the ceiling with books in many different tongues. The child knows that someone must have written those books. It does not know who or how. It does not understand the languages in which they are written. But the child notes a definite plan in the arrangement of the books – a mysterious order which it does not comprehend, but only dimly suspects.[2]

"Who are we?" An American astronomer, planetary scientist, cosmologist and astrophysicist, Carl Sagan, wondered. "We find that we live on an insignificant planet of a humdrum star lost in a galaxy tucked away in some forgotten corner of the universe in which there are far more galaxies than people."[3] Earlier, Italian astronomer Galileo Galilei had one day observed: "The sun, with all those planets revolving around it and dependent on it, can still ripen a bunch of grapes as if it had nothing else in the universe to do."[4] That was in the 17th century, years before space exploration accelerated from the mid-1950s.

---

2   V. Alexander Stefan (ed), *Thus Spoke Einstein on Life and Living: Wisdom of Albert Einstein in the Context* (La Jolla, CA: Stefan University Press, 2011), p. 368.

3   Vladan L. Kuzmanovic, *Kuzmanovic's Spacebook: 2500 Quotes About Space, Stars, Constellations and Universe* (Morrisville, NC: Lulu Press, Inc., 2018), p. 8.

4   Ibid.

Scientists tell us the Universe is 879,873 followed by 18 zeros kilometres across. On 15 November 2017 in the *Forbes* magazine, Robert Frost, an instructor and flight controller at NASA, gave an insight at the number of stars that constitutes the Universe. There are about 100 billion stars in our galaxy and up to 10 trillion galaxies in the universe. This equals to one followed by 24 zeros stars in the universe. About 7.6 per cent of those stars are class G stars (like our sun). Almost all class G stars have at least one planet giving 76 followed by 21 zeros stars similar to ours and almost all of them have some form of planets. A quarter of those stars have at least one rocky planet similar in size to the Earth and in the habitable zone. This means there are up to 19 followed by 21 zeros stars similar to ours with at least one planet similar to Earth… we can – with some confidence – say that there are likely billions of other solar system structurally somewhere like ours.

In 1989, NASA Voyager I spacecraft, one of the many projects made for space exploration and the most distant human-made object from earth, billions of kilometres away, was hurtling towards the edge of the Solar System, and its cameras were almost shutting down. Carl Sagan, a member of the mission's imaging team, asked officials to direct the cameras to take a picture, the only one chance Voyager I had. The resulting iconic image, captured on Valentine's Day, 14 February 1990, a very tiny place within vast space less than 0.12 pixels in size became known as the "pale blue dot". It was the most distant image of the earth ever taken. Some thirty-four minutes after capturing the Earth, the cameras turned off, forever.

The stunningly pale blue image of Planet Earth changed the way humanity view its world, how small and fragile it is, a dot, an extremely tiny fraction of the Universe. In 1994, Sagan wrote a book titled, *Pale Blue Dot: A Vision of the Human Future in Space.*

> From this distant vantage point, the Earth might not seem of any particular interest. But for us it's different. Consider again that dot. That's here. That's home. That's us.

> On it everyone you love, everyone you know, everyone you ever heard of, every human being who ever was, lived out their lives.

> The aggregate of our joy and suffering, thousands of confident religions, ideologies, and economic doctrines, every hunter and forager, every hero and coward, every creator and destroyer of

civilization, every King and peasant, every young couple in love, every mother and father, hopeful child, inventor and explorer, every teacher of morals, every corrupt politician, every 'superstar', every 'supreme leader', every saint and sinner in the history of our species lived there-on a mote of dust suspended in a sunbeam.[5]

The Earth is a very small stage in a vast cosmic arena. Think of the rivers of blood spilled by all those generals and emperors so that in glory and triumph they could become the momentary masters of a fraction of a dot. Think of the endless cruelties visited by the inhabitants of one corner of this pixel on the scarcely distinguishable inhabitants of some other corner.

How frequent their misunderstandings, how eager they are to kill one another, how fervent their hatreds. Our posturings, our imagined self-importance, the delusion that we have some privileged position in the universe, are challenged by this point of pale light. Our planet is a lonely speck in the great enveloping cosmic dark.

In our obscurity – in all this vastness – there is no hint that help will come from elsewhere to save us from ourselves.

The Earth is the only world we know, so far, to harbour life. There is nowhere else, at least in the near future, to which our species could migrate…

To me, it underscores our responsibility to deal more kindly with one another and to preserve and cherish the pale blue dot, the only home we've ever known.[6]

The Pale Blue Dot. That's mankind's home. The only home. For ages man has been fighting for resources and power. Slavery, colonialism, two great wars, genocides. Hatred. Blood spilled and human rights abuses. Today there are stockpiles of nuclear weapons that can destroy every living thing on Earth in a flash. And now Covid-19, the pandemic that has shaken the whole world than any other in history is around. And yet so far no other planet has been found to sustain human life. In the event of the very worst on earth, where would humanity migrate to?

---

5   Quoted in Michael Marett-Crosby, *Twenty-Five Astronomical Observations That Changed the World: And How To Make Them Yourself* (New York: Springer, 2013), p. 226.

6   Quoted in Sujan Sengupta, *Worlds Beyond Our Own: The Search for Habitable Planets* (New York: Springer, 2015), p. 140.

Modern medical research will no doubt come up with a vaccine and cure for Covid-19. But how soon and what next? Appreciating the technological wonders created during World War II, *Time* magazine science writer, Gerald Wendt, in 1946 envisioned a future in which, "Science will have freed the human race not only from disease, famine and early death, but also from poverty…"[7] Seven decades later science is still struggling to find solutions to various diseases that abound on earth, among other problems.

That Covid-19 first broke out in China does not really matter. What really matters is that experts are pointing to one specific direction as the genesis of the pandemic: abuse of Mother Nature. Stopping deforestation will prevent pandemics since contact with wild animals, where most viruses originate, will be minimal, they say. Climate change could increase respiratory illness, stroke and heart disease especially due to environmental pollution, they add. What came out immediately during lockdowns? There were noted decrease in air pollution. Due to lessened human activity there was decrease in the Earth's seismic vibration and the oceans were quiet. And more notably, global carbon dioxide emissions had dropped by 17 per cent in four months, what scientists said could be the largest decline in recorded history. In short since 1988 when NASA scientist James Hansen introduced the concept that global warming was not (with 99 per cent confidence) natural, but human-caused, the world has learned that addressing climatic change results in healthier life with less instances of viral attacks.

Is Mother Earth in a kind of revenge through Covid-19? It seems. How do you pretend to know the meaning of the word *love* if you cannot extend the same to the only home you own? Planet Earth want to be loved. And perhaps to teach humanity a lesson it banned all shaking hands, kissing and hugging, the gestures of affection, through Covid-19. The Earth want these gestures to be directed to it as well.

Mata Amritanandamayi commonly known as Amma, or simply Mother, is one teacher the world need badly. Amma does not only show genuine love to humanity, but also to planet earth. She believes between

---

7   Paul Boyer, *By the Bomb's Early Light: American Thought and Culture at the Dawn of the Atomic Age* (Chapel Hill, NC: University of North Carolina Press, 1994), p. 137.

the two types of poverty – financial poverty and poverty of love – the latter needs more addressing. Since the 1970s, Amma has kissed and embraced more than 37 million people across the globe. The Indian Hindu spiritual leader and humanitarian – she is called the Miracle Hug Lady, or the Hugging Saint – inspires, uplifts and transforms through her embrace and whispered words. Known worldwide for her selfless love and compassion for all people, she dedicates her time to alleviating the pain of the poor and those suffering physically and emotionally. Amma also runs global charities under Embracing the World, which include in hospitals, schools, temples, houses for the poor and elderly, and an orphanage. In 1993 she served as President of the Centenary Parliament of World Religions in Chicago, US, and also spoke at the UN Jubilee Anniversary in 1995. Amma has visited Kenya a total of four times.

What has been the Hugging Saint's reaction to Covid-19? She donated USD 1.7 million to help combat and contain Covid-19 as well as to provide relief to those physically, mentally and economically affected by the virus. "The virus is filling us internally and externally with the poison of fear and anxiety." She lamented. "To destroy it, we have to ignite our inner flame, our inner light."[8]

On the 29th anniversary of the Pale Blue Dot, an article in *Forbes* magazine by Dr Ethan Siegel, an astrophysicist, concluded: "Now is the most important time to reinvest in the future of the human enterprise. Let us never forget that we are in the grand scheme of things. It is up to us to make the future of humanity the greatest one we are capable of creating."[9]

Carl Sagan died of pneumonia, a respiratory disease, on 20 December 1996, aged 62. Some of his best quotes are deeply relevant in the Covid-19 era: "We are like butterflies who flutter for a day and think it is forever."[10] And, "The universe is not required to be in perfect harmony with human ambition."[11] On the latter, mankind ought to be

---

8   Amma, "Light the lamp of hope, compassion and unity", Global News, 5 April, 2020, Amritapuri, India. Available at: https://amma.org/news/light-lamp-hope-compassion-and-unity-amma. Accessed on 25 June 2020.

9   Ethan Siegel, "The Pale Blue Dot celebrates its 29th anniversary, reminding us how small and fragile we are", *Forbes*, 14 February, 2019.

10 Davidji, *Sacred Powers: The Five Secrets to Awakening Transformation* (Carlsbad, CA: Hay House Inc., 2017), p. 58.

11 Kuzmanovic, *Kuzmanovic's Spacebook*, op cit, p. 124.

shaped by the earth and to operate within its laws – not the other way round. As the saying goes, God always forgives, we forgive sometimes, but Nature never forgives.

"It is during our darkest moments that we must focus to see the light."[12] Greek Philosopher Aristotle famously said. Covid-19 is humanity's darkest hour. Protecting the Planet Earth is the only light. Until the Americans and the Russians and the Chinese and others discover some other planet that can host human life, if any, and this could take ages, humankind must agree that Earth is the very best home there is. Instead of constantly searching for flaws in it, recognise the goodness in abundance. Instead of forever complaining that rose bushes have thorns, it is logical to rejoice that bushes have roses. The Chinese, whose country Covid-19 was first reported, have a poem whose one line was told by their President Xi Jinping at the World Economic Forum, Davos, Switzerland, 17 January 2017: "Honey melons hang on bitter vines; sweet dates grow on thistles and thorns."[13]

Carl Sagan's story on the Pale Blue Dot teaches that the earth is so tiny but dear to humanity. And how could a mere virus make man to run to the hills? Coronavirus' lesson is that one man, out of seven billion human inhabitants, is absolutely tiny, fragile, a Black/White Dot. A man could be a political, economic or religious titan, but he remains merely a collection of bones, flesh and blood sustained by God's breath. The 5ft 10in 150-pound brutal tyrant Adolf Hitler, he who caused deaths of dozens of millions of people then committed suicide, required only 180 litres of petroleum to turn his and that of wife Eva bodies into ash. Ashes to ashes, dust to dust. Félicien Kabuga, the 84-year old Hitler of Africa, was nabbed on 16 May 2020 after 26 years on the run and, instead of enjoying his retirement in peace, he will be thinking how to extricate himself from accusation of involvement in the 1994 Rwandan genocide where close to one million people lost their lives.

Interrogating leadership amidst Covid-19

Did the world descend to an unwarranted scare due to the coronavirus visitation? This is a question that will dominate debates for long times ahead. Because locking down virtually all human activities globally is

---

12 Isa Singh, *The Essence of Aristotle Life* (Mahesh Dutt Sharma, 2018), p. 56.

13 François Bougon, *Inside the Mind of Xi Jinping* (London: Hurst & Company, 2018), p. 1.

not a laughing matter. At the top of research and conversations will be the massive economic and political loss and change of lifestyles as the world run against time to save human lives. Of course, the winner will emerge that: you don't put a shilling value on an individual; human life is priceless and protecting it should be a priority over other issues.

Yet a South-African-born Nobel Prize winner took a different position on the lockdown. Michael Levitt, a chemistry scientist at Stanford University, said the lockdown was a huge mistake, a waste of time and was not the best plan of action. Levitt added that the decision to keep people inside was motivated by "panic" rather than better science. "For reasons that were not clear to me," he noted, "I think the leaders panicked and people panicked."[14] Levitt went on that for two months most expert predictions were wrong and deaths projections were overestimated, suggesting that the lockup could have caused more deaths than saved. "I think the lockup has not saved lives. I think it may have cost lives. It will have saved a few lives from traffic accidents, things like that, but the social damage-domestic abuse, divorce, alcoholism-have been extreme. And then you have those who have not been treated for other reasons."[15]

Calling blockages effective but "medieval," Levitt opined that countries like Germany and Sweden were the world's big winners as they did not practice too much lockdown. Instead, he offered, the world would have insisted on face masks, disinfecting substance and some form of payment system that does not involve touching (i.e. phones) and only isolating the elderly. He predicted "that countries that have implemented a hard lockdown will be harshly judged by future generations for their mistakes."

However, two studies published in *Nature* magazine later gave a different view. The first, from the Imperial College of London, concluded that lockdowns had a dramatic effect in reducing transmissions and that three million people would have died in eleven European countries had the lockdowns not been put in place. The second at the University of California, Berkeley, analysed six countries – China, South Korea, Iran, France, Italy and the US and found that lockdowns and closing of non-

---

14 Tom Morgan, "Lockdown saved no lives and may have cost them, Nobel Prize winner believes", *The Telegraph*, 23 May 2020.

15 Ibid.

essential businesses and schools averted 530 million confirmed cases. One day, the truth will be known.

Whether the leaders over-reacted to the Covid-19 invasion or not, one thing came out clearly. Populations heeded them, put everything aside and on hold at great sacrifice and cost and followed the rule of the day. It is better to prevent than to cure or, as the Agĩkũyũ puts it, "*Kĩguoya kĩainũkũire nyina*" (a coward returned home safely). If only people can be so committed to the true religion, beneficial politics and economics as they diligently adhered to the commandments brought about by Covid-19 as preached by their leaders! The world would be a better place.

Meanwhile there emerged those leaders whose guidance was exemplary and those who goofed terribly. "…In a crisis, placing faith in a strong leader can save psychological needs whose importance to us can outweigh our desire even for physical safety… as long as mortal peril lurks in people's lives, the appeal of believing in one's leader and seeking solace in the idea of national unity will be hard to resist."[16]

From the day WHO announced Covid-19 a global pandemic, President Kenyatta got on top of things. He monitored closely how the pandemic unfolded both locally and globally and issued guidance to the nation accordingly. Together with Deputy President Ruto, he led the country on a National Day of Prayer saying that, "we cannot ignore the need to turn to God in these circumstances" of Covid-19. With the President and Deputy fully in charge, there was no vacuum in the management of Covid-19.

But it was from the Ministry of Health itself that Kenya came out as among the world's leading countries in the management of Covid-19 crisis. *The Wall Street Journal* recognised Cabinet Secretary Mutahi Kagwe for his solid crisis leadership in the fight against the crisis and one of the best handlers of the pandemic in the world. "The leaders who have distinguished themselves under pressure are rarely the bold, charismatic, impulsive, self-regarding, politically calculating alphas we have elected. The real heroes have been, for lack of a better term, career deputies." The Journal continued: "Kenya's unlikely coronavirus

---

16 Max Fisher, "Rattled by a Pandemic, People Turn to Leaders — Any Leaders", *New York Times*, 23 May, 2020.

hero is Health Minister Mutahi Kagwe… Mr. Kagwe projects calm, emphasize evidence and urges Kenyans to face facts, a style one senator described as a 'breath of fresh air.'"[17] Other international persons hailed as heroes were Jung Eun-Kyeong, a South Korean doctor, and Jenny Harries, UK deputy chief officer.

Dancing with Covid -19

It will be hard to dispute this: that Raila Odinga was the most sinned against politician by nature. The BBI was launched at the Bomas of Kenya on 27 November 2019. Ten days earlier, the first coronavirus case in the world had struck in Hubei Province, China. Within no time the virus had spread across the world like bush fire, outlawing hugs and handshakes and crowding, among other restrictions.

Before the world, including Kenya, implemented the lockdowns, the BBI was nearing its peak season. The Handshake, its mother, had now been declared human poison, persona non grata. The countrywide rallies to propagate the BBI, where reggae had become the signature anthem, were no more. "Nobody can stop reggae", Raila was decreeing everywhere. "I want to assure you we are going to stop this reggae!" Deputy President Ruto was responding. "We are going to have the Referendum in June, *wapende wasipende*!" That was Senator James Orengo, Raila's right-hand man, making the declaration as he grinned from ear to ear as if he had just announced the greatest discovery on earth.

Raila was the saddest man on earth. With Covid-19 lockdown he could not dance to Lucky Dube's "Nobody Can Stop Reggae" tune. His Canaan journey was being delayed by the pandemic, hence the mourning. He was perhaps now humming, "Who Let The Dogs Out", wondering who brought Covid-19 and why at that inappropriate time. Raila could not sing, "*Mapambano, mapambano*". He could not mobilise the youth to the streets to protest and demonstrate: Corona Must Go! The virus was not his political party like Cord-13 he so easily dismantled when it failed to put the Jubilee government into total lockdown. Covid-19 and Cord-13 were as different as day and night. The virus was invisible and dangerous.

---

17 Sam Walker, "Thank God for Calm, Competent Deputies", *The Wall Street Journal*, 4 April, 2020.

In 2016, South African Economic Freedom Fighters (EFF) party leader, Julius Malema, had threatened to overthrow President Jacob Zuma's government "through the barrel of a gun." Its members donned red overalls and berets as uniform. Perhaps in imitation, Raila's Cord-13 opposition members came up with a new code of dressing of navy blue berets with a *filimbi* (whistle) emblazoned on them. Now you cannot defeat Covid-19 through guns or a military coup d'état or through a Cord-13. Raila was like a trapped wild animal.

But Raila had nicknamed himself Joshua, one of the Israelites' most famous liberators. Could he do a Joshua? On 30 October 2017 (after Raila boycotted repeat election of 26 October 2017) *The Times of Israel* reported that University of Cambridge researchers had been able to pinpoint the exact date when Joshua stopped the sun as 30 October 1207 BCE, some 3,224 years ago calling it the earliest recorded annual eclipse of the sun.[18] Joshua had just entered the Promised Land and he desperately needed more time before the sunset to battle and defeat several armies. God lengthened the day for almost 24 hours. "Sun, stand still over Gibeon; And Moon, in the Valley of Aijalon" (Joshua 10:12 – NKJV). Raila: "God, hear my deep-hearted prayer. Can you kindly stop Covid-19 until the Referendum and General Election in Kenya are over, like you did to the sun and moon to help Joshua defeat his enemies? Lord, I know you can!

Today, unfortunately, is not the biblical Joshua's times when the sun would still in the middle of the day. Although Covid-19 was playing with fire by interrupting "Nobody Can Stop Reggae", Raila had no choice but to wait for God's appointed time of lifting the lockdowns.

Seriously, Covid-19 is hell on earth. During the very first days of its landing in particular the world was scared stiff. It was like an apocalypse in the happening. One could imagine a scenario if Jesus Christ were to be sighted in the clouds with his heavenly outriders headed to the Earth for judgment day. What instructions would one expect to hear? Keep maximum social distancing from all sins! Hugs, kisses and handshakes allowed only when accompanied by repeated loud chants of Praise the Lord! Sanitise your hearts and minds with the strongest Bible verses and glorious hymns! Tie your tongues with rubber bands; cover mouths

---

18 David Sedley, "'Joshua stopped the sun' 3,224 years ago today, scientists say", *The Times of Israel*, 30 October 2017.

with tight cello-tapes-made masks-these are the organs from where sins originates! Stay at Church; I repeat stay at Church, all of you! If you treat this Jesus' Second Coming normally (like you treated the First) it will treat you abnormally!

Apparently Raila did not know Covid-19 is not a respecter of political giants; it knows no kings or queens, presidents, hustlers, age, creed or profession. All can provide a habitat to the virus and get infected. However, he was still calling himself Tinga (Tractor) and Nyundo (Hammer), a titan; ""*Kwani Corona kitu gani?*" On 13 April, 2020, together with Senator James Orengo, Cabinet Secretary Eugene Wamalwa and Jubilee Vice-Chairman David Murathe, he broke the lockdown and the two-passenger per vehicle rules, and were cleared at a roadblock on their way to visit COTU Secretary-General Francis Atwoli in Kajiado County. This would have been okay if they were Essential Services Providers. Definitely they were not. And this was a man crying to be President or Prime Minister of Kenya through the BBI violating a matter of life and death proportion. His important mission was probably to go make more ropes for hanging Deputy President Ruto and building more bricks to strengthen the wall he had already constructed to separate Ruto and President Kenyatta to his advantage. This was the leader of building bridges project sneaking across a forbidden border like a village chicken thief jumping over a fence in the dead of the night while even President Kenyatta's wife and mother could not leave the Coast due to the lockdown. This trip to Atwoli's home was irresponsibility of the gravest order; as a leader, it was the lowest Raila could sink. The act was a disgrace to the country.

When the world leaders had come together to face Covid-19, the Global Great Equalizer common enemy, Raila opted to be an exception. If he cannot dance with his followers during the BBI rallies why couldn't he dance with coronavirus? Breaking the universal coronavirus restrictions was tantamount to promoting Covid-19. It demonstrated grandiose sense of self-importance, lack of empathy for others, preoccupation with fantasies about power; these are among the traits associated with people suffering from Narcissistic Personality Disorder (NPD). Considering that the BBI, which he leads, will most likely co-exist with the Covid-19 era, Kenyans must be very afraid of his NPD's characteristics during the critical period.

An article in the *Forbes* magazine on how narcissistic leaders could destroy organisations (and countries) during the Covid-19 period gives a timely caution:

> …narcissistic leaders can be hugely enticing. Their confidence and ability to self-promote can make them hugely attractive, especially to organizations in the midst of turmoil. The researchers analyze over 150 previous studies on the topic, and find that narcissistic leaders can be hugely risky for any organization… "That [they] tend to be most attractive in times of turmoil should be especially worrying given the huge turmoil the coronavirus pandemic has wrought on the world. It can be hugely tempting to plump for a leader who says they have the solution to all of our problems, but such self-confidence can be highly damaging… With the impact of the coronavirus enormous, the stakes involved could not be bigger, so we're duty bound to make sure we hire the right people. Tempting though the narcissistic leader might be in these times of crisis, we need to think past that temptation and select leaders who can leave a lasting impression in the right way.[19]

There were other leaders who too danced with Covid-19. Nairobi City County Governor, Mike Sonko, distributed care packages which included Hennessy cognac believing that alcohol kills coronavirus. He called it the "throat sanitiser". Tanzanian President John Pombe Magufuli got angry that donated testing kits were faulty after samples from goat, sheep and paw paws tested positive. He also suspended the daily updates on Covid-19 and surprised everyone by maintaining that the most effective panacea was prayers in addition to steam therapy and consumption of lemons, which he claimed helped her infected daughter to recover. On 7 June 2020, Magufuli declared Tanzania free of Covid-19. "The Corona disease has been eliminated thanks to God," he told worshippers in a church in the capital, Dodoma. "I want to thank Tanzanians of all faiths. We have been praying and fasting for God to save us from the pandemic that has afflicted our country and the world. God has answered us."[20] He also commended the priest and worshippers for not wearing gloves and

---

19   Adi Gaskell, "How Narcissistic Leaders Can Destroy Organizations During Covid-19", *Forbes*, 19 May, 2020.

20 BBC, "Coronavirus: John Magufuli declares Tanzania free of Covid-19", British Broadcasting Corporation, 8 June 2020. Retrieved from: https://www.bbc.com/news/world-africa-52966016. Accessed on 25 June 2020.

masks and warned that the donated masks could be used to transmit the virus. "I want to urge you Tanzanians not to accept donations of masks, instead tell the donors to go and use them with their wives and children."

What a president to have, a PhD holder in chemistry no less, in a time of crisis such Covid-19 and in the 21st century? His name "Pombe" in Kiswahili means alcohol. This president was intoxicated. The President encouraged religious services in church sometimes without social distancing. "Coronavirus is a devil. It cannot live in the body of Christ." The devout Catholic must have forgotten that even the Vatican, the seat of the Catholic Church, had closed services and that the Devil sometimes visits heaven (Job 1:6) leave alone a church!

Madagascar President Andry Rajoelina claimed that an herbal concoction called Covid-Organics (CVO) manufactured in the country was capable of preventing and curing Covid-19. Several countries imported the drug.

President Donald Trump called Covid-19 "Chinese virus" and "a very bad gift from China." He termed WHO a "puppet of China" and withdrew grants for Covid-19. Tragically, he shook hands and avoided face masks on various occasions. He considers climate change, claimed to be the main cause of Covid-19, a hoax. Meanwhile, former US President, Barack Obama, called the US government's handling of coronavirus "an absolute chaotic disaster."[21] In some world countries, police officers embarked on a human rights abuse spree as they terrorised people and demanded bribes in the name of enforcing Covid-19 restrictions measures.

An economist's tips on post-Covid-19

At the international stage, leaders outside governments provided outstanding leadership on Covid-19 crisis. Prof. Muhammad Yunus, the 2006 Nobel Peace Prize Laureate for his efforts to use micro-credit to lift millions of women in Bangladesh out of poverty, was one of them. Addressing the post-Covid-19 scenario, he said: "Do we take the world back to where it was before the crisis or do we redesign the world?… If we don't make a social and environmentally conscious plan post-

---

21 Jeff Zeleny, "Obama says White House response to coronavirus has been 'absolute chaotic disaster'", CNN Business, 9 May, 2020. Retrieved from: https://edition.cnn.com/2020/05/09/politics/obama-trump-coronavirus-response-flynn-case/index.html

Covid-19, a bigger catastrophe await us."[22] He explained: "We can hide in our homes from coronavirus, but if we fail to address the deteriorating global issues, we will not have any place to hide from the angry Mother Nature and angry citizens all around the world."[23]

In yet another forum, Prof Yunus delivered a powerful message on the recovery (he likes to call it reconstruction) programme for the Covid-19 crisis. In a lecture sponsored by the Pontifical Lateran University on the global economy after the Covid-19 pandemic, he spoke of the "recovery full of opportunities if the world embrace a new social and environmental awareness, a use of the economy not as a mere science, useful for maximizing profits, but as a tool to achieve the greatest possible happiness of individuals and the community."[24] Noting that before the pandemic the world faced crises of global warming and climate change, massive unemployment, wealth inequality and artificial intelligence, Covid-19 pushed the world to reset, to start over, an opportunity to find new and creative solutions to these issues in addition to creating "a strong moral and religious leadership capable of overcoming tribalism."

After the pandemic, Pope Francis predicted at a sermon (*Crux*, 19 April 2020) that there was bound to emerge a worse virus of selfish indifference. He advised:

> We may be profoundly shaken by what is happening all around, the time has come to eliminate inequalities, to heal the injustice that is undermining the health of the entire human family… To everyone: Let us not think only of our interests, our vested interests. Let us welcome this time of trial as an opportunity to prepare for our collective future, because without an all-embracing vision, there will be no future for everyone.[25]

---

22 Muhammad Yunus, "Going Back to That World Is Equal to Committing Suicide: The Opportunity Presented by COVID-19", Yunus ScialBusiness, 20 May, 2020. Available at:https://www.yunussb.com/blog/2020/5/20/professor-muhammad-yunus-opportunity-covid-19. Accessed on 25 June 2020.

23 Ibid.

24 The theme of the lecture was, "No Going Back: The World Economy after the Covid-19 Pandemic", and was held on 16 May, 2020. See "Yunus: In wake of pandemic, we must create a better world", Vatican News, 16 May 2020. Available at: https://www.vaticannews.va/en/vatican-city/news/2020-05/yunus-in-wake-of-pandemic-we-must-create-a-better-world.html. Accessed on 26 June 2020.

25 Carol Glatz, "Now is time to build new world without inequality, injustice, pope says", Catholic News Service, 19 April 2020. Available at: https://www.catholicnews.com/services/englishnews/2020/now-is-time-to-build-new-world-without-inequality-injustice-pope-says.cfm. Accessed on 26 June 2020.

Pope Francis, whose heart is very close to the subject of global warming and climate change (said to be the genesis of Covid-19), was named Time Person of the Year 2013. On his heroic spiritual leadership on the pandemic he may not require the Nobel Peace Prize – he has already earned a bigger award – but deserves prayers and a big thank you for emerging number one overall mankind shepherd during the Covid-19 storm.

Now to the nations of the Earth on leadership. The UN bodies refers to themselves to as organisations born out of the fire of World War II. In the UN Security Council Chamber is a colourful mural depicting a central image rising like the Greek Phoenix from the ashes. The artistic work symbolised a world being rebuilt after the war, the promise of peace and individual freedom. Norwegian artist Per Krogh, who drew the mural, noted: "The essence of the idea is to give an impression of light, security and joy. The world we see in the foreground is collapsing, while the new world based on clarity and harmony can be built up."[26]

There is a world war, call it the Third World War. This is not being fought between man and man, but between man and a virus. Apparently man is being punished for destroying his very own and only habitat despite having held numerous international conferences over the years on global warming and climate change. There has never been a fierce urgency for the United Nations members and bodies, especially UNEP, to redouble its efforts and find better solutions to pollution, climate change and biodiversity loss. And an improved earth should be a global war cry as the world rises from the ashes of Covid-19 devil. And in memory of the terrible experience humanity has undergone through coronavirus, the UN global headquarters in Nairobi, UNEP, could do with a mural proclaiming: "In The Year of Our Lord Twenty Twenty, Coronavirus Coronaized Planet Earth". It is time to build bridges to reach out to Planet Earth and embrace it. And from Carl Sagan's story on the Pale Blue Dot, it is apparent that time on earth is limited. It pays for the leaders to make the most of it by leading their subjects well.

---

26 UNSC Admin, "U.N. Security Council Chamber Still Most Important Room in The World Maintains 'Norwegian Identity'", Diplomatic Times, 23 November, 2018. Retrieved from: https://diplomatictimes.net/2018/11/23/u-n-security-council-chamber-still-the-most-important-room-in-the-world-with-norwegian-identity/. Accessed on 26 June 2020.

God's Cabinet, a belt around Earth

At no other time in history did the international community held numerous, elaborate, mind-straining and long conversations on one subject like in early 2020. People of all background across the world talked and asked about Covid-19 endlessly with a view to finding an urgent solution. Did God just sit there watching the painful events as they unfolded? No! The following is a stretch of imagination of God convening an Extra-ordinary Cabinet meeting one day consisting of the Holy Trinity and his 24 elders (God likes a lean Cabinet despite the massive size of his government) and a selected number of Heavenly Saints and Advisors. (God is omniscient – all knowledge, all power – but for the sake of setting an example of governance and democracy he formed a Cabinet and appointed advisors.)

When God convened the Cabinet, he called the Covid-19 issue a "matter of universal importance". The meeting opened with prayers led by Jesus after which God commenced by reading from a paper titled, "The State of Coronavirus Coronaisation on Earth". He began by updating the audience on the global Covid-19 circumstances. He lamented about humanity's age-long ignorance of the beauty and goodness of creation and wished people could understand Him better. They know very little. That way, he confirmed, the relationship between man and God would be more productive and effective. He dwelt at length in the explanation of the Johari Window technique developed by American Psychologists Joseph Luft and Harry Ingham in 1955 that help people understand better their relationship with themselves as well as with others and even recalled the US Secretary of State Donald Rumsfeld's famous quote on 12 February 2002 with in relation to the ignorant mankind: "…as we know, there are known knows; there are things we know we know. We also know there are known unknowns; that is to say we know there are some things we do not know. But there are also unknown unknowns – the ones we don't know we don't know…"[27]

"You know why I dispatched JC (that's how they call Jesus Christ up there) to the Earth some 2,000 year ago?" God demanded from the attendants. He proceeded to explain that even with God Himself appearing and speaking to man and doing miraculous things, the angels'

---

27 Norbert Georg Schwarz, *The Pandora Principle: The Destructive Power of Creation* (Hamburg: Norderstedt, 2019), p. 16.

visitations, the prophets and the Scriptures, man proved extremely hard to educate. Man was like a group of people chained to the wall of a dark cave since childhood and facing a blank wall. Behind them is an invisible big fire some people are using to project shadows on the wall. (God was using the Allegory of the Cave story found in *The Republic* and authored by Greek philosopher Plato in 375 BC.) The prisoners have no motivation to leave the cave for they know nowhere else better.

"What the earthly people perceive," God elaborated, "at face value they accept as reality, through obstructions and manipulations of Satan. They are unaware of the reality that is the truth outside the cave. I sent JC on a special mission to educate mankind to transit from the darkness to light. True education would help him escape from bondage of ignorance and discover his special place in the creation. For converting his character and hence his soul man would become what he was meant. Unfortunately to date, lack of knowledge is still part of his nature.

"Mankind must understand that while the Earth is a speck in the Universe, but very special to me, it is the only place where I created an organism in my own image. Why would I send my only Son to save it if I held no love for it? The Earth is the only place that can sustain human life. And one of the things that delights me most is to see people taking care of it, especially planting the trees. This is the reason I appointed Wangari Maathai as Chief Advisor on Global Warming and Climate Change the moment she arrived here from Kenya through the Pearl Gates on 25 September 2011. You realise that she is the senior-most female in my entire government.

"Talking of Kenya, the country is greatly dear to me. On 19 April, 1903, I caused the allocation of 13,000 sq km in the Mau Plateau (part of the Uasin Gishu Plateau) for the establishment of the Jewish state. Kenya would be today the Promised Land hadn't the Jews not got scared of the bands of Maasai warriors and fierce lions inhabiting the region. Out of almost 200 world countries, I caused Kenya to be the global headquarters of UNEP and Habitat with a mind that it will lead in the conservation of the Earth. I caused President Moi to introduce an ambitious tree-planting and conservation campaign across the country through the Permanent Presidential Commission on Soil Conservation. Sadly he put an illiterate, sycophant, story-teller Mulu Mutisya, as the Chair thereby collapsing the whole project. And in the year 2004, I caused Wangari Maathai to win the Nobel Peace Prize for environment conservation to demonstrate my seriousness of protecting Mother Nature. In fact, pictures of Prof Maathai hugging a tree are some of my best. And how do you think the country's name became Kennia, like Canaan, or has a map resembling a heart, the manifestation of love or produced the first black American President? Kenya is a wonderful country, the land of great marathoners like First Lady Margaret Kenyatta and Eliud Kipchoge, who calls himself unlimited, like God. If God were to be asked one wish before his birth, I would have wished to be born in Kenya.

"Moving on, how does the Kenya BBI treat global warming and climate change? By the way I hear the initiative has dethroned Deputy President William Ruto, the guy who has built a prayer altar at his Karen home. Human beings and power! Honestly, I agonise for the man. Imagine (turning to JC) if I were to kick out my Principal Assistant in building global bridges and label him *Tanga Tanga* for his three years' work on earth, and replace him with Lucifer? That would be tantamount to God overthrowing himself. (JC exchanged knowing glances with St. Albino Luciani, known while on Earth as The Smiling Pope. Here both have a moniker of the 33-figure guys. The former for the 3 years of preaching and 33 years stay on earth and the latter for the shortest papacy period of 33 days.) And isn't the man spearheading the BBI not the one who tried to overthrow President Moi in a military coup in 1982? The one who governed the largest slum in Africa? That one, he left Kibra in a worse state than he found it. This man is truly a human political virus. See how he has politically distanced President Kenyatta and his Deputy Ruto. See how he has politically lock-downed the latter. And see how mercilessly he is spoiling the Jubilee Party's party just when it was approaching its climax. Anyway, now to the main issue.

"I created the universe. I said 'It is good' six times. I am not amused when humanity destroys any component of the creation package, especially the Earth. If climate change continue at the current rate, humanity will have no place to call home. Where will I take them? Furthermore, the concept of creation will lose meaning as I alone keep the timetable ahead of the end times. The Earth has enough for mankind to last him until the last days. Take Israel for instance. (JC smiles. Though Judaism, the religion and way of life of the Jewish people does not recognise Him, he still adores the land of his forefathers.) Measuring a mere 22,000 square kilometres and mostly desert, the country is one of the most durable economies. With an average annual precipitation of about 4mm, it is a leading authority in agricultural technology and pioneer in drip irrigation and water cycling. A desert exporting food! A case study of praise is not because I called them the chosen nation. Israelites uses their God-given brains extremely well.

"Not that I can't create another Earth if I feel like. An awesome Earth like the first to replace what is currently there. I am *Unlimited*. (Why would God make a finite world, if he could make an infinite one? The answer is: God did not want to do anything else than what He did – this however will not prevent us from believing He is all powerful, as we distinguish in God the work and the will – *le faire et le vouloir* – Marin Mersenne, French 17th century theologian). I am the author of all creation, including coronavirus. And I can stop the virus instant. But since humans (even those with PhDs) cannot understand and obey God-made laws or man-made laws like the UDHR, SDGs or their countries' constitutions, a baby-class lesson becomes inevitable. To shake mankind a little bit, try to get him out of the dark cave of ignorance and rebellion. The language of coronavirus. Coronaisation is doing exactly that.

"Some think Covid-19 is a precursor to the apocalypse, the end of the world. Indeed, I am shocked by the stream of prayers entering my inbox every second due to the pandemic. So people can be so panicky and humbled so? Covid-19 is just a tip of an iceberg. Humans have no clue how the end will be; a world turned upside-down where some people shall emerge happiest and others saddest. Of course Covid-19 has wrecked immense suffering and death. This is part of the healing, the cleansing process of the earth that I desire. Tears brings healing. I am very particular about trees so right from the beginning, there was the tree of knowledge of good and evil. There was the tree of life. Why did I decide to put knowledge and life in trees?

"Trees are food for all living things the reason I initially gave them to the First Family as their only source of food. Trees bring salvation, the reason JC was crucified on a tree and not stoned to death by the insane mobs, to save mankind. Covering the entire Earth with a green belt of trees and attainment of zero-carbon status is a grand vision closest to my heart. For humans are awfully selfish and have no regard for future generations. And as Prof. Wangari Maathai taught mankind, the Earth will henceforth enjoy peace. How I wish mankind can extract their brains from their crania, wash them with soap and running water and sanitise them before they think of WHO Covid-19 measures...

Revisiting Wangari Maathai

"I love the trees, I love the colour." Prof. Wangari Maathai remarked during an UNEP documentary interview sometime in 2004. "To me they represent life, and they represent hope. I think it is the green colour. I tell people I think heaven is green."[28]

For many years, Maathai preached and practised one important gospel: trees bring rain, oxygen and food for both humans and animals. Trees prevent soil erosion, and provide human shelter and beauty. Trees are life. Human existence and well-being are directly proportional to the conservation of environment. Conservation brings about peace and democracy. Degradation invites competition of resources, which eventually leads to human to human conflict and human to wildlife conflict. Wildlife, including lethal snakes (and of course viruses) invades peoples' habitats when theirs have been destroyed.

But few listened to Maathai, a case of a prophet going around unrecognised in her home country. For her activism Maathai was ridiculed. When she opposed the construction plan of a 60-storey tower at Nairobi Uhuru Park, President Daniel arap Moi said she had *dudus* (worms) in her head. When she joined mothers who were pressuring the government to release political prisoners, Moi called her a mad woman. And when she protested against the destruction of Kenya's forests he termed her a threat to the order and security of the country. "What can a divorced woman tell us?" The powers that be wondered. Maathai was severally harassed and beaten.

The world applauded Maathai and her work. Zackie Achmat, South Africa AIDS campaigner, said the Nobel moment was "a happy day for every blade of grass in Africa." BBC World Service Richard Black elaborated on what the Nobel citation meant: "It's not just planting trees –

---

28 "UN applauds awarding of Nobel Peace Prize to Kenyan environmental activist", UN News, 8 October 2004. Available at: https://news.un.org/en/story/2004/10/117382-un-applauds-awarding-nobel-peace-prize-kenyan-environmental-activist. Accessed on 26 June 2020.

it's the reasons why trees are planted… the vision that sees loss of forest as translating into loss of prospects for people down the track." Before the Nobel moment, Maathai had planted trees at Uhuru Park and put a plaque reading: "Freedom Corner: Memorial Trees of Peace, Lest we Forget!"

The Covid-19 came in the 16th year of Maathai's Nobel win. More than ever, climate change is currently the biggest threat to life on the planet. Maathai's message on that memorable December 10 is more relevant than ever. She said: "Today we are faced with a challenge that calls for a shift in our thinking, so that human stops threatening its life-supporting system. We are called to assist the Earth to heal her wounds and in the process heal our own."[29] Lest We Forget!

Since Prof Maathai passed on, her Green Belt Movement has planted some 50 million trees to date. But this is just a drop in the ocean. Watching from up there she shudders as many more millions of trees are mercilessly destroyed across the world as if there is no tomorrow. Want God to smile? Want God to make a purely holidaying (not judgment) mission to earth? God touring Maasai Mara and Diani Beach in Kenya! Want to eradicate the human-viruses (including novel Coronavirus) conflict? Then girdle the whole planet Earth with a green belt.

Our children are very afraid

> My first diary entry appeared on 3 January 2009 under the heading "I am Afraid": "I had a terrible dream last night filled with military helicopters and Taliban. I have had such dreams since the launch of the military operation in Swat." I wrote about being afraid to go to school because of the Taliban edict and looking over my shoulder all the time. I also described something that happened on my way home from school: "I heard a man behind me saying – I will kill you! – I quickened my space and after a while I looked back to see if he was following me. To my huge relief I saw he was speaking on his phone, he must have been talking to someone else".[30]

The above passage is from Malala Yousfzai's book, *I Am Malala*. The Taliban in Pakistan had banned girls from attending school and

---

29 Ibid.

30 Malala Yousafzai, *I Am Malala: The Girl Who Stood Up for Education and Was Shot by the Taliban* (London: Weidenfeld & Nicolson, 2013), p. 130.

blown more than a hundred girl schools. This was the beginning of her activism for the right to education for women. Then she started receiving death threats from the militants.

"How dare the Taliban take away my basic right to education?" The Pakistani girl complained bitterly.

"Our annual exams are due after the vacations, but this will only be possible if the Taliban allow girls to go to school… I am really bored because I have no books to read…I think of it often and imagine the scene clearly. Even if they come to kill me, I will tell them what they are trying to do is wrong, that education is our right… I have a new dream… I must be a politician to save this country…. There are so many crises in our country. I want to remove these crises…"[31]

The Taliban militants meant business. On 9 October 2012, while riding home with other pupils in a bus from school, Malala was shot by a Taliban gunman. After a three-hour hospital operation, she remained in a comma for a week. Exactly two years later on 10 October 2014, the 17-year old, jointly with the 60-year old Satyarthi Kailash from India, won the Nobel Peace Prize "for their struggle against the suppression of children and young people and for the right of all children to education."

After the award at the Oslo City Hall, Malala poured her mind's confusion about conflicts and education among the priorities of grown-ups. "The so called world of adults may understand it," she said, "but we children don't… Why is it that giving guns is so easy but giving books is so hard? Why is it that making tanks is so easy, but building schools is so difficult?" The Taliban were not done yet. Two months after Malala's Nobel moment, on 16 December 2014, seven Taliban insurgents stormed an army-run school in Peshawar city and killed 141 people – nine staff members and 132 children – in the eight-hour onslaught. (In June 2020, eight years after the Taliban gunned her in an attempt to lock-down her from her education, the 22-year old Malala graduated with a degree in Philosophy, Politics and Economics (PPE) at UK's prestigious Oxford University.)

"You see, I must repeat again, it is a peculiar characteristic of many people, this love of torturing children, and children only…" wrote Russian Fyodor Dostoevsky in *The Brothers Karamazov*. "It's just their

---

31 Ibid, p. 118.

defenselessness that tempts the tormentor, just the angelic confidence of the child who has no refuge and no appeal, that sets his vile blood on fire. In every man, of course, a demon lies hidden-the demon of rage, the demon of lustful heat at the screams of the tortured victim, the demon of lawlessness let off the chain, the demons of diseases that follow on vice gout, kidney disease and so on"[32]

Flashback some 80 years. In 1934, Anne Frank, a Jewish girl enrolled in school. Her dream was to be either an actress or a journalist when she grows up. Ten years later, the whole world was in a mess on the account of World War II, and the Jews were being persecuted en mass in Europe. On 12 June 1942 Anne had started writing her experiences in a diary. She wrote about how she "can't build up my hopes on a foundation consisting of confusion, misery and death..." where "...The earth is ploughed by their bombs..."[33] On 5 April 1944, she jotted down her love for education and career path: "I finally realized that I must do my schoolwork to keep from being ignorant, to get on in life, to become a journalist, because that's what I want... And if I don't have the talent to write books or newspaper articles, I can always write for myself. But I want to achieve more than that... I need to have something besides a husband and children to devote myself to..."[34]

Sadly, Anne did not manage to become a journalist. She died of typhus in a Nazi concentration camp on 31 March 1945, just a few months before the war she dreaded so much came to an end. But she did write something great. Her book, *The Diary of Anne Frank*, is one of the world's most popular dream by a child in a time of war.

And in Kenya mid-2013, Pauline Atieno, a 16-year old Standard Seven pupil at Amani Primary School in Mikindani, Mombasa, had broken down in tears. First she had heard an unusual assembly bell, then when the school gathered, the head teacher sent home all pupils following a nationwide teachers' strike that had started on 25 June. Later she explained the reason to her reaction: "I have no conducive

---

32 Fyodor Dostoevsky, *The Brothers Karamazov* (New York: Farrar, Straus & Giroux, 2002), p. 766.

33 Anne Frank, *Anne Frank: The Diary of a Young Girl* (Kampen, Ned: LRV-info, 1992), p. 49.

34 Ibid, p. 39.

environment at home. I am the only girl at home and whenever I plan to study there is a lot of interruption from my younger brother and cousin."[35]

The above three girl examples, but also representing boys, demonstrates how seriously children take their education. They know it is their right and a ticket to their careers and fulfilment of their dreams. Yet the children, who make the biggest proportion of the world population, oftentimes meet roadblocks emanating from actions of adults. Wars, conflicts, teachers' strikes, sexual abuse, preventable diseases, physical violence… They feel let down by those who are supposed to ensure their visions come true, since most problems they encounter are preventable or curable.

Today the children are very afraid. Covid-19 brought with it an assortment of challenges to their education and future. Worst, they have witnessed the don't-care attitude with which some adults have handled the Covid-19 crisis. If grown-ups, including leaders like Raila Odinga, can violate the Covid-19 measures laid by international authorities with abandon, whom shall they emulate, and who will protect them? The children wonder: will the policies and programmes put in place for their protection be sound enough? Will the school-going and bonding with other children be ever the same again? Because to school they must go and do their exams since it is their right rather than bow down to Covid-19 fears. Or would the world say, like Raila in September 2017: "*Kwani watoto watakufa kama hawatafanya mtihani* (shall the children die if they miss to sit their exams?)[36]

Children are the riskiest and every day they leave the door for school or out to play will leave the world in suspense. Never in the history has the world been called upon to respond with all its might to: "A Child's Prayer". For due to their social nature, children will be more vulnerable to Covid-19; the children being infected will bite the world where it hurts most. For the children, the Covid-19 period will be the cruellest.

---

35 "Why I cried after school sent us home", The Latest Kenyan News, Friday, 28 June, 2013. Available at: http://kenyauptodate.blogspot.com/2013/06/why-i-cried-after-school-sent-us-home.html. Accessed on 26 June 2020.

36 Raila was calling for a delay in national exams in favour of a repeat General Election. See Fay Ngina, "There's no harm in pushing the exams by two weeks, the children are not going to die- Raila Odinga", U Report, 5 September, 2017. Available at: https://www.standardmedia.co.ke/ureport/story/2001253664/there-s-no-harm-in-pushing-the-exams-by-two-weeks-the-children-are-not-going-to-die-raila-odinga. Accessed on 26 June 2020.

Humans are diverse, yet they are the same

"The problem of the Twentieth Century is the problem of colour line," wrote American human rights defender, W.E.B Du Bois.[37] This prophetic remark from his 1903 book, *The Souls of Black Folks*, was evident throughout the said century and even spilled over into the next as anti-black racism continued to be witnessed in various countries across the world.

Two recent instances: From China where Covid-19 was first reported, images of blacks being mistreated travelled online across the globe. A negative-tested person forced into quarantine; an evicted student sleeping under a bridge; an employee holding up a sign that the restaurant is no longer serving black people; Chinese on social media calling Africans ungrateful, foreign migrants, carriers of disease, criminal elements. And from the US, on 25 May 2020, George Floyd, a 46-year old black American, was killed by white police officers triggering demonstrations and protests in most US cities and around the world. What is that so horribly bad as to be of black colour?

When it became real that the Covid-19 was a global pandemic, all fingers from the Western world were suddenly pointing to Africa. In early April two French doctors suggested the vaccine for the disease be tested in Africa. "If I can be provocative" one doctor allowed, "shouldn't we be doing this study in Africa, where there are no masks, no treatments, no resuscitation? A bit like it is done elsewhere for some studies on AIDS."[38] According to the French TV Channel LCI, the other doctor nodded in agreement at the idea. "You are right. We are in the process of thinking about a study in parallel in Africa." The idea sparked an outrage with WHO Director-General Tedros Ghebreyesus calling it a hangover from "colonial mentality." "Africa can't and won't be a testing ground for any vaccine. It was a disgrace, appalling to hear during the 21st century, to hear from scientists that kind of remark," he stated.

---

37 W. E. B. Du Bois, *The Souls of Black Folk* (New York: Dover Publications, 1994), p. 24.

38 Anne Mawathe, "Coronavirus: Why Africans should take part in vaccine trials", BBC News, 18 May 2020.

Africa is a continent of disease and deaths, so it seems. On 10 April 2020, American billionaire philanthropist, Melinda Gates, in an interview with CNN predicted an apocalyptic virus outbreak, total doom in Africa. "If the world does not act fast enough," she said, "there will be dead bodies all over the streets of Africa." Gates added that the continent might not be able to handle the devastating effect of the virus.

Hot on heels within the same month, a research conducted by the UN Economic Commission for Africa (UNECA), headquartered in Addis Ababa, Ethiopia, revealed that, "Anywhere between 300,000 and 3 million Africans could lose their lives as a direct result of Covid-19 depending on the intervention measures taken to stop it."[39] Colonial mentality? Backward Africa with fragile healthcare systems… mass deaths?

Surprise, surprise. About two months after Gates and UNECA doom prediction, Africa, home to 17 per cent of world population, had fewer diagnosed coronavirus cases accounting for less than 1.5 per cent of global total and 0.1 per cent deaths. The storyline began to change. That coronavirus thrives more in cold climate, Africa had a younger population, has lower population density, its people have better genetic immunity… as justification of the low infection rate. An article in *The African Report* magazine concluded a story on this subject quoting Francine Ntoumi, a Congolese biologist: "In certain countries on the continent, people eat bats and live on top of one another… in fact, all the conditions for a disaster are reunited, but we haven't seen one happen. It's up to scientists to find out why."[40]

This is the African continent, home of the blacks. The Heart of Darkness, the Dark Continent or the Hopeless Continent has variously been referred to by the whites at different ages. Coronavirus first sprang from a developed world. One could imagine if the virus originated from Africa, once referred to as "The White Man's graveyard". Aircraft-loads and shiploads of the whites would be heading out of Africa and not a single white person would be left in the continent.

---

39 Colin Dwyer, "U.N. Agency fears 'vulnerable' Africa may suffer at least 300,000 Covid-19 deaths", NPR [National Public Radio], 17 April, 2020.

40 Olivier Marbot, "Coronavirus: Unpacking the theories behind Africa's low infection rate", theafricareport, Tuesday, 5 May 2020. Available at: https://www.theafricareport.com/27470/coronavirus-unpacking-the-theories-behind-africas-low-infection-rate/. Accessed on 26 June 2020.

Travelling back in time – approximately 700 years– a picture of the continent as perceived by the whites is described by Adam Hochschild in *King Leopold's Ghost*:

> … a Benedictine Monk who mapped the world in 1350 claimed that Africa was inhabited by one-eyed people who used their feet to cover their heads. A geographer in the next century announced that the continent held people with one leg, three faces and the heads of lions. In 1459, an Italian monk named Fra Mauro declared Africa "the home of the Roc, a bird so large that it could carry an elephant through the air… and as for trying to sail down the African coast everyone knew that as soon as you passed the Canary Islands, you would be in the Mare Tenebroso, the Sea of Darkness[41]

Hochschild continues:

> This was a region of uttermost dread… where the heavens fling down liquid sheets of flames and the water boils… where serpents rocks and ogre islands lie in wait for the marines, where the giant hand of Satan reaches up from the fathomless depths to seize him, where he will turn black in face and body as a mark of God's vengeance for the insolence of his prying into this forbidden mystery. In case he survives, he will then arrive in the Sea of Obscurity and be lost forever in the vapours and slime at the edge of the world.[42]

What was the inhabitants of the African continent's greatest crime? Black colour of skin. Throughout history black has been linked to everything bad: black magic, black sheep, black cat, black market, blackmail, blacklisted, black-hearted, black book, black day, etc. The devil, the night, mourning, uncleanliness, ugliness, have similarly been associated with black, on one hand, and on the other, white colour has been related to all the good things in life and the afterlife.

Yet blacks remained proud of their skin colour and saw no significant differences between themselves and the whites. Black is beautiful, the saying was born. In Kenya, Raila Odinga has been using Lucky Dube's, "You Can't Stop Reggae" as the signature to build bridges. A more appropriate one from the same artist would be "Different Colours, One

---

41 Adam Hochschild, *King Leopold's Ghost: A Story of Greed, Terror, and Heroism in Colonial Africa* (Boston: Houghton Mifflin Company), p. 6.

42 Ibid.

People", the word colours substituted with tribes or "One Love" by Bob Marley.

"I suppose there is no stronger argument against racism," noted Professor Philip Tobias, a South African Anthropologist "and in favour of the brotherhood of man than the evidence that we all come from one African ancestor, whether it is the ancient Australopithecus, or possibly, the not so ancient proposed Eve. Whoever it was wasn't just the ancestor of African man, or just this man, or the other, but of us all."

Despite past and present prejudice about blacks on account of their skin colour Covid-19 taught the world an important lesson. The virus did not attack selectively based on ethnicity, people's colour, social-political-economic status, age, creed or geographic location. Every human being was a potential target. And while millions were infected and thousands died across the globe, the whole world came forward together to fight against this common enemy. The lesson: Humans' diversity notwithstanding, all are one and the same.

Embrace God much more

In the beginning, God created man. "You can eat fruits from any tree except from the tree of knowledge of good and evil in the middle of the garden, lest you die." God commanded Adam. But the crafty Serpent came around to Eve, Adam's wife. "Eat it, your eyes will be opened and you will be like God, knowing good and evil." They both ate, instantly triggering the fall of man. (Pray, tell why didn't God warn Adam not to eat from the tree of life in the middle of the garden only to have it guarded after the fall of man?)

For the first couple trusted in their own strength, knowledge and wisdom. They became the know-it-all, *wajuaji*. By wilfully choosing to disobey God, Adam opted for independence over a lasting relationship with God. "Colonialism or dictatorship will not reign in Eden," perhaps this is what Adam was thinking, having now grown horns "here is politics of socialism and self-reliance." *Siasa za ujamaa na kujitegemea*. Reading his mind, God asked him: "Is that so, so soon? Then from now henceforth, there is nothing for free, *hakuna cha bure*. It will be sweat, sweat and lots of prayers." Things would never be the same again for mankind.

Considering the devastation Covid-19 has wrought around the world, it is extremely difficult to convince, even the most religious that God can allow such suffering. So is God in control then?

Yet, hard questions remain troubling – the whys, whats, and hows. How can an organism unseen by a naked eye devastate the whole world in such magnitude? "And we know that all things work together for good to them that love God…" (Romans 8:28) Doesn't the world love God? And if so what is good about Covid-19? What kind of a world was this? A world of limitations. Various theories concerning the "from where," "by whom" and "for what" started emerging. Behold this: The Devil thrives better in times of great crises. One day he sat down and felt lonely and idle. For quite sometimes he had not rendered a real bombshell to the Earth. And for a long time he had not performed the Handshake with God. Then he recalled the fruits of one of the best Handshakes when he caused Job's household into a total lockdown. Then, Job received messengers in quick succession who carried only the worst news: "Your servants have been slain…! Your oxen have been taken away…! Sheep and servants have been burned by fire from heaven! Camels have been taken away and servants slain…! Your sons and daughters have been killed by great wind!" Then Job was "smitten with sore boils from the sole of his foot unto his crown." This prompted his wife to shout at him: "Dost thou still retain thine integrity? Curse God, and die." Job was quarantined for days.

So the Devil, in his sly, calculating nature approached God, calling him Sir, and Your Excellency. "I need some real, big job to do." He told God. "Of late, I haven't had anything meaningful to do with myself." God thought for a moment then asked him, "What theme do you have in mind this time around?" The Devil find great satisfaction where God has been wronged most. He replied: "Rescuing of Planet Earth From Climate Change Annihilation,", and added, "to make humans build genuine bridges between themselves and Planet Earth, not walls of pollution and forests degradation, a kind of the BBI."

God thought the Devil had never produced a nobler idea. "Yes, permission granted. But on one condition. Don't hit them too hard, especially the children and the elderly." Both shook hands and sealed the BBI. The Devil, feeling as if on cloud nine left for his archives, got hold of coronavirus and fast headed to the Earth. Then he unleashed the havoc…

Economic and political activities became limited. And Jesus' children whose kingdom of God is theirs could not go to school. The children could not go to Sunday school to sing to their Jesus and pray him. Even their playing was limited. And when people needed consolation most, houses of worship-churches, synagogues, temples and mosques were almost closed. Prayers, baptisms, weddings and funeral services became limited. How could a minute virus limit religious freedom in countries' constitutions and also limit the way to God's kingdom? The Devil never got a better experience.

Accepting that the health authorities (the sciences are like the rays of divinity/science serve us as a ladder to climb towards God – Marin Mersenne) led by WHO were justified in demanding restrictions, the world had been denied the greatest weapon to fight against the evil: Worship. As a result the world sensed too weak to fight.

In an article appearing in *The New York Times* on 10 March 2020, Italian journalist, Mattia Ferraresi, wrote:

> Holy water is not a hand sanitizer and prayer is not a vaccine… But for believers, religion is a fundamental source of spiritual healing and hope. It's a remedy against despair, providing psychological and emotional support that is an integral part of well-being… At a deeper level, religion for worshippers, is the ultimate source of meaning. The most profound claim of every religion is to make sense of the whole of existence, including, and perhaps especially, circumstances marked by suffering and tribulation. Take such claims seriously enough, and even physical health, when it is devoid of greater purpose, starts to look like a hollow value.[43]

The world wanted to know the truth, the gospel truth concerning Covid-19, to set their mind free. Some things don't just appear from the blues. Someone, somewhere must have been sinned against mightily. Could the Holy Scripture provide the truth about the pandemic?

Hope is what is desperately needed in the Covid-19 times, like the following sermon provided by Pope Francis on 27 March 2020, teaches:

> When evening had come (Mark 4:35)…For weeks now it has been evening. Thick darkness has gathered over our squares, our streets

---

[43] Mattia Ferraresi, "God vs. Coronavirus", *New York Times*, 10 March, 2020. Retrieved from: https://www.nytimes.com/2020/03/10/opinion/coronavirus-church-religion.html. Accessed on 20 June 2020.

and our cities; it has taken over our lives, filling everything with a deafening silence and a distressing void, that stops everything as it passes by; we feel it in the air, we notice in people's gestures, their glances give them away. We find ourselves afraid and lost. Like the disciples in the Gospel we were caught off guard by an unexpected, turbulent storm. We have realized that we are on the same boat, all of us fragile and disoriented, but at the same time important and needed, all of us called to row together, each of us in need of comforting the other. On this boat… are all of us. Just like those disciples, who spoke anxiously with one voice, saying 'We are perishing' (v. 38), so we too have realized that we cannot go on thinking of ourselves, but only together can we do this.

It is easy to recognize ourselves in this story. What is harder to understand is Jesus' attitude. While his disciples are quite naturally alarmed and desperate, he stands in the stern, in the part of the boat that sinks first. And what does he do? In spite of the tempest, he sleeps on soundly, trusting in the Father; this is the only time in the Gospels we see Jesus sleeping. When he wakes up, after calming the wind and the waters, he turns to the disciples in a reproaching voice: 'Why are you afraid? Have you no faith?' (v. 40)...[44]

Humans' finite understanding cannot comprehend why and how God works. And therefore the world has no choice other than return to God more dedicatedly through the Holy Scriptures. Satan never wrote or commissioned any author to write his manifesto. Could you follow a leader without a manifesto who only operate from the underground and in darkness? You may have your god of evolution or god of the Big Bang, but the God of creation comes supreme. It is only God who has wisdom on how to battle the evil Covid-19, among other human challenges.

In the *Crux* publication April 19, 2020, Pope Francis allowed:

God never tires of reaching out to lift us up when we fall. He want us to see him, not as a taskmaster with whom we have to settle accounts, but as our father who always raises us up…. We need the Lord, who

____

44 For the full sermon, see ""Urbi Et Orbi" Blessing: Extraordinary Moment of Prayer Presided Over by Pope Francis", Sagrato of St Peter's Basilica, Friday, 27 March 2020. Available at: http://www.vatican.va/content/francesco/en/messages/urbi/documents/papa-francesco_20200327_urbi-et-orbi-epidemia.html. Accessed on 30 June 2020.

sees beyond that fragility (Covid-19) an irrepressible beauty. With him we discover how precious we are even in our vulnerability.[45]

As the world rush against time to put their house in order, what next? John Lennox Professor of Mathematics at Oxford University authored a book titled, *Where is God in a Coronavirus World?* He proposed that "Coronavirus is evidence that both our relationship with creation and creation's relationship with us are disordered; and that is not an accident. But hope is found in another Corona: The crown of thorns that was forced on Jesus Christ's head at his trial before execution."

In the midst of the dangerous Covid-19, the world cannot afford to lose faith in God and throw insults to Him like Job was advised by his wife. There are no two ways! It is either the money or the box, or rather take either God or the Devil.

The barrel of a pen

Prof. Ngũgĩ wa Thiong'o, Kenya's foremost novelist with over 50 titles to his credit, has been, since the publication of his first work, *Weep Not, Child* in 1964, the loudest and most consistent literary voice against abuse of human rights both in colonial and independent Kenya. In nearly all his books, some terms are particularly dominant: Colonialism. Imperialism. Foreign domination. Exploitation. Freedom struggle and fighters. Neo-colonialism. Women's liberation. Theft of public funds... Ngũgĩ's *Barrel of a Pen* has been truly potent.[46]

On 29 December 1977, a detention order was issued "for the preservation of public security" by the Minister for Home Affairs, Daniel arap Moi (of course from an Executive Order XYZ issued by President Jomo Kenyatta) and thereafter a statement signed by senior police officer Muhindi Munene giving reasons for his imprisonment as, "you have engaged yourself in activities and utterances which are dangerous to the good government of Kenya and its institutions..." was a cruel fight against what Ngũgĩ had been propagating. Out of the

---

45 See "Pope Francis' homily on Divine Mercy Sunday", Catholic News Agency, Vatican City, 19 April, 2020. Available at: https://www.catholicnewsagency.com/news/full-text-pope-francis-homily-on-divine-mercy-sunday-21849. Accessed on 30 June 2020.

46 Ngugi wa Thiong'o, *Barrel of a Pen: Resistance to Repression in Neo-Colonial Kenya* (Trenton: Africa World Press, 1983).

prison gate one year later the government could not allow Ngũgĩ to get back his university teaching job and he was eventually forced into exile. Some 37 years later – on 8 June 2015 at a State House reception – President Uhuru Kenyatta told him that Kenya had changed into a country "that needs all your talents. It is time for you to come back and help us build the country."[47] How things can change!

It seems Covid-19 brought Ngũgĩ a new job as it resonates strongly with where his passion lies: To rescue a people ravaged by economic, political and social bondages. The British colonialism and the novel coronavirus 'coronalism' bears some striking similarities. *Oxford Dictionary* defines colonialism as the policy or practice of acquiring full or partial political control over another country, occupying it with settlers, and exploiting it economically. Covid-19 is a kind of a colonist.

From 1895 Kenya was a protectorate of the British Empire until 1920 when it was declared a colony (comes from Latin colonus, a farmer settler). During the colonisation period the British engaged in massive exploitation of both human and natural resources that led to the birth of freedom fighters and struggle fronted by Dedan Kimathi. On 20 October 1952, the colonial government enacted emergency legislation that provided restrictions on freedom of association, and on speech, meeting, writing and movement. Curfew was imposed in districts adjacent to European communities. Security forces were reinforced and armed police increased.

The neo-coronalism or '*ukoroni mambo leo*' in Kiswahili, has caused a global State of Emergency never seen anywhere else or before. Just like the Europeans forced Africans' way of living into a lockdown, this coronaisation has restricted freedom of association, meetings and movement, and has had curfews imposed. Some people have been put into concentration camps (quarantines) for screening just like the Wazungu did to Africans. There has been heightened security and a huge increase of police officers on duty. All in all this coronaisation has brought global economy to its knees, besides costing human lives and the unprecedented suffering.

The major positive thing about this new coronalism is that people will take more interest in their personal hygiene and rethink their

---

47 PSCU, "It is time to come back home, Uhuru tells Ngugi wa Thiong'o", *Daily Nation*, 8 June 2015.

relationship with Nature and God. To regain its independence, there will emerge in the world committed freedom fighters as well as home guards and traitors…

Coronavirus is a story that will excite singers, film makers and writers. Coronaisation is a subject that would interest Ngũgĩ greatly, especially having researched and written widely on British colonialism in Kenya as well as Kenyans re-colonising themselves. Having been detained without trial for one year, Ngũgĩ knows a lot about a lockdown. A novel on novel (comes from Latin, meaning new) coronavirus coronaisation will help the world, even minimally, shake off the yoke of Covid-19. For how can a tiny virus measuring approximately 50 nanometers (about 1/1000th the width of a typical human hair) across drag along its whole tribe to terrorise the whole global community (it knows no apartheid) without triggering creativity in a writer's mind? Following the path of his earlier work, *Decolonising the Mind*,[48] Ngũgĩ would enlighten readers through the barrel of a pen on ways to decoronaise their minds in order to break the chains of coronaisation.

And what is in a name? William Shakespeare said "that which we call a rose but any other name would smell as sweet." Take Ngũgĩ's family tree, for instance. Somewhere around 1870s, a young Maasai boy was captured by Agĩkũyũ during one of the tribal wars and taken to Murang'a. During the abduction, the boy resisted all he could and was beaten thoroughly. Meanwhile, the new masters would ask him things in the Gĩkũyũ language, which he could not understand. "Aatooshoki! Aatooshoki!" He was replying in the Maa language. (I have been beaten! I have been beaten!) To the captors, this sounded like *ntũũcũ, ntũũcũ*. Henceforth, they gave the boy a new name, Ndũũcũ. This ancient Ndũũcũ would eventually birth Ngũgĩ's father, Thiong'o wa Ndũũcũ and this writer's grandfather, Kariũki wa Ndũũcũ. This is going back to the roots, to revert to it in a moment.

The British colonialism in Kenya brought a kind of *sheng* language where some English words and phrases were Gĩkũyũnised: *turungi* (true tea), *thuruarĩ* (trouser), *igooti* (coat), *igooti* (court), *mũringamu* (blue gum), *rũmande* (remand), *thamanji* (summons), *manjeneti* (emergency), *ngaati* (home guard), *mairĩrĩ* (my lady), *ndaimono*

---

48 Ngũgĩ wa Thiong'o, *Decolonising the Mind: The Politics of Languages in African Literature* (Nairobi: East African Educational Publishers, 1986).

(demon), *ndamiucĩrĩ* (damn you silly), *mburarĩbuu* (bloody fool), *candabu* (shut up), *baga* (bugger), *niga* (nigger), *rĩthithi* (racing), *bakini* (fxxing), Warubaga (Elburgon), *mbaathi* (bus), *miitha* (Mass) and many others. Similarly the novel coronavirus coronaisation came with new names and phrases and those that existed before became known to the larger global population: Covid-19 (Coronavirus disease 2019); SARS (Severe Acute Respiratory Syndrome); zoonotic (transmission between humans and animals); pandemic (spreading to all); symptomatic (showing symptoms of disease); PUI (Person Under Investigation for disease); PCR (Polymerase Chain Reaction)testing, a testing protocol to identify disease; herd immunity (reduction in risk of infection within a population); patient zero (first person to become infected); essential business (those that serve critical purpose); PPE (Personal Protective Equipment); social distancing, self-quarantine, lockdown… The world dictionaries were immediately updated to accommodate the new normal of terms. Other non-scientific names will also join the list: *Hii kitu* (This Thing); *Hii ni Shetani* (This is the Devil)…

In the early 1960, with two novels – *Weep Not, Child* and *The River Between* – already accepted for publication, Ngũgĩ used to run a regular column for the Nation Media Group of newspapers under the title, "As I see It". The media, also known as the Fourth Estate or the Fourth Power, is one partner that will be crucial in victory over coronaisation. Celebrating the World Press Freedom Day on 3 May, 2020, the Nation Media Group's Mutuma Mathiu and one of Kenya's finest journalist, outlined the qualities of the kind of the media people required in the fight against Covid-19 in an article, "Journalism Doesn't Always Have a Point; It is The Point". A (good) journalist has:

> …an inborn sense of justice, the courage to be unpopular and disliked and an instinctive willingness to gravitate towards the defence of the underdog… Love people, have a great sense of community and a willingness to fight lost causes, make sacrifices without expectation of reward and throw your own interests down the toilet for the benefit of people… great journalists have a naïve, almost suicidal, belief in the truth and integrity.[49]

---

49 Mutuma Mathiu, "Journalism doesn't always have to have a point; it is the point", *Daily Nation*, Wednesday, 13 May 2020.

First an inspiring story 40 years old. On 2 November 1978, President Julius Nyerere declared war on Uganda after President Idi Amin invaded Tanzania and annexed Kagera region on 27 October 1978. Besides mobilising the Tanzania People Defence Force, the Police, National Youth Service and Prisons Service, with the total at the war's peak numbering 100,000, he "enlisted" all 18 million citizens in the war through media propaganda. The President devised a lethal machinery where quotes, phrases and messages of war propaganda were coined. Radio Tanzania Dar-es-Salaam earnestly picked up the battle cries and aired them several times a day. Amin was called "that syphillic lunatic" and "a snake."

One of the weapons in use by the Tanzanian forces, the BM-21 multiple rocket launcher was known as Baba Mtakatifu (Holy Father). In so doing, the President galvanised millions of Tanzanians to unity of purpose. Everyone gave support either by enlisting in the war or donating foodstuffs, money, services and property that could help to pay for the war. The effect of conquering the demented aggressor, Amin, in just five months was due in part to the government collaborating with the media in bringing the masses on board. President Nyerere had gone on air to assure his nation and delivered his famous speech:

> We have the capacity to hit him;
> We have the reason to hit him; and,
> We have the determination to hit him."[50]

But we understand this: novel coronavirus cannot be fought with tankers, jet fighters, bombs or guns. And it would care less to hear human propaganda and insults. The media too cannot provide a blueprint for its vaccine. But President Nyerere's radio statement about the "resources", the "reasons" and "will" can be a great driving force.

Going back to the roots… This is not charting a person's lineage like Ngũgĩ would to reach ancestor Ndũũcũ or Alex Haley in *Roots*, tracing his forefather, Kunta Kinte, through seven generations to a village in the Gambia or Luke in the Gospels recording the genealogy of Jesus Christ 70 generations backwards and ending with "the Son of

---

50 Quoted from Simon Chesterman's, *Just War Or Just Peace?: Humanitarian Intervention and International Law* (Oxford: Oxford University Press, 2001), p. 77.

God." This is going back to the roots of Covid-19. The media are one of the most important tools in the Covid-19 campaign. First, they will communicate broadly that Covid-19 is not a myth, a dream or some peoples' imagination. Covid-19 is real and is definitely not a passing cloud any time soon. Secondly, the media will take the world back to their roots. Despite the modern advanced scientific knowledge, when did the rain started beating mankind? For, despite priding themselves as moon-going, planets explorers or nuclear missiles makers, mankind of the 21st century knows very little of what takes place in or around Planet Earth. This is one mighty lesson that coronavirus taught.

For what reasons, for instance, did the coronavirus hold their "Berlin Conference" to survey the whole world for coronaisation? And moving forward why did the rivers, ice in mountains, clean sky and clean oceans disappear? Trees are on their way out, for real. See how the soil has been polluted by pesticides and fertilisers. How often do you hear coo-coos from the doves, screeching from bats, twitters from birds, chatters from monkeys, trumpets from elephants, laughs from hyenas, or croaks from frogs? When did you see last beautiful butterflies and bees hovering over stunning flowers as it used to be long ago? And why do eggs, chicken, beef, sausages, fruits and vegetables taste differently from what they used to be, say 40 years ago?

Networking with credible researchers, the media will hammer and hammer in the message that Mother Nature is terribly wounded and exploited; and she is reacting. Covid-19 is a kind of human-made human extinction. Re-loaded with energy and great passion the media will communicate that Mother Nature is crying for restoration to her former glory, and can mankind act urgently to avoid an imminent annihilation? Additionally, the media will continue without break to give accurate and balanced coverage as well as aiding the global health organisations in the Covid-19 campaign.

While the media will be leading the campaign, the war against novel coronavirus will be for everyone, requiring all relevant talents. In a letter addressed to The Students of Workers and Peasant's Faculty, German poet, Bertolt Brecht, noted: "Your science will be valueless you will find; And learning will be sterile, if inviting; Unless you pledge your intellect to fighting; Against all enemies of all mankind."[51] Covid-19 is a story for everyone.

This chapter opened with a poem by Ngũgĩ, "Dawn of Darkness", giving comfort to the world citizens that the coronaisation darkness shall for sure pass away and humanity will once again bond: handshake, hug and sing. American poet, Walt Whitman's "On the Beach at Night" also urge that people should never give up hope because the clouds of any adversity always will pass and the stars shine again:

> Weep not, child
> Weep not, my darling
> With these kisses let me remove your tears,
> The ravening clouds shall not be long victorious,
> They shall not long possess the sky....[52]

We shall sing and dance post-Covid-19

The fruits of independence do not ripen overnight. The battle against Covid-19 is bound to be a long painful trek requiring global political, economic and social goodwill. It will need prayerful and spiritually inclined people. Ultimately, unprecedented economic loss will be recorded. Thousands of human lives lost. Tears and unending fears will torment millions in the four corners of the earth. But at some point in time will the world rise from the ashes of Covid-19 and back to its former *inglorious* past? Field Marshal Covid-19 will surely be floored and people liberated from its bondage. Humanity will survive and thrive. But after coronavirus coup d'état aborts, mankind will have to revolutionalise treatment of their health, environmental health and planetary health. Things will never be the same again, ever.

Much later the future generations will listen in awe as grandparents tell bedtime stories: Once upon a time there came a human-eating ogre from God knows where that devastated the world until people thought the Armageddon was around the corner. The monster created a new world order. World citizens pulled together to confront it. Defeated, the virus fled back to its bunker. American writer, Maya Angelou's poem,

---

51 John Willett and Ralph Manheim, *Bertolt Brecht Poems* (London: Eyre Methuen, 1976), p. 450.

52 Walt Whitman, *Selections from the Prose and Poetry of Walt Whitman* (Boston: Small, Maynard and Company, 1898), p. 162.

"Still I Rise" (1978) gives the assurance of humans' ability to cope with adversity:

> You may write me down in history
> With your bitter, twisted lies,
> You may trod me in the very dirt
> But still, like dust, I'll rise.
> { … }
>
> Just like moons and like suns
> With the certainty of tides,
> Just like hopes springing high,
> Still I'll rise.
>
> Do you want to see me broken?
> Bowed head and lowered eyes,
> Shoulders falling down like teardrops,
> Weakened by my soulful cries?
> { … }
>
> Out of the huts of history's shame
> I rise
> Up from a past that's rooted in pain
> I rise
> { … }
>
> Leaving behind nights of terror and fear
> I rise
> Into a daybreak that's wondrously clear
> I rise…
> I rise
> I rise
> I rise[53]

And after the world liberates itself from coronavirus coronaisation will it be able to sing songs? Yes, like whales' songs. "Whale songs become hits that can spread halfway around the globe. All the males in a humpback whale population usually sing just one song at any given time. But once they get bored of that song, an innovator in the group

___

53 Maya Angelou, *The Complete Collected Poems of Maya Angelou* (New York: Random House, 1994), p. 163.

will start singing a new one … Once a new song catches on, every hip male in the community will start singing it too…"[54] Yes, the world will sing about the gone coronaisation era and liberation as Bertolt Brecht, a German poet, while in exile from Nazi Germany, wrote:

> In the dark times,
> Will there also be singing?
> Yes, there will also be singing.
> About the dark times.

Music is food for the soul. And what songs will Kenyans sing? They will sing their songs of freedom and patriotism: from the National Anthem; from Mwakigwena Choir's "Kenya Yetu"; from Daudi Kabaka's "Harambee Harambee"; from Kakai Kilonzo's "Kenya Nchi Yetu"; from Eric Wainaina's "Daima"; and to other glorious melodies, for they believe, heaven is a place on earth. And they will remember an appeal for "one and all to arise" and be brand ambassadors of Kenya.

Kenyans shall also sing and dance when the country's top political leaders learn an important lesson. Hopefully, through God's mercies they will have learned that the art of use-and-dump of able and patriotic leaders for selfish reasons clothed with nationalistic names denies the country the best of brains as some of those thrown out of the establishment spend years wasting their talents elsewhere. (A reminder of the KANU disciplinary committee of the 1986-1987 that terrorised leaders and made grown up men shed tears for fear of expulsion as they were grilled on issues of loyalty to the Party, government, President Daniel arap Moi and Nyayo Philosophy.) Germans have an idiom that goes: "…you must empty-out the bath-tub, but not the baby with it. Fling out your dirty water with all zeal, and set it careening down the kennels; but try if you can to keep the little child." In other words, do you throw away the lemon peels after squeezing the lemon juice? The Daily Inspiration for Healthy Living say that lemon peels contain about five to 10 times more vitamins than lemon juice. They are also an excellent source of fibre, potassium, magnesium, calcium, folate and beta carotene. Lemon peels

---

54 Kristi Harrison, Fady Labib and Eddie Rodriguez, "Six Things You Won't Believe Animals Do Just Like Us", Cracked, 28 August, 2011. Available at: https://www.cracked.com/article_19388_6-things-you-wont-believe-animals-do-just-like-us.html. Accessed on 30 June 2020.

should never be thrown away.[55] And we shall sing even more when we manage to build genuine, stronger bridges.

Finally, the world shall sing the biggest song and dance the biggest dance. When humanity will desist from inflicting more wounds on Planet Earth and let her be, as Norwegian Halldis Moren Vesaas, urged so beautifully in a poem, "The Woman is Planting", presented in Oslo at Prof Wangari Maathai's Nobel Peace Prize award ceremony on 10 December 2004:

> The woman is planting a tree in the world,
> On her knees, like someone in a prayer,
> Among the remains of the many trees,
> That the storm has broken down.
> She must try again, perhaps one at last,
> Will be left to grow in peace…
> She sees the hands outspread on the earth,
> As if trying to impose her calm,
> On its threatening tremors.
> Oh, earth, be still,
> Be still, so my tree can grow.

And that is the story of our emerging as new form from coronavirus coronaisation, our great songs and great dances and most importantly, of building better, genuine, stronger bridges. Amen and Amen.

---

55 See "Do you throw away the lemon peels after squeezing the lemon juice?" Daily Inspirations for Healthy Living, 28 May, 2013. Available at: http://suhanijain.com/2013/05/28/do-you-throw-away-the-lemon-peels-after-squeezing-the-lemon-juice/. Accessed on 30 June 2020.

Epilogue

In the early production stages, a few people saw the manuscript of this book. Some, visibly shaken but equally sympathetic, posed some questions: "How can you be that bold? Isn't this not trending on dangerous grounds? Doesn't the content largely constitute satanic verses?" – the latter referring to author Salman Rushdie's novel, *The Satanic Verses,* published in 1988, and which was considered by many Muslims as blasphemous. It resulted in the then Iranian leader Ayatollah Khomeini, declaring a *fatwa* against him.

In Chapter One of the *The Satanic Verses* Rushdie asks: "How does newness come into the world? How is it born? Of what fusions, translations, conjoinings is it made? How does it survive, extreme and dangerous as it is? What compromises, what deals, what betrayals of its secret nature must it make to stave off the wrecking crew, the exterminating angel, the guillotine?"[1] Well...

The BBI is a project that was meant to bring "newness" into the country, the remaking that would bring on board, to use the UN 2030 Agenda term, to ensure "no one will be left behind" and the endeavour to "reach the furthest behind first." Unfortunately, even before its official departure from the station, some passengers were being mercilessly and violently thrown out of the window and lock-downed Covid-19 style. Additionally, the initiative was surprisingly reaching the furthest in front first. As subsequent events unfolded, a testament was unveiled once again of how humans can be selfish, treacherous, and loaded with other hearts that hurts hearts shamelessly without blinking an eye.

Prof Evan Mwangi, a Kenyan US-based scholar, called the BBI "shoddily written," "designs they (the leaders) had for themselves at the expense of their weakened leaders and the rest of the nation," "wasn't meant to be better than a Primary Class Five composition" and "a reflection of the low intellectual capacity of the clowns in charge of our country's affairs and the public that follows them blindly."[2] Another

---

1   Salman Rushdie, *The Satanic Verses* (Dower, DE: The Consortium Inc., 1988), p. 8.

2   Evan Mwangi, "Take it easy, the BBI report was not meant to be all that serious", *Daily Nation*, 18 March, 2020.

scholar, Dr Wandia Njoya, in an online article on 30 November 2019, titled, "BBI: From "We the People" to "Fix the People"" termed it a "narrow diagnosis of Kenya's social problems" that identifies the people rather than the leadership as the problem that is torturing our land and therefore the solution must be to "fix their behaviour, the values and the souls of Kenyans."[3] She called the initiative as "largely a declaration of war by the political class against the people of Kenya." And yet another online article on the BBI by Alfred Kiti was headlined as *"Ni Msitu Mpya, Nyani ni Wale Wale."* (New forest, same monkeys)?

Therefore, such questions about this book like being "bold," "dangerous grounds" and "satanic verses" were neither here nor there since millions of Kenyans were of the same stand posted in the work and had logical answers waiting: We are Kenya and Kenya is us. We are stakeholders in this country with a duty to inspire the building of genuine bridges. To many, King David's Psalm 115:5-6 had been rewritten in their minds. "We have mouths, so we speak; we have eyes, so we see; we have ears, so we hear; we have noses, so we smell…" After all, who will sing our song, however nasty it is, if citizens constantly develop cold feet or give in to being taken for a ride by their leaders endlessly?

Biblical Noah was one day lying naked and drunk. Two of his three sons, Japheth and Shem, fetched a blanket quickly and covered him up. The other named Ham burst out laughing at the sight of his father. Waking up later, Noah found out what had happened. He punished Ham by cursing him and his children to be slaves forever and ever. Fast forward in Kenya. By not trying to find a way of erasing the shameful, naked and drunken leadership in the BBI you invite a national curse. Put it differently in this era of novel coronavirus: a political leadership's crown constitutes thousands or millions of citizens' votes and goodwill. What do you do on finding the leadership has lost the crown and replaced it with one synonymous with the coronavirus one thereby risking to infecting people with social-economic-political Covid-19? Logically, you act with speed.

They say a pen is mightier than an army and can help change a worse situation before it turns worst. You cannot also underrate the

---

3 Wandia Njoya, "BBI: From "We the People" to "Fix the People"", Wandia Njoya, 30 November 2019. Retrieved from: https://www.wandianjoya.com/blog/bbi-from-we-the-people-to-fix-the-people. Accessed on 26 June 2020.

source, however small or weak it may seem, from where a message is coming. Jesus Christ taught in the synagogue and people got astonished at his wisdom and wondered: "Is not this the carpenter's son?"

Then look at this: A writer develops a concept after forecasting a national initiative of catastrophic proportions in the making. He puts other things aside and embarks on an energy-sapping extensive research and consultation with a view to producing a literary piece of monumental importance. Thousands of man-hours later, exhaustion and huge finances expended notwithstanding, a 142,633 word count first draft manuscript emerges. After further trimming and the editor's refining the end product is this book of 140,000 words. An undertaking of this magnitude can only be conceived, done and completed by a person profoundly passionate about his country. Now, it is left to the reader to make a verdict on the Satanism or otherwise contained in the book. The cardinal mission of this work has been principally like John the Baptist: perparing the way for better times in Kenya.

The starting point of this book is a quote by Ivo Andric, a Yugoslav novelist and the winner of the 1961 Nobel Prize for Literature. The Nobel committee cited "the epic force with which he… traced themes and depicted human destinies drawn from his country's history." On the occasion of the Nobel Banquet at the Stockholm City Hall on 10 December 1961, Andric noted: "My country is indeed a 'small country between the worlds'… a country which, at breakneck speed and at the cost of great sacrifices and prodigious efforts, is trying in all fields, including the field of culture, to make up for those things of which it has been deprived by a singularly turbulent past."[4]

This work is about a Kenyan destiny that will be shaped by genuine bridgings, particularly in politics and economics of the people so that every citizen will come to enjoy a full humane life. And like Andric's country, Kenya is small and on the run trying to correct a worse situation that has been brought about by an unpatriotic leadership in the past.

The BBI will by all standards not get Kenyans to the desired destiny. However, all is not lost. There is hope. Every day Kenyan mothers birth genuine bridge builders who will at an appropriate time rise up to

---

4   Ivo Andric, "Ivo Andric Banquet Speech", The Nobel Prize, City Hall in Stockholm, 10 December, 1961. Retrieved from: https://www.nobelprize.org/prizes/literature/1961/andric/speech/. Accessed on 20 June 2020.

build them and they, to borrow Andric's words in his acclaimed book, *The Bridge on the Drina*, "will be firm... existence will be passed in happiness... and will never know sorrow."[5] Thus, this book ends with a triumphant note of what every Kenyan dreams of, again to source from the same Andric's novel:

"You will see...you will see. We shall create a state which will make the most precious contribution to the progress of humanity, in which every effort will be blessed, every sacrifice holy, every thought original and expressed in our own words, and every deed marked with the stamp of our name... we will bridge greater rivers and deeper abysses... we will build new, greater and better bridges... There cannot be any doubt any longer. We are destined to realize all that the generations before us have aspired to; a state, born in freedom and founded in justice, like a part of God's thought realized on earth."[6]

---

5   Ivo Andric, *The Bridge on the Drina*, translated by Lovette F. Edwards (London: George Allen & Unwin, 1919), p. 68

6   Ibid, pp. 245-246

Index

9 798748 582032